New Femininities

Also by Rosalind Gill

THE GENDER-TECHNOLOGY RELATION (*with Keith Grint*)

TECHNOBOHEMIANS OR THE NEW CYBERTARIAT

GENDER AND THE MEDIA

SECRECY AND SILENCE IN THE RESEARCH PROCESS (*with Róisín Ryan-Flood*)

Also by Christina Scharff

REPUDIATING FEMINISM: YOUNG WOMEN IN A NEOLIBERAL WORLD

New Femininities

Postfeminism, Neoliberalism and Subjectivity

Edited by

Rosalind Gill
King's College London, UK

Christina Scharff
King's College London, UK

First published in hardback 2011
First published in paperback 2013 by
PALGRAVE MACMILLAN

Palgrave Macmillan in the UK is an imprint of Macmillan Publishers Limited,
registered in England, company number 785998, of Houndmills, Basingstoke,
Hampshire RG21 6XS.

Palgrave Macmillan in the US is a division of St Martin's Press LLC,
175 Fifth Avenue, New York, NY 10010.

Palgrave Macmillan is the global academic imprint of the above companies
and has companies and representatives throughout the world.

Palgrave® and Macmillan® are registered trademarks in the United States,
the United Kingdom, Europe and other countries.

ISBN 978–0–230–22334–9 hardback
ISBN 978–1–137–33986–7 paperback

This book is printed on paper suitable for recycling and made from fully
managed and sustained forest sources. Logging, pulping and manufacturing
processes are expected to conform to the environmental regulations of the
country of origin.

A catalogue record for this book is available from the British Library.

A catalog record for this book is available from the Library of Congress.

For Angela McRobbie

Contents

List of Figures

Acknowledgements

This collection started life as an ESRC seminar series entitled New Femininities? We are grateful to Jane Arthurs, Ann Phoenix, Merl Storr, Estella Tincknell and Valerie Walkerdine who jointly organized the programme of talks with us, as well as to everyone who presented their work and made the seminars the stimulating, enjoyable and productive occasions they were. We would also like to formally acknowledge our gratitude to ESRC for award number RES 451 26 0783 as well as to a follow-up award from British Academy reference SG-43703.

The chapters presented here are all original pieces of work, prepared specifically for this volume. We would like to express our appreciation to all the contributors for what we believe is a collection of outstandingly interesting and challenging essays that struggle to 'think' and understand the contours of gender, sexuality, race, class and neoliberalism in this contradictory moment. Without exception, the contributors have been a delight to work with, and have made the process of editing far easier than it might have been. We would also like to thank Alice Gavin and Chloe Preece for all their assistance with editing and preparing the manuscript and Christabel Scaife, Catherine Mitchell, Felicity Plester, Chris Penfold and their team at Palgrave for all their support. Our thanks also go to Joanne Kalogeras for her insightful comments on the introduction to this volume, and to Bridget Conor for being such a source of support and inspiration. We would also like to express our huge gratitude to Ana Sofia Elias for all her hard work on the Index, to Sara de Benedictis for her help with the publication of the paperback edition, and to the team at Newgen for everything they did 'behind the scenes'.

In addition, we each have people we would like to thank individually. Ros would like to thank colleagues, family and friends for their mix of support, good humour and intellectual sustenance – in particular Andy Pratt, Bruna Seu, Róisín Ryan-Flood, Shani Orgad, Stephanie Taylor, Gail Lewis, Meg Barker, Clare Hemmings, Imogen Tyler, Hazel Johnstone, Laura Harvey, Lynda Preston and Tom and Katarina Gill. She would also like to thank Christina for being such a pleasure to work with in preparing this volume, taking a long-standing intellectual collaboration to new levels of collegiality and friendship.

Christina would like to thank her colleagues for their intellectual and personal support, particularly Clare Hemmings, Sadie Wearing, Hazel Johnstone, Maria do Mar Pereira, Btihaj Ajana, Patrizia Kokot, Jonathan Dean, Natasha Marhia, Carolyn Pedwell, Marina Franchi, Amy Hinterberger, Deborah Finding, Joanne Kalogeras, and Rebekah Wilson. Her thanks also go to her friends Charles Jandreau, Leena Crasemann, Katharina Gnath, Olga Jugov, Nele Kirchner, Ana Hozyainova, Sarah Jones, Hyo Yoon Kang, David Saha, Eddie Cass, Sheila Cass as well as Maria Hoffmann-Lüning and Gisela Zenz. Her special thanks go to her family – Anna Georgi, Philipp Scharff, Tim-Owe Georgi, Christiane Scharff-Woelfing, Mae Georgi, Ada Georgi, Eve Georgi, Luisa Scharff, Emma Scharff and her parents Heidi Scharff and Jörg Scharff. Christina really enjoyed working on this volume with Ros Gill, who she would like to thank for being such an inspiring, and supportive, colleague and friend.

Finally, both of us would like to express our admiration, affection and respect for Angela McRobbie who is, in our view, the leading figure working in this field, and a feminist intellectual whose scholarship has consistently taught us, challenged us and inspired us. In recognition of her enormous contribution to feminist cultural studies we would like to dedicate this book to Angela McRobbie.

Preface to the Paperback Edition

Perhaps the most surprising idea of contemporary feminism is that women are female impersonators (Carol Ann Tyler, 2003)

Being, as Butler would have it, 'culturally intelligible' as a girl makes one ill. But by today's standards, that is almost acceptable (Angela McRobbie, 2009)

Is it just us, or has the notion of 'femininities' captured imaginations in the last few years? When we were developing this collection, and the seminar series on which it was based, we were surprised by the paucity of research on femininities, especially when contrasted with the burgeoning of scholarship on masculinity/ies, and we questioned the bifurcated logic that produced an interest in girls and young women, but on masculinity. By using the notion of 'new femininities' we sought to challenge this and to bring an anti-essentialist perspective that would highlight the social production and construction of gender and its intersection with class, race, age, sexuality and location. What new questions, we wondered, might the notion of femininities allow us to ask? What new insights or possibilities might it open up?

Several years on, we are struck by the proliferation of uses of the term, and by the flourishing of research on femininities. It may just be that our own interests have sensitized us to this, and, to be sure, we have retrospectively come across publications that predated our work on this volume such as Nina Laurie et al.'s (1999) book *Geographies of New Femininities* which we think may be the first use of this term, and Liz Conor's (2004) work on 'spectacular' femininity in the 1920s, that has offered us important new historical insights.

But beyond this, an interest in femininities seems now to be in the air in gender and cultural studies, generated in part by contemporary concerns with performativity and postfeminism. Angela McRobbie's work articulates both traditions, speaking to the difficulty (in Western culture) of inhabiting femininity in this postfeminist and neoliberal moment. Today, McRobbie (2009) writes, being 'culturally intelligible' as a girl makes one ill, as femininity becomes pathologized, and gender melancholia normalized, under conditions in which patriarchal culture retains a brutal effectivity yet is 'dissolved, decentralised and nowhere to be seen' (McRobbie, 2009: 122).

But despite the seeming 'impossibility of femininity', an exciting range of research in recent years has pointed to the sometimes ironic, parodic or resistant ways in which women 'do' or live femininity – from tomboys to burlesque to genderqueer (Renold, 2009; Ferreday, 2007). There has also been a growth of interest in how young women negotiate or resist normative femininities: Claire Charles (in press) and Alexandra Allan (2010) interrogate 'new femininities' in schools in Australia and the UK; Catherine Elzerbi's (forthcoming) research on menstrual art explores how young, feminist artists subvert patriarchal discourses of menstruation, the female body and femininity; B. McClure (2012) looks at the international Salsa community to ask how 'being in movement' allows Salsa dancers to move in and out of gendered scripts; Rachel O'Neill (2013) traces feminist becoming and offers an auto/biographical account of female political subjectivity, understanding 'willfulness' as a form of politics (Ahmed, 2010); Amy Dobson (in press) examines how the 'performative shamelessness' of young women's self-presentations in social networking sites may offer a bulwark against pathologization; and Nada Albunni's (2012) work on 'geek girls' from Damascus both speaks back to the West's fantasies of young Arab women, and offers accounts of grassroots collective organizing. This research highlights the need to explore femininities in light of recent technological innovations and, in particular, the growth of social media as a fast-changing domain that is shifting meanings and experiences of gender.

Not all of this work emerges from Anglo or even Western contexts, and it is exciting to see research on contemporary Chinese masculinities and femininities (Brownell and Wasserstrom, 2002), on 'new femininities' in Korea (Kim, 2011), and on postfeminist femininities in Nigeria (Dosekun, 2012) – as well as transnational work that explores how gendered subjectivities may be mediated by place (Elias, 2013). Feyza Akinerdem's research explores the emergence of televisual 'marriage shows' in Turkey as a forum for producing new femininities and masculinities in the context of changing understandings of nation and family. As Mary Jane Kehily and Anoop Nayak (2008: 325) have argued more broadly, 'globalisation may provide opportunities for the emergence of new femininities'.

One aspect of globalization that has had a profound impact in the years since we worked on this book is the global financial crisis. Not only has this been unevenly gendered in its economic impact, disproportionately inflicting suffering on the world's poorest women, but it has also produced new mediations of gender. Diane Negra and Yvonne Tasker (2014) argue that 'recessionary femininity is not routinely associated with crisis in the manner of masculinity; rather it is often presented as adaptive and resourceful'. Examining the post-crash London riots of 2011, Sara de Benedictis (2013: 1) contends that a new gendered figure emerged: the 'discourse of the "feral" parent emerged to position the blame for the riots on a class of "feral" children borne of "feral" parents. Specifically, this blame was centred upon the lone, working-class mother.' In turn, Laura Harvey et al. (2013) examine the role of consumer goods and social media in constructing and sustaining particular kinds of masculinities during the riots.

Finally, we have noted a dramatic proliferation of terms being used as modifiers of the notions 'femininity' or 'femininities' – 'hybrid', 'ambivalent', 'negotiated', 'global', 'ageing', 'young', 'power', 'alternative', etc. The remarkable upsurge of use of these terms points to a renewed interest in femininity/ies as culturally constructed and lived/experienced in diverse ways. If we were pulling together the collection today, three years on, much of this work would have a place in here.

We are delighted that this book is now available in paperback. It is a vibrant collection of interesting and stimulating essays, and we are proud that the work collected here has become part of an ongoing conversation about gender – and its intersections – in the 21st century.

Rosalind Gill and Christina Scharff

March 2013

Bibliography

Ahmed, S. (2010) 'Feminist Killjoys (and Other Willful Subjects)', *The Scholar and Feminist Online* 8(3) [online]. Available at: http://barnard.edu/sfonline/polyphonic /print_ahmed.htm [accessed 25 March 2013].

Akinerdem, F. (2012) 'Yeni Bir Güven Alanı Olarak Evlilik Programları ve Makbul Aile Hayali/Feeling Secure in Marriage Show: A New Space for Negotiating the Family Norms in Turkey', Kadın, Şiddet ve Güvenlik Çalıştayı/Women, Violence and Security Symposium, İstanbul Şehir University, Turkey, 25 May 2012.

Allan, A.J. (2010) 'Picturing Success: Young Femininities and the (Im)possibilities of Academic Achievement in Selective, Single-sex Schooling', *International Studies in Sociology of Education*, 20(1): 39–54.

Albunni, N. (2012) 'Damascus Girl Geeks: From Segregation to Global Identity', paper presented at Girls and Digital Culture: Transnational Perspectives, King's College London, 13–14 September.

Brownell, S. and J.N. Wasserstrom (2002) *Chinese Femininities/Chinese Masculinities: A Reader* (Berkeley, CA: University of California Press).

Charles, C. (in press) *Girls' Schooling, Social Class and Sexualised Popular Culture* (London and New York: Routledge).

Conor, Liz (2004) *The Spectacular Modern Woman: Feminine Visibility in the 1920s* (Bloomington, Indiana: Indiana University Press).

De Benedictis, S. (2013) '"Feral" Parents: Austerity Parenting under Neoliberalism', *Studies in the Maternal* 4(2).

Dobson, A. (in press) 'Performative Shamelessness on Young Women's Social Network Sites: Shielding the Self and Resisting Gender Melancholia', *Feminism and Psychology*.

Dosekun, S. (2012) 'Neither Phallic Nor Factory Girl: Thinking Transnationally About Girls Online', paper presented at Girls and Digital Culture: Transnational Perspectives, King's College London, 13–14 September.

Elias, A.S. (2013) 'On and Beyond Body Modification: "Technologies of Sexiness" as a Threefold Entrepreneurship', paper presented at Body Projects: Body Modification and the Female Body, York, 9 March 2013.

Elzerbi, Catherine (forthcoming). 'How to do things with Art: A Discourse Analytic Examination of Menstruation in the Talk of Feminist Artists', PhD Dissertation, Culture, Media and Creative Industries, King's College London.

Ferreday, D. (2007) 'Adapting Femininities: The New Burlesque' *M/C Journal* 10(2).

Harvey, L., J. Ringrose and R. Gill (2013) 'Swagger, Ratings and Masculinity: Theorising the Circulation of Social and Cultural Value in Teenage Boys' Digital Peer Networks', *Sociological Research Online* special issue on Collisions, Coalitions and Riotous Subjects: Reflections and Repercussions.

Kehily, M.-J. and A. Nayak (2008) 'Global Femininities: Consumption, Culture and the Significance of Place', *Discourse: Studies in the Cultural Politics of Education*, 29(3): 325–42.

Kim, J. (2011) *Women in Asia: New femininities and Consumption* (London: Routledge).

Laurie, N., C. Dywer, S.L. Holloway and F. Smith (1999) *Geographies of New Femininities* (New York: Longman).

McClure, B. (2012) 'Thinking in Movement: Theoretical and Methodological Implications', conference paper for 'Theorizing the Body, Embodiment and Body-Practices, Annual Conference of the Canadian Society for Women in Philosophy, Mount Royal University, Calgary, 26–28 October 2012.

McRobbie, A. (2009) *The Aftermath of Feminism: Gender, Culture and Social Change* (London: Sage).

Negra, D. and Y. Tasker (in press) *Gendering the Recession* (Duke University Press).

O'Neill, R. (2013). 'Impressions of my Mother: On Wilfulness and Passionate Scholarship' in V. Reimer and S. Sahagian (eds) *Mother of Invention: How our Mothers Influenced us as Feminist Academics and Activists* (Toronto: Demeter Press).

Renold, E. (2009) 'Tomboys and "Female Masculinity": (Dis)embodying Hegemonic Masculinity, Queering Gender Identities and Relations' in W. Martino, M. Kehler and M. Weaver-Hightower (eds) *The Problem with Boys: Beyond Recuperative Masculinity Politics in Boys' Education* (New York: Routledge).

Tyler, C.A. (2003) *Female Impersonation* (London and New York: Routledge).

Preface

It gives me enormous pleasure to provide some words as a preface to this volume, and I regret that questions of space make it impossible for me to offer a response to every single chapter in this collection. The contents advance our understanding of current developments and permutations in the conditions of (mostly young) womanhood, the production of gendered subjectivities, and the various requirements to perform a kind of sexuality which will be compliant with the changing needs of a global economy. The authors all recognize and engage with the changes which have come to characterize the distinctive modalities of power that comprise flows and luminosities and formations of attention which attend to young women in contemporary sociality. Most vivid here is the expectation of 'equality'. Where there is no question of this being fulfilled in socio-economic terms, or even of it becoming a lively subject for discussion, nevertheless it is promulgated as a prevailing cultural norm, as though to say in capital letters 'Girls and Women Are Now Equal'. This provides a new horizon of power against which all sociological analyses must now proceed. Some might see this as an intensification of power through tropes of imaginary freedom, others as the gender logic of neoliberal governmentality. Certainly this equality norm has become a notional feature of social, political and corporate institutions through the last twenty years. Yet this has proved intractable, refusing to yield itself for analysis until recently. Maybe the reason for this was a 'double entanglement', a seemingly progressive push-forward factor which has seen gay and lesbian partnerships recognized and legitimated, and girls and young women being provided with new avenues and opportunities for achievement in education and employment and with sexual freedoms in leisure. At the same time, indeed as part of this same package, modes of patriarchal retrenchment have been digging in, as these conditions of freedom are tied to conditions of social conservatism, consumerism and hostility to feminism in any of its old or newer forms.

Perhaps I should say at this point that I owe all of my own writing on these topics from about 2003 onwards, to the slim volume by Judith Butler titled *Antigone's Claim* where she lays out the terrain of exactly this kind of scenario (Butler, 2000). Indeed I appropriated her re-reading of Antigone to reflect on how sexuality, family and kinship were being reconfigured to incorporate some of the strengths and achievements of feminism (Antigone's courage and strength). But in doing so such values were also, at the same time being discredited and repudiated, being literally entombed in a darkened cave with the effect that a whole range of sentiments, desires and attachments were to be forgotten about, abandoned. Desires that could not be fitted into the family unit were considered irregular and increasingly unthinkable. This included, for example, political desires for feminist collectivity, for communality, for non-familial forms of kinship, for shared childcare, for a politicized non-monogamy, all of which no longer have a place in the polity, giving rise to a sense of loss and to a haunting melancholia.

One way in which this mode of neoliberal governmentality has more recently been discussed by Butler, by Joan Scott and others, is through the idea of instrumentality, where feminist ideals are hijacked by governments and agencies of the state in order to pursue a completely different agenda which often entails the denigration of other cultures where it is argued women are degraded or their human rights are violated (Butler, 2004; Scott, 2007). And consistent with this instrumentalization is a celebratory rhetoric in regard to the high levels of sexual visibility and the seeming enjoyment factor accruing to women in Western capitalism, as the fruits of secular modernity and the benevolent state, as though to say to those of us living in the West, that we should remind ourselves of 'how lucky we are'. Joan Scott has recently dissected the way in which such instrumentalization by government of 'women's rights' is currently played out in France through the 'politics of the veil' and her argument can be extended to the banning of the burkha. Here we see something similar, if more aggressive, to what I argued in *The Aftermath of Feminism* (McRobbie, 2009). The UK government during the Blair years offered itself as the preferred agency for delivering women's rights, such that self-organized feminism might wither away. In France we see the Sarkozy government in effect become champion of women's freedoms directly at the expense of migrant communities, already marginalized and suffering from poverty and from being targets for endemic racism. In the current volume this development is vividly described in the essay by Sadie Wearing in her discussion of the film *Vers le Sud*. The 'liberated' older woman who enjoys sexual encounters with a young man in Haiti emerges in the film as a blame-free neocolonizer inattentive to the consequences of her pursuit of sexual satisfaction. Likewise in Carolyn Pedwell's chapter there is a detailed analysis of some dangers which are attached to a desire by feminists to bring together debates about the veil with those about hyper-sexualization of young women through the rise of what has been called 'porno-chic'. Pedwell argues that these versions of intersectionality nevertheless confirm underlying essentialisms; Sheila Jeffreys, for example, takes the 'oppressive nature of 'non-Western' practices for granted and proposes a universalist feminism which would see women as both 'bareheaded and barefaced' (I myself recall my own fury as a young woman at the anti-make-up and anti-fashion stance of the radical feminists of the early 1980s; indeed such a stance encouraged myself and others to go to further extremes of flaunting the love of fashion, make-up, etc.) And Pedwell also argues that Duits and van Zoonen, in bringing the veil and the thong or G-string together, through a cross-cultural analogy with reference to sexual regulation, are themselves also creating an axis of intelligibility which has its own limits and constraints. It feeds into a sense of how girls nowadays are to be understood, either as veil-wearing or thong-wearing. Pedwell is suggesting that unwittingly perhaps they are consolidating a trope in contemporary discourse, feeding into the moral panic and into a conventional manner of thinking which needs to be reconsidered.

Sexuality is of course a major theme throughout this volume; this entails, for example, our attention being critically drawn to the eroticization of the pregnant mother's body, and, in Róisín Ryan-Flood's article, to the realms of pain and injury which emerge at the social interface of the experiences of lesbian couples who are embarking on the process of becoming pregnant. As Ryan-Flood poignantly notes, this 'remains to some degree an "underground" activity'. The trajectories of openness and of new possibilities in reproductive technology are foreclosed or circumscribed by the sheer discrepancy between the commercialized and celebratory discourses which are now targeted at the newly pregnant woman and her male partner and the realms of subterfuge activity and, at the very least shameful discomfort, on the part of lesbians who want to have their own children. And so what prevails across the boundaries of lesbian, queer and heterosexual is the intensification of disciplinary practices as part of a new moral economy of reproduction where an absence of feminism within public policy discourse results in the privatization of interests according to sexual preferences. For 'well behaved' heterosexual couples who have almost 'left it too late' to have children, there are government agencies supporting their needs for fertility treatment, in sharp contrast to the few specialist agencies who are even aware of the needs of gays and lesbians in this regard and for whom the words 'reproductive rights' barely exist.

Across the chapters in this volume we see the subtle ways in which heterosexuality becomes more assertive, more expansive and ebullient than ever. Many of the chapters convey the mechanisms through which this occurs, even when, as in the many popular television shows which address the issues of love, sex and desire, there is an incorporation of gay and lesbian people. Laura Harvey and Ros Gill show how popular TV programmes like *The Sex Inspectors* endorse a notion of female performance which corresponds with the practices and rhetoric of pornography, and this theme reappears in many of the other chapters where the focus is on pre-teen and teenage girls, so much so that it becomes in effect the dominant vocabulary for popular sexual discourse, something which the abundant provision of pornography through the internet has made more possible than would have been the case prior to the growth of the new media. It is fitting then that I should conclude this preface with a more concentrated look at the way in which sexuality is reconfigured within the realms of the 'new femininities'. One thing that is overwhelmingly apparent is the way in which the internet and new media along with popular culture have created a space of sexuality which borrows its vocabulary from the world of pornography and the sex industry. This then informs the everyday sex talk of teenagers, and studies referred to in this volume report the widespread practices of girls' own self-description as 'sluts'. Many of these girls talk dirty among themselves and with boys across the social networking sites in a way that would have been unthinkable ten or fifteen years ago. The prevalence of explicit talk about oral sex, for example, or of girls posting pictures of their breasts onto websites (not just the more usual bikini shots) seems to me to point to the need for more in-depth analysis of what this all means culturally. The authors here make an impressive start on this task; there is a recognition of class, age and ethnic differences and how they play out in these sexualized friendships; there is also recognition of the pervasive use of irony and humour as in one girl calling her best friend her 'whore'. There is also lurking somewhere in the background a feminist-influenced destigmatization of sex work. This active taking up of pornography as a mainstream part of everyday life must have the effect of depathologizing the sex work which is entailed in its production, since so many people could hardly be active consumers whilst simultaneously condemning those who create it or bring it to their computer screens. At the very least this reduces the scope for old-fashioned hypocrisy. There is a strand of popular feminism which unites young women's investment in this kind of porn-scene as a buttress against the reappearance of the old sexual double standard. And as is shown with great clarity in the chapter by Feona Attwood the genre of 'altporn' provides sexually explicit material (e.g. Furry Girl who does not remove her body hair) some of which takes its benchmarks from queer activist and sex positive groups and sub-cultures.

I am totally in agreement with Jessica Ringrose that a feminist pedagogy dealing with these topics and brought directly into the classrooms for teenage girls and boys is an urgent requirement, that they might be exposed to the range of debates and the different arguments made by second-wave feminists and now also by their contemporary counterparts. This would give girls better ammunition with which to deal with some of their doubts and misgivings, with their uncertainties about how to engage with this pornographic popular culture which is perhaps in the first instances appealing precisely because it is 'bad' or 'shocking' especially to parents and teachers. And finally I welcome the chapter by Jin Haritaworn on the racialized slur of prostitution which sticks onto the bodies of second-generation, mixed race Thai-English and Thai-German women. Haritaworn's account of the Mail.Order.Brides/M.O.B.s, a group of Filipina-American artists who challenge the dominant imaginary which places such women as 'maids', 'brides' or 'prostitutes', draws attention to the ability of art to function as critique in a context where more conventional organizational structures for political resistance have become exhausted.

Angela McRobbie

Bibliography

Butler, J. (2000) *Antigone's Claim: Kinship between Life and Death* (New York: Columbia University Press).
Butler, J. (2004) *Precarious Life: The Power of Mourning and Violence* (London: Verso).
McRobbie, A. (2009) *The Aftermath of Feminism: Gender, Culture and Social Change* (London: Sage).
Scott, J. W. (2007) *The Politics of the Veil* (Princeton, NJ: Princeton University Press).

Notes on Contributors

Editors:

Rosalind Gill is Professor of Social and Cultural Analysis at the Centre for Culture, Media and Creative Industries at King's College London. She worked previously at the Open University, where she was Professor of Subjectivity and Cultural Theory. Before that she spent ten years working in the LSE's interdisciplinary Gender Institute. She is known for her work on gender, media, cultural industries and new technologies as well as for longstanding interests in discourse and narrative analysis and visual methods. Underlying all her interests is a concern with theorizing the relationship between culture, subjectivity and change. She is the author of *Gender and the Media* (Polity, 2007). Her latest book (with Róisín Ryan-Flood) has just been published by Routledge, entitled *Secrecy and Silence in the Research Process*.

Christina Scharff is Lecturer in Culture, Media and Creative Industries at the Centre for Culture, Media and Creative Industries, King's College London. Her research interests include young women's engagements with feminism, entrepreneurial subjectivities and cultural labour. Christina's work has been published in international journals such as *Sociology, Feminism & Psychology*, and the *European Journal of Women's Studies*. She is editor (with Natasha Marhia and Maria do Mar Pereira) of the journal special issue 'Lost (and Found) in Translation'. Her monograph *Repudiating Feminism: Young Women in a Neoliberal World* appeared in 2012 as part of the Ashgate series 'The Feminist Imagination – Europe and Beyond'.

Contributors:

Feona Attwood is Professor of Media at Middlesex University, UK. Her research is in the area of sex in contemporary culture; and in particular, in onscenity; sexualization; sexual cultures; new technologies, identity and the body; and controversial media. She is the editor of *Mainstreaming Sex: The Sexualization of Western Culture* (2009), *porn.com: Making Sense of Online Pornography* (2010) and (with Vincent Campbell, I.Q. Hunter and Sharon Lockyer) *Controversial Images* (2012) and the co-editor of journal special issues on Controversial Images (with Sharon Lockyer, *Popular Communication*, 2009), Researching and Teaching Sexually Explicit Media (with I.Q. Hunter, *Sexualities*, 2009), and Investigating Young People's Sexual Cultures (with Clarissa Smith, *Sex Education*, 2011). Her recent publications have focused on online culture, aesthetics, sex and the media, and public engagement. Her current book project is *Media, Sex and Technology*.

Gargi Bhattacharyya is Professor of Sociology at the University of East London, UK. Her work examines issues of racism, sexuality and globalization. Her recent publications include *Dangerous Brown Men, Exploiting Sex, Violence and Feminism in the War on Terror.*

Brinda Bose is Associate Professor of English at Delhi University, and has recently been a Fellow of the Nehru Memorial Museum and Library, New Delhi. She researches in postcolonial, gender and cultural studies, with a focus on South Asia. She is the editor of *Translating Desire* (2003), *Gender and Censorship* (2006) and the co-editor of *The Phobic and the Erotic: The Politics of Sexualities in Contemporary India* (2007). She is currently working on a manuscript on cities, sexualities and contemporary Indian visual cultures.

Shelley Budgeon is Senior Lecturer in Sociology at the University of Birmingham. She has published on the formation of gender identity within the context of social change in *Choosing A Self: Young Women and the Individualisation of Identity* (2003); postfeminism and constructions of femininity; the relationship between young women and feminism; and the practice of non-normative intimacy. Her most recent book, *Third Wave Feminism and the Politics of Gender in Late Modernity* (2011), evaluates thirdwave feminism and its implications for feminist theory and politics.

Dawn H. Currie completed her PhD at the London School of Economics, London in 1988. She is currently Professor of Sociology at the University of British Columbia, and past Chair of the Women's Studies Program. Her main areas of teaching include feminist theory and methodologies, girls' culture, and more recently International Service Learning. She is author of *Girl Talk: Adolescent Magazines and Their Readers* (1999) and co-author of *'Girl Power': Girls Reinventing Girlhood* (2009), as well as author of several journal articles on girl culture, feminist theorizing and teaching for social justice.

Umut Erel's research interests are in gender, migration, ethnicity and class, culture and representation empirically and theoretically. She is interested in how these issues play out in practices of citizenship, differentiated along gender and ethnic lines. Her recent monograph on *Migrant Women Transforming Citizenship* (Ashgate, 2009) addresses these issues through the lens of the life-stories of migrant women from Turkey in Britain and Germany. She is currently exploring migrant women's mothering practices as citizenship practices in their own right and with respect to shaping their children's ethnic, cultural, political identities and modes of citizenship. Her recent publications include 'Migrating Cultural Capital: Bourdieu in Migration Studies', *Sociology* (forthcoming); 'Constructing Meaningful Lives: Biographical Methods in Research on Migrant Women', *Sociological Research Online*, 12(4) 2007 (reprinted in: *Life Story Research*, edited by Barbara Harrison, Sage, 2008); and with Jin Haritaworn, 'Encarnación Gutiérrez

Rodríguez, Christian Klesse: On the Depoliticisation of Intersectionality Talk. Conceptualising Multiple Oppressions in Critical Sexuality Studies', in Kuntsman et al. (eds) *Out of Place* (Raw Nerves Publishers, 2008).

Lisa Guerrero is Associate Professor in Critical Culture, Gender, and Race Studies at Washington State University. Her areas of research include black masculinity, African American popular culture, the commodification of racialized identities, and African American literature. She is the editor of *Teaching Race in the 21st Century: College Teachers Talk About their Fears, Risks, and Rewards* (Palgrave Macmillan, 2008), and has published essays on African American 'Chick Lit', the Bratz dolls, irony in African American film, and the space of black bodies in the wars on terror and same-sex marriage. Currently she is at work on a book-length project on satire and the commodification of black masculinity in contemporary popular culture.

Jin Haritaworn is Assistant Professor of Gender, Race and Environment at York University in Toronto. They just had their first monograph published *The Biopolitics of Mixing: Thai Multiracialities and Haunted Ascendancies* (Ashgate, 2012) and a second one tentatively titled *Queer Lovers and Hateful Others* is in contract with the Pluto series 'Decolonial Studies, Postcolonial Horizons'. Jin is the editor and co-editor of several special issues and clusters on the intersection of race, gender and sexuality, including 'Women's Rights, Gay Rights and Anti-Muslim Racism in Europe', *European Journal of Women's Studies* 19(1/2) 2012, 'Polyamory and Non-Monogamies', *Sexualities* (2006, 9(5)), 'Murderous Inclusions', *International Feminist Journal of Politics* 15(4) 2013, as well as the book collection *Queer Necropolitics* (ed. with Adi Kuntsman and Silvia Posocco, forthcoming with Routledge). They have also just joined the board of the Critical Ethnic Studies Association.

Laura Harvey is Research Assistant at Brunel University, working on an ESRC-funded project about young people's aspirations and celebrity culture, and also works as a Teaching Fellow at King's College London. Laura recently completed her PhD, which explored the negotiation and representation of condom use. Her research interests include feminist methodologies, discourse analysis and understanding inequalities.

Sue Jackson is Senior Lecturer in the School of Psychology at Victoria University of Wellington, New Zealand, a post she has held since completing her PhD at the University of Auckland in 1999. Much of her previous research and publication work has centred on young women's negotiation of sexuality and ways sexuality is represented in girls' popular culture. Currently her research centres on the project from which material in the chapter is drawn: the NZ Royal Society Marsden funded a three year project examining pre-teen girls' engagement with popular culture in their everyday lives.

Deirdre M. Kelly is Professor of Sociology of Education in the Department of Educational Studies at the University of British Columbia. With Dawn Currie and Shauna Pomerantz, she is author of *'Girl Power': Girls Reinventing Girlhood* (2009) for Peter Lang's *Mediated Youth* series. She recently co-edited a special issue on *The Popular Media, Education, and Resistance* for the *Canadian Journal of Education* (http://www.csse.ca/CJE/Articles/CJE29–1. htm). She is the author of *Last Chance High: How Girls and Boys Drop In and Out of Alternative Schools* (1993) and *Pregnant with Meaning: Teen Mothers and the Politics of Inclusive Schooling* (2000), which won a 2003 American Educational Studies Association Critic's Choice Award.

JongMi Kim is a Senior Lecturer at the Department of Media and Communication, Coventry University. She received her PhD on Global Media, Audience and Transformative identities: Femininities and Consumption in South Korea at the London School of Economics. Her current research interests are new femininities in the East-Asian context and medical tourism, particularly, plastic surgery in East Asia and digital media in transnational families. She is now working on a book project focusing on New Femininities in South Korea.

Michelle M. Lazar is Associate Professor in the Department of English Language and Literature at the National University of Singapore. Her research interests include critical discourse analysis, feminist and gender studies, media and political discourse, and multimodal discourse analysis. She is the editor of *Feminist Critical Discourse Analysis: Gender, Power and Ideology in Discourse* (Palgrave 2005/2007), and series editor of *Routledge Critical Studies in Discourse*.

Carolyn Pedwell is Senior Lecturer in Media and Cultural Studies at Newcastle University. She is author of *Feminism, Culture and Embodied Practice: The Rhetorics of Comparison* (Routledge, 2010) and *Affective Relations: The Transnational Politics of Empathy* (Palgrave, forthcoming). Carolyn's current AHRC-funded research explores the transnational politics of emotion and affect, with a focus on feminist, queer and postcolonial approaches.

Shauna Pomerantz is Assistant Professor of Child and Youth Studies at Brock University. Her research interests include girls and girlhoods, youth culture, popular culture, sociology of education, constructions of academic success, qualitative research and feminisms. She is author of *Girls, Style and School Identities: Dressing the Part* (Palgrave, 2008), has co-authored articles on girl skateboarders, computer girls, and popularity in the school, and has contributed to the anthologies *Girlhood: Redefining the Limits* (Black Rose, 2006) and *Girl Culture: An Encyclopedia* (Greenwood Press, 2007).

Andrea Press is Chair of the Department of Media Studies and Professor of Sociology at the University of Virginia, and has taught at the University of Illinois and the University of Michigan. She is internationally known for her interdisciplinary scholarship on the media audience, on feminist media issues, and on media and social class in the US. She is the author of *Women Watching Television: Gender, Class and Generation in the American Television Experience* (University of Pennsylvania Press), and the co-author (with Elizabeth Cole) of *Speaking Of Abortion: Television and Authority in the Lives Of Women* (University of Chicago Press), and (with Bruce A. Williams) of *The New Media Environment* (Blackwell), and she co-edits the journal *The Communication Review* with Bruce A. Williams. She has published numerous essays, articles and chapters on feminist media theory, social class and the media and media audiences. Her new project looks at representations of feminism in popular media and their reception among women of different ages.

Jessica Ringrose is Senior Lecturer at the Institute of Education, University of London. Recent research projects have explored gender and sexual identities among teens in secondary school, including uses of digital technology and issues related to 'sexting' and cyber-bullying. Theoretically and methodologically her work develops feminist poststructural and psychosocial approaches to understanding subjectivity and affect. Her recent books are: *Rethinking Gendered Regulations and Resistances in Education* (Routledge, 2011, edited); *Post-Feminist Education? Girls and the Sexual Politics of Schooling* (Routledge, 2012, research monograph); and *Deleuze and Research Methodologies* (Edinburgh University Press, 2013, co-edited with Rebecca Coleman).

Róisín Ryan-Flood is a Senior Lecturer in Sociology and Director of the Centre for Intimate and Sexual Citizenship (CISC) at the University of Essex. Her research interests include gender, sexuality, citizenship, kinship and critical epistemologies. She is the author of *Lesbian Motherhood: Gender, Families and Sexual Citizenship* (Palgrave, 2009) and co-editor (with Rosalind Gill) of *Secrecy and Silence in the Research Process: Feminist Reflections* (Routledge, 2010), as well as numerous journal articles and book chapters. She recently completed a project on sexual citizenship and diaspora. Her current research explores the experiences of donor egg recipients. She is co-editor of the journal Sexualities: Studies in Culture and Society (Sage).

Estella Tincknell is Reader in Media and Cultural Studies at the University of the West of England, Bristol. She is the joint author of *The Practice of Cultural Studies* (2004) and author of *Mediating the Family: Gender, Culture and Representation* (2005), and of *Reading Jane Campion: Angels, Demons and Voices* (forthcoming). She has contributed to p.o.v. *Feminist Media Studies, Gender and Education, Journal of Sociology of Education, Journal of European Cultural Studies, Journal of Popular Film and Television*, and is on the editorial board of *Body and Society*. She is the co-editor of *Film's Musical Moments*

(2006) and of the forthcoming *Aging Femininities: Troubling Representations*. Her most recent publications are on the figure of the female secret agent in *Revisioning 007: James Bond and Casino Royale* (2009), and on adolescence and witchcraft in *New Gothic Cinema in Horrorzone: The Cultural Experience of Contemporary Horror Cinema* (2010).

Imogen Tyler is Senior Lecturer in Sociology and co-Director of the Centre for Gender and Women's Studies at Lancaster University. She specializes in the area of marginal social identities, a topic which brings together research on asylum and migration, borders, sexual politics, motherhood, race and ethnicity, disability, social class and poverty. Her book is titled *Revolting Subjects: Social Abjection and Resistance in Neoliberal Britain* (Zed, 2013). Other recent publications include a special issue of *Feminist Review* (with C. Gatrell) on the theme of 'Birth', a special issue of *Studies in the Maternal* (with T. Jensen) on the theme of 'Austerity Parenting', a special issue of *Citizenship Studies* on the theme of 'Immigrant Protest' (2013) and a book (with K. Marciniak) *Immigrant Protest: Politics, Aesthetics, and Everyday Dissent* (forthcoming SUNY).

Tiina Vares is Senior Lecturer in Sociology and Gender Studies at the University of Canterbury. Her research is in the area of audiences and popular culture with a current focus on 'tween' girls' engagement with popular culture.

Sadie Wearing is Lecturer in Gender Theory, Culture and Media at the Gender Institute, London School of Economics. Her research interests are in the critical analysis of literary, visual and film culture with particular emphasis on conceptualizations of aging, temporality and memory in both historical and contemporary contexts. She is currently working on a book manuscript entitled *Age, Gender and Sexuality in Contemporary Culture*.

Introduction

Rosalind Gill and Christina Scharff

This is a book about the politics of gender, sexuality, race, class and location in contemporary culture, at a moment that, we argue, is, in many places, distinctively neoliberal and postfeminist. The book brings together 20 original essays in which scholars were asked to reflect on the changes and continuities in gender relations and other intersecting axes of power, across a range of different texts, sites and practices. The collection traverses disciplines, geopolitical spaces and approaches. It is marked by an extraordinarily wide focus – from analyses of North American and British celebrity magazines and makeover shows to examinations of the experiences of young female migrants to Europe; from readings of diasporic Indian cinema to an analysis of the complicated positioning of African American First Lady Michelle Obama; from examinations of alternative female-produced pornographies, to new, Third Wave and critical race feminisms. What unites the contributions is not their substantive focus, nor their disciplinary 'take', but their attempts to think critically about the contours of the current moment in all their troubling complexity.

The book was inspired by a series of seminars and an international conference held in the UK between 2005 and 2007 (see acknowledgements) that aimed to examine the contradictoriness of the landscape of gender relations. Our initial call for participation pointed to some of the paradoxes we observed, perhaps most notably the way in which a discourse of 'girl power', 'top girls' (McRobbie, 2007) and 'can-do girls' (Harris, 2004) seemed to coexist alongside the reinvigoration of inequalities and the emergence of new forms and modalities of power. Crucial to the genesis of our project was the desire to formulate a response to this, when little feminist writing seemed to be doing so. 'No one uses the word sexism any more', as Judith Williamson put it in conversation in 2005. 'It has an old-fashioned, almost quaint ring about it.' Instead the *mots de jour* were terms like 'choice' and 'empowerment', and the word 'feminism', when it was used at all, was either prefixed by 'post' or 'power' in a way that seemed to threaten to evacuate the terrain of politics altogether – or, in a neocolonialist dynamic, projected on to 'Others' in need of rescuing from 'harmful cultural practices' (Arthurs, 2011; Gill, 2006; Pedwell, this volume; Scharff, this volume).

The notion of 'new femininities' is designed to be wrapped in scare quotes and followed by an interrogative. It seeks to open up questions about the ways in which gender is lived, experienced and represented. For us, speaking of 'femininities' is a way of highlighting the *social production and construction of gender* and avoiding essentialism. It also points up an interesting contrast within gender and cultural studies in which we noted a tendency to study *girls and women*, but *masculinities*. Why has there been a relative lack of interest in femininities? This despite the very interesting early psychoanalytic conceptions of 'womanliness' as a 'masquerade' designed to rebut or defend against male attack (Riviere, 1929), as well as the work by artists such as Cindy Sherman that reveal femininity as a tightly policed set of practices, dispositions and performances. There has been, to our knowledge, no investigation of 'hegemonic femininity', yet a wealth of writing about 'hegemonic masculinity'. What new questions, we wondered, might the notion of femininities allow us to ask? What new insights or possibilities might it open up?

The putative *newness* of the 'femininities' discussed is also included in the spirit of questioning. We are wary of a world saturated by consumerist logics and an attention economy in which a premium is placed (even in academia) on the 'new' (if not improved!). Indeed, this volume is itself published (we suspect) partly because of the word 'new' in the title, and our attempts to reinstate the question mark after 'new femininities' were met with resistance and ultimately refusal by our publisher. Yet this preoccupation with the new seems in danger of producing a sociology of accelerated transformation, a version of social relations as speeded up and in constant flux, in which nothing ever stays still. By contrast, we asked our contributors about both change *and* continuity, facilitating an engagement both with what might be understood as novel, but also with the old, unchanging and stubbornly persistent (not least, of course, the continued force and power of the very idea of binary gender difference).

Despite the divergent foci of interest amongst contributors there is a surprising convergence around the terms used to characterize contemporary culture. There is, in this volume, a sustained concern with exploring postfeminism, neoliberalism and subjectivity (the words which make up the subtitle of the book) and, moreover, amongst some contributors, an attempt to think transnationally in ways that are informed by critical race studies, queer and postcolonial scholarship. In the remainder of this chapter, we introduce each of these key terms in order to set the context for the essays that follow. We conclude by discussing the structure and organization of the book.

Postfeminism

Postfeminism has become a key term in the lexicon of feminist cultural critique in recent years. Its taken-for-granted status belies very real disputes and contestations over its meanings. Or perhaps it is more accurate to say that it is used with *such* a lack of specificity, to signal *such* a wide range of meanings, that interlocutors might not even know that they are disagreeing! We have found it helpful to think about the notion being used in four broad ways. First, it can be used to signal an *epistemological break within feminism*, and marks 'the intersection of feminism with a number of other anti-foundationalist movements including post-modernism, poststructuralism and post-colonialism' (Brooks, 1997, p. 1). 'Post' as it is used in this sense, implies transformation and change within feminism that challenges 'hegemonic' Anglo-American feminism 'with its dominant and colonizing voice' (Alice, 1995, p. 11). In this sense, postfeminism is understood as an analytical perspective, and a kind of maturing or 'coming of age' of academic feminism (Yeatman, 1994).

Somewhat differently, postfeminism is also used to refer to *an historical shift after the height of Second Wave feminism*. Tasker and Negra (2007, p. 1) describe postfeminism as based around 'a set of assumptions, widely disseminated within popular media forms, having to do with the "pastness" of feminism, whether that supposed pastness is merely noted, mourned or celebrated'. Sometimes, particularly in the US, the term is used synonymously with Third Wave feminism to mark out a time not after feminism *per se*, but after a particular moment of feminist activism (usually in the 1970s), against which all others are judged and found wanting (Hollows, 2000).

A third way of using the term is to refer to a *backlash against feminism*. Backlash discourses take many contradictory forms. They often work by attributing all women's unhappiness to feminism, but may also suggest that 'all the battles have been won' or, conversely, that 'you can't have it all – something has to give'; that 'political correctness' has become a new form of tyranny; that (white) men are the real victims, and so on (Faludi, 1991). Imelda Whelehan (2000) argues that contemporary postfeminist discourses are often characterized by 'retrosexism', premised on real fears about the collapse of masculine hegemony. She has explored the nostalgic quality of much contemporary media, which harks back to a time and place peopled by real women and humorous 'cheeky chappies', and argues that representations of women 'from the banal to the downright offensive' are being 'defensively reinvented against cultural changes in women's lives' (Whelehan, 2000, p. 11).

These arguments are valuable for trying (unlike the other two approaches considered so far) to say something about the normative or ideological *content* of postfeminist discourses, but they do not tell the whole story. In particular, the focus on harking *back* may miss what is *new* about contemporary depictions of gender, as well as tending to underplay the extent to which the entire history of feminist struggle has been characterized by 'strategies of resistance, negotiation and containment' which a linear model of 'achievements won and then subsequently lost' cannot illuminate (Tasker and Negra, 2007, p. 1). Moreover, whilst notions of backlash and retrosexism have been crucial in highlighting the reactive (as well as reactionary) nature of many contemporary representations, the elision of postfeminism with anti-feminism misses a crucial feature of current media discourses: namely the *entanglement* of feminist and anti-feminist ideas within them (McRobbie, 2004).

It is this notion of entanglement that the fourth approach develops through its elaboration of *postfeminism as a sensibility* (Gill, 2007) characterizing large parts of contemporary culture. In an influential essay, Angela McRobbie (2004) argued that what is distinctive about postfeminist culture is the way in which a selectively defined feminism is both 'taken into account' and repudiated. Drawing on Judith Butler's work, McRobbie argues that this double entanglement facilitates both a doing and an undoing of feminism. (Young) women are offered particular kinds of freedom, empowerment and choice 'in exchange for' or 'as a kind of substitute for' feminist politics and transformation (McRobbie, 2009). There is not space to discuss McRobbie's important argument in detail here (see her book of essays *The Aftermath of Feminism*) but its significance in this context is the way in which it positions postfeminism as *an object of critical analysis*, rather than as a theoretical orientation, new moment of feminism or straightforward backlash. In this sense postfeminism becomes a term that can be used analytically – with which we must work hard in order to specify its nature and content. Elsewhere, Rosalind Gill suggested that a postfeminist sensibility includes the notion that femininity is increasingly figured as a bodily property; a shift from objectification to subjectification in the ways that (some) women are represented; an emphasis upon self-surveillance, monitoring and discipline; a focus upon individualism, choice and empowerment; the dominance of a 'makeover paradigm'; a resurgence of ideas of natural sexual difference; the marked 'resexualization' of women's bodies; and an emphasis upon consumerism and the commodification of difference. These themes coexist with, and are structured by, stark and continuing inequalities and exclusions that relate to race and ethnicity, class, age, sexuality and disability as well as gender (Gill, 2007), a fact that is underscored by the preoccupation with using the term to analyse a very restricted number of media texts, focused on the lives of largely white, middle-to-upper class North American or European women (for example *Sex and the City, Ally McBeal, Bridget Jones's Diary, Desperate Housewives* and *Girls*).

Many aspects of this sensibility emerge in the essays presented here. Michelle Lazar examines adverts in a Singaporean daily paper, showing how they construct beauty as an extension of women's 'right' to freedom and liberation. She calls attention to the language of choice and empowerment deployed, and, following McRobbie, highlights the ways in which these postfeminist adverts simultaneously take feminism into account and repudiate it. Estella Tincknell looks at the British makeover show *Ten Years Younger*, foregrounding the way it constructs the older female body as inevitably abject and in need of radical reconstruction – which frequently now includes surgery. Lisa Guerrero also focuses on makeover, but in this case examines the complicated and contradictory ways in which the figure of Michelle Obama needed to be reconstructed and reinscribed in particular ways as the US's first African American First Lady. Andrea Press's attention is caught by the postfeminist consciousness she identifies among young female viewers of *America's Top Model* – a consciousness she describes as schizophrenic.

Neoliberalism

Alongside postfeminism, neoliberalism is a concept that animates many of the chapters in this collection. Broadly speaking, it is understood as a mode of political and economic rationality characterized by privatization, deregulation and a rolling back and withdrawal of the state from many areas of social provision that rose to prominence in the 1980s under the Reagan administration in the US and Thatcher's premiership in the UK. It expanded its economic reach globally through international organizations such as the IMF, the World Trade Organization and the World Bank. Equally significant as its geographical reach, however, was its expansion across different spheres of life to constitute a novel form of governance. As David Harvey puts it 'neoliberalism is, in the first instance, a theory of political economic practices that proposes that human well-being can best be advanced by liberating individual entrepreneurial freedoms and skills within an institutional framework characterized by strong private property rights, free markets and free trade' (Harvey, 2005, p. 2). It sees market exchange as an ethic in itself, capable of acting as a guide to all human action, and it holds that the social good will be maximized by maximizing the reach and frequency of market transactions.

This 'ethic' spreads wide, as neoliberalism, in Aihwa Ong's words, 'is reconfiguring relationships between governing and governed, power and knowledge, sovereignty and territoriality' (Ong, 2006, p. 3). Governing is recast as a technical, rather than political activity. Neoliberalism is a mobile, calculated technology for governing subjects who are constituted as self-managing, autonomous and enterprising. George W. Bush's inaugural speech to mark his second term in office captured this vividly. His address was about 'preparing people for the challenges of life in a free society...by making every citizen an agent of his or her own destiny'. Significantly, neoliberalism is no longer associated simply with Republicans in the US or Conservatives in the UK but was as central to the Clinton administration as it was to New Labour's period in office in the UK until mid-2010. Lisa Duggan (2003) argues that Clinton extended the Reagan/Bush Sr. era, while Ong contends that Clinton's government marked a new second phase of neoliberal governance in which the *psychological internalization of individual responsibilization* was stressed. Significant discursive elements remain the same in the Obama administration, though perhaps tempered by a more welfare-concerned ethic seen most vividly in the project of health-care reform.

This resonates with Peck and Tickell's (2002) periodization that discerns proto-, rollback- and rollout-neoliberalism – the latter being a more advanced form in which quasi-market mechanisms expand over an ever-widening range of activities. Indeed it would seem that many of the different ways of periodizing neoliberalism point to its deeper penetration over time and its intensification as a force for creating actors who are rational, calculating and self-motivating, and who are increasingly exhorted to make sense of their individual biographies in terms of discourses of freedom, autonomy and choice – no matter how constrained their lives may actually be (Rose, 1999).

Spatially, neoliberalism is ever expanding its geopolitical reach, though, as Ong (2006, p. 1) cautions, 'neoliberalism means many different things depending on one's vantage point' and it may become something different as it travels (say) from the US to the fast-growing BRIC economies (Brazil, Russia, India and China). Nevertheless, it is striking how global actors are disseminating neoliberal ethics transnationally, not simply through the 'brute force' of structural adjustment policies and the like, but also through development initiatives in which bodies such as the UN and World Bank work increasingly with private corporations and 'brands', exporting particular modes of entrepreneurial subjectivity. A case in point is the 'Girl Effect' in which Nike's Coalition for Adolescent Girls is directing 30 organizations including leading NGOs, the Bill and Melinda Gates Foundation and UNICEF in promoting a notion of 'girl power' borrowed directly from the UK pop group the Spice Girls. The Nike Corporation's branding experts played a pivotal role in creating the media, internet and social networking campaign, with its bold claim that investing in adolescent girls holds the key to ending world poverty (Koffman and Gill, 2013).

One of the criticisms levelled at neoliberalism is that it has become a 'catch-all' term incapable of explaining or illuminating anything. In an important paper paralleling Stuart Hall's famous interrogation of postcolonialism ('When was "the Postcolonial?"' (Hall, 1996)), John Clarke (2008) critiques the sweep and 'omnipotence' of the term neoliberalism and effectively challenges us to answer 'what *isn't* neoliberal?' His arguments are important and should give us pause. But rather than abandoning the term we want to use it here – as do contributors to this volume – in three ways.

First we want to push for more careful, detailed empirical studies of neoliberalism 'on the ground' and 'in action' – to argue for research that relates the grand theoretical claims to the lived realities of people's lives. Secondly we want to explore neoliberalism in relation to subjectivity.

Thirdly, we want to open up and investigate the relationship between neoliberalism and postfeminism. As argued elsewhere (Gill, 2007), this remains underexplored. But it appears that there is a powerful resonance between postfeminism and neoliberalism which operates at at least three levels. First, and most broadly, both appear to be structured by a current of individualism that has almost entirely replaced notions of the social or political, or any idea of individuals as subject to pressures, constraints or influence from outside themselves. Secondly, it is clear that the autonomous, calculating, self-regulating subject of neoliberalism bears a strong resemblance to the active, freely choosing, self-reinventing subject of postfeminism. These two parallels suggest, then, that postfeminism is not simply a response to feminism but also a sensibility that is at least partly constituted through the pervasiveness of neoliberal ideas. However, there is a third connection which might imply that the synergy is even more significant: in the popular cultural discourses examined in this volume it is *women* who are called on to self-manage, to self-discipline. To a much greater extent than men, women are required to work on and transform the self, to regulate every aspect of their conduct, and to present all their actions as freely chosen. Could it be that neoliberalism *is always already gendered*, and that women are constructed as its ideal subjects?

Here, several essays pay close attention to the relation between neoliberalism and gender. Imogen Tyler looks at the way in which pregnancy no longer operates as a period of 'escape' from the strictures that require women to be compulsorily beautiful and heterosexually desirable, arguing that this signals the deeper commodification of maternity under neoliberalism. Pregnant beauty becomes a disciplinary technology that occludes or obscures the tensions between maternity and the neoliberal workplace, as well as the class inequality that supports middle-class motherhood. Laura Harvey and Rosalind Gill examine the construction of a postfeminist and neoliberal subject whom they call the 'sexual entrepreneur', elaborating their discussion through notions of sexual subjectification and technologies of sexiness. Shelley Budgeon explores the contradictions of successful femininity, arguing that Third Wave feminism is at risk of remaining trapped in discourses of choice, freedom and empowerment that are complicit with, rather than critical of, postfeminism and neoliberalism.

Subjectivity

We want to argue that a focus on the psychosocial seems to be missing from most work on neoliberalism – though Nikolas Rose (1999) and Wendy

Brown (2003) are obvious exceptions. Most writers on neoliberalism quote Foucault on 'governmentality': 'governmentality covers a range of practices that constitute, define, organize and instrumentalize the strategies that individuals in their freedom can use in dealing with each other' (Foucault, 2003, p.128). As Nikolas Rose (1999, p. 4) puts it, 'to govern human beings is not to crush their capacity to act, but to acknowledge it and utilize it for one's own objectives'. However, what often seems to be missing from writing about neoliberalism – as Derek Hook (2007) has pointed out – is the emphasis in Foucault's later work on the *mentality* part of governmentality – the ways in which these governing practices quite literally 'get inside us' to materialize or constitute our subjectivities. Along with the lack of attention to experiences, this seems to be a significant omission in writing about neoliberalism to date.

Our third key term, then, is subjectivity – a term we have selected over the obvious and more readily accessible alternative 'identity' in order to signal the extent to which we see contemporary modes of power operating increasingly on and through the making and remaking of subjectivities, and through 'governing the soul' (Rose, 1989). This is a theme taken up in multiple chapters in this volume (some already mentioned). Tyler, for example, argues that the new figure of pregnant beauty is literally reconfiguring the experience of maternity, while Harvey and Gill look at the uneven ways in which sexual entrepreneurship plays out on male and female bodies – while for men it is presented primarily in terms of 'technique', for women becoming the normatively demanded sexual entrepreneur requires a remaking of subjectivity itself.

The new femininities under discussion here need to be situated in the wider context of 'individualization' and risk that some have understood as pre-eminent features of late capitalism, late modernity or liquid society (Bauman, 2007; Beck, 1999; Beck and Beck-Gernsheim, 2001). Central among these changes are the gradual 'desacralization' of social life, the erosion of grand political narratives or certainties, and the rise of both individualism and consumerism (Shilling, 1993). Giddens (1991) argues that the dissolution of tradition in late or high modernity has been accompanied by 'ontological insecurity' and a reflexive concern with identity and the body. Secure and stable self-identity no longer derives automatically from one's position in the social structure, and in its place some argue that we are seeing attempts to ground identity in the body, as individuals are left alone to establish and maintain values with which to live and make sense of their daily lives. Shilling (1993) argues that high modernity has produced an unprecedented 'individualization', in which meanings are privatized and individuals become preoccupied with 'projects of the self' (Featherstone, 1991). In late modernity, it is argued, 'we have become responsible for the design of our bodies' (Giddens, 1991, p. 102) – yet insufficient attention has been paid to the ways in which this plays out across differently gendered, racialized, aged, classed and abled bodies.

In feminist writing (some of which has contested these accounts (Skeggs, 2004; Smart, 2007)), questions of agency have been of particular concern in postfeminist and neoliberal contexts in which women (particularly young women) are often presented as autonomous, agentic and empowered subjects, and in which, even in feminist scholarship, an older vocabulary that spoke of structures, domination, inequality and oppression sometimes seems to be giving way to something more celebratory, as though the feminist theorizing were itself inflected by a postfeminist sensibility and had come to believe the hype. Thus, while some scholars insist that we must think female agency in a wider context of persistent coercion and inequality (Madhok, 2012), others deploy a more upbeat language of freedom and choice (Duits and Van Zoonen, 2006).

Such debates are animated here across a range of chapters. Feona Attwood's discussion of alternative pornographies highlights women's active agency in making different forms of erotica and argues that 'camgirls' can be understood as defying objectification and controlling the gaze. Sue Jackson and Tiina Vares draw attention to girls' critical engagements with the 'sexualized' self-presentation of pop stars and celebrities, even while the girls are keen to distance themselves from anything they regard as 'slutty'. By contrast, Ringrose's study of girls' self-presentation on the Bebo social networking site, points to their struggles to fashion a viable subjectivity amongst its increasingly hypersexualized and pornified discourses. Dawn Currie, Shauna Pomerantz and Deirdre Kelly's chapter on skater girls is interesting because it examines how the capacity to invest in 'alternative' or counter-hegemonic modes of femininity is contingent and unstable, as well as based in particular sets of material and cultural advantages that are not available to all.

Thinking transnationally

This book contains essays from and/or about a number of different national contexts. Whilst it is dominated by British and North American studies it also includes chapters that focus beyond 'Anglo' contexts. JongMi Kim examines the figure of the 'Missy' as a 'new femininity' taking root in South Korean culture, in a way that challenges the de-sexualization and domestication of married women; Christina Scharff's chapter critically engages with the 'new feminisms' that have emerged in Germany in the last few years; and Michelle Lazar analyses advertisements in Singapore and traces how they both displace local–global disjunctures and build upon a distinctive history of Singaporean gender politics.

But more than this, a number of the chapters (including Lazar's) draw on ideas from critical race studies and postcoloniality to attempt to *think transnationally*, to think across borders in a way that does not simply 'add in' countries previously 'overlooked' by Western/Northern scholarship, but to address the transnational as a field structured by power relations. They begin what Aniko Imre, Katarzyna Marciniak and Aine O'Healy (2009, pp. 386–7) call 'a contemporary transcultural dialogue' in which 'feminism needs to reconstitute itself in a time of global interconnectedness, when the economic and political processes of representations of media culture' inevitably permeate everything, including feminisms. The chapters ask difficult questions about differences, mediation and translation – highlighting the tensions produced. In doing so they play what Ien Ang (2001) regards as the appropriate role for the postcolonial intellectual: that of 'party pooper':

> The diasporic intellectual acts as a perpetual party pooper because her impulse is to point to ambiguities, complexities and contradictions, to complicate matters rather than provide merely for solutions, to blur the distinctions between colonizer and colonized, dominant and subordinate, oppressor and oppressed. (Ang, 2001, p. 2)

This is not an easy mingling or a smoothing out, nor is it a call to some sort of comforting 'global sisterhood'. It is not, as Trinh Minh-Ha has argued, a project in which 'the margins can easily comfort the centre in its goodwill and liberalism' (1991, p. 17). Rather, it starts from the recognition of a transnational field as structured by radically uneven power relations, differences and even perhaps incommensurabilities (Imre et al., 2009).

Sadie Wearing explores the complex racial, sexual, geopolitical, postcolonial and generational politics generated by the film *Vers le Sud*. Carolyn Pedwell critically examines the very politics of transnational cultural comparisons, asking not only what it means to continually compare and juxtapose differently located subjects – for example veil-wearing young Muslim women or others who 'flaunt' their bodies in heterosexy dress – but also what political work such comparisons do. Jin Haritaworn looks at how the figure of the 'Thai prostitute' haunts and shapes performances of Thai femininities across national borders. Umut Erel's chapter critically engages with migrant women from Turkey in Britain and Germany, and the ways they challenge constructions of non-Western cultures as 'backward' and less progressive. Brinda Bose explores Indian diasporic cinema as the 'Other' of Indian cinema, tracing the ways in which nostalgia about 'home' plays out in the films, but also how such films construct new possibilities for sexual subjectivities. Róisín Ryan-Flood explores, amongst other things, the transnational networks that have developed for lesbians seeking fertility services in contexts in which these are primarily or exclusively reserved for heterosexual couples.

All of the representations, subjectivities and practices explored here are located in a New World (Dis)Order that includes punitive structural adjustment policies, aid tied to political reform or access to mineral resources, nation building, the 'liberalization' of the global economy – to say nothing of increasingly aggressive Anglo-American foreign policy and the 'War on Terror'. As Anne McClintock (1995) has argued, the 'post' in postcolonial may be prematurely celebratory, and a variety of neocolonialisms and new forms of transnational power and domination are in play. In her chapter, Gargi Bhattacharyya draws attention to these processes, looking particularly at economic crisis, securitization and militarization, and challenging feminist thinkers to generate ways of engaging that will take seriously the 'emergencies' of the current moment, both within nation states and across borders.

The structure and organization of the book

Part I: Sexual subjectivity and the makeover paradigm

New Femininities is divided into five thematically organized sections. In the first, 'Sexual Subjectivity and the makeover paradigm', themes of postfeminism, compulsory beauty and heterosexiness are discussed alongside consideration of the makeover as a disciplinary gender, race, class and agemaking technology.

'Pregnant Beauty' begins with the observation that there has been a proliferation of representations of the maternal. Placing these representations within the context of neoliberalism, **Imogen Tyler** argues that the emergence of pregnant beauty signals the deeper commodification of maternity under neoliberalism, a process that transforms maternal experience and contributes to lived gender inequalities. Concluding her chapter with reflections on an anti-neoliberal feminist politics, Tyler discusses the work *Contemplation Time* of artist/activist Lena Simic as a possible maternal response to neoliberalism.

Michelle Lazar's chapter analyses beauty advertisements in a Singaporean English daily, exploring how advertisers link the normative practice of beautification with an emancipated identity. Her chapter, 'The Right to be Beautiful', demonstrates how local/global disjunctures are effaced in the advertisements by the prevalence of a universalizing individualist discourse. On the other hand, the advertisements build on a distinctive history of gender equality in Singapore, where the government tended to mute feminist struggles by introducing gender equality measures. In that sense, decades of enjoying government-driven rights and opportunities make mainstream Singapore fertile ground for the postfeminist distancing of feminism.

Laura Harvey's and **Rosalind Gill's** chapter 'Spicing it Up' explores the emergence of a new feminine subject: the 'sexual entrepreneur'. Harvey and Gill begin with a discussion of the 'sexualization of culture', and then elaborate the theoretical notions of sexual subjectification, technologies of sexiness and sexual entrepreneurship. They suggest a way of reading the rise and proliferation of sexual entrepreneurship that tries not to fall back into old binaries (for example, either unproblematic liberation or wholesale recuperation). The chapter examines the new subjectivity of the sexual entrepreneur through a detailed discussion of the British television makeover show *The Sex Inspectors*.

Lisa Guerrero's chapter '(M)other-in-Chief' explores the meaning of American womanhood as embodied in the role of the First Lady of the United States, and discusses various forms of gender and racial oppression that create a complex terrain in which Michelle Obama has had to forge a different model of idealized American womanhood. Suggesting that Michelle Obama presents an interesting amalgam of various models of 'First Lady' womanhood alongside models of black womanhood, Guerrero illustrates her analysis of the particular challenges that Michelle Obama faces in transforming, or being transformed by, the role of the first black First Lady.

The genre of the makeover show constitutes the focus of **Estella Tincknell's** chapter on the British television programme *Ten Years Younger*. Exploring representations of the ageing female body, Tincknell foregrounds the problematic ways in which the television makeover programme has helped to reconstruct contemporary femininity as an abject condition waiting to be renewed and redeemed by cosmetic surgery. Arguing that femininity has become represented almost entirely in terms of fragmentation as well as objectification, Tincknell concludes by asking critical question about women's agency in postfeminist culture.

Part II: Negotiating postfeminist media culture

The second section of the book moves from textual analysis (broadly conceived) to studies of how girls and women negotiate postfeminist culture.

In her chapter 'Are You Sexy, Flirty or a Slut?' **Jessica Ringrose** draws on findings from a UK study of young people's use of the online social networking site Bebo. Through analysis of both online and interview data, Ringrose explores how social networking sites are spaces where increasingly normalized hypersexualized and pornified discourses and visual imagery circulate rapidly. Ringrose provides a nuanced, feminist analysis that takes seriously the power dynamics of 'sexualization' processes, but that does not oversimplify the complexity of teen girls' responses to the postfeminist media context.

Andrea Press's chapter '"Feminism? That's so Seventies"' examines the particular configuration of feminist and postfeminist consciousness characterizing the way many young women think and speak today. Drawing on data collected from a larger research project on young women's discussion of the popular television show *America's Next Top Model*, Press explores how young women react to the ironies of the postfeminist sensibility, a sensibility rather schizophrenic in its acceptance both of women's career identities paired with the continuing foregrounding of bodily transformation and appearance.

Drawing on a wider research project that explores how pre-teen New Zealand girls make sense of the popular culture they engage with, **Sue Jackson and Tiina Vares** trace how girls negotiate 'hypersexualized' femininities. Their chapter 'Media Sluts' foregrounds girls' critical engagement with postfeminist media, challenging notions that girls are easily influenced by popular culture. At the same time, Jackson and Vares highlight that girls' sexuality continues to be kept under surveillance and regulated, and thereby provide a nuanced analysis of girls' talk about hypersexualization.

JongMi Kim's chapter 'Is the 'Missy' a New Femininity?' explores the figure of the 'Missy' in a Korean context. The term 'Missy' refers to a young married woman who presents herself as an unmarried woman. Seeking to examine whether the 'Missy' can be understood as a new femininity, Kim describes the origins of the concept in the media and controversies surrounding its rapid spread. Moreover, the chapter analyses empirical interviews to discuss how women construct their femininities using the concept of the 'Missy'.

Part III: Textual complications

The third section foregrounds questions of race, nation and postcoloniality in relation to 'new femininities'.

Brinda Bose's chapter 'Of Displaced Desires' presents a reading of films that focus on the Indian diasporic space in the United States and in England. Regarding cinema as a 'close-up' that reveals new formations of the subject, Bose attempts to read shifting patterns of sexualities in the context of shifting spaces. She traces multiple ways in which nostalgia about 'home' plays out in the films, but also explores how contemporary diasporic cinema constructs a vision of possible new diaposric sexualities. Diasporic cinema flirts with radical stances and actions, but fails to sustain its promise in order to maintain a status quo that is delicately created through the trope of nostalgia for the homeland.

Sadie Wearing's 'Notes on Some Scandals' constitutes a critical reading of the film *Vers le Sud*. Wearing explores the workings of shame in the narrative trope of a sexual encounter between an 'older' woman and a younger man that is embedded in a complex web of racial, sexual, geopolitical, postcolonial and generational politics. She suggests that there is something new in the specific way that the management of shame is implicated in broader questions of race, class and postcolonial dynamics. While earlier versions of intergenerational sexual encounters tended to focus on the injustice of norms of sexual conduct that render an encounter between an 'older' woman and a younger man illegitimate, *Vers le Sud* exposes the shameless injustice of economic privilege and inequality.

In 'The Limits of Cross-Cultural Analogy' **Carolyn Pedwell** critically examines feminist texts that draw cross-cultural analogies between Muslim veiling and so-called Western fashion and beauty practices. Pedwell's chapter reveals the limitations of cross-cultural analogies as a critical tool. Porno-chic and veiling, for example, become defined predominantly through their relationship to gendered norms which means that the analogies encounter difficulties in tracing multiple and intersecting axes of differentiation that are constitutive of these practices.

Part IV: New femininities: agency and/as making do

The fourth section picks up on the discussion of agency, mentioned already. Borrowing Atwood's phrase of 'making do', it seeks to locate new feminini-ties in the context of debates about autonomy and power.

Feona Attwood's chapter 'Through the Looking Glass?' focuses on alter-native pornography in the contemporary Western context where the rapid development of media and communication technologies offers women unprecedented access to various forms of cultural production. She shows that these cultural and technological shifts also open up a space for the presentation of new feminine sexualities that are not simply responses to male desires or forms of self-policing. Arguing that agency is always a form of 'making do', Attwood shows that there are new ways of doing femi-ninity and making culture in the context of women's online sexual self-representation.

Jin Haritaworn's 'Reckoning with Prostitutes' demonstrates how the fig-ure of the 'Thai prostitute' haunts and shapes performances of Thai femi-ninities. Drawing on interviews with people in Britain and Germany who were raised in 'mixed' Thai/'interracial' families, Haritaworn shows that the interviewees never got away from the haunting presences of the 'Thai prostitute', and yet they were not one-sidedly defined by the prostitute dis-course. Haritaworn concludes by underscoring the importance of exploring how the interviewees discussed their gender identities in order to restore sexual agency to female-assigned people of Thai descent.

Umut Erel's chapter 'Migrant Women Challenging Stereotypical Views on Femininities and Family' is based on a biographical study of skilled and educated migrant women from Turkey in Britain and Germany. Erel explores how some migrant women's articulations of their sexual identi-ties challenge gendered and racialized public representations. Her chapter presents a range of ways in which migrant women negotiate heteronorma-tive and family-centred female subjectivities, thereby foregrounding the need to move beyond dichotomous constructions of traditional versus pro-gressive femininities to an acknowledgement of internal differentiation and multiple identifications.

Róisín Ryan-Flood's chapter 'Negotiating Sexual Citizenship' explores the implications of choosing to parent outside heteronormative parameters at different spatial scales. Drawing on interviews with 68 lesbian parents in Sweden and Ireland, Ryan-Flood explores the practical challenges facing lesbians embarking on parenthood and the transnational networks that develop for lesbians seeking fertility services abroad. The chapter examines lesbians' experiences of reproductive health care and their constant negotiation of heteronormative assumptions about 'the family'.

Part V: New feminisms, new challenges

Finally, the book turns from 'new femininities' to new feminisms and new challenges.

Christina Scharff's chapter critically analyses 'The New German Feminisms'. By discussing their characteristic features, Scharff argues that the new feminisms exhibit some problematic tendencies. The emancipatory potential of the new feminisms is limited by their homophobic representation, and repudiation, of 1970s feminism. This, in addition to the uncritical uptake of individualist rhetoric as well as the focus on privileged, white, heterosexual and 'German' women, means that the new feminists fail sufficiently to interrogate the very social constellations that initially gave rise to the felt need for a 'new' feminist politics.

Shelley Budgeon explores 'The Contradictions of Successful Femininity'. Her chapter investigates characterizing features of Third Wave feminism in order to understand new femininities and their relationship to both feminism and postfeminism. She highlights that Third Wave feminism frequently promotes an individualist politics that is based on self-definition and projects of selfhood. However, argues Budgeon, Third Wave feminism must provide opportunities to transcend the incitement to an uncritical project of self-definition in order to produce feminist articulations of femininity.

Investigating the themes of feminism and femininity in the context of 'Skater Girlhood', **Dawn Currie, Deirdre Kelly** and **Shauna Pomerantz** draw on semi-structured interviews with young Canadian girls. Being specifically interested in 'alternative' modes of femininity, they focus on skateboarding and explore the unstable and contingent nature of girls' identities. They show that some girls move freely between and among competing ways of doing girlhood, but underline that the ability to belong to several social groups is linked to material and cultural privileges.

Gargi Bhattacharyya's chapter 'Will These Emergencies Never End?' outlines a programme of study of recent global changes. Bhattacharyya examines how the economic crisis and processes of securitization affect mundane practices in Britain (and beyond), and explores the impact of the economic crisis on migrant workers. She concludes her chapter by asking about the complementarities between economic exploitation and securitization, and the suitability of feminist theoretical frames to grasp recent global developments and changes.

Bibliography

Alice, L. (1995) *What is Postfeminism? Or, Having it Both Ways: Feminism, Postmodernism, Postfeminism* (New Zealand: Massey University).

Ang, I. (2001) *On Not Speaking Chinese: Living between Asia and the West* (London: Routledge).

Arthurs, J. (2011) 'Deliciously Consumable: The Use and Abuses of Irony in Counter-Trafficking Campaigns' in K. Ross (ed.), *The Blackwell Handbook of Gender, Sexualities and the Media* (Oxford: Blackwell).

Bauman, Z. (2007) *Liquid Times: Living in an Age of Uncertainty* (Cambridge: Polity Press).

Beck, U. (1999) *World Risk Society* (Cambridge: Polity).

Beck, U. and E. Beck-Gernsheim (2001) *Individualisation: Institutionalised Individualism and its Social and Political Consequences* (London: Sage).

Beck, U., J. V. Loon and B. Adam (2000) *The Risk Society and Beyond: Critical Issues for Social Theory* (London: Sage).

Brooks, A. (1997) *Postfeminisms: Feminism, Cultural Theory and Cultural Forms* (London: Routledge).

Brown, W. (2003) 'Neo-liberalism and the End of Liberal Democracy', *Theory and Event* 7(1): 1–19.

Clarke, J. (2008) 'Living with/in and without Neo-liberalism', *Focaal: European Journal of Anthropology* 51: 135–47.

Duggan, L. (2003) *The Twilight of Equality: Neoliberalism, Cultural Politics and the Attack on Democracy* (Boston: Beacon Press).

Duits, L. and L. Van Zoonen (2006) 'Headscarves and Porno-Chic: Disciplining Girls' Bodies in the European Multicultural Society', *European Journal of Women's Studies* 13(2): 103–17.

Faludi, S. (1991) *Backlash: The Undeclared War Against Women* (London: Chatto & Windus).

Featherstone, M. (1991) *Consumer Culture and Postmodernism* (London: Sage).

Foucault, M. (2003) *The Essential Foucault: Selections from the Essential Works of Foucault 1954–1984*, ed. P. Rabinow and N. Rose (New York and London: Free Press).

Giddens, A. (1991) *Modernity and Self-Identity: Self and Society in the Late Modern Age* (Cambridge: Polity Press).

Gill, R. (2006) *Gender and the Media* (Cambridge: Polity Press).

Gill, R. (2007) 'Postfeminist Media Culture: Elements of a Sensibility', *European Journal of Cultural Studies* 10(2):147–66.

Hall, S. (1996) 'When was "the Postcolonial"? Thinking at the Limit', in I. Chambers and L. Curti (eds), *The Post-Colonial Question: Common Skies, Divided Horizons* (New York: Routledge).

Harris, A. (2004) *Future Girl: Young Women in the 21st century* (New York and London: Routledge).

Harvey, D. (2005) *A Brief History of Neoliberalism* (Oxford: Oxford University Press).

Hollows, J. (2000) *Feminism, Femininity and Popular Culture* (Manchester: Manchester University Press).

Hook, D. (2007) *Foucault, Psychology and the Analytics of Power* (London: Palgrave Macmillan).

Imre, A., K. Mariniak, et al. (2009) 'Transcultural Mediations and Transnational Politics of Difference', *Feminist Media Studies* 9(4): 385–90.

Koffman, O. and Gill, R. (2013). 'i matter. And so does she: Girl power, (post)feminism and the Girl Effect' in Buckingham, D., Bragg, S. & Kehily, M. J. (eds). *Youth Cultures in the Age of Global Media*. London: Palgrave.

Madhok, S. (2012) *Rethinking Agency: Developmentalism, Gender and Rights* (New York and London: Routledge).

McClintock, A. (1995) *Imperial Leather: Race, Gender and Sexuality in the Colonial Conquest* (New York and London: Routledge).

McRobbie, A. (2004) 'Post-Feminism and Popular Culture', *Feminist Media Studies* 4(3): 255–64.

McRobbie, A. (2007) 'Top Girls?', *Cultural Studies* 21(4): 718–37.

McRobbie, A. (2009) *The Aftermath of Feminism: Gender, Culture and Social Change* (London: Sage).

Minh-ha, T. (1991) *When the Moon Waxes Red* (New York: Routledge).

Ong, A. (2006) *Neoliberalism as Exception: Mutations in Citizenship and Sovereignty* (Durham, NC and London: Duke University Press).

Peck, J. and A. Tickell (2002) 'Neoliberalizing Space' in N. Brenner and N. Theodore (eds), *Spaces of Neoliberalism* (Oxford: Blackwell).

Riviere, J. (1929) 'Womanliness as a Masquerade', *International Journal of Psychoanalysis* 10: 303–13.

Rose, N. (1989) *Governing the Soul: Technologies of Human Subjectivity* (London: Routledge).

Rose, N. (1999) *The Powers of Freedom* (London: Routledge).

Shilling, C. (1993) *The Body and Social Theory* (London: Sage).

Skeggs, B. (2004) *Class, Self, Culture* (London: Routledge).

Smart, C. (2007) *Personal Life: New Directions in Sociological Thinking* (Cambridge: Polity Press).

Tasker, Y. and D. Negra (eds) (2007) *Interrogating Postfeminism: Gender and the Politics of Popular Culture* (Durham, NC and London: Duke University Press).

Whelehan, I. (2000) *Overloaded: Feminism and Popular Culture* (London: Women's Press).

Yeatman, A. (1994) *Postmodern Revisionings of the Political* (New York: Routledge).

Part I
Sexual Subjectivity and the Makeover Paradigm

1
Pregnant Beauty: Maternal Femininities under Neoliberalism

Imogen Tyler

> Fourteen weeks pregnant with her first child, Margot Tenenbaum secretly wished she were a bit more nauseous. As it was, she controlled her mild bouts of queasiness with pasta and pizza, but if she'd been just a notch sicker every once in a while, she might have felt too bad to eat at all.
>
> (Laurie Abraham, *New York Times Magazine*, 2005)

> HOTmilk celebrates the sexy, sensual woman inside the loving mother.
>
> (HOTmilk, advertising copy, 2009)

Since the mid-1990s there has been an extraordinary proliferation of representations of maternity within popular culture, arts, literature, politics, consumer culture and 'everyday life'. The fascination with celebrity pregnancy and motherhood, the emergence of 'momoir' literary genres, a new emphasis on the maternal in the visual and performance arts and the ascendance of 'Maternal TV' reality formats, are indicative of this new visibility. The maternal is no longer confined to traditionally domestic or child-orientated spaces, such as private homes, hospitals, parks and playgrounds,[1] but is present in spectacularly public forms: think of British artist Marc Quinn's 12ft statue of a naked, heavily pregnant, disabled artist Alison Lapper, in Trafalgar Square, London in 2005 (see Betterton, 2006) or pregnant beauty contests (see Longhurst, 2000).

Pregnancy and motherhood have even taken centre stage in mainstream politics: a global media storm surrounded the French Justice Minister Rachida Dati when she announced her pregnancy as a lone mother, and later made a very public and glamorous return to work five days after a Caesarean section in January 2009.[2] In the United States the 2009 presidential election produced some striking maternal imagery: pro-life Republican vice-presidential candidate Sarah Palin went on the election trail brandishing a four-month-old son and a pregnant teenage daughter, whilst pro-choice

Ivy League educated attorney Michelle Obama declared herself the nation's rightful 'mom in chief'. This plethora of maternal publicity is not simply a matter of representation, but signals the emergence of a range of new maternal identities and practices. For example, the internet has enabled the rise of a phenomenal 'digital motherhood'; in Britain millions of mothers are online, creating blogs, sharing foetal scans and 'celebrity style' pregnant photographs in 'bump galleries', swapping tips and commiserating with each other in the chat rooms of sites such as Mumsnet, and uploading childbirth movies to video-sharing platforms (see Longhurst, 2009).[3] So whilst it has been claimed that girls are the 'privileged' subjects of neoliberalism (see McRobbie, 2009) this is also the era of 'maternal femininities'. Maternity has never been so visible, so talked about, so public and so deeply incoherent.

This chapter will examine the sexual politics of maternity under neoliberalism through a focus on one key contemporary maternal figure, which I will term 'pregnant beauty'.[4] One of the defining contradictions of neoliberalism is that it is packaged as concerned with individual freedom, choice, democracy and personal responsibility. In reality, as David Harvey argues, neoliberalism is a class-based economic project that systematically strips assets from the poor (including welfare provisions) and concentrates wealth within a tiny global elite (individuals and corporations). As a system of governance neoliberalism has fabricated new subjectivities capable, as Nikolas Rose phrases it, 'of bearing the burdens of liberty' (1999, p. viii). Within a neoliberal society the ability (and desire) to work and to spend are key measures of value and ideal neoliberal subjects cooperate with their subjectification within these markets (and compulsive consumption and workaholism are symptomatic pathologies).

As Angela McRobbie argues, popular culture is a privileged terrain for the production of neoliberal values (2009, p. 29). This terrain becomes legible through the appearance of specific figurative types, figures who move across and through different popular media and accrue meaning, form and value as they travel. In this chapter I will argue that pregnant beauty represents a particular neoliberal amalgam of maternity and femininity, and is deserving of closer analysis. In the last decade, feminist theorists have successively argued that young motherhood, especially lower-class lone motherhood 'carries a whole range of vilified meanings associated with failed femininity' (ibid., p. 732; see Tyler, 2008). Maternity is understood in this context as a 'failed femininity', in relation to a specific neoliberal femininity determined by economic productivity and flexibility. Young motherhood is constituted as a site of failure, not primarily because of a perceived sexual immorality, but because maternity signifies an unwillingness to work (or shop). It is the imagined economic redundancy and welfare dependence of this population which is repugnant. Thus the idealisation and celebration of youthful maternity in the figure of pregnant beauty may appear anachronistic. In what follows I will consider how pregnant beauty complicates feminist accounts of young motherhood, and reconfigures maternity as a neoliberal femininity. I will argue that pregnant beauty is highly spectacular and contradictory 'maternal femininity' that combines signifiers of (sexual) freedom, consumption, choice, agency and futurity in a powerful and seductive post-feminist cultural ideal. This chapter traces the origins of this figure within Anglo-American celebrity culture; it then outlines some of the consumer practices through which pregnancy has been reconfigured into an aesthetic 'project of self'. It argues that the emergence of pregnant beauty signals the deeper commodification of maternity under neoliberalism, a process which is reshaping maternal experience and contributing to lived gender inequalities. I will conclude by reflecting on politics and aesthetics and asking whether a political maternal aesthetic might, nevertheless, form the basis of an anti-neoliberal feminist politics.

Out and proud

> I love Nicole Richie's pregnancy look. Sorta makes me wanna get pregnant myself.
>
> ('Harley', 2007)

In the early 1990s a representational shift took place within popular culture. The visual spectacle of the pregnant body, previously confined to clinics, hospitals and the scientific or healthcare manuals – or to the avant-garde or pornographic margins – was suddenly and shamelessly everywhere, on the catwalk, dancing in pop videos, reading the news, acting in soap operas, featuring in advertising campaigns and spectacularly visible on cinema screens. As the name of the US-based pregnant clothing company 'Preggers n' proud' beautifully illustrates, pregnant women were now 'out and proud'. The figure of pregnant beauty emerged out of and is still driven by celebrity culture. The publication of Annie Leibovitz's photograph of a naked and heavily pregnant Hollywood actress, Demi Moore, on the front cover of the American magazine *Vanity Fair* in August 1991 was the 'celebrity event' that marked the breaking of the powerful cultural taboo around the representation of pregnancy (see Tyler, 2001). The palpable shock, intense controversy and global public debate that 'More Demi Moore' generated is, 20 years later, difficult to comprehend.[5]

Since 1991 there have been thousands of high-profile publicity photo shoots of pregnant celebrities. By the mid-1990s specialist pregnancy photographers had emerged to meet the demand for pregnancy photography amongst 'ordinary' women. As journalist Hilary Stout notes, 'the maternity photograph is becoming a rite of pregnancy for an increasing number of women, many of them over 30, with money to spend and a yearning to savor every part of the experience' (Stout, 2005). If pregnancy was previously imagined as a passive, abject and ordinary physical state to be stoically borne in private, the pregnancy photo shoot reconfigured pregnancy into a sexy bodily performance: a 'body project' to be coveted and enjoyed. Alongside professional photographic services, pregnant photography has become central to everyday photographic practices. Family photographic albums, which would have previously marginalized pregnant bodies, now feature them, carefully staging changing body shape in poses which mimic celebrity photo shots. Within online communities, women document their changing attitudes to their pregnant bodies: hundreds of thousands of 'belly shots' can be found in specially created 'pregnancy galleries'. Whilst a closer examination of these photographic practices is beyond the scope of this chapter, these online spaces offer rich data which reveal some of the ways in which the new ideology of pregnant beauty is being actively negotiated.[6] In one typical online pregnancy diary 'Anastasia' reflects on why she has decided to visually document her pregnant body and share her experiences online:

> I can remember being mildly revolted by the naked image of a very preg-nant Demi Moore in Vanity Fair all those years ago and now I feel like I was a traitor for thinking she looked anything but beautiful. My first pregnancy I felt sensual and bought lingerie and made my husband take pictures of my version of 'Mama Demi'.[7]

Anastasia's reflections track the shift from abjection to idealisation which I am interested in thinking about in this chapter (see also Tyler, 2009). Indeed, this kind of insight into how women relate to celebrity pregnan-cies, exemplifies the ways in which the celebrity body has become a cen-tral means through which contemporary social values are distributed and through consumption, identification and mimicry become hardwired into everyday practices of subjectivity (see Tyler and Bennett, 2010). Pregnant beauty has not only transformed how we see the pregnant body, but has impacted on women's experience of pregnancy. For the 'bump chic' genera-tion pregnancy is not an embarrassing or abject physical state but an oppor-tunity to have a differently fashionable and sexy body shape. In the context of older ideologies which compelled women to conceal their pregnant bod-ies in public, the new visual culture of pregnancy is a site of pleasurable identifications and consumption and is imagined as a new freedom.

Fertile fashion

If being photographed whilst pregnant became *de rigueur* in the mid-1990s, by the end of the decade pregnant women were also becoming more vis-ible 'on the streets' as (young) pregnant woman stopped concealing their pregnant bodies and adopted 'skintight' fashions, designed to cling to and emphasise pregnant women's swollen abdomens. Proud pregnancy fashions are epitomised by T-shirts marketed to pregnant women which advertise pregnancy with logos as such 'Baby Under Manufacturing Process', 'Sexy Mama', 'Under Construction⇓' and 'I'M A BABY: Get Me Out Of Here!',[8] whilst self-help guides, such as *Hot Mamma: How to Have a Baby and Be a Babe* (Salmansohn, 2003) educate women in 'pregnancy style'. Successful pregnancy chic is dependent on the ability to remain 'taut' during pregnancy – to minimise weight gain and, as a recent New York magazine article put it, acquiring that 'perfect little bump' (Abraham, 2005). As pregnant bodies have become subject to aesthetic and sexual scrutiny there has been a qualitative shift in the intensity of (self-) surveillance pregnant women now experience, a shift which has changed the meaning of pregnancy itself.[9] As Julia Becks, founder of 40 Weeks, a business that provides 'consulting and branding advice to companies targeting the expectant and new-parent market', writes: 'pregnancy is no longer just a means to an end' (in Stout, 2005).

Pregnant pornography, historically a marginal sub-category of pornography, is now mainstream. In 1998, the US soap actress Lisa Rinna was the first pregnant woman to feature in a *Playboy* photo shoot (see Rebecca Huntley, 2000). A decade later, 'Lad's mag' features such as 'Maxim's 9 Hottest Pregnant Women Ever' (*Maxim*, November, 2007) are evidence of how openly pregnant bodies are marketed to a male sexual gaze.[10] Pregnant sex is also aimed at female consumer. For example, a feature in British women's magazine *Scarlet*, entitled 'How to Grind with a Bump!', instructs women in how to have great sex whilst they are pregnant. The advertising imagery of the maternity lingerie company HOTmilk is notable for its role in the development of a visual vocabulary of pregnant sexuality. HOTmilk's print advertisements often feature pregnant women in playful, dominating sexual poses, for example the advertisement 'Seduction' (Figure 1), which depicts a bronzed and blonde pregnant woman dressed in black lingerie and straddling a male torso (his head is out of the frame). The model gazes directly at the camera/viewer, the implication being that she is *in control*, that sexual agency resides with her. It is difficult to imagine a more dramatic example of the shift in the visual culture of pregnancy from 1990 to the present time.

Developing this theme, HOTmilk's first screen commercial features a pregnant women stripping in the hallway for her husband as he steps through the door on his return from work: this short film intercuts shots of her sexually wanton face, his surprised expression and abstract close-ups of her body, before finally revealing 'the surprise' – her exposed large tight pregnant belly (see Figure 2). The striptease also involves the hedonistic shattering of domestic ornaments, staging pregnancy as a comic, excessive bodily performance: 'a tantalizing sexy striptease with a shattering twist'.

The sexualisation of pregnant bodies can easily be read as part of a more general 'pornographication' of culture (Attwood, 2006). However, it is

Figure 1   'Seduction' HOTmilk advertising image, 2008, with permission

important to note, as Rosalind Gill (2009) argues, that this process of sexualisation is uneven and has different effects, depending on how a body is marked in relation to class, age and race. Only specific types of pregnant bodies are beautiful and/or sexually desirable – white, tight, youthful bodies with social capital and appropriate aspiration; 'lower-class' pregnant celebrities, for instance, are deemed trashy and sluttish if they bare their bumps. Historically, middle- and upper-class mothers were granted a social position 'safe from sex' (Kaplan, 1992 in Huntley, 2000, p. 348). Until the 1990s, pregnancy provided even the most famous women with some respite from the scrutiny and documentation of their bodies, clothing and personal lives.[11] However, this 'sex-safe' status has always been contradictory; on the one hand pregnancy has been constructed as sacred, on the other pregnant bodies are indelibly marked by sex, hence the embarrassment and shame these bodies have historically elicited. In this respect, pregnant women, in common with low-status groups such as working-class women and black women have often been viewed as morally flawed bodies. Indeed, as sexualised bodies, pregnant women were 'excluded from the beauty category on moral grounds. *They lacked the innocence of true beauties'* (Craig, 2007, p. 168, my emphasis). The liberalisation of culture in the 1960s enabled the taboo on pregnant representation to be broken – a taboo still referenced within commercial imagery, with HOTmilk, for example, declaring that 'young mothers that look this hot should be banned' (Figure 2). In terms of women's everyday lives, the most significant consequence of this representational shift from confinement to pregnant beauty, is that in fundamental ways pregnant women are no longer released, however briefly, from either the relentless pursuit of beauty or the pressure to perform sexual availability: in this case *sexual freedom is in actuality sex work.*[12]

The ideology of pregnant beauty reaches its apotheosis in the post-partum photo shoot, the aim of which is to demonstrate how rapidly celebrities can shrink back to a pre- pregnant size and shape. It was another Leibovitz and Moore collaboration which inaugurated this trend, provoking yet more controversy when a naked body-painted Moore was shot for front cover of *Vanity Fair* in August 1992 (exactly a year after 'More Demi Moore'), framed by the caption 'Demi's Birthday Suit'. Magazines, newspapers and celebrity websites now engage in a relentless documentation of post-partum celebrity bodies. Dieting products, magazines and fitness DVDs (and from US reality TV host and celebrity mother Brooke Burke, a post-pregnancy girdle, 'Taut'), promise to help women in their battle to 'shed' pregnancy weight and achieve optimum 'body bounce back'.[13] Shari Dworkin and Faye Linda Wachs' analysis of the magazine *Shape Fit Pregnancy* led them to conclude that:

Ideals of contemporary motherhood now prescribe a new set of tasks beyond the first shift of work and the second shift of household labor

Figure 2   'HOTmilk presents' 2009, with permission

and child care. There is now a required third shift of bodywork. After birth, there are clear warnings that 'letting the body go' constitutes failed womanhood and motherhood. (2004, p. 616)

As this short overview suggests, pregnant beauty is a disciplinary figure, which is symptomatic of a deeply entrenched 'disciplinary neoliberalism' in which the most intimate bodily experiences have become thoroughly capitalised (see S. Gill, 1995). In this respect pregnant beauty fits within the classic feminist theoretical accounts of beauty developed by Susan Bordo, in which beauty produces norms 'against which the self continually measures, judges, "disciplines," and "corrects" itself' (1993, p. 25). Certainly, contemporary culture is so saturated with pregnant beauty that it is now difficult to function as a pregnant or post-partum subject without sub-jecting oneself to these technologies of self. And whilst women may find pregnant beauty pleasurable, the new maternal markets I have illustrated in this chapter are lucrative because they activate the kinds of 'negative narcissism' (emptiness, anxiety and guilt) upon which consumer culture is predicated (Tyler, 2005). One of the most disturbing symptoms of these new disciplinary ideals is the growing demand for plastic surgery amongst postnatal women, a trend which has led the American Society of Plastic Surgeons to coin the term 'mommy makeover' to describe procedures such as tummy tucks, breast augmentations and breast lifts.[14] Gossip columnists and bloggers also speculate that pregnant celebrities are now routinely opt-ing for early elective Caesareans (from 35 weeks' gestation), as a means of limiting late pregnancy weight gain).[15] In Britain and the US health experts have argued that 20 per cent of pregnant women suffer from an eating disorder, triggered or heightened by the fear of pregnancy weight gain. The term 'pregorexia' is now widely used to describe a range of eating disorders in pregnancy (see Bruton, 2008).[16] It seems that the weight of the new ide-ology of pregnant beauty has for some women, made pregnancy itself *an unbearable weight.*

Maternal fetish

The plasticity of the figure of pregnant beauty communicates the demand that pregnant woman 'snap back' into shape after birth, returning as soon as possible to paid work: *why, you don't look like you have just had a baby.* In actuality pregnant beauty is a foil which masks the persistence of work-based inequalities: the fact, for instance, that despite a raft of equal oppor-tunities legislation since the 1970s, 7 per cent of all pregnant women in Britain lose their jobs each year as a consequence of becoming pregnant and women with children under 11 are the most discriminated group in the British workforce (Equalities Review, 2007). The celebration of mater-nity through the figure of pregnant beauty masks these lived inequalities. Indeed, pregnant beauty is extraordinary in terms of its ability to hold in place the highly conflictual and contradictory place of maternity under neo-liberalism: the high levels of anxiety and depression amongst women who are pressured and pressurise themselves to return to work immediately after birth. As Jessica Ringrose and Valerie Walkerdine argue, 'the feminist politi-cal dilemmas of housewife versus career woman...have been replaced by narratives of renaissance women who juggle thriving careers...with moth-erhood' (2008, p. 232). Pregnant beauty is a shining embodiment of this post-feminist ideology of 'having it all'. Pregnancy has been reconfigured as a neoliberal project of selfrealization, a 'body project' to be directed and managed, another site of feminine performance anxiety and thus ironically a new kind of confinement for women.

According to Sigmund Freud, a fetish arises when the child realizes that the mother doesn't have a penis (she is castrated), the horror of this discovery is such that the child generates substitutes for this lost object, to 'cover over' this gaping absence. Thus, as Sarah Kofman (1985) argues fetishism is both the recognition *and* the disavowal of reality, through the constitution of a substitute. As the visual culture of pregnant beauty suggests, this is a highly fetishistic figure; the question is what this figure is a substitute for, and what is being disavowed and recognised in this process. Some of the tensions and contradictions which this figure effectively conceals and holds in place include: the incompatibility of maternity with the neoliberal workplace, the hidden class exploitation (the armies of nannies, cleaners, childminders) which supports middle-class motherhood, nostalgia for an imaginary era of 'blissful motherhood' and anxiety about infertility amongst middle-class women. However, it is important to note that Freud's account only makes sense from the perspective of a male child, and as a narrative of loss I would argue that it in fact conceals another much more horrific recognition, that the mother is lost to the child: a loss which Luce Irigaray theorizes as primary matricide (1991). In this account fetishism arises as a consequence of an unconscious but unbearable recognition of the loss of the (imaginary) mother. The fetish then is always already a maternal object, a means of warding off the loss of the mother, and the anxiety which (knowledge of) this separation generates. Understanding fetishism in terms of mother loss is incredibly productive, as Roland Barthes illustrated in *Camera Lucida* (1981), his beautiful essay on photography written after the death of his mother. However, in terms of pregnant beauty I want to argue something different still: I want to suggest that *the figure of pregnant beauty is a fetish substitute for motherhood itself.*

As Christian Metz notes, 'a fetish has to be kept, mastered, held, like the photograph in the pocket' (1985, p. 86). Understood as a fetish, pregnant beauty figures the (impossible) mastery of the maternal body; it communicates the impossibility of a neoliberal maternity and as a consequence produces the perverse and bizarre spectacle of *maternity without children*. Indeed, it is worth noting that even in the post-partum photo shoot the baby is almost always either absent, or marginal, a mere footnote. Pregnant beauty offers women a skintight, attractive consumer-orientated version of maternity abstracted from the turbulent and messy realties of motherhood: the radical bodily changes and fluid body boundaries, the extraordinary emotional physical demands that accompany the radical dependency of a child and the never-ending social judgement of motherhood. Furthermore the reconfiguration of pregnancy as an individual identity marks the disavowal of any recognition of the maternal as a relation *between* a mother and a child (see Baraitser, 2009). Pregnant beauty is a perverse maternal fetish which wards off the maternal realities, but in doing so nevertheless bears witness to the fundamental incompatibility of maternity and neoliberalism.

Maternal art/activism

Under neoliberalism, maternity, like femininity, has been thoroughly capitalised – international 'maternal markets' trade not only in clothes, beauty products, pregnancy belly casts, photo shoots and foetal film, but in fertility treatments, eggs, foetuses and children. However, I want to conclude by contending that this examination of the figure of pregnant beauty has also revealed that there is something about the maternal, understood as a relation *between* subjects, that troubles neoliberalism. Indeed, I want to suggest that we might begin to theorize that something as a site of resistance to the capitalization of social life and subjectivity. Maggie Humm writes that 'although a resisting approach to aesthetic objectification is always necessary, there have been few productive feminist accounts [of] maternal beauty' (2006, p. 238). This chapter has traced the limitations of the aesthetic of pregnant beauty, yet I want to conclude by suggesting that the development of a *counter-cultural maternal aesthetic* might counter the hegemony of pregnant beauty. As Jacques Rancière (2004) suggests, the redistribution of visibility is critical to all radical social and political change. For Rancière visibility is not only a question of aesthetics but of democracy, hence the need for counter-cultural accounts of 'maternal beauty' are needed to trouble the new disciplinary ideals of pregnant beauty.

Since 2003 the Croatian-born, Liverpool-based, art/activist Lena Simic has begun to develop an extraordinary body of artistic work which draws on a history of feminist performance art to offer some alternatives to the hegemony of contemporary representations of the maternal. Simic's marginality as a recent immigrant to Britain, the particular radical historical vein of working-class politics she has 'married into' and her life within in an Everton council house in the city of Liverpool, combined with her experiences of being a mother to three young children, has given rise to an overtly political maternal aesthetic in Simic's work. This aesthetic captures something of the lived realities and contradictions of contemporary motherhood as well as the deeper psycho-social marginality, foreignness and displacement which is peculiar to maternal experience.

'Contemplation Time: A Document of Maternity Leave' (2007–2008) consists of the written and visual documentation of 32 visits by Simic and her newborn baby, Sid, to a local park and a specific park bench between 5 July 2007 and 27 April 2008. During these visits Simic takes photographs, writes down her thoughts, 'performs being a mother', or gets baby Sid 'to perform being a baby', or just sits and *does nothing*. This notion of maternity as a performance is central to Simic's understanding and development of a political maternal aesthetic. Everyday motherhood restaged as a relation, between mother and children, in order to reveal the codes, structures and relations of power at stake. Indeed, this overt and deliberate 'mimicry' of maternal practices is one of Simic's central critical and political strategies.

An estrangement which enables a focus on the ways in which the maternal operates relationality is always a spatio-temporal relation: 'Contemplation Time' is in this respect a Lena–Sid collaborative production, even whilst their relationship is radically unequal.

This photograph of the pram in the park is one of the 'Contemplation Time' documents (Figure 3). I find this a deeply affective and strangely melancholic image. It draws the viewer into a nostalgic maternal topography: the pram is set apart at some distance on the grass, the mother remains out of the frame (the lost object), but at the same time you are positioned with/ as her, perhaps sitting on the bench looking towards the pram, contemplating the scene, *doing nothing*. The old-fashioned blue and chrome of the pram and the startling rich colours in the photograph have a dream-like quality – out of time – *if only you could experience it again, that being in your pram, the feel and smell of it, the wonder of being in the park with your mum.* In fact, Simic isn't interested in romanticizing infancy or motherhood, her art explores the alienation, despair and anguish of maternity, as well as the banality of maternal labour. She is interested in documenting the bitchy judgements and ambivalence as well as the extraordinary solidarities of mothers and the sheer joy of some moments of maternal experience.

'Contemplation Time' is also, as the title suggests, about *doing nothing*. As Rosalind Gill and Andy Pratt argue in their account of autonomist Marxism, doing nothing is an important political strategy in the context of 'a system

Figure 3   Lena Simic, 'Contemplation Time' (2007)

in which life is arranged around, and subordinated to work' (2008, p. 6). Indeed, 'Contemplation Time' can be read as a specific maternal response to neoliberalism; it explores the aesthetics of *doing nothing together*, an experience which is resolutely marginal to 'the social factory' of neoliberal motherhood. Simic is part of a new generation of art/activists who are engaged in deliberate 'strategic valorization' of the maternal (see Baraitser, 2009, p. 6). It is perhaps this process which just might enable the unmarketable and the anti-capitalism within the maternal to be politically mobilised. As Simic writes: 'I think about the daily routines mothers are expected to maintain. I think about parents who only want what's best for their kids. I think about the impossible expectations placed on mothers. I feel trapped. I feel out of the game. I feel like an outsider. *It feels good'* (Lena Simic, 'Contemplation Time', 2007, my emphasis).

Notes

1. See also Baraitser (2009) on 'maternal publics'.
2. Dati, who had allegedly described maternity leave as 'for wimps', was sacked by President Sarkozy shortly after her spectacularly early return to work.
3. What, for example, are the psycho-social implications of being able to watch films of your own inter-uterine life and birth?
4. Methodologically, this chapter draws on earlier work in which I develop a figurative approach to the analysis of media culture (see Tyler, 2008).
5. These celebrity photographs very often directly reference 'More Demi Moore', through, for example, the use of nude profile, similar background colour, soft lighting and/or a punning caption. This citation re-establishes Leibovitz's photograph as the iconic origin of the new visual paradigm of pregnant beauty.
6. Indeed, it is clear that within some of these online spaces women are engaging in collective projects of maternal self-representation which could certainly be argued to counter the hegemony of pregnant beauty I am describing in this chapter. However, my survey of online entertainment blogs and discussion groups suggests that the dominant meanings encoded in celebrity pregnancy images are consolidated rather than challenged within the majority of interactions.
7. This is an excerpt from a pregnancy diary posted on ivillage.co.uk.
8. From the 'Blooming Marvellous' maternity range autumn 2003.
9. In 2009, an undergraduate student in the Sociology Department at Lancaster University, Allison Kirby, undertook an empirical study on the impact of the new visual culture of pregnancy upon British women's experiences of pregnancy and early motherhood. I am very grateful to Allison for allowing me to have access to this data which has helped shape my argument in this chapter.
10. It is important to note that the sexiness attributed to pregnant women within popular culture is often pubescent, naïve 'naughty school girl' imagery which infantilizes the pregnant woman. Examples include the front-cover photograph of Pamela Anderson, wearing a nappy and sucking a lollypop on the cover of the British celebrity magazine *OK!* (May, 1996), Sadie Frost doe-eyed and flashing her knickers in a Lolita schoolgirl pose on the front cover of the *Sunday Telegraph*'s style supplement (21 June 2002) and Britney Spears in a polka-dot bikini, seductively sucking a lollypop on the cover of *Q* (November, 2006).

11. When the privacy allowed to pregnant women was breached it caused public outrage. For example, in 1982, two British tabloid newspapers followed Princess Diana and Prince Charles to the Bahamas and subsequently published long-lens photographs of a five months' pregnant Diana in a bikini. Queen Elizabeth unusually released a statement, read in Parliament, which described this intrusion as 'the blackest day in the history of British journalism'.
12. This was a key finding of Kirby's 2009 study (see note 10).
13. See http://www.babooshbaby.com/tauts.html.
14. See http://www.amommymakeover.com/ for information about mommy makeovers.
15. See also urban mythology about the existence of the mythic C-tuck operation (a combination tummy tuck/Caesarean section).
16. Professor John Morgan, head of the Yorkshire Centre for Eating Disorders estimates that 1 in 20 pregnant women have an eating disorder. For press coverage see Bruton, 2008 and also a 2007 BBC Radio Four *Women's Hour* discussion on this topic in which I participated: http://www.bbc.co.uk/radio4/womanshour/01/2008_34_fri.shtml.

References

Abraham, L. (2005) 'The Perfect Little Bump', *New York Magazine*, 21 May, online at: http://nymag.com/nymetro/health/features/9909/.
Attwood, F. (2006) 'Sexed Up: Theorising the Sexualization of Culture', *Sexualities* 9(1): 77–94.
Baraitser, L. (2009) *Maternal Encounters: The Ethics of Interruption* (London and New York: Routledge).
Baraitser, L. (2009) 'Redundant Groupings and the Ethico-Political Subject: Mothers Who Make Things Public', *Feminist Review* 93: 8–23.
Barthes, R. (1981) *Camera Lucida: Reflections on Photography*, trans. Richard Howard (New York: Hill & Wang).
Betterton, R. (2006) 'Promising Monsters: Pregnant Bodies, Artistic Subjectivity, and Maternal Imagination', *Hypatia* 21(1): 80–100.
Bordo, S. (1993) *Unbearable Weight: Feminism, Western Culture, and the Body* (Berkeley: University of California Press).
Bruton, C. (2008) 'Pregorexia: Does This Bump Look Big on Me?', *The Times*, 18 August, online at: http://www.timesonline.co.uk/tol/life_and_style/health/features/article4541959.ece.
Colebrook, C. (2006) 'Introduction', *Feminist Theory* 7(2): 131–42.
Craig, M. (2007) 'Race, Beauty, and the Tangled Knot of a Guilty Pleasure', *Feminist Theory* 7(2): 159–77.
Duden, B. (1993) *Disembodying Women: Perspectives on Pregnancy and the Unborn* (Cambridge, MA: Harvard University Press).
Dworkin, S. and Wachs, F. (2004) '"Getting Your Body Back": Postindustrial Fit Motherhood in Shape Fit Pregnancy Magazine', *Gender & Society* 18(5): 610–24.
Equalities Review (2007) 'Fairness and Freedom: The Final Report of the Equalities Review', online at: http://archive.cabinetoffice.gov.uk/equalitiesreview/.
Gill, R. (2009) 'Beyond the "Sexualization of Culture" Thesis: An Intersectional Analysis of "Sixpacks", "Midriffs" and "Hot Lesbians" in Advertising', *Sexualities* 12(2): 137–60.
Gill, R. and Pratt, A. C. (2008) 'In the Social Factory? Immaterial Labour, Precariousness and Cultural Work', *Theory, Culture and Society Annual Review* 25(7–8): 1–30.

Gill, S. (1995) 'Globalisation, Market Civilisation, and Disciplinary Neoliberalism', *Millennium – Journal of International Studies* 24(3): 399–423.

'Harley' (2007) 'Pregnant Beauty and the Beast', online at: http://www.celebslap.com/pregnant-beauty-and-the-beast/.

Harvey, D. (2006) *A Brief History of Neoliberalism* (Oxford: Oxford University Press).

Harvey, D. (2009) 'Is This Really the End of Neoliberalism?', Counterpunch, 13 March, online at: http://www.counterpunch.org/harvey03132009.html.

Humm, M. (2006) 'Beauty and the Wolf', *Feminist Theory* 7(2): 237–54.

Huntley, R. (2000) 'Sexing the Belly: An Exploration of Sex and the Pregnant Body', *Sexualities* 3(3): 347–62.

Irigaray, L. (1991) 'The Bodily Encounter with the Mother' in M. Whitford (ed.), *The Irigaray Reader* (Oxford: Blackwell).

Jensen, T. (2009) 'Why Study the Maternal?', *Studies in The Maternal* 1(1), online at: http://www.mamsie.bbk.ac.uk/editorial.html.

Kaplan, E. A. (1992) *Motherhood and Representation: The Mother in Popular Culture and Melodrama* (New York: Routledge).

Kofman, S. (1985) *The Enigma of Woman: Woman in Freud's Writings*, trans. C. Porter (Ithaca, NY: Cornell University Press).

Longhurst, R. (2000) ' "Corporeographies" of Pregnancy: "Bikini Babes" ', *Environment and Planning D: Society and Space* 18(4): 453–72.

Longhurst, R. (2009) 'Youtube: A New Space for Birth?', *Feminist Review* 93: 46–63.Mckay, S. and D. Baxter (2007) ' "Your Kids Say 'Mom.' Your Clothes Say Otherwise": Pregnant Fashion Dolls and Visual Culture', *Visual Culture & Gender* 2: 49–61.

McRobbie, A. (2006) 'Yummy Mummies Leave a Bad Taste for Young Women', *The Guardian*, 2 March, online at: http://www.guardian.co.uk/world/2006/mar/02/gender.comment.

McRobbie, A. (2009) *The Aftermath of Feminism* (London: Sage).

Marion-Young, I. (1990) 'Pregnant Embodiment: Subjectivity and Alienation', in *Throwing Like a Girl and Other Essays in Feminist Philosophy and Social Theory* (Bloomington: Indiana University Press).

Metz, C. (1985) 'Photography and Fetish', *October* 34: 81–90.

Oakley, A. (1980) *Women Confined: Towards a Sociology of Childbirth* (Oxford: Martin Robertson).

Rancière, J. (2004) *The Philosopher and His Poor*, Andrew Parker (ed.), trans. John Drury, Corinne Oster and Andrew Parker (Durham, NC: Duke University Press).

Ringrose, J. and Walkerdine, V. (2008) 'Regulating the Abject', *Feminist Media Studies* 8(3): 227–46.

Rose, N. (1999) *Governing the Soul* (London: Free Association Books).

Salmansohn, K. (2003) *Hot Mama: How to Have a Babe and Be a Babe* (San Francisco, CA: Chronicle Books).

Selinger-Morris, S. (2006) 'The Bump and How to Wear It', *Sydney Morning Herald*, 8 June, online at: http://www.smh.com.au/articles/2006/06/07/1149359820133.html.

Stout, H. (2005) 'Letting It All Hang Out: Pregnant Women Pose for a New Type of Family Portrait', *The Wall Street Journal*, 11 August, online at: http://online.wsj.com/article/NA_WSJ_PUB:0,SB112372315198410490,00-search.html.

Traister, R. (2004) 'Pregnancy Porn', *Salon.com*, online at: http://dir.salon.com/story/mwt/feature/2004/07/31/pregnancy_porn/index.html.

Tyler, I. (2000) 'Reframing Pregnant Embodiment' in S. Ahmed et al. (eds) *Transformations: Thinking Through Feminism* (London and New York: Routledge).

Tyler, I. (2001) 'Skin-tight: Celebrity, Pregnancy and Subjectivity' in S. Ahmed and J. Stacey (eds), *Thinking Through the Skin* (London and New York: Routledge).

Tyler, I. (2005) 'The Sexual Politics of Narcissism', *Feminist Theory* 6(1): 25–44.

Tyler, I. (2006) '"Welcome to Britain": The Cultural Politics of Asylum', *European Journal of Cultural Studies* 9(2): 185–202.

Tyler, I. (2008) '"Chav Mum, Chav Scum": Class Disgust in Contemporary Britain', *Feminist Media Studies* 8(1): 17–34.

Tyler, I. (2009) 'Against Abjection', *Feminist Theory* 10(1): 77–98.

Tyler, I. and Bennett, B. (2010) 'Celebrity Chav: Fame, Femininity and Social Class', *European Journal of Cultural Studies* 13(3): 375–93, online at: http://ecs.sagepub.com/content/13/3/375.abstract.

2
The Right to Be Beautiful: Postfeminist Identity and Consumer Beauty Advertising

Michelle M. Lazar

Introduction

The relationship between beauty practices, femininity and feminism is well documented in the scholarly literature. In many societies, 'doing' beauty is a vital component of 'doing' femininity: being beautiful, as defined by the norms of a society – for example, in terms of skin type and complexion, and body shape, size and appearance – and working towards achieving those conventional standards are an accepted (and expected) part of what women do by virtue of being 'women'. Some feminists (associated, especially, with the 'second wave') have criticized normative beauty practices, and the highly profitable commercialized beauty industry that drives those practices, as oppressive upon women generally. The beauty industry has been targeted for upholding narrow and restrictive definitions of beauty, for reinforcing the burden of 'lookism' upon women (namely, women are constantly judged by how they look), and for promoting unhealthy body image obsessions and potentially harmful beauty procedures (Bordo, 1995; Coward, 1984; Kilbourne, 1999). However, other feminists (identified with the 'third wave' and whose views quite easily fit within that of postfeminism), have reclaimed beauty practices as enjoyable, self-chosen and skilled feminine pursuits (e.g. Jervis and Zeisler, 2006).

In this chapter, my focus is on the strategic positioning by advertisers in the dialogue concerning commercial beautification, normative femininity and feminist perspectives. Specifically, I examine how advertisers, known for their opportunistic ability to read a society's pulse and respond adroitly by selectively appropriating social discourses (Dyer, 1988; Goldman, 1992), link the normative practice of beautification with an emancipated identity. This approach maintains the connection between beautification and femininity construction, but resignifies the latter as productive of a 'new' kind of femininity that blends with a feminist consciousness. This deflects second-wave feminist positions, which imply a polarization of 'feminist' and 'feminine' identities, while it is allied with third-wave and postfeminist-friendly perspectives that erase the distinctions between the two identities (Hollows, 2000; McRobbie, 2007).

The emancipated new femininity is a subject effect of a broader, global neoliberal postfeminist discourse. Originating in Western media and popular culture, the discourse of postfeminism involves the popularization of feminist ideas, presented as if widely accepted and assumed, even while (as McRobbie, 2007 has noted) taking distance from feminism as a politics of the past. Certain themes associated with postfeminism have acquired common currency in the mainstream, such as personal empowerment, entrepreneurship, sexual agency, entitlement to pleasure and emancipation (Akass and Mccabe, 2004; Gill, 2009; Jackson 2006; Lazar, 2009). In this chapter, the focus is on the theme of emancipation in beauty advertising, namely, a construction of women's right to be beautiful, which is explored in two ways. First, the beauty project is signified as an extension of women's right to freedom and liberation. Second, beauty practices are represented as offering women self-determined choices. The consumerist discourse of emancipation – centring on rights, freedoms and choices – purportedly 'speaks to' the concerns of feminists generally, regardless of their identification with second- or third-wave feminisms.

The chapter examines the production of the emancipated new femininity in a set of beauty advertisements, collected randomly in Singapore's English daily, *The Straits Times*, from 2001 to 2007,[1] as part of a larger project on beauty and postfeminism. The ads pertain to the marketing of cosmetics, fragrances, skincare, hair and body management products and services, and feature a mix of international and local beauty brands. As will become evident from the data and analysis presented below, the ads predominantly enunciate a Western-style discourse of emancipation based on individual rights, even though the concept of individual rights is antithetical to the Asian-Confucian national and cultural ethos of Singapore. The latter is enshrined, for example, in a government-formulated 'national ideology' in 1991, which emphasizes obligations to the community and nation above self-interest and, in the process, clearly de-emphasizes individuals and rights. Moreover, the history of gender equality is also quite distinctive in Singapore, whose long-standing ruling government has tended to mute local feminist struggles for social change, by (selectively) initiating gender equity measures of its own, largely, out of economic pragmatism. In fact, in the 1960s, when women's struggles for equal rights were actively fought for in the West, the Singapore government had already instituted a "Women's Charter" to protect Singapore women's interests in several areas. The resulting perception, thus, has been of a benevolent government bestowing 'gifts' of equality upon women (Lazar, 2001; Purushotam, 1992). On the one hand, the local–global disjuncture in terms of cultural and feminist histories gets effaced by the prevalence of a universalizing postfeminist discourse circulated in the ads. Yet, on the other hand, decades of enjoying government-given rights and opportunities makes mainstream Singapore fertile ground for the postfeminist distancing of feminism to take root so well.

This study is undertaken from the perspective of critical discourse analysis (Fairclough, 1995; van Dijk, 1993; Wodak and Meyer, 2009) – developed within a socially conscious linguistics – adopting, in particular, a 'distinctively feminist politics of articulation' (Lazar, 2005; Wetherell, 1995). Taking 'discourse' to mean a systematic, socio-historically contingent signification practice (à la Foucault, 1972), my approach is oriented towards the close analysis of the semiotic expression of discursive meanings via language and other meaning-making resources (e.g. visual images, colour and typeface). In the following section, an analysis-cum-discussion of advertisers' articulations of 'the right to beauty' is provided, first, in relation to 'freedoms' and then, in terms of 'choices'. The chapter concludes with remarks about this consumer-oriented, globalized emancipated new femininity.

Emancipated new femininity: the right to be beautiful

The right to be free

An 'emancipated femininity' is construed in the ads as liberation and freedom from women's *self*-restrictions. Self-restrictions, which hold women back from living fully and freely, may be embodied or attitudinal. Embodied constraints, as examples (1) to (4) below show, involve perceived imperfections of the body, which in the ads may be particularized in terms of 'oily skin', 'stubborn fat', '[bodily] hair', or more generally categorized as 'beauty concerns' and 'effects of stress', from which women need releasing.

> (1) FREEDOM FROM OILY SKIN. (Nivea Visage 3/6/07)
> (2) Live Free from stubborn fat! (Mayfair Slimming 28/10/03)
> (3a) '[...] I am hair-free for evermore'. (Bio Hair Jet 15/8/01)
> (4a) FIL [...] frees you of your beauty concerns and the effects of stress. (FIL 22/7/04)

What the ads promise is the freedom to be beautiful. This is entry into a world in which women have 'pristine complexion', 'a stunning body' (example 4b) and have no restrictions on the clothes they may wear (examples 3b, 5 and 6). See the examples below.

> (3b) 'Now I feel completely liberated to live my life because I am hair-free for evermore.' You can be like Mathilda, Director of Bio Skin Concept. She is free to wear anything she fancies to show off her arms and silky smooth legs. (Bio Hair Jet 15/8/01)

(4b) Discover the freedom of being beautiful. FIL's complete custom-ized beauty solutions for your skin, body and wellness, frees you of your beauty concerns and the effects of stress. Welcome your new pristine complexion, a stunning figure and a refreshed body and mind [...]. (FIL 22/7/04)

(5) The sweet, sensual freedom to wear anything you want. And look good in it. The all-natural bust enhancement programme [...]. (Beauty Express 11/4/06)

(6) I Can. Can you? ... put on ☐ a bikini ☐ those hot pants ☐ that mini skirt ☐ all of the above. Thanks to Hair Away I don't have to worry about my hair! Ever! (Hair Away 16/4/08)

The freedom to 'wear anything', contrary to suggesting limitless options, refers to a particular category of attire that allows women to flaunt their bodies – as example (3b) says, 'to show off her arm and silky smooth legs', or in the case of (6), all the boxes to be checked list body-revealing clothes. These are construed in terms of women's own desires (note the verbs denot-ing affect: 'fancies', 'want', and the emphatic expressive clause 'Thanks to Hair Away ... !'), and in terms of how attractive such a freedom is: it is con-ceptualized as an exciting journey – 'discover', 'new' and 'welcome' (4b); pleasurable – 'sweet and sensual' (5); and enduring – 'evermore', 'Ever!' The freedom to be beautiful is implicitly set against the 'tyranny of ugliness' through presuppositions. The clauses 'The sweet, sensual freedom to wear anything you want. And look good in it' (5) and 'I Can. Can you?' (6), for instance, presuppose as culturally understood that 'showing skin' is judged inappropriate for women who do not fit the conventional standards of beauty. Therefore, conformity to the (narrow) beauty ideals, paradoxically, is represented as freedom of expression for women; the liberating promise of beauty is to gain access to ways of life and styles of dressing otherwise 'denied' them, which does nothing to challenge the prevailing norms of beauty and fashion. Indeed, this (skewed) freedom only works because of the fact that the narrow beauty standards are all that exist gets elided.

Furthermore, in some ads the liberating promise of beauty suggests that unless a woman achieves beautification goals, she is not wholly emanci-pated. The presuppositions in the statement: 'Now I feel completely liber-ated to live my life because I am hair-free for evermore' (3b), and a question posed separately by a Clinique ad: 'Are your lips living up to their full poten-tial?', reveal that these women have already realized some measure of libera-tion and of their (or their lips') potential. Yet, the qualifiers in *'completely* liberated' and *'full* potential' suggest that total emancipation is possible only through practices of self-aestheticization. Construed thus, the ads extend feminist notions of social and political emancipation to the domain of per-sonal grooming, where the latter's achievement becomes the hallmark of full emancipation.

In some ads, the achievement of the body beautiful is overtly represented as a feminist right. Consider the examples below:

(7) Exercise your right to health and beauty. (Philip Wain 13/10/03)
(8) FIGHT FOR YOUR RIGHT TO OWN THE PERFECT BODY. Fend off the extra pounds with the women's empowerment package. Women around the world, unite. The struggle against the flab is coming to an end. With our new Women's Empowerment Package, you can now slim down and shape up in 10 effective sessions. [...] So take a step towards liberation. Give us a call to sign up for the Women's Empowerment Package today. (Slimming Sanctuary 10/3/04)

In both these ads, knowing references to feminist struggles for rights are placed prominently in caption position (and in the case of (8) also in large capital letters), accompanied by arresting visual images of models in fighting poses, who engage the viewer through direct gaze. In the Philip Wain ad (7) for a fitness-cum-beauty centre, the model is clad in exercise gear and boxing gloves which, through the inter-semiosis of the headline, carries meaning at two levels. Literally, the word 'exercise' in complementary relationship to the pugilistic image denotes a kind of physical fitness and training regime. At the same time, the lexical item 'right[s]' together with the fighting pose (indexed by raised clenched fists) evokes reference to feminism's struggle for women's rights, with 'exercise', in this context, assuming the sense of 'putting into effect'.

'Feminist-speak' is more comprehensively performed throughout the Slimming Sanctuary ad (8) which combines resonances of second-wave feminist sentiments with popular postfeminist ones. Semblance of a second-wave feminist discourse is rehearsed linguistically in the headline and copy of the ad; note the semantic field constitutive of such expressions as 'fight for your right', 'women's empowerment'; 'women ... unite', 'the struggle' and 'liberation'. Popular postfeminist sentiments are visually carried in the image of a young woman featured in a 'kick ass' pose – with clenched fists, and arms raised to throw punches and a knee lifted to kick an invisible assailant. In Singaporean culture, which encourages Confucian values, and its political climate, which emphasizes obligations rather than rights of citizens, the overt invocation of a rights discourse, interestingly, 'takes feminism into account' (in McRobbie's terms), yet does this in politically distancing ways. The tenor of the language – viva la revolución! – suggests a throw-back to a bygone 'militant' era. For a contemporary audience, for whom feminism's battles are thought to be over, its ideology is rendered harmless by virtue of being out-of-date (Macdonald, 1995; McRobbie, 2007). The 'retro' sense is accentuated by the large font size and capital letters of the headline which lend stridency to the words, as well as through a two-tone red background – a colour generally associated with leftist political sentiments (Archer and Stent forthcoming) – presented as rays, radiating outwards from behind the model. The distancing effect is not only tempo-ral, but also cultural in that the overall stridency of tone, for a Singaporean audience, belongs to a perceived Western feminist style of rhetoric. Unlike the language (and colour) in the ad, the visual image of the model is con-temporary, yet also 'safe' from the political critique of feminism. In the ad, the popular postfeminist image of a woman, dressed in black leather and poised to fight, indexes an action movie genre, in which modern women (like men) are depicted as tough action heroes. While achieving popular appeal among a young modern female audience, the fictional aspect of the movie genre allows the audience to consume popular cultural images of female empowerment from a political distance.

Apart from establishing a direct link between liberation and the achieve-ment of the body beautiful, an 'emancipated femininity' is also presented as a form of consciousness or attitude. Following Gill (2009), this involves a transformation of the self, which is less about acting or performing than about remodelling one's interior or psychic sense of self – in this case involv-ing the embracing of an attitude of self-belief. For example,

(9) To say the sky's the limit isn't too much of a stretch. [Headline]
Try and you will see. Reach and you will achieve. At Amore Fitness, it's about taking that all important step towards achieving a healthy and attractive body. [...] The sky's the limit. So go for it at Amore Fitness now. (Amore 1/4/08)
(10) The greatest freedom is to believe in yourself. [Headline]
BRITNEY SPEARS. believe (believe March 2008)

These ads draw upon a motivational, self-help discourse that suggests to women that emancipation lies in the hands of women themselves. Example (9) is from an ad for a fitness and beauty centre, which like (7) depends on wordplay. In this case, the play is on the words 'stretch' and 'reach', which reference the domain of body extension exercise as well as motivational talk – that the goal is not far-fetched (a 'stretch') and is some-thing women can realistically strive for ('reach'). In this latter context, women are told that possibilities are endless and that no obstacle is insur-mountable, if only they apply themselves, as evident from agentive verbs – 'try', 'reach', 'achieve', 'taking that...step' and 'go for it'. Thus, even though the goal ultimately is the achievement of the body beautiful ('a healthy and attractive body'), what is made textually salient is for women to embrace the go-getting attitude.

Example (10) is the caption (and only linguistic text) in an ad for a fra-grance named 'believe' by Britney Spears. As Williamson's (1978) classic semiotic analysis showed, the juxtaposition of a celebrity referent with a product seeking signification involves transference of meaning associated with the referent on to the product. The process of signification, Williamson argued, not only 'aestheticizes' the product, but also 'ideologizes' it by situating it in an ideological context which the product imbues. Britney Spears as the chosen referent in the ad represents a popular image of postfeminism (cf. Gauntlett, 2008, p. 230) associated with young women, financial independence, fame and success, and individualism – the essence of which is bottled in the fragrance, named 'believe'. In particular, textually performed in the ad is an emancipated postfeminist identity based upon the concept of freedom. This is metaphorically realized in the visual scenario of Spears surrounded by caged birds, with the exception of an unfettered small bird resting on her hand. Less obvious, in small print, a caption reads, 'The greatest freedom is to believe in yourself'. In keeping with popular postfeminism, the kind of freedom that is enacted is personal and individual, rather than social and collective, as evident in a number of ways. For instance, the caption is presented as Spears's personal philosophy, which appears next to her name and the name of her fragrance; a personalized website address is also provided for viewers to browse and learn more (www.britneyspearsbelieve.com). Also, the letter 'i' in the product name 'believe' is singled out for emphasis, which may be interpreted as a singular first-person pronoun. Rendered in bright pink, 'i' visibly corresponds to the colour used for Britney Spears's name just above it. A semiotic reading of this suggests that just as reference to Spears is literally (i.e. orthographically) central to the fragrance, so too the individual consumer ('i') is central to unlocking its 'sense'. This works well with the reader, further, personally addressed as an individual, in the singular second-person pronoun – '...believe in yourself'.

The right to choose

Related to rights and freedoms is the question of choice. Although a signifier of women's emancipation, the term 'choice', at the same time, is a source of much debate and contention among feminists. Closely associated with the US landmark case *Roe* vs. *Wade* in the 1980s concerning women's rights to safe and legal abortions, the issue of women's reproductive *rights* became framed instead as a matter of choice. Rickie Solinger explains that 'choice' was a deliberately apolitical use of language (substituted for the more militant sounding 'rights'), which became a way for US liberal feminists to talk about abortion at a time when people had become weary of rights claims (cited in Zeisler, 2008, p. 130). The language of choice gradually permeated women's decision-making in other domains and paved the way for a culture of 'choice feminism'. Coined by Hirschman, 'choice feminism' indexes the shift to personal (rather than social and political) choices made by women in domains such as paid work, domesticity and parenting, sexuality, as well as grooming (Cohen, 2006). As Wolf remarks about beautification practices, 'we deserve the choice to do whatever we want with our faces and bodies'

(1991, p. 2). In sum, the notion of a woman's right to her own body has extended from 'pro-choice' abortion debates to the pursuit of feminine self-aestheticization.

Not surprisingly, choice feminism supports and is supported by a late capitalist culture replete with consumer lifestyle choices. 'Choice' standing in as a shorthand for 'feminism' thus can be easily appropriated to fit into consumerist imperatives so that the implied message is that women may reach feminist goals through their consumer choices (Mascia-Lees and Sharpe, 2000; Zeisler, 2008).

In some ads, the assumption that the modern emancipated woman/consumer is used to having choices at her disposal is presumed as a 'given'. Such messages as 'What are your make-up choices?' (Clinique 28/4/06) and 'giving women all the options they want' (Prescriptives 28/2/03) presuppose that women do have (make-up) choices and that they want to be able to exercise options, respectively. More commonly, however, consumer feminism makes the exercise of choice an explicit part of the ad copy in order to appeal to the target consumer directly:

(11) Two shades, two different textures in a single, definitive fashion and jewel-inspired product. *Choose one texture or feel free to associate them* to create a multitude of colour and shine effects...(Yves Saint Laurent 18/5/07)

(12) *Choose from 3 pampering treats* at $68. Pampering Body Treat. Radiant Facial Treat. Body Contouring Treat. (Amore 5/3/07)

(13) All you need and must-have to maintain beautiful skin, and more – *yours to choose. Select your customized 4-piece skincare gift*, plus Projectionist High Definition Mascara, Pure Color Lipstick in Rosewater and a Pleasures EDP Spray all in a cosmetic pouch. [Below the text are images of four sets of items: two pouches in chocolate and plum with the caption '*Choose* your Pouch'; two bottles captioned '*Choose* your Cleanser'; two other bottles captioned '*Choose* your Repair; and two small containers captioned '*Choose* your Moisturizer'.] (Estée Lauder 2/10/08)

(14) *Your choice* of coverage and benefits. *You pick the type of coverage you want.* Would you like a foundation that gives you *sheer, medium or full coverage? Custom Blend lets you choose.* [...] as with the foundation, *you choose the skincare benefits and finish you want.* (Prescriptives 28/2/03)

In these ads, women are positioned as subjects who exercise choice – expressed either in the nominal form 'your choice' or through the verbs 'choose', 'select', 'pick'. In sync with choice feminism, the advertiser could arguably claim that as long as women choose, the choices count as 'feminist' (Cohen, 2006). The experience of choosing varies with ads. In some cases, women may exercise a single choice only (for example, in (12) the choice ends with the selection of one of three treats), whereas in others multiple choices are offered (for example, (13) gives an impression of exhilarating, never-ending choices). Moreover, the choice exercised may be among discrete items (e.g. 'a body treat', 'a body contouring treat' – presumably different from the former – or 'a facial treat'); along a continuum ('sheer', 'medium' or 'full'); or of a pick-and-mix type ('Two shades, two different textures... Choose one texture, or feel free to associate them').

No matter how the choices are packaged, however, underlying all the ads is the obligatory imperative to consume. The choices offered to women are to decide what (and how) to consume from a fairly limited and indistinguishable range of products, as if this is the kind of choice that matters. The option not offered to women is the one *not* to consume and, in turn, the freedom not to comply with the commercialized beauty rituals and ideals entailed by the consumption of those products.

Although one could quite reasonably argue that non-consumption is not an option for advertisers driven by a consumerist ideology, an ad for Hairaway (a hair removal brand) seems to suggest just such a possibility. In a segment overtly titled 'Choice', the ad copy reads:

(15) You know your mind better than anyone else. At HAIRAWAY, *you have total freedom of choice*. No set course of treatments, no compulsory programmes, no minimum visits, no forced sales and no empty promises. [...] And *you can choose to stop* treatment after one session if you are satisfied. It's entirely your call.

It would appear that Hairaway expresses a pro-feminist attitude, which respects women's freedom to choose, even if that means to stop being a consumer. Yet, Hairaway's of course, is a clever recuperative strategy, which while manifestly distancing itself from the strategies associated with other competitors, through multiple uses of negation, persuades women to remain consumers 'volitionally'. The sentence 'And you can stop treatment after one session if you are satisfied', even while telling women that they have a way 'out', requires that women must first become consumers. By phrasing the dependent conditional clause positively (instead of negatively), the efficacy of the product cannot be faulted; rather, the onus is on whether the customer achieves satisfaction. Because permanent hair removal is not possible after a single session, a customer satisfied with the short-term results will likely return voluntarily for repeat treatments for longer-term effectiveness.

The availability of consumer choices in advertising can be related to the idea of providing for a diversity of women and their needs, which parallels third-wave feminist theorizations that have shifted away from 'women' as a monolithic category to accounting for the diversity of social positions and concerns of women across space and time. Ads marked for Asian-ness relate best to this point: for instance, 'Developed for Asian skin, the new range brings together the best in cosmetic dermatology' (Clinique 17/3/06) and

'9 Asian skin-true shades' – copy which is accompanied by close-up images of Asian women's faces arranged in a row (L'Oréal 21/10/05). Catering to diversity is a trend within contemporary consumer culture also, as reflected in cosmetics entrepreneur Bobbie Brown's words: 'It is not about cookie cutter beauty anymore. There are a lot more options now' (quoted in Weingarten, 2006, p. 12). Unlike the social nature of diversity as envisaged by feminists (namely, pertaining to social groups of women), the kind constructed in consumer feminism emphasizes the personal and individual, which is congruent with the achievement of individualized identities through the consumption of goods. See the examples below:

(16) *Custom-fit* brightening. [...] *There is no one solution* to a more radiant skin. Because the causes of discolouration are as varied as *skin types are unique*. That's why Clinique introduces new Derma White™ custom-fit brightening range. Developed for Asian skin, the new range brings together the best in cosmetic dermatology. For a *personalized approach* to brightening. [...] *No matter what your concerns may be.* (Clinique 17/3/06)

(17) Catering to *the different needs of individuals*, you may choose from [...] (Beauty Express 20/3/07)

(18) Time to Choose. At Clarins, we understand that *not all skin are similar*. Which is why, with the exclusive Time to Choose programme, you have the freedom to pick 4 free travel size products [...] (Clarins 27/8/04)

(19) *There's one to match every personality*, whether you're a girl-next-door, party diva, flower child or quirky boho chick! You can choose from 3 different powder foundations [...]. Choose from 4 designs to *match your style and personality*! (ettusais 26/11/04)

(20) You can have your foundation and powder *tailor-made* before your eyes, *to your exact shade, your skin's needs, your ideal coverage ...* (Prescriptives 28/2/03)

In these examples, the diversity among women is reduced to physical differences: 'skin types are unique' (16); 'not all skin are similar' (18). Diversity is also presented in terms of individualization, cut off from any social or political collective. Note the lexical choices 'personalized', 'individuals', 'unique', 'signature style' and 'every personality' and the metaphors 'custom-fit' and 'tailor-made'. The use of the singular second-person pronoun, especially where this is repeated in a three-part list (see (20), contributes to the similar effect. It could be argued that personalized choices afforded by consumer feminism allow women the freedom to create their own unique beauty (Weingarten, 2006). While this may be true, the depoliticization of choice is what makes consumer feminism problematic. The commercialization of choice, in Baudrillard's terms, offers only a simulation of freedom. Yet, the depoliticization of choice is exactly what makes choice feminism itself so deeply contentious. As Hirschman critically notes, while choice feminism apparently promises liberation, it leaves much of the traditional gender order undisturbed (Cohen, 2006). Especially in a world where women are in real danger of losing the original choice granted by Roe, Zeisler (2008, p. 132) asks 'could less-substantial choices remain a viable stand-in for feminist ideology?'

Although choice in consumer feminism is largely about the provision of and selection from a range of product options, there are ads that steer women towards exercising a single preferred choice. For example, 'The one choice for total health, fitness and beauty' (Philip Wain 16/12/03) and 'Choose the power of Water Science™ and see the difference' (Laneige 3/10/03) refer to the brand – Philip Wain, and a particular product by Laneige, respectively. Typically, the recommended choice is positively appraised. Following Martin and White (2005), the appraisal here expresses the text producers' attitude of judgement about the action taken – in this case, regarding the exercise of choice.

One way the appraisal is communicated is via depersonalized 'objective' claims that are seemingly factual, even though no empirical evidence is offered in support. In the nominal phrases below, the definite article preceding the epithets 'top' (21) and 'smart' (22), and the inclusive possessive noun 'everyone's' (23a) ranks these choices definitively as universal and true. By implication, therefore, the prospective consumer ought to embrace these choices as her own as well.

(21) *The top choice* for the most effective BUST enhancement! Even celebrities come to Slim Fit! (Slim Fit 3/1/05)

(22) BEAUTY EXPRESS. Still *the smart woman's choice* since 1988. (Beauty Express 6/10/04)

(23a) Bioskin – *Everyone's Choice!* (Bioskin 18/10/05)

The recommended choice can also be expressed as a subjective, personalized one, which is attributed to a represented participant in the ad. See the examples below.

(24) 'I realized that trying to hide my body's flaws doesn't work. That's why *I made a savvy decision and chose the new Marie France CPT slimming program*. After only two weeks, I was lighter, sleeker, and had a slim, trim waist. Now I don't have to cover up my bulges any more. I've got nothing to hide!' [...]. *Choose savvy slimming*. Call Marie France for the details of CPT today. (Marie France Bodyline 24/4/02)

(25) *Make Your Intelligent Choice* Now! In just 2 months, 80% of her skin problems solved! Ng Wen Xu, 20 years old, a Bio Science undergraduate [...] found a remedy for her skin problems at Bionn International Beauty Clinique – the Skin Remedy System! 80% of her skin problems solved [sic] after 2 months of treatment. Most importantly, *her intelligent choice* makes

her become a more confident person! *So make your right choice*, call 6100 0661 for your skin remedy NOW! (Bionn International 19/9/03)
(26) 'Choose confidence. Choose assurance. Choose the way you want to re-experience your life. *I've chosen mine with Mary Chia, have you?'* – Ivy Lee, MediaCorp Artiste. Client of Mary Chia. (Mary Chia 26/11/02)

Although clearly subjective (cued by personal pronouns, named individuals, and/or personal testimonies), such ads trade on the endorsement of actual women – celebrities and 'ordinary' women – who have chosen wisely. Based on these women's choices evaluated as 'savvy' and 'intelligent', the prospective consumer also must make her choice, similarly judged as 'savvy', 'intelligent' and 'right'. The positively appraised choice is one that must be personally exercised and owned by the consumer. Note, the second-person singular pronouns (explicit or implicit) in the exhortations: '[you] choose savvy slimming' (24), 'make your intelligent choice'/'make your right choice' (25), and 'I have chosen mine...have you [chosen yours]?' (26).

Indeed, not only do the personal choices of celebrities and other women encourage and ratify readers' similar personal choices, so, too, the depersonalized and universalized types of claim. In example (23b) below, the copy starts with the brand as 'everyone's choice', and ends with the injunction to personally act – for the personally invested volitional act is necessary in the enactment of an emancipated femininity.

(23b) Bioskin – *Everyone's Choice!* [...]. So if you have any skin problems, don't wait! Treat it early with any Bioskin's signature face treatment! Be the first 50 to sms your name and password – *'My Choice!'* to 9119 9115 now [...].

Drawing upon Nicholas Rose's idea of 'the ethic of freedom', McRobbie (2007) considers such popular discourses of personal choice and self-improvement as new means of re-regulating the lives of 'modern' young women. As McRobbie explains, choice within lifestyle culture is a modality of constraint, for the individual is compelled to be the kind of subject who can make the 'right choices'. By these means, new lines and demarcations are drawn between those subjects who are judged responsive to the regime of personal responsibility, and those who fail miserably (2007, pp. 35–6).

Conclusion

To sum up, I shall highlight two points, pertaining to the nature of the emancipated new femininity and the global aspect of this identity, before ending with some thoughts on what is 'new' about this kind of femininity. In this chapter, I hope to have shown how advertisers have discursively resignified women's relationship to commercial practices of beautification as 'doing' an emancipated feminine subjectivity. The notion of emancipation is based on a discourse of rights (namely, being free and able to exercise choices), which is central to most second- and third-wave feminist perspectives, albeit the emphasis of the former is on the social/collective, while the latter orientates towards the personal/individual. The latter, moreover, fits particularly well with capitalist-consumerist imperatives that are underscored by individualism. A consumer-based emancipated feminine identity not only rides on the notion of emancipation which originates within feminism but, at the same time, is also premised upon *emancipation from (second-wave) feminism*, as misguided and curtailing of women's realization of their 'true' feminine selves.

On the point of emancipated femininity being a globalized identity for women today, it can be said that regardless of whether beauty brands are Western or Asian/Singaporean in origin, the consumerist discourse of emancipation is strikingly universal. Although the 'local' is indexed in a number of ways – for example, Clinique's (US brand) reference to Asian skins; Bionn International's (local brand) use of Asian models with Asian sounding names; and Slimming Sanctuary's (local brand) use of a pseudo-feminist strident tenor that is clearly marked from a Singaporean discourse style – in all cases, the commodification of emancipation remains consistent.

In conclusion, as many contemporary feminist scholars have asked of purported 'new femininities', what is 'new' about this represented emancipated identity? Certainly, the regime of representation has shifted ostensibly to one of progressivism, while maintaining the normalization of beauty practices as fundamentally constitutive of feminine selves. However, this is not merely a rhetorical change only, but involves quite substantively a change in disposition as well. The disavowal of feminism, even while strategically deploying it, I suggest, radically reverses feminist efforts to make the personal political, by repeatedly and universally reducing the political to the personal.

Note

1. In citing the ads in the chapter, I have provided the name of the brand, and a string of numbers which indicate sequentially the date/month/year in which the particular ad appeared in *The Straits Times*.

Bibliography

Akass, K. and J. Mccabe (eds) (2004) *Reading Sex and the City* (London: I. B. Tauris).

Archer, A. and S. Stent (forthcoming) 'Red Socks and Purple Rain: The Political Uses of Colour in Late Apartheid South Africa', submitted to *Visual Communication*.

Bordo, S. (1995) *Unbearable Weight: Feminism, Western Culture and the Body* (Berkeley: University of California Press).

Cohen, P. (2006) 'Today, Some Feminists Hate the Word "Choice"', *The Nation*, 15 January.

Coward, R. (1984) *The Female Desire* (London: Paladin).

Dyer, G. (1988) *Advertising as Communication* (London: Routledge).

Fairclough, N. (1995) *Critical Discourse Analysis* (London: Routledge).

Foucault, M. (1972) *The Archaeology of Knowledge* (London: Tavistock).

Gauntlett, D. (2008) *Media, Gender and Identity* (London: Routledge).

Gill, R. (2003) 'From Sexual Objectification to Sexual Subjectification: The Re-sexualisation of Women's Bodies in the Media', *Feminist Media Studies* 3(1): 100–6.

Gill, R. (2009) 'Mediated Intimacy and Postfeminism: A Discourse Analytic Examination of Sex and Relationships Advice in a Women's Magazine', *Discourse and Communication* 3(4): 345–69.

Goldman, R. (1992) *Reading Ads Socially* (London: Routledge).

Halliday, M. A. K. (1978) *Language as a Social Semiotic* (London: Edward Arnold).

Hollows, J. (2000) *Feminism, Femininity and Popular Culture* (Manchester: Manchester University Press).

Jackson, S. (2006) 'Street Girl: "New" Sexual Subjectivity in a NZ Soap Drama?', *Feminist Media Studies* 6(4): 469–86.

Jervis, L. and A. Zeisler (eds) (2006) *Bitchfest* (New York: Farrar, Straus and Giroux).

Kilbourne, J. (1999) *Can't Buy My Love: How Advertising Changes the Way We Think and Feel* (New York: Simon & Schuster).

Lazar, M. M. (2001) 'For the Good of the Nation: "Strategic Egalitarianism" in the Singapore Context', *Nations and Nationalism* 7(1): 59–74.

Lazar, M. M. (2005) *Feminist Critical Discourse Analysis* (Basingstoke: Palgrave Macmillan).

Lazar, M. M. (2009) 'Entitled to Consume: Postfeminist Femininity and a Culture of Post-critique', *Discourse and Communication* 3(4): 371–400.

Macdonald, M. (1995) *Representing Women* (London: Edward Arnold).

Martin, J. R. and P. R. R. White (2005) *The Language of Evaluation* (Basingstoke: Palgrave Macmillan).

Mascia-Lees, F. and P. Sharpe (2000) *Taking a Stand in a Postfeminist World* (Albany: State University of New York Press).

McRobbie, A. (2007) 'Postfeminism and Popular Culture: Bridget Jones and the New Girl Regime' in Y. Tasker and D. Negra (eds), *Interrogating Postfeminism* (Durham: Duke University Press).

Purushotam, N. (1992) 'Women and Knowledge/Power: Notes on the Singapore Dilemma' in K. C. Ban et al. (eds), *Imagining Singapore* (Singapore: Times Academic Press).

Van Dijk, T. A. (1993) 'Principles of Critical Discourse Analysis', *Discourse and Society* 4(2): 249–83.

Weingarten, R. C. (2006) *Hello Gorgeous! Beauty Products in America '40s–'60s* (Portland, Oregon: Collectors Press).

Wetherell, W. (1995) 'Romantic Discourse and Feminist Analysis: Interrogating Investment, Power and Desire' in S. Wilkinson and C. Kitzinger (eds), *Feminism and Discourse* (London: Sage).

Williamson, J. (1978) *Decoding Advertisements* (London: Marion Boyars).

Wodak, R. and M. Meyer (eds) (2009) *Methods in Critical Discourse Analysis. Second Edition* (London: Sage).

Wolf, N. (1991) *The Beauty Myth: How Images of Beauty Are Used against Women* (New York: Anchor Books).

Zeisler, A. (2008) *Feminism and Pop Culture* (Berkeley, CA: Seal Press).

3
Spicing It Up: Sexual Entrepreneurs and *The Sex Inspectors*

Laura Harvey and Rosalind Gill

Introduction

The aim of this chapter is to discuss the emergence of a new feminine subject who we call the 'sexual entrepreneur'. We will argue that the 'modernization' of femininity over the last two decades in the wake of the 'sexual revolution' and women's movement, alongside the acceleration and intensification of neoliberalism and consumerism, has given rise to a new and contradictory subject position: the sexual entrepreneur. This 'new femininity' constitutes a hybrid of discourses of sexual freedom for women, *intimately entangled with* attempts to recuperate this to (male-dominated) consumer capitalism. This makes this figure difficult to read, and helps to account for the familiar polarization between those feminists who appear hopeful and optimistic about the spaces that have opened up in recent years for female sexual self-expression and sexual pleasure in Western societies, and those who interpret the same phenomena as merely old sexual stereotypes wrapped in a new, glossy postfeminist guise. Contextualizing our argument in discussions about the 'mainstreaming of sex' (Attwood, 2009), we seek to develop notions of 'sexual subjectification' (Gill, 2003) and 'technologies of sexiness' (Radner, 1993, 1999) to explore the rise and proliferation of discourses of sexual entrepreneurship, and suggest a way of reading this that does not – or at least tries not to – fall back into the old binaries (e.g. either unproblematic liberation or wholesale recuperation).

Evidence for the new sexual entrepreneur is widespread. She can be seen in magazine sex advice, in advertising, and across social networking sites. In this chapter, however, we seek to explore the contours of this subject through consideration of one of several 'sex makeover' shows, airing on British television: *The Sex Inspectors*. *The Sex Inspectors* draws on conventions from self-help, confessional and reality TV. Each episode takes a (heterosexual) couple, films them in the bedroom and uses two 'sexpert' presenters to intervene to makeover their 'dysfunctional' sex lives. The programme, in its third series at the time of writing, owes some of its success to its ability to blend explicitly 'sexy' content with legitimating discourses of self-help, self-improvement and sex education (cf. Arthurs, 2004). Its fast-paced, involving, generic format also plays a part, and will be familiar to anyone who has watched *Supernanny* or other parenting makeover programmes, which have a similar show structure and also deploy the same visualization strategies to capture moments of intimate life, complete with the use of night-vision cameras. Its popularity is due, too, in no small part, to the intertextual identity of Tracey Cox, its primary presenter, who is author of at least fifteen self-help books and also a sex and relationship adviser for *Glamour* magazine, the UK's best-selling monthly glossy. In many ways Cox herself represents a 'new femininity', one of the new breed of 'celebrity agony aunts' (Boynton, 2009). In what follows we first discuss the 'sexualization of culture', then move on to elaborating our theoretical notions of sexual subjectification, technologies of sexiness and sexual entrepreneurship, and finally explore this new subjectivity through detailed discussion of *The Sex Inspectors*.

The 'sexualization of culture'

Over the last decade the 'sexualization of culture' has become a major focus of interest and concern. The phrase is used to capture the growing sense of Western societies as saturated by sexual representations and discourses, and in which pornography has become increasingly influential and porous, transforming contemporary culture. It speaks to something more than the idea that 'sex has become the big story' (Plummer, 1995, p. 4) but denotes a range of different things: 'a contemporary preoccupation with sexual values, practices and identities; the public shift to more permissive sexual attitudes; the proliferation of sexual texts; the emergence of new forms of sexual experience; the apparent breakdown of rules, categories and regulations designed to keep the obscene at bay; [and the] fondness the scandals, controversies and panics around sex' (Attwood, 2006, p. 77). Porn stars have emerged as best-selling authors and celebrities; a 'porno chic' aesthetic can be seen in music videos and advertising; and practices once associated with the sex industry, e.g. lap dancing and pole dancing have become newly 'respectabilized', promoted as mainstream corporate entertainment or fitness activity.

Feminist arguments about this are polarized. While some contemporary (radical) feminist positions are reminiscent of the anti-porn positions taken by Andrea Dworkin and Catherine MacKinnon in the 1980s (e.g. Jeffreys, 2008) other ('Third Wave') positions build from the 'sex positive' feminism of the same period (Johnson, 2002; Juffer, 1998). Moreover, another distinctive perspective is found among a growing number of writers who examine contemporary sexualization as a distinctively postfeminist phenomenon linked to discourses of celebrity, choice and empowerment (Coleman, 2008;

Gill, 2006, 2008, 2009a; McRobbie, 2004, 2009; Pinto, 2009; Ringrose, this volume; Ringrose, forthcoming).

Popular (trade rather than academic) books are largely critical of 'sexualization'. Pamela Paul's (2005) *Pornified* is a polemical treatise about the damage to psychological well-being, relationships and contemporary culture caused by the widespread availability of pornography. Another of the most well-known popular feminist critiques of sexualization is Ariel Levy's (2005) searing attack on 'raunch culture' which, she argues, extends pornography into mainstream media. Levy asserts that the sexual objectification of women is being repackaged as empowerment, but contends that 'raunch culture is not essentially progressive, it is essentially commercial. Raunch culture isn't about opening our minds to the possibilities and mysteries of sexuality. It's about endlessly reiterating one particular – and particularly saleable – shorthand for sexiness' (2005, p.29). *The Lolita Effect* (Durham, 2009) makes a similar argument in relation to children, indicting commercial culture for posing children (but particularly girls) 'as sexual objects of the adult gaze' – a set of concerns that resonate with reports such as the APA's (2007) Task Force on the Sexualization of Girls, and the Australia Institute's (2006) report on Corporate Paedophilia, both of which received extensive media coverage and discussion.

More generally, it seems to us that the binary arguments of feminism's so-called 'sex wars' in the early 1980s have given way to a situation in which divergent positions should be located across *multiple axes of difference*, which may or may not map on to each other. Alongside the familiar 'anti-porn' versus 'pro-sex', we might situate people in relation to libertarianism versus authoritarianism, according to whether they focus on texts or on audiences, their disciplinary location in psychology or media studies, whether they research effects or meanings, their tendency to be 'media positive' or hostile to media – and a whole range of other axes, all of which tend, nevertheless, to be polarized.

A new binary opposition that has emerged in the last decade among feminist scholars attempting to make sense of a Western postfeminist landscape relates to whether the proliferation of representations of women as desirable and sexually agentic represents a real and positive change in depictions of female sexuality, or whether, by contrast, it is merely a postfeminist repackaging of feminist ideas in a way that renders them depoliticized and presses them into the service of patriarchal consumer capitalism. From one perspective, recent representations of women – from the humorous 'sex bombs' of bra advertising to the stars of 'alt porn' sites (see Attwood, this volume) – constitute a clear break with representations from the past in which women were passive and objectified, now showing them as active, desiring and 'taking charge' sexually in a way that clearly reflects feminism's aspirations for female sexual self-determination. As Attwood has argued 'a whole series of signifiers are linked to promote a new, liberated, contemporary sexuality for women; sex is stylish, a source of physical pleasure, a means of creating identity, a form of body work, self-expression, a quest for individual fulfilment' (2006, p. 86). What's not to like, we might very well ask? But others see in precisely the same shift not a positive transformation towards a more feminist sexual future, but a turning backwards, a 'harking back' (Whelehan, 2000), a 'retro sexism' (Williamson, 2003) in which old, objectifying representations are simply wrapped up in a feisty, empowered sounding discourse. How can we move beyond this binary to a space that is less polarized and more productive for feminist debate and activism?

Sexual entrepreneurship

In this chapter, we want to attempt this through the notion of sexual entrepreneurship, which builds upon Foucault's ideas about technologies of selfhood, and also on the potential for feminist research of Deleuze's notion of 'becoming', identified by Coleman (2008; see also Ringrose and Walkerdine, 2008). Sexual entrepreneurship is the latest in a number of Foucaultian-influenced concepts used to capture gender–power–resistance. In Foucault's later work he moved away from his focus on 'techniques of domination', which, he argued, promoted a view of the subject as overly 'docile' and passive. Instead, towards the end of his life, he developed the notion of 'technologies of the self'. These

> 'permit individuals to effect, by their own means or with the help of others, a certain number of operations on their own bodies and souls, thoughts, conduct and way of being, so as to transform themselves' (Foucault, 1988, p.18)

Of course, the transformations possible are not open or infinite, and are constrained by the availability of circulating discourses and the resistances that might – intelligibly – be made to/within these. Nevertheless, this later work opened up a space for theorizing agency, as well as for considering the 'psychic life of power' (Butler, 1997), and there have been numerous productive feminist attempts to use this focus on technologies of selfhood – amongst them the works of Bordo (1993), Butler (1990), de Lauretis (1987) and McRobbie (2009).

In relation to sexualization, two notions have been developed from Foucault's work that help to establish the ground for the notion of sexual entrepreneurship. The idea of 'sexual subjectification' (Gill, 2003) draws on Foucault's later work to reject a view of modern power as overbearing domination, and to highlight instead the way in which power works *in and through subjects*. New knowledges and new visual regimes, Gill argues, literally helped to bring into being or materialize the new feisty, playful, desiring (heterosexual) subject of postfeminist advertising. This is not a matter of patriarchal conspiracy, but the outcome of a variety of changes – amongst them the significance of feminism and sexual liberation but also the intensified consumerism of fast capitalism – which created space for a new hybrid subject who was both invited – and incited (as we will show below) – into being.

Hilary Radner's concept of a 'technology of sexiness' is also central to our notion of sexual entrepreneurship. Writing about the 'modernization' of romance narratives in the 1990s, Hilary Radner argued that, whereas the classical romantic heroine offered 'virtue', innocence and goodness as the commodities she brought to the sexual/marriage marketplace, contemporary romances demand a 'technology of sexiness'. For Radner 'the task of the Single Girl is to embody heterosexuality through the disciplined use of make-up, clothing, exercise and cosmetic surgery, linking femininity, consumer culture and heterosexuality' (1999, p. 15). In fact we would go further: in the postfeminist, post-*Cosmopolitan* West, heroines must no longer embody virginity but are required to be skilled in a variety of sexual behaviours and practices, and the performance of confident sexual agency is central to this technology of the self.

Through the notion of sexual entrepreneurship, we seek to build on these two ideas to capture the way in which a new mode of femininity organized around sexual entrepreneurialism is emerging. This modern, postfeminist subject, we contend, is incited to be compulsorily sexy and always 'up for it', and is interpellated through discourses in which sex is work that requires constant labour and reskilling (as well as a budget capable of stretching to a wardrobe full of sexy outfits and drawers stuffed with sex toys). Beauty, desirability and sexual performance(s) constitute her ongoing projects and she is exhorted to lead a 'spiced up' sex life, whose limits – not least heterosexuality and monogamy – are tightly policed, even as they are effaced or disavowed through discourses of playfulness and experimentation.

To argue this is not to suggest a process of imposition, domination or false consciousness. Nor is it to deny the agency or creativity of those who may take up or choose to inhabit this 'new femininity'. Nor still is it to doubt the pleasures which that may involve. Indeed, what makes *The Sex Inspectors* a particularly good example of constructions of sexual entrepreneurship is both that the show is itself concerned with *bringing into being this new feminine subject*, and because in doing so it shows – vividly – the agency and dedication required, as well as sometimes pleasure too. To note the extent to which this subject has become a normative ideal, then, is resolutely not to deny agency, but is instead to open up a language in which subject–object, power–pleasure, discipline–agency are no longer counterposed as antithetical, binary opposites. In this sense, our aim is similar to Coleman's (2008) development of the Deleuzian notion

of 'becoming' in which she seeks to open up 'feminist research to consider the ways in which bodies are not separate to images but rather are
known, understood and experienced through images'. As Coleman notes,
'if feminist research take[s] seriously this conception of bodies as becoming, its task is to account for how bodies become through their relations
with images; what becomings of bodies do images limit or extend?' (2008,
p. 163).

In our analysis of *The Sex Inspectors* we explore the nature of sexual
entrepreneurship – the kind of bodies and subjectivities it brings into being.
We highlight its premise upon binary sexual difference and the asymmetri-
cal nature of the transformations it advocates. We also explore how it brings
into being not simply different bodily practices and sexual performances,
but also a 'made over' sexual subjectivity for women. Finally, we discuss
the limits of the 'spiced up' sexuality it promotes. By conducting a textual
analysis we do not assume a homogeneous reading of the text. We are mind-
ful of the potentially diverse readings and patterns of consumption of television (Bragg and Buckingham, 2004; Morley, 1992) but consider that a
feminist textual analysis provides important points of discussion about the
changing construction of feminine sexual subjectivity.

The Sex Inspectors: gendered sexual entrepreneurship

Aired on Channel 4 in 2004, 2005 and 2007, *The Sex Inspectors* combines the
genres of sex self-help, confessional reality TV and makeover. Each episode
takes a heterosexual couple in a long-term monogamous relationship, films
them over the course of a week and offers tips for them to improve their sex
lives. Participants are overwhelmingly, but not exclusively, white, none have
visible disabilities and most are aged between their mid-twenties and forty.
The producer, Daisy Goodwin, transferred the surveillance self-help format
from her previous work on the dating show *Would Like to Meet* and the home
improvement show *How Clean is Your House?* She states the purpose of the
show is to 'encourage couples to stay together' and has subsequently measured the show's success based on the number of couples who are now married (Goodwin, 2004).

The sex and relationships self-help genre has grown into an ever-expanding
market across both traditional and new media. Central in this market is the
role of the 'sexpert'. Drawing on Foucault and Gramsci, Melissa Tyler (2004)
has explored the key role that the 'expert' plays in the production of 'common-sense' discourses of sexuality. Tyler contends that experts engage in
managerial discourses to incite a sexual subjectivity that requires constant
performance appraisals and skills acquisition. Such 'sexpertise' is exemplary
of a shift within the self-help industry towards celebrity columnists and presenters who do not have the training or experience of qualified therapists,
but rather have an interest in promoting their own books, websites and toys
(Boynton, 2009).

'The Sex Inspectors' are two such sexperts, Tracey Cox and Michael Alvear. *The Sex Inspectors* consistently uses scientific and therapeutic discourses and legitimizes the 'facts' given by its sexperts with statistics. For example,

'Six out of ten couples split up because their sex life goes wrong'
  '95% of women want more kissing'
  '47% of women worry about their figure during sex and want the lights off'
  '75% of women rate foreplay as more important than intercourse'
(*The Sex Inspectors*, Channel 4, February 2007)

This authoritative-sounding discourse presents the show, and the advice given in the show, as a 'common-sense' and neutral approach by qualified experts, obscuring the very particular brand of performance-based 'great sex' produced and regulated throughout the series. It is underscored by the confident presence of the sexperts themselves. Tracey Cox is described on her website as 'an international sex, body language and relationships expert' with an 'academic background in psychology' (2009, www.traceycox.com). While in interviews with the press, she is quick to point out that she has never claimed to be a therapist (Wignall, 2008), the format of the show, which addresses emotional and physical problems, powerfully positions her as such in relation to the participants, often distressed by what they perceive to be sexual failure (Hall, 2005). She offers soothing advice which echoes familiar discourses of the body and individualized, commodity-based sexual empowerment from women's magazines. Tracey Cox is a best-selling self-help author, who has sold over two million books, and features regularly on sex self-help features on the television, radio and in women's magazines. She is a brand herself, with her own range of lubricants and vibrators. She has not undertaken formal training in sex or relationships therapy, her degree was in Journalism and Psychology (BBC, 2009; Rudebeck, 2004); her career as sexpert was launched from her time as Assistant Editor of Australian *Cosmopolitan Magazine*. Michael Alvear is described by the show as a 'gay agony uncle'. Also an author, but less prolific than Tracey, he has written two sex self-help books, one of which is a *Sex Inspectors* spin-off.

The sexperts' power operates not only through implicit authority and expertise, but also through a combination of techniques including surveillance and confessions. We are exhorted to watch alongside – and through the eyes of – Cox and Alvear, who use thermal imaging and night-vision cameras to peer into the most intimate moments of the participants' lives. Participants are invited to confess by video diary their fears of sexual failure or their sexual frustrations, in a way which profoundly resonates with Foucault's claim that 'confession is at the heart of the procedures of the individualization of power' (1978, p. 59). A sometimes sympathetic but nevertheless disciplinary gaze calls upon the couple, and by extension the viewer, to solve their problems through improved sexual performance, usually broken down into a specific repertoire of 'skills' to practise and perfect. In women's case, however, the changes involve not only new sexual techniques but frequently the *remaking of sexual subjectivity*. The sexual subject must transform herself, her attitude to her body, her comfort/discomfort with range of sexual practices in order to emerge, made over, as a 'sexual entrepreneur'.

His 'n hers sexual entrepreneurship: technique, performance, subjectivity

The particular episode we draw upon here (season 3, episode 2) focuses on Sarah (28) and Nick (31), who have been married for ten years. He is presented as an extrovert, while she is labelled as 'insecure'. The programme introduces their relationship difficulties as a 'mismatch' between Nick's 'experience' and 'sexual confidence' and Sarah's sexual 'inhibition'. We see CCTV footage from their home in which Nick continually rates Sarah's sexual performance and puts her down, comparing her to the perfect sexual subject he wants her to be. In language that echoes mainstreamed narratives from pornography, he wishes that their weekly sex was more adventurous and laments that:

> She'll never sort of like, sit on top of me, you know, and really sort of, go for it like this and, you know, start really going for it, throwing her head back and stuff, like she's not got a care in the world, because, that would turn me on so much more. (February 2007)

Sarah is concerned about her perceived sexual failure, and wants to improve their sex life so that she doesn't lose him. She repeatedly mentions dissatisfaction with her body – which means that she prefers to have sex with the lights off:

> I'm not happy with my body so I don't want Nick – I don't like Nick, looking at me, so much, 'cause I just feel uncomfortable in myself, that he, he wouldn't find me attractive. (February 2007)

Rather than address Sarah's concerns about her body image, repeating a familiar body-image mantra of women's lifestyle magazines, Tracey informs Sarah that 'sex is about what's happening on the inside, not the outside' while nevertheless promptly instructing her that overhead lighting is unflattering, so she should always put the bedside lamp on the floor for maximum effect! This contradictory construction of feminine sexual subjectivity has been analysed elsewhere in women's magazines (Gill, 2009b) and constructs sexual entrepreneurship in a way that often reinforces more 'traditional' goals such as 'finding and keeping a man' (Gill, 2009b). In *The Sex Inspectors* this occurs through the adoption of feminist discourses closely tied in with discourses of neoliberal individualism, in which emancipation is achieved through the effective and repeated production of an appropriately com-modified sexual subjectivity.

In their analysis of sexual discourses in *Cleo* and *Cosmo* women's maga-zines, Farvid and Braun (2006) note that female sexuality is often discur-sively produced in natural opposition to male sexuality. They show that while female sexuality was constructed as increasingly active and desiring, it requires acquisition of skills in order to prevent their male partner from 'straying' (Farvid and Braun, 2006, p. 295). Female sexuality, in this con-text, is constructed in what Potts (1998) has identified as 'Mars and Venus' accounting, particularly where a normalized 'male sexual drive' (Hollway, 1989) is presented as in conflict with female desire to maintain a romantic relationship. *The Sex Inspectors* reproduces this binary construction in its presentation of the naturalized differences in Nick and Sarah's relationship, in which Tracey diagnoses that Sarah would like more 'intimacy' and Nick would like more 'lust'. The entrepreneurialism required to navigate such 'nat-ural' differences is presented as qualitatively different for men and women. As Tyler (2004) and Rogers (2005) have noted, mediated constructions of masculinity in lifestyle magazines present male sexuality as unproblematic, experienced and skilful, with efficiency as a marker of success. Men are advised on how to 'streamline' and make their sex more 'productive' (Tyler, 2004, pp. 95–6) in order to be at their 'peak', whereas women's sexuality is constructed as primarily *responsive* to male sexuality, in which the acquisi-tion of skills should never threaten the lead of the male partner (Gavey and McPhillips, 1999).

The sex advice given to Nick and Sarah on *The Sex Inspectors* reproduces this distinction. While there is much to be welcomed in a mainstream tel-evision show which advocates female-centred pleasure such as cunnilingus, the ways that such knowledges are produced by the show's experts reveals the gendered construction of the 'technicalities' of sex. Holding up a large clock, Michael instructs Nick that he should

> picture Sarah's vagina as a clock. This whole area is a hot zone, what you're looking for, is the nuclear zone. So, as your tongue goes across, what you're looking for is a moan [...] you can freeze it in your mind – three o'clock, so when you're looking at her vagina you're going – three o'clock sends her to the moon. (February 2007)

Empowering women? remaking sexual subjectivity

Like Nick, Sarah is instructed in the 'techniques' of fellatio, but is also instructed in the skilful *performance* of sex, where she must look and behave – indeed, better, *become* – the part of the confident, actively desiring sexual subject in order to prevent Nick from leaving her. Her entrepreneurialism is about much more than learning and practising skills; it requires the management of the self as an alluring, confident woman who always has another 'trick' to keep her partner enticed (Farvid and Braun, 2006, p. 302). This is presented, within the discourses of the show, as becoming more powerful.

On the one hand, Tracey criticizes Nick's constant put-downs, and talks with Sarah about empowering herself to make decisions – she should do things for herself, not for Nick. Yet on the other hand, the things Sarah should do 'for herself' turn out to be all about pleasing Nick so that he doesn't leave her. This is a postfeminist moment, in which activities which might in an earlier era have been explicitly presented in terms of 'pleasing your man' are discursively repackaged as all about 'pleasing yourself'. (As Tracey puts it: 'I want you to think to yourself, am I doing what Nick wants, or is it what Sarah wants.') It is difficult not to see in this a further, more pernicious twist of ideology at work – in which a continued preoccupation with fulfilling men's sexual desires now has to be thought of as authentically self-chosen and, what's more, as empowering.

More generally, the programme repeatedly tells both participants and viewers that it is not enough to enter into a long-term relationship, the relationship must be intimately governed as 'spiced up' through tireless work and skills acquisition in order to avoid slipping into that sexual no man's land, 'the rut'. The brand of entrepreneurship produced through the visual sexualization of *The Sex Inspectors* provides a very specific shopping list of activities to produce a normal sexual subjectivity, which is heterosexual, monogamous and bound up with Western consumer culture. Such a shopping list reflects what Jackson and Scott (1997) term 'the Taylorization of sex' as requiring classification and rational management. Faced with an enormous pile of self-help books, both Sarah and Nick are invited, separately, to choose the activities that would make up their ideal sexual repertoire, including 'blindfolds, masturbating, oral sex, handcuffs, spanking, photographs, sex outdoors, dress up/role play, sex in the kitchen'. A selection of these activities are written on a flipchart, and Nick is amazed as Alvear writes 'YES' in big red letters next to each of the activities that Sarah would be willing to engage in, revealing a moment of discursive tension. Sarah seems to be getting pleasure from these revelations and fantasies, but perhaps we could also examine this in relation to the compulsory sexual agency the programme incites in which 'normal' feminine sexual subjectivity *requires* being 'up for it' or at least 'willing to try'. Within the terms of reference of the programme, is there really a choice for Sarah? To say 'no' would be to reveal her out of date, unmodernized (read: frigid, or at the very least 'inhibited') subjectivity, to position herself outside the show's framing, beyond their 'help', a sexual failure. It's worth noting too how perfectly this strategy, this psychosocial materialization, complements the advice given in 'lad mags', much of which centres on how to get her to do things she doesn't want to, e.g. let you photograph her in the buff, do anal, have a threesome, etc. (Boynton, 2009; Gill, 2006).

(The limits of) spicing it up

In this particular moment of sexualization, references to pornography and sexual subcultures such as BDSM are made, but 'softened around the edges' to preserve the boundaries of taste around *The Sex Inspectors*, as strictly educational, strictly heterosexual and monogamous. Sarah and Nick are asked if they like spanking, handcuffs, and taking 'saucy' photographs of each other. It is interesting to see how these boundaries are policed throughout the series. In two similar episodes from the first and third series, couples are advised to take a break from dressing up and using bondage accessories and toys to 'encourage more loving sex' (*Gary and Rea*, December 2004). In both cases the female participants would regularly 'dress up' for sex, but had become uninterested in sex or no longer wanted to use toys or costumes. While we would argue that the show does address both female participants' sexual desires and needs by advocating a change from their usual sexual behaviours, the way in which this change is constructed by *The Sex Inspectors* reveals the marked boundaries around 'spiced up' heterosexuality, and the resulting sexual exclusions. Cox explains exactly where the boundaries lie:

> We actually recommend dressing up, but what's not good is if you start using it every single time, 'cause then that can turn into what's called a fetish, meaning that you can't actually get aroused unless the person has that item of clothing on. (*Sally-Ann and Paul*, February 2007)

The Sex Inspectors' boundaries (experimentation is fine, but fetish is 'not good') are reflected in the kinds of products available to buy on Tracey Cox's website. In particular, the 'Supersex Beginners Soft Bondage Kit', complete with 'faux fur tie blindfold sash' and 'velvety soft cuffs' (2009, traceycox.com/products) illustrates this 'softened' version of sexual subculture as strictly *experimentation* within clearly defined limits. This presents the ideal feminine sexual entrepreneur as inhabiting a space on a precarious tightrope of sexuality; on one side looms 'sexual failure' and 'the rut' and on the other is a dark world of sexual addiction.

The very particular, policed limits of sexuality in *The Sex Inspectors* operate through a number of silent exclusions. Presenting long-term monogamous heterosexuality as the unquestioned 'goal' of sexual management, the show ignores sexualities and bodies that do not conform to this rigid model. There is no space for gay, lesbian or bisexual desire, and no space for bodies that do not fit the sexual binary of male or female. In addition, heterosexual desire outside of the show's narrow boundaries (whether that be being part of a fetish scene or enjoying sex outside of a long-term relationship) is excluded from the norms of 'great sex' constructed in the language and visualization of the show. The sexual entrepreneurialism of *The Sex Inspectors* is thus about keeping heterosexual monogamous relationships spiced up through an engagement with a repertoire of commodified acts.

By drawing attention to the contradictory nature of this new mode of feminine sexual entrepreneurialism, we do not aim to dismiss the advice of *The Sex Inspectors* as merely a brand of 'commodity feminism' (Goldman, 1992). The advice of *The Sex Inspectors* has a clear impact on Sarah's confidence. She starts to assert herself in the bedroom, practising her new skills in an almost theatrical production that requires preparation with lighting, costume and photography in a performance not just for Nick, but for us, the voyeur, the viewer. We watch as she choreographs their own form of soft-core, amateur pornography through night-vision cameras. She takes control during sex. Outside the bedroom, she argues back when Nick shouts at her. However, Tracey's simplistic solution for Sarah (she must simply 'tip the see-saw back the other way' by taking control in the bedroom) is starkly highlighted towards the end of the episode, when Nick continues to put Sarah down despite her efforts to perform for him, interrupting sex to complain 'I've gone right off this now' (February 2007).

The way that this new feminine subject is brought into being through discourses of self-improvement in *The Sex Inspectors* is complex, and cannot be explained by dismissing the show as a mediated tool of patriarchy. Tracey and Michael do not accept Nick's self-centred desire for a sexually performing, but passive wife. They insist that he takes time to listen to Sarah's needs and stop undermining her confidence through his persistent sexual performance appraisals. Michael, watching a clip of Nick interrupting sex, complains 'he's asked for more effort and then slaps it down when he gets it!' (February 2007). However, it is clear that in the narrative of the sex makeover, the solution for Sarah is to continue to maintain the performance in the bedroom in order to preserve their relationship and avoid the ever-present threat of failure: sexual dysfunction. By positioning feminine sexual entrepreneurialism as a means to maintain the relationship, rather than a source of pleasure for Sarah, the discourses of self-management produce a feminine subject that is required to be 'up for it' as a response to male needs, in which her own pleasure is a secondary concern.

As a show which aims for bite-size solutions, there is never a deeper exploration of the psychological and social factors underlying the problems in Sarah and Nick's relationship. *The Sex Inspectors* does not explore whether Sarah might be better off without the constant grading, shouting and whining of Nick, presenting female sexual subjectivity as unintelligible without a male partner. Power is presented as something individualized, rather than bound up in the structures of society. Tracey's message, while initially calling upon Sarah (and viewers in a similar situation) to take back control, couches this as a simple choice in terms of sexual performance – get better grades. Sarah should become the porn-star performer that Nick has always wanted, but of course, internalizing the policing gaze of the inspectors, and buying their products to help her along the way, she will be doing it for herself.

Conclusion

The new feminine sexual entrepreneur is made intelligible through discourses of sex produced by the mainstream self-help genre. While the 'sexualization of culture' has undoubtedly facilitated access to information about sexual desires and problems, there is a complex relationship between such mediated knowledges, power and subjectivity. Although sexual entrepreneurship allows for a desiring, knowing female sexuality, it must be at once 'up for it' yet sensitive to male needs and fears, and 'spiced up' but maintaining the boundaries of heterosexual monogamy. Such a contradictory mode of femininity intimately entangles the struggles and gains of feminism and sexual liberation with the neoliberal incitement to constant self-improvement through hyper-consumption. The representation of such sexual self-improvement as a matter of 'choice' and 'empowerment' obscures the narrow, tightly policed boundaries that remain around feminine intelligibility, and the symbolic and material violence that women can suffer if they do not 'perform'. Importantly, shifting our analysis away from binary characterizations of feminine sexual subjectivity is not to deny the power that operates through the discourses of sex self-help. Nor is the exploration of such power a denial of the agency and pleasure felt in the taking up of sexual entrepreneurialism. Rather, as feminists we aim to critically explore the discursive constraints and resistances available to women as we work towards the production of inclusive and positive sexual representations.

Bibliography

American Psychological Association (2007) *Report of the APA Task Force on the Sexualization of Girls* (Washington, DC: American Psychological Association).

Arthurs, J. (2004) *Television and Sexuality: Regulation and the Politics of Taste* (Maidenhead: Open University Press).

Attwood, F. (2006) 'Sexed Up: Theorising the Sexualization of Culture', *Sexualities* 9(1): 77–95

Attwood, F. (ed.) (2009) *Mainstreaming Sex: The Sexualization of Western Culture* (London: I. B. Tauris).

BBC (2009) 'Becoming a Body Language Expert', bbc.co.uk. Available at http://www.bbc.co.uk/relationships/singles_and_dating/techniques_becomeblexpert.shtml#how_i_got_there [accessed 26 May 2009].

Bordo, S. R. (1993). *Unbearable Weight: Feminism, Western Culture, and the Body* (Berkeley: University of California Press).

Boynton, P. (2009) 'Whatever Happened to Cathy and Claire? Sex, Advice and the Role of the Agony Aunt' in F. Atwood (ed.), *Mainstreaming Sex: The Sexualization of Western Culture* (London: I. B. Tauris).

Boynton, P. and W. Callaghan (2006) 'Understanding Media Coverage of Sex: A Practical Discussion Paper for Sexologists and Journalists', *Sexual and Relationship Therapy* 21(3): 333–46.

Butler, J. P. (1997) *The Psychic Life of Power: Theories in Subjection* (Palo Alto, CA: Stanford University Press).

Butler, J. P. (1990) *Gender Trouble: Feminism and the Subversion of Identity* (New York and London: Routledge).

Buckingham, D. and S. Bragg (2004) *Young People, Sex, and the Media: The Facts of Life?* (Basingstoke and New York: Palgrave Macmillan).

Coleman, R. (2008) 'Girls, Media Effects, and Body Image', *Feminist Media Studies* 8(2): 163–79.

Durham, M. G. (2004) 'Constructing the "New Ethnicities": Media, Sexuality, and Diaspora Identity in the Lives of South Asian Immigrant Girls', *Critical Studies in Media Communication* 21(2): 140–61.

Durham, M. G. (2009) *The Lolita Effect: The Media Sexualization of Young Girls and What We Can Do About It* (London: Gerald Duckworth Press).

Farvid, P. and V. Braun (2006), '"Most of Us Guys Are Raring to Go Anytime, Anyplace, Anywhere": Male and Female Sexuality in Cleo and Cosmo', *Sex Roles* 55(5–6): 295–310.

Foucault, M. (1978) *The History of Sexuality* (New York: Pantheon).

Foucault, M. (1988) 'Technologies of the Self' in L. H. Martin et al., *Technologies of the Self: A Seminar with Michel Foucault* (London: Tavistock).

Gavey, N. and K. McPhillips (1999) 'Subject to Romance: Heterosexual Passivity as an Obstacle to Women Initiating Condom Use', *Psychology of Women Quarterly* 23(2): 349–67.

Gill, R. (2003) 'From Sexual Objectification to Sexual Subjectification: The Resexualisation of Women's Bodies in the Media', *Feminist Media Studies* 3(1): 99–106.

Gill, R. (2006) *Gender and the Media* (Cambridge: Polity Press).

Gill, R. (2008) 'Empowerment/Sexism: Figuring Female Sexual Agency in Contemporary Advertising', *Feminism & Psychology* 18(1): 35–60.

Gill, R. (2009a) 'Beyond the "Sexualization of Culture" Thesis: An Intersectional Analysis of "Sixpacks","Midriffs" and "Hot Lesbians" in Advertising', *Sexualities* 12(2): 137–60.

Gill, R. (2009b) 'Mediated Intimacy and Postfeminism: A Discourse Analytic Examination of Sex and Relationships Advice in a Women's Magazine', *Discourse and Communication* 3(4): 1–25.

Goldman, R. (1992) *Reading Ads Socially* (London: Routledge).

Goodwin, D. (2004) 'A Sex Inspector Calls', telegraph.co.uk, 23 November 23. Available at http://www.telegraph.co.uk/culture/tvandradio/3632286/A-sex-inspector-calls.html [accessed 10 March 2009].

Hall, P. (2005) 'Who Do They Think They Are?', *Counselling and Psychotherapy Journal* 16(1): 40–1.

HM Government (2009) *Together We Can End Violence against Women and Girls: A Consultation Paper* (London: Home Office).

Hollway, W. (1989) 'Making Love Without Contraception: Towards a Theory for Analysing Accounts' in W. Hollway (ed.), *Subjectivity and Method in Psychology: Gender, Meaning and Science* (London: Sage).

Jackson, S. and S. Scott (1997) 'Gut Reactions to Matters of the Heart: Reflections on Rationality, Irrationality and Sexuality', *The Sociological Review* 45(4): 551–75.

Jeffreys, S. (2008) *The Industrial Vagina* (London: Routledge).

Johnson, M. L. (ed.) (2002) *Jane Sexes It Up: True Confessions of Feminist Desire* (New York: Four Walls Eight Windows).

Juffer, J. (1998) *At Home with Pornography* (New York: New York University Press).

Lauretis, T. de (1987) *Technologies of Gender* (Bloomington, IN: Indiana University Press).

Levy, A. (2005) *Female Chauvinist Pigs: Women and the Rise of Raunch Culture* (New York: Free Press).

McRobbie, A. (2004) 'The Rise and Rise of Porn Chic', *The Times Higher Education Supplement*, 2 January.

McRobbie, A. (2009) *The Aftermath of Feminism: Gender, Culture and Social Change* (London: Sage).

Morley, D. (1992) *Television, Audiences and Cultural Studies* (London: Routledge).

Paul, P. (2005) *Pornified: How Pornography is Transforming our Lives, our Relationships and our Families* (New York: Times Books).

Pinto, P. (forthcoming) 'From Post-*Feminism* to "Dildocracy": Sex Industries and Happy Woman's Biopolitics', *Feminism and Psychology*.

Plummer, K. (1995) *Telling Sexual Stories: Power, Change and Social Worlds* (London: Routledge).

Potts, A. (1998) 'The Science/Fiction of Sex: John Gray's Mars and Venus in the Bedroom', *Sexualities* 1(2): 153–73.

Radner, H. (1993) 'Pretty is as Pretty Does: Free Enterprise and the Marriage Plot' in H. Collins, H. Radner and A. Preacher (eds), *Film Theory Goes to the Movies* (New York: Routledge).

Radner, H. (1999) 'Queering the Girl' in H. Radner and M. Luckett (eds), *Swinging Single: Representing Sexuality in the 1960s* (Minnesota: Minnesota University Press).

Ringrose, J. (forthcoming) 'Beyond Discourse? Using Deleuze and Guattari's Schizoanalysis to Explore Affective Assemblages, Heterosexually Striated Space, and Lines of Flight Online and at School', *Educational Philosophy & Theory*, Special Issue: The Power In/Of Language.

Ringrose, J. and V. Walkerdine (2008) 'Regulating the Abject: The TV Make-over as Site of Neo-liberal Reinvention toward Bourgeois Femininity', *Feminist Media Studies* 8(3): 227–46.

Rogers, A. (2005) 'Chaos to Control: Men's Magazines and the Mastering of Intimacy', *Men and Masculinities* 8(2): 175–94.

Rudebeck, C. (2004) 'About Last Night', *The Independent*, 22 November. Available at http://www.independent.co.uk/life-style/health-and-families/health-news/about-last-night-534175.html [accessed 26 May 2009].

Rush, E. and A. La Nauze (2006) *Corporate Paedophilia: Sexualisation of Children in Australia* (Canberra: The Australia Institute).

The Sex Inspectors (2004) 'Gary and Rea' (Channel 4, 7 December).

The Sex Inspectors (2007) 'Nick and Sarah', (Channel 4, 13 February).

The Sex Inspectors (2007) 'Sally-Ann and Paul', (Channel 4, 14 February).

Tracey Cox (2009) Available at www.traceycox.com [accessed 10 March 2009].

Tyler, M. (2004) 'Managing between the Sheets: Lifestyle Magazines and the Management of Sexuality in Everyday Life', *Sexualities* 7(1): 81–106.

Tyler, M. (2008) 'Sex Self-help Books: Hot Secrets for Great Sex or Promoting the Sex of Prostitution?', *Women's Studies International Forum* 31(5): 363–72.

Whelehan, I. (2000) *Overloaded: Popular Culture and the Future of Feminism* (London: Women's Press).

Wignall, A. (2008) 'The Joy of Sexperts', guardian.co.uk, 25 February. Available at http://www.guardian.co.uk/media/2008/feb/25/pressandpublishing.relationships [accessed 26 May 2009].

Williamson, J. (2003) 'Sexism with an Alibi', *The Guardian*, 31 May.

4
(M)Other-in-Chief: Michelle Obama and the Ideal of Republican Womanhood

Lisa Guerrero

On 4 November 2008, the people of the United States witnessed something that had never occurred in the nation's history. For the first time since its founding, a black woman was set to become the First Lady of the United States. (It's fair to say that the election of her husband as the first African American President of the United States was an auspicious occasion as well.) With the historic event of Barack Obama's election to the presidency, and to the title of the leader of the free world, the attention given to Michelle Obama as the new First Lady was, to say the least, extensive and rapt. But among all of the discussions of J. Crew and Target, biceps, hairstyles, and inaugural gowns, much less was being made of the significance of a black woman as First Lady, than of a black man as President. While it is obvious why focus has been largely aimed at President Obama concerning the momentous intersection of race, manhood, citizenship and the meaning of the presidency,[1] the role to which Michelle Obama has ascended is arguably far more complicated and fraught, and one in which it could be far more challenging to 'succeed'. This essay looks at the meaning of American womanhood as embodied in the role of the First Lady of the United States, and the complicated ways in which Michelle Obama must work to inscribe those meanings onto the overdetermined terrain of black womanhood. In doing so, it also reveals some of the larger contours of new femininities, in particular, the primacy of a performative consciousness that has evolved as a mode through which to suture together the disparate social demands of imagined womanhood in the new millennium in order to forge a coherent, translatable identity of femininity.

Ladies and gentlemen ... the First Lady of the United States

Before looking at the ways in which the position of First Lady, called by Margaret Carlson 'the most tradition-bound and antiquated model of

American womanhood' (Carlson, 1992, p. 31), presents unique challenges to Michelle Obama, it is critical to look at the position itself, its symbolic functions and its complicated political purposes. As Karrin Vasby Anderson has said in her essay 'The First Lady: A Site of "American Womanhood"' (2004) regarding the role of the First Lady:

> Historically, first ladies have functioned as 'symbols' of traditional white middle- to upper-class femininity in America, a condition that has both constrained and empowered them. (Mayo and Meringolo, 1994)...My argument...is that first ladies also influence conceptions of 'American' for all women. Indeed, by virtue of their husbands' elections, first ladies become 'sites' for the symbolic negotiation of female identity. (Wertheimer, 2004, p. 18)

One of the most significant aspects of Anderson's assessment is that First Ladies have 'functioned as "symbols" of traditional *white* middle- to upper-class femininity in America' (emphasis added). The role of the First Lady begins with a naturalized assumption of whiteness, including the way in which femininity is a uniquely white domain, which means that Michelle Obama, and the type of womanhood that she 'represents', begins by being imagined *outside* of the role of the First Lady. In other words, the function of blackness has never been to serve as a symbol for traditional whiteness so that that modus must, out of necessity, be reconceived from the outset for Michelle Obama. And though Anderson also sees the First Lady as a ' "site" for the symbolic negotiation of female identity', that negotiation isn't assumed to be inclusive and remains contained in notions of whiteness. Both of these particular symbolic functions of the First Lady are intrinsically linked to the concept of the 'ideal of republican womanhood' that came to prominence at the end of the eighteenth century, and which 'sought to infuse women's domesticity with intense political meaning' (Kann, 1999, p. 47). The women who advanced this idea:

> ...felt that female influence on male family members was the single most important determinant of the nation's future. They gradually developed the doctrine of 'republican womanhood', which called on domestic women to take responsibility for breeding, teaching, and sustaining good citizenship in America. (Kann, 1999, p. 47)

Again, black women are left out of this equation as their domesticity has never been viewed by dominant power structures as having intense political meaning. If viewed as anything, black female domesticity has been viewed as an economic commodity unlinked to any conceptions of traditional femininity, and therefore outside of the ideal of republican womanhood.

These symbolic functions are but one side of the role of First Lady that must be negotiated by all women who fill the role, but that pose a singular challenge to a woman who is black. The other side of the role of First Lady is the political purposes she must serve. Politically, the First Lady must strike what is viewed as an appropriate balance between being a wife and mother, and being a political asset, a balance that oftentimes erases the *actual* identity of the woman inside the role. Or as Grace Coolidge remarked in her post-White House memoir, 'this was I and yet not I, this was the wife of the President of the United States and she took precedence over me' (Coolidge, 1992, p. 62, as quoted in Wertheimer, 2004, p. 1). The erasure of a personal identity for the purpose of an effective political identity is a problematic enterprise that reproduces certain social systems of gender oppressions that work to contain femininity in specific ways that are meant to serve dominant male power structures. These dominant male power structures have been historically white, which is to say that they have supported the maintenance of a white supremacist[2] social, political and economic order (and actually, remain so, despite the fact that the current President of the United States is a black man), so that the containment of *black* femininity in service of the (white) power structures necessarily takes on a different ideological meaning wherein both her race *and* her gender have to be 'kept in check' so as to not distract from political messages. For Michelle Obama, the simultaneous containment of blackness and womanhood potentially creates in her a kind of modern-day slave, where the master is the message. She isn't really to be seen or heard as herself per se, like the First Ladies before her, but additionally, she must make sure to not be seen or heard as a *black woman*, or she risks distracting people away from the message. So not only must she strive, as all First Ladies have had to do, to be feminine, but not *feminist*, she must also strive to be raceless even as she appears black since the role of First Lady has never been forced to be understood through the lens of race as the whiteness of its character has long been naturalized. To be interpreted as raceless while being seen as black exposes what is, unfortunately, a common struggle of the paradoxical performances demanded of people of colour in an American society that increasingly naturalizes colour-blind racism. The other struggle, to be feminine and not *feminist* stems from the long-held social conflation of feminism with anger, and subsequently, with the 'anti-feminine'. Despite the fact that being 'womanly' (which itself is not a straightforward exercise, except in the most stereotypical terms), and believing in the political, social and economic equality between men and women are *not* mutually exclusive, being 'feminine' and being 'feminist' remain polar opposites in the larger national imagination. And though this tension between feminine and feminist isn't particular to Michelle Obama – all First Ladies (and, in fact, all women) – are forced to negotiate it, Michelle Obama's race makes this tension particularly precarious as her race is always already suspected of irrationality and anger in the ways in which it has been historically constructed in the American social imagination. Consequently, Michelle Obama must consciously work on two fronts to confine even the slightest hint that she may be anything *other* than content in her assimilated privilege. However fraught these demands, she must accomplish these things to fulfil her role as a domestic centre for her husband, as well as a goodwill messenger of her husband's, and the party's, political agenda. Historically speaking, the systematic erasure of black womanhood in American society is nothing new, but in the context of the most prominent role of American womanhood this erasure is given an even greater ideological legitimacy that not only works to contain a singular black woman, Michelle Obama, by amputating her racial identity, but is sure to have larger social repercussions for women of colour as a model of 'deracialized' womanhood becomes an increasingly normalized model. In other words, as the United States becomes further convinced of the ideological merits of the myth of 'equality through colour-blindness', models of women (and men) of colour who 'transcend' (read: appear to ignore – or, in the very least, perform as if they do) the social and physical mantles of race to reach permissible levels of assimilation[3] will, with more frequency and impact, be used to justify the radical reduction and outright dismissal of social, political and economic theories and policies aimed at addressing the realities of racial inequity in the country. For women of colour, this impending social trajectory poses a uniquely insidious threat. Since women of colour, especially black women, find themselves at, or near, the bottom of many of the most significant socio-economic indicators of prosperity and longevity in disproportionate numbers, the trend of this largely performative deracialization removes race as a factor for critical consideration when proposing solutions to these disproportionate numbers even as it remains as one of their primary causes, the consequences of which promise to be the social legitimation and codification of the continued and deepening marginalization of black women in the United States.

Unfortunately, it seems nearly impossible that Michelle Obama would be able to challenge this rhetorical and ideological move of deracialization since in the role of First Lady, she is, in many respects, *owned* by the American public, an experience that is clearly fraught with historical irony, but also one that demands strict performances. As Molly Meijer Wertheimer states: 'With the public's sense of ownership have inevitably come expectations of what a first lady can and cannot say and do' (Wertheimer, 2004, pp. 10–11). These expectations transcend the individuals who hold the office, that is, 'the office itself carries a heavy symbolic burden' (Wertheimer, 2004, p. 3). Nowhere was this idea made more apparent in the context of Michelle Obama, than the events that transpired on 18 February 2008.

Pride and prejudice

On 18 February 2008, during a campaign stop in Madison, Wisconsin, Michelle Obama, the woman who would be First Lady, said to a crowd 'For the first time in my adult lifetime, I'm really proud of my country, and not just because Barack has done well, but because I think people are hungry for change.' This sentiment caused a furor among conservative pundits, voters and politicians, and contributed welcome fuel to the anti-American flame that opponents of Barack Obama's candidacy were trying to ignite around the first truly viable black candidate for president the country had ever seen. Wanting to paint him into the threatening role of the other, opponents jumped on every opportunity, no matter how slight, to impeach his American citizenship and belonging. They saw the words spoken by his wife as a fecund demonstration of their own rampant suspicions: Barack Obama and his family weren't *real* Americans because the respect and appreciation they showed for the country was never respectful or appreciative *enough*. Because of the fact of their blackness, any statement that was critical of any aspect of the American nation was interpreted by detractors, the majority of whom were white, as ungrateful or elitist. (Although, it remains unclear just *how* grateful and humble a black man in America, with a successful, close-knit family is supposed to be when it only took a mere 232 years for the United States to acknowledge the leadership potential of a man of colour.)

Obama's campaign spokespeople were quick to do their jobs and address this apparent misstep by Mrs Obama, by emphasizing 'Of course Michelle is proud of her country, which is why she and Barack talk constantly about how their story wouldn't be possible in any other nation on Earth.' Which story exactly is *their* story? The story of successful black people in a nation founded on ideologies of white supremacy? More likely, the spokesperson, Bill Burton, was making reference to a more romanticized story of meritocracy, where two people, no matter their race or class, work hard and are rewarded with success. Of course, race and class did matter – do matter still – but there was no room for that in the public relations spin. The campaign just needed to be put back on course, and with the momentary restoration of pride and gratitude on the part of the candidate's wife, it was.

But there are several significant things about this instance that are central to my consideration of the figure of Michelle Obama. The first is that conservative constituencies used this line by Michelle Obama to re-establish the 'true' model of republican womanhood in the figure of Cindy McCain who, on the day after Michelle Obama's remark, stated, 'I just wanted to make the statement that I have and always will be proud of my country.' In other words, don't worry; I'm a *real* American. What is truly interesting about these two remarks is the juxtaposition of notions of ownership. McCain's bald retort comes from a position of entitlement.

As a white woman of class privilege, when she states '*my* country', it actually means just that...the country has historically been meant for people of her race and her class. And even her racialized gender identity, though not always on equal footing with white men, has always been at the heart of the United States ideologies of the preservation and maintenance of the democratic republic. The protection of white womanhood, both literally and symbolically, has stood at the centre of most of the endeavours enacted in the name of American democracy. Alternatively, Michelle Obama's statement hinted at (in my mind, intentionally) the ways in which African Americans, especially African American women, have been systematically marginalized in a country that was their own, but never one that they have been allowed *to own*. Her words seemed to be less about being proud for the first time, and more about seeing the country, 'my country', as something she could claim for the first time, because it finally seemed to being claiming *her*. So unlike Cindy McCain's snide comment that appeared to be based largely in its use as a rhetorical move, Michelle Obama's comment seemed to be based, not in a bitter, anti-Americanism, but rather in a critical acknowledgement of varied systems of hegemony, privilege and oppression on which the United States has relied to justify and maintain unfair practices, unequal access, unconstitutional policies and unjust wars. Because of her race and gender, Michelle Obama came to the notion of 'American pride' just a little differently than a white woman like Cindy McCain might. For Mrs Obama, national pride was not something to be given automatically, rather it was something to be earned, just as her acceptance as a black woman in America was something the country constantly made, and continues to make her earn. This underlying sense of Michelle Obama's comments leads to the next significant point of consideration: her sense of, and operation within, what Patricia Hill Collins has termed the 'matrix of domination'.

In *Black Feminist Thought: Knowledge, Consciousness, and the Politics of Empowerment* (1990) Patricia Hill Collins introduces the concept of the 'matrix of domination' by saying:

> Black feminist thought fosters a fundamental paradigmatic shift that rejects additive approaches to oppression. Instead of starting with gender and then adding in other variables such as age, sexual orientation, race, social class, and religion, Black feminist thought sees these distinctive systems of oppression as being part of one overarching structure of domination. Viewing relations of domination for Black women for any given sociohistorical context as being structured via a system of interlocking race, class, and gender oppression expands the focus of analysis from merely describing the similarities and differences distinguishing these systems of oppression and focuses greater attention on how they interconnect. (Hill Collins, 1990, p. 222)

Thinking about oppressions, (1) as plural, and (2) as interconnected, interdependent and simultaneous, provides a broader theoretical frame to begin to imagine the significant implications of a black woman assuming the position of *the* exemplar of American womanhood. Collins's 'matrix of domination' becomes a useful way through which to examine the rhetorical choices that have circulated around Michelle Obama, of which the 'proud of my country' remark is but one. An interesting aspect of the 'proud of my country' remark not yet noted was the audience response in the instant that she made her statement. Though she was speaking to an 'Obama' crowd, when she made the first part of her comment there was a momentary, awkward silence that was emphasized by the one or two tentative claps of support for the sentiment. This was compared to the thunderous applause that erupted just seconds later when she ended the statement with the surefire invocation of change. Using Collins's idea of interlocking oppressions we can see a double image of Michelle Obama emerge in the national imagination almost instantaneously within this moment. First, there is the image of the assimilated black woman, who is well-spoken and dressed appropriately, and is supporting her husband, himself another example of black assimilation. But as she begins to address her qualified pride in her country, the image of the assimilated black woman melts into the image of the angry black woman who carries a racial grudge. It's a quick, almost imperceptible shift, but a telling one. In one brief moment she exposes both myriad oppressive stereotypes regarding black women, as well as white liberal relationships to those stereotypes.

Before she starts speaking, her warm acceptance by the mainly white crowd is predicated on very complicated issues of assimilation as they regard blackness, specifically black femininity. People respond to her because they *like* her, feel comforted by her...as if she were their mom. They feel comforted by her because she appears to be much like them, in other words, not black. She speaks well. She dresses fashionably, yet, appropriately conservative. She doesn't highlight race (except in her body), because she is assimilated and no longer needs to rely on the 'excuse' of race. She doesn't pose a threat, because she isn't *seen* as black. She's *almost* one of them. In fact, in many respects, she's *better* than them. She's Princeton and Harvard educated. She's upper-middle class. She's an exception, which *does* pose a certain ideological threat to assumptions about blackness. This one paradoxical response is indicative of the complicated systems of racial oppression in the US through which Michelle Obama is forced to navigate daily.

Further, people's response to her as motherly is a very tenuous one that she must play on very carefully. She *is* a mother, and a demonstratively good one. And as First Lady, it is necessary to play into the role of the nation's mother. However, at the same time, the motherly image as associated with black womanhood cannot help but be linked to historical ideas of the mammy, a space in which both her race and her gender become dually vilified, which is an experience that has continued to follow Michelle Obama even in her short tenure as First Lady, and which will likely not disappear.[4] But it is the 'mother' role that Michelle Obama continues to foreground for herself, in part because she must understand that, however complicated, it is the most comforting (historically) normal role for many Americans, white and black, to see her in.

The one role they *don't* want to see her in is 'angry black woman'. And even though her comment was not delivered in anger, and was not, by and large, an angry statement, the interpretation of it, even by many Obama supporters, connected it to notions of black anger. In that moment in the national imagination, her assimilated self took a backseat to her 'black' self, one that spoke 'out of turn', one that was 'ungracious', one that made white people feel guilty/responsible/threatened. She wasn't even speaking about race explicitly, but the implication of her statement hinted at race enough to cause confusion to a country that doesn't want to see race...even when it is looking at a black woman.

Finally, this rhetorical misstep resulted in a mind/body split being conducted on the image of Michelle Obama within the popular media. After this comment, most of the attention given to Michelle Obama was focused on her body and not on her intellectual contributions, as if people didn't want to risk 'unleashing' any black rage. The kind of focus on her body has teetered on the fetishistic, and has been largely unprecedented for an American First Lady, but not so for American black women. The fascination, especially over her arms and hair, recalls the disembodied fascination with the bodies of black women that began in slavery and have continued into the twentieth and twenty-first centuries with various images including the welfare queen and the video vixen. As Patricia Hill Collins has said 'Objectifying Black women's bodies turns them into canvases that can be interchanged for a variety of purposes' (Hill Collins, 2004, p. 129). But in this instance this was the woman who would be 'First Lady' being bodily scrutinized. Should she not be immune? Again drawing on Collins's 'matrix of domination', we can understand that she is *not* immune. It is the fact of her blackness, and its interconnection to her gender, that makes this attention not only acceptable, but also *normal*. Couched in terms of 'admiration', the continued portrayal of Michelle Obama through her black female body manages to further compromise any ability she may have to ascend to the 'ideal of republican womanhood', as well as further distinguish the challenges she faces as First Lady from those of all of her First Lady predecessors.

Role models in black and white

As I write this, Michelle Obama has been First Lady for only about ten months. There is no real way to predict the direction her role in the White

House will take, or the ways in which the combination of her race and gender will continue to characterize the nation's response to her performance in that role. However, what we may consider are the ways in which Michelle Obama presents as an interesting amalgam of various models of 'First Lady' womanhood alongside various models of black womanhood, and how this amalgam may serve her as she is forced to negotiate her time as America's first black First Lady.

Though space does not allow for an extensive look at the women who provide certain critical groundings for understanding the complexities of becoming 'Michelle Obama, the first black First Lady of the United States', it is enough to simply introduce them because they each come with such strong references in the national imagination that the picture of influence takes shape very quickly and critically. Michelle Obama's reflection of this gallery of disparate women not only demonstrates the challenge of fitting blackness into a role imagined expressly in whiteness, but also exposes the tension of the traditional role of First Lady, or as Karlyn Kohrs Campbell puts it: 'presidential wives face insuperable obstacles arising out of expectations that they are to represent what we pretend is a single, universally accepted ideal for U.S. womanhood' (Campbell, 1996, p. 191 as quoted in Wertheimer, 2004, p. 3). Whereas a singular ideal of American womanhood doesn't exist, it becomes one of the main charges of the First Lady to shape that conception in a way that truly takes American women into consideration, but that is also allowable inside the small arena of elite politics and is embraced by the American public. The question for Michelle Obama is how does she do that through the historically vilified space of blackness? Which models does she call upon?

In the figure of Michelle Obama we witness the collision between archetypes of the First Lady and archetypes of modern black womanhood. Two former First Ladies and three icons of black womanhood form a useful genealogy through which to map Michelle Obama's challenge in performing the role of the First Lady. Though there are most certainly other women who might be considered part of this genealogy, I believe these five make up central facets of the ways in which Michelle Obama appears to be shaping her identity into the identity of the first black First Lady. Jacqueline Kennedy and Hillary Rodham Clinton, and Angela Davis, Kathleen Cleaver, and Claire Huxtable, are not necessarily women that are immediately associated with one another, but the template that their combined characteristics create offers several insights into some of Michelle Obama's sartorial, rhetorical and political choices.

In many ways, the link to Jacqueline Kennedy is apparent. Many have likened Obama's candidacy and election to that of John F. Kennedy, and his presidency as the promise of the new 'Camelot'. The connection between Jackie and Michelle are obvious on the one hand, especially the clamour around each woman's fashion, but in other ways more subtle. Jackie Kennedy is considered the first 'televisual' First Lady. Her role became more 'consumable' than other First Ladies' because the public's 'access' to her became more intimate with the use of the television medium. Similarly, Michelle Obama is the first true 'new media' First Lady.[5] Not only is the public's 'access' to her instantaneous through modes of new media, but also the potential for the manipulation of images and stories is endless, as are the routes of their circulation. This kind of proliferation of 'nano accesses' gives the perceived ownership of Michelle Obama a more tangible foundation, one that she must confront in order to not be consumed by it. So just as Jackie Kennedy gave a tour of the White House on television in an effort to control the boundaries and tenor of the public's access to her, so too has Michelle Obama invited particular kinds of access to her, most notably in magazines and television programmes, to try to firmly set the tone for people's view of her as First Lady, including the framing of people's sense of 'entitlement' over the ways in which she performs her womanhood and her race.

In sharp contrast to Jackie Kennedy, Hillary Rodham Clinton is largely an anomaly when it comes to the role of First Lady. With only a few exceptions, including Edith Wilson and Eleanor Roosevelt, no other First Lady has played such a large role in the politics of their husbands' presidential administrations. Her insistent portrayal of a First Lady whose credentials matched those of her husband, was instructive in the ways in which American society largely responded to intelligent, capable, aggressive womanhood, which is to say, not well. Hillary Clinton's time as First Lady vividly demonstrates Edith Mayo's comment on controversies regarding First Ladies being about 'America's continuing, deep-seated ambivalence, even hostility, toward power in the hands of women' (Anderson, 2004, p. 21). It is the reception of Hillary Clinton as First Lady that seems to temper Michelle Obama's performance as a 'high-powered' First Lady, despite her credentials being not only as impressive as Hillary Clinton's, but also as impressive as her own husband's. Not only is it precarious to be viewed as 'feminist' (a highly misunderstood and vilified term in the American lexicon), but as a black woman, it is also dangerous to 'flaunt' her accomplishments too much or else be racially characterized as 'uppity' (as both she and the President have often been characterized throughout the campaign and well into his presidency). As a result, Michelle Obama appears to strategically pull out the 'Ivy-League' aspect of herself only in support of her husband and his administration. Even then she makes sure to balance it out with her domestic identity so as not to threaten the American people with the simultaneity of her race and gender. But it is the ways in which she chooses, even subtly, to deploy her racialized gender that we can identify several influences of models of modern black womanhood.

On 21 July 2008, the cover of *The New Yorker* magazine depicted a cartoon of Barack and Michelle Obama as identifiably marked as 'threats to America' engaged in the over-hyped 'terrorist fist jab' (so named by Fox News).

Barack's depiction as a Muslim was less inspired than Michelle's depiction as a fantastical image of the 1960s version of Angela Davis. Though I won't offer a critical narrative analysis of the cover itself (that is an article in and of itself), I do want to stress that the connecting of Michelle Obama to Angela Davis, and by association to Black Power and 1960s revolutionaries including Kathleen Cleaver (who was married to Eldridge Cleaver, a leader in the Black Panthers and well-documented misogynist, and was, herself, a black power leader in her own right), perhaps said more about the fear of black womanhood than anything else that came out during the campaign or since. The fear, as depicted in the cover, was twofold: (1) fear of a strong black woman who was *ready for a fight*, demonstrated through the weaponry she wore, and (2) fear of a black woman who clearly supported black men as represented through her husband. Though Michelle Obama is, in many substantive ways, removed from the Black Power image represented by Angela Davis and Kathleen Cleaver, they do remain some of the few and most powerful models of modern black womanhood as resistant and transformative, even in the face of racial hegemonies and oppressive systems of patriarchy, both largely and in the black community specifically. And through the synecdoche of Michelle Obama's arms and their show of strength and power, as well as the public's simultaneous offence and fascination with them, we can trace a small ideological connection to the model of modern revolutionary black womanhood, one that, perhaps most importantly, served to support *black manhood*... one of the most revolutionary moves there is in twenty-first-century America. Of course, Michelle Obama tends to dilute this aspect of black womanhood (even as she *does* subtly call upon it in various occasions) with a more palatable model of modern black womanhood: Claire Huxtable.

The model of middle-class black womanhood that the character of Claire Huxtable represents is clearly one of the closest influences we can recognize in Michelle Obama's performance as First Lady of the United States. As the successful attorney wife to Bill Cosby's Cliff Huxtable, and the mother of the large Huxtable family, Claire Huxtable became *the* black version of proprietous white womanhood. She, like Michelle Obama, combined professional success with domestic success and did it all while remaining almost completely 'raceless'. It was largely the middle-class, deracinated nature of Claire Huxtable that allowed people to accept her wholeheartedly as a very close approximation of ideal republican womanhood.[6] This is the same condition that enables Michelle Obama to assume the mantle of First Lady, even as she's forced to reconceive it. But what Claire Huxtable was not allowed to show then, and what Michelle Obama is not allowed to show now, is the complicated palimpsest that defines black womanhood in the United States, despite both of them, a fictional character and the First Lady, being forced to continue to live *inside* of that complicated web.

Ain't I a woman?

Though the seemingly infinite portraits of Michelle Obama and the first family show a model of American domestic 'normalcy', they belie the fact of racial and gender oppressions that still shape the United States, and that Michelle Obama, as a black woman, and the first family, as a black family, are intrinsically formed by. Several individual aspects of the systematic oppression of black womanhood have already been discussed throughout this essay, including the vilification of the black female body and the exploitation of black female domestic identities. These things, in conjunction with issues of patriarchy and the historical view of the black family, round out the terrain on which Michelle Obama is forging a different model of idealized American womanhood.

As a modern (black) American matriarch, Michelle Obama must live in the wake of the image of the mammy, a de facto, yet demonized, matriarch; the welfare queen, the greedy, fertile chimera of social programmes; and of the dysfunctional black family, or what Daniel Patrick Moynihan deemed 'the tangle of pathology'. Even as a 'Claire Huxtable' model of black womanhood, Michelle Obama is still the inheritor of these notions. It is her job to try to keep these ideas from touching her family, and more importantly, from touching the Obama presidency. And it is a Sisyphean task. The first family ostensibly serves as the model for the national family; however, black families have been historically defined as transgressive due in large part to the role played by black mothers, a role that has been deemed non-normative.[7] How then does Michelle Obama, a black mother, turn the non-normative (the black family) into the hyper-normative (the first family) without necessarily having to deny racial identity on some level and without threatening the patriarchal status quo to which black mothers are, apparently, a constant threat?

Another complex negotiation is the ways and means of 'communication', with which Michelle Obama, as a black woman, but also as the First Lady, is confronted. The historical silencing of black women has taken many forms, both violent and non-violent, all in service to both white and black patriarchal orders. In other words, the rhetorical and intellectual space for black women has been severely limited in most social and political arenas enforced by both ideological repression and bodily harm. Now alternatively, and with different consequences, as First Lady, *everything* is considered communication. There is no such thing as 'silence'. 'For better or worse, a first lady cannot *not* communicate. Whatever she says or does not say and whatever she does or does not do reflect upon her husband and herself. It is the ethos of the presidential couple in the public mind that defines the president's administration' (Wertheimer, 2004, p. 12). So how do you communicate 'effectively', and at all times, to a public that has been historically socialized to not let you communicate at all? How do you transform yourself from an invisible woman to an everywoman?

Conclusion: black like me

It is clear that even during this short period of Barack Obama's presidency, people do seem to genuinely like Michelle Obama. Even as President Obama remains relatively popular with the American public (with a few hits taken by healthcare debates), his wife is still *more* popular. Granted, she isn't the face of policy, the economy or war, but it is still a notable feat. She has strived vigorously for accessibility, from buying her clothes at popular mall retailers like J. Crew, Target and Black Market/White House, to planting the first White House garden since Eleanor Roosevelt's victory garden, to emphasizing nightly family dinners, to hugging the Queen of England, to controversially wearing shorts on the family trip to the Grand Canyon.[8] And much of her striving has seemed to rely, as has been discussed, on an air of 'racelessness'. However, Patricia Hill Collins provides another way to understand this modus of accessibility as something perhaps utterly 'raced'.

> The spheres of influence created and sustained by African-American women are not meant solely to provide a respite from oppressive situations or a retreat from their effects. Rather, these Black female spheres of influence constitute potential sanctuaries where individual Black women and men are nurtured in order to confront oppressive social institutions. Power from this perspective is a creative power used for the good of the community...By making the community stronger, African-American women become empowered. (Hill Collins, 1990, p. 223)

Using Collins's notion we can see the nation as the community for which Michelle Obama is working to create her spheres of influence. Most recently we can see these spheres of influence in her 'humanizing' of the healthcare debate and her hosting of the G20 spouses. But it is unclear whether or not these small moments of 'success' in Michelle Obama's tenure as the First Lady will ever alter the conception of the ideal of republican womanhood as the whiteness of womanhood. We'll have to wait to see how far Michelle Obama can transform the preconceived notions of the First Lady as inalterably white...or how far those notions of the First Lady will transform Michelle Obama.

Notes

1. Even one of the earliest moments of his presidency was marked with the symbolic residue of this intersection as he took his oath of office on what was being called the 'Lincoln Bible', the bible on which Abraham Lincoln took his oath of office. What went largely unsaid about that particular bible is that it was the bible that belonged to Chief Justice Roger Taney, the Supreme Court Justice who wrote the decision in Dred Scott v. Sanford that declared that no person of African descent,

slave or free, could ever be citizens of the United States, and that stated that blacks had 'no rights which the white man was bound to respect'.

2. I use the term 'white supremacist' here in its most fundamental connotation to mean the belief in white racial superiority and in the positioning of the white racial population at the top of the social order. I am not using it in its more inflammatory and extreme connotation that takes the fundamental notion and attempts to enact it through systematic violence and hatred, though I readily acknowledge the interrelationship between the two connotations.

3. The jury is still out for many white Americans as to whether or not President of the United States is a 'permissible' level of assimilation.

4. The editors of this collection, Rosalind Gill and Christina Scharff, insightfully questioned this 'trap' in which I argue Michelle Obama finds herself: 'Will Michelle Obama always, inevitably, be situated in (at the very least) an implicit relation to this figure? Where might this leave the possibility of change?' My belief is that she, like all black women, unfortunately will always, inevitably, find herself situated in relation to this figure. Such is the effect of socio-historic trauma used in service of white power structures. New black femininities may travel further and further away from the history of this image, but they will never escape its power to control and contain. Unfortunately, what this says about the possibility of change is that it can, likely, as continues to be proven, only go so far.

5. Though Laura Bush is the first First Lady of the twenty-first century, the role that new media played in politics remained developing during the eight years of the Bush administration. It wasn't until the 2008 election that the power of new media played a central, even decisive, role in the way in which politics was engaged.

6. She, again like Michelle Obama, could not totally be accepted as the ideal of republican womanhood because she remained physically marked as 'black'.

7. See Moynihan (1965); also Franklin Frazier (1939).

8. One is forced to ask, what was she supposed to be wearing?

Bibliography

Anderson, K. V. (2004) 'The First Lady: A Site of "American Womanhood"' in M. M. Wertheimer (ed.), *Inventing a Voice: The Rhetoric of American First Ladies of the Twentieth Century* (Lanham, MD: Rowman & Littlefield Publishers).

Beasley, M. H. (2005) *First Ladies and the Press: The Unfinished Partnership of the Media Age* (Evanston: Northwestern Illinois Press).

Carlson, M. (1992) 'All Eyes on Hillary', *Time*, 140 (11): 31–8.

Desmond-Harris, J. (2009) 'Why Michelle's Hair Matters', Time.com, 7 September. Available at http://www.time.com/time/magazine/article/0,9171,1919147,00.html

Franklin Frazier, E. (1939) *The Negro Family in the United States* (Chicago: University of Chicago Press).

Gregory, S. (2009) 'J. Crew and Talbots: Can Michelle Obama Save Fashion Retail?' Time.com, 6 May. Available at http://www.time.com/time/business/article/0,8599,1895631,00.html

Hill Collins, P. (1990) *Black Feminist Thought: Knowledge, Consciousness, and the Politics of Empowerment* (Boston: Unwin Hyman).

Hill Collins, P. (2004) *Black Sexual Politics: African Americans, Gender, and the New Racism* (New York: Routledge).

Kann, M. E. (1999) *The Gendering of American Politics: Founding Mothers, Founding Fathers and Political Patriarchy* (Westport: Greenwood Publishing Group).

Mayo, E. P. and Meringolo, D. D. (1994) *First Ladies: Political Role and Public Image* (Washington, DC.: Smithsonian Institution).

Moynihan, D. P. (1965) *The Negro Family: The Case For National Action*, Office of Policy Planning and Research, United States Department of Labor (March).

Mundy, L. (2008) *Michelle* (New York: Simon & Schuster).

Noveck, J. (2009) 'Why All the Fuss Over a First Lady's Bare Arms?', Huffingtonpost.com, 24 March. Available at http://www.huffingtonpost.com/2009/03/24/why-all-the-fuss-over-a-f_n_178728.html

Swarns, R. L. (2009) '"Mom-in-Chief" Touches on Policy; Tongues Wag', NYTimes.com, 8 February. Available at http://www.nytimes.com/2009/02/08/us/politics/08michelle.html?_r=1&scp=1&sq=rachel+swarns+february+8+2009&st=nyt

Watson, R. P. and A. J. Eksterowicz (eds) (2006) *The Presidential Companion: Readings on the First Ladies* (Columbia: University of South Carolina Press).

Wertheimer, M. M. (2004) 'First Ladies' Fundamental Rhetorical Choices: When to Speak? What to Say? When to Remain Silent?' in M. M. Wertheimer (ed.), *Inventing a Voice: The Rhetoric of American First Ladies of the Twentieth Century* (Lanham, MD: Rowman and Littlefield).

5
Scourging the Abject Body: *Ten Years Younger* and Fragmented Femininity under Neoliberalism

Estella Tincknell

The profoundly toxic character of neoliberalism's recuperation of feminism has rarely been more powerfully articulated than in the television genre that promises to make women look better while making us feel worse. It is a genre whose pervasiveness and proliferation within broadcasting schedules has helped renew the hegemony of beauty culture as the apex of femininity at a historical juncture when women (in parts of Western society at least) are ostensibly more economically independent, socially engaged and politically visible than ever before. And it is a genre whose history is thoroughly tied into the changes in broadcasting structures and reception partly produced by the impact of neoliberal government policies on media ownership and regulation. That genre is the makeover show, the staple of contemporary television schedules and the progenitor of a thousand merchandising opportunities.[1]

Perhaps it should not be surprising that the achievement of a limited social and political autonomy in the twenty-first century for (admittedly, mainly white, middle-class, Western) women has been paralleled by a renewed discursive emphasis on femininity as a pathological condition, this time recast as a relentless drive for physical perfectibility. Not surprising, but deeply troubling. Indeed, while the educational and economic achievements of young women are frequently cited as evidence of feminism's triumph under late modernity, this progressive narrative is always accompanied by its monstrous siblings: the ugly sister stories of eating disorders and bodily anxiety amongst those same young women and an increasingly pervasive celebrity culture in which the physical appearance of female stars is hungrily picked over and brutally pilloried for minute signs of imperfection. As Anita Harris observes, this is a society in which 'the never good enough girl ... must perpetually observe and remake herself', finding herself and her behaviour 'relentlessly pathologised in the therapeutic language of self-esteem' (2004, pp. 34–5).

83

It is, however, the shift of that pathologizing discourse onto older women, and in particular the ageing female body as it appears in popular media, which is the focus of this essay. In Kathleen Woodward's words (1999, p. xvi), these bodies have become both 'invisible and hypervisible' within contemporary culture, increasingly and excessively represented as sites of disgust and fear, and cast as the corporeal signifiers of an inevitable mortal decay that the youth and consumer-orientated culture of late modernity can address only through narratives of punitive physical transformation.[2] This chapter, then, is about the problematic ways in which the television makeover show has helped to reconstruct contemporary femininity, this time as a fragmented and abject condition waiting to be renewed and redeemed by the postmodern Prometheus of cosmetic surgery.

Pathologizing the penitent

Nowhere are the contradictory discourses around the female body more fully played out, rehearsed and recast than in those television makeover shows which week by week promise to transform 'ordinary' women into an acceptable version of femininity through the relentless application of the transformative powers of surgery and dentistry, fashion advice, hairstyling and expert make-up. Women's bodies are pulled apart and then cosmetically reconstructed, sealed up and smoothed over, their gaps and apertures sutured to produce a boundary-less object. Yet this process is presented as the solution to what has already been cast as an essential and immutable pathology of femininity – its lack, in an emotional as well as a physical sense. It is simply in order to enhance their fragile self-esteem and improve their social confidence, that these women must undergo such procedures, according to the discursive framing of the makeover show, and this is a claim that is legitimized by the quoted comments of the women participants themselves, who seem thoroughly convinced of the necessity of such radical intervention. 'It will give me back my life', says Pandora Ankers, the subject of the programme discussed here.

My specific focus therefore is on one episode of the British television programme, *Ten Years Younger*, a show which has appeared on a relatively mainstream terrestrial channel, Channel 4, since 2004 (although there is also a US version which has run on Living TV since 2005).[3] The particular edition discussed here was chosen precisely because its operation at the extreme end of the makeover show's rigid formula reveals the underlying discursive and ideological assumptions which have shaped the genre more generally. Not only does this episode of *Ten Years Younger* present its radical physical transformation of a middle-aged divorced woman as a process of emotional and spiritual redemption in which self-esteem is collapsed into sexual self-objectification in the habitual style of the genre, but it was explicitly billed as a 'Christmas Special'. Pandora's transformation was thus presented as an appropriate kind of seasonal re-packaging – just in time for the festivities. Indeed, this curious foregrounding of the Christmas season as the rationale for the programme's project – it's just helping those lonely laydees get a bit of lurve in time for Xmas – actually functions to remind the viewer of *Ten Years Younger's* profoundly moralistic discourse in the context of a dominant culture (that of white middle-class Britons) which has become increasingly uncomfortable with organized religion. As we will see, *Ten Years Younger's* fetishization of bodily suffering represents a curious recovery and reworking of Christianity's own discourse of abjection, in which the scourging of the physical, bodily self becomes the route to redemption and transformation, effected by powerfully patriarchal practitioners. Perhaps, then, in the absence of a single set of religio-moral beliefs or institutions and in the light of a tendency towards 'pick and mix' spirituality which has been incoherently tied into Western beauty culture (scented candles, Reiki massage and the healing power of hot stones), the makeover show offers its viewers the promise that physical and spiritual renewal are both necessary to femininity and wholly dependent on appropriate forms of consumption in a world in which consumer culture looks like rescue if there's nothing else on offer.

Gendered identities and the fragmented self

Victor Seidler (1989, p. 5) amongst others has pointed out that the development of what we call 'modernity' during the eighteenth century involved an increased emphasis on an ideal human subject who was rational, autonomous and highly individualized. Yet women's ability to produce themselves in terms of a modern self has always been compromised; by the way in which the ideal was itself implicitly gendered and by the social and cultural limitations placed on women's access to self-determination. Furthermore, masculine agency and autonomy was never explicitly predicated on an aesthetics of the male body – if anything, the 'ideal subject' of modernity was constructed in abstract, disembodied terms.

Femininity has thus been the implied 'other' of modernity: where the modern subject was cerebral, autonomous, rational, exercising a confident mastery of public space and expert knowledge, femininity was figured as its opposite – bodily, private, emotional, responsive – dependent rather than autonomous. The intensification and proliferation of consumer culture in late modernity with its emphasis on women as expert consumers (with a specialized if unclear kind of expertise) has facilitated greater female participation in the public sphere, but this has often also been bound into the hyper-commodification of the female body itself and its availability as an object of an evaluative gaze, whether that body belongs to a lap-dancer or a nurse. Furthermore, as David Bell and Joanne Hollows point out (2005, p. 5), the 'aestheticisation of everyday life' during the late twentieth century identified by Mike Featherstone (1991) has also been associated with an increasingly reflexive and stylized mode of consumption in which the 'self' is a privileged site, especially for women.

Cosmetic surgery's increasing popularity and respectability in the twenty-first century is therefore perhaps an inevitable consequence of the consumer logic of late capitalism and femininity's position in late modernity. As these twin forces have extended to incorporate women, while also individualizing them, they have done so on the largely corporeal terms in which image and 'to-be-looked-at-ness' define a certain kind of postfeminist femininity. So, as Kenneth Dutton (1995, p. 177) argues (echoing Marshall McLuhan), while generally in late modern culture the body does not simply carry the message, it *is* the message, this remains more 'true' for women than for men since for women the self has been insistently recast almost entirely in corporeal and objectifying terms. Once even the most apparently insignificant component of the female body – a line around an eye, shall we say – has been experienced and made sense of as part of a larger entity that is inherently flawed, it can be no surprise that surgery seems a logical solution to the problem of decay.

The emphasis on the 'reflexive project of the self' that is characteristic of late modernity as defined by Anthony Giddens, thus seems to offer 'a plurality of options' to everyone while continuing to exclude women in particular from 'full participation in the universe of social activity which generates those options' (1991, p. 106). One consequence of this contradictory process for Giddens, is the proliferation of bodily disorders linked to anorexia or bulimia amongst young women, disorders which are grounded in a desire for mastery over the body through the punitive control of appetite, and which entail the production of a 'new self' through rigid discipline. Yet as Giddens points out, fasting and self-denial have also been a central part of female spirituality, in particular within the Western Christian tradition (1991, p. 104), so that regulating, managing and controlling the female body became consonant with spiritual purification. The residual traces of those beliefs, however incoherently recast within the postmodern spiritual supermarket, may continue to structure both the kind of social agency women can exercise and the way in which it is represented.

In addition, as the project of feminism has itself been recuperated by postfeminism and the maelstrom of postmodern culture, femininity has become systematically represented almost entirely in terms of fragmentation as well as objectification, so that the 'self' has become a collection of disparate body parts to be endlessly worked on or even replaced as part of the plenitude of consumer choice. In this way, 'wholeness' for the female human subject can only be a temporary and contingent condition achieved through her participation in consumer culture.

The television makeover show promises to achieve a kind of wholeness, then; its premise is that the female subject can be 'made new'. As Brenda R. Weber points out, the US show, *Extreme Makeover* (ABC, 2002–7), effectively suggests that its interventions will produce 'a classical sense of the subject, one that is internally coherent and fully autonomous; [the subject] feels fractured no longer, a new-found state that strikes her as liberating and empowering' (2005). *Ten Years Younger* also promises that physical renewal will ensure psychological and subjective coherence and the recovery of what has been – apparently – lost. As Pandora says, 'I've been given my youth back'. The version of youth being cited here and the one that is central to contemporary femininity is, however, entirely figured in terms of sexual desirability. After all, nobody has commissioned a television show in which Pandora joins a band, takes a gap year or abandons her children in order to recover her youth, if that is really what she wants. Instead, Pandora's personal dissatisfaction has been stitched into the larger discourse of fragmented femininity within late modernity, and it has been facilitated through the apparently innocent, supposedly empowering, vehicle of the makeover show.

The makeover show: a cultural history

Makeover shows are effectively a hybrid sub-genre of perhaps the most successful and widespread variant of contemporary popular television, the 'reality' and lifestyle show, both of which date from the mid-1990s, in which 'ordinary' members of the public were shown at work, at leisure, or undergoing some sort of personal journey or quest. The forebears in the UK at least included institution-based series such as *Airport* (BBC, 1996–2008) and *Driving School* (BBC, 1997) in which a weekly narrative would be constructed around the quotidian activities of everyday life and work. The home and garden makeover programmes such as *Ground Force* (BBC, 1997–2005), *Changing Rooms* (BBC, 1996–2004), *60 Minute Makeover* (ITV, 2003–) and the mother of them all, *Home Front* (BBC, 1992–6), all emphasized lifestyle, taste, domestic space and even relationships as sites for personal transformation effected through new kinds of consumption, and helped shift television's discursive focus away from the public to the private sphere, and thence to the body as the object of transformation.[4]

As Charlotte Brunsdon points out (2003, p. 8), the development of this 'TV for me' during the 1990s was in part a response to enormous social changes that had taken place in the latter part of the twentieth century through the shifts engendered by late modernity, including the expansion in home ownership, changes in the class structure and women's entry into the workforce, especially into professional and well paid jobs. The makeover show was also – arguably – merely one outcome of fundamental structural changes in broadcasting as the demographic for terrestrial television channels was fragmented by cable and satellite television and then the internet, and family viewing habits diminished under pressure from changes in entertainment culture. This complex cultural and economic mix of changing forms of leisure, the emphasis on the project of the 'self' and the difficulty of securing and maintaining audiences for terrestrial channels have all, then, contributed to a move towards what has been characterized as a 'feminization' of mainstream television as it struggles to compete with a changing media landscape. Yet this 'feminization' has, paradoxically, led to an intensification of the *policing* of femininity, exemplified by the dramatic rise in the makeover show over the last two decades and culminating in a proliferation of competing texts offering graphic depictions of female bodies undergoing increasingly invasive surgical procedures as part of the regular nightly TV entertainment schedule.

However, it was only towards the mid-2000s that the endorsement of invasive surgery began to appear in British editions of the genre. Earlier versions such as *What Not to Wear* (BBC, 2001–6), had significantly avoided any mention of such procedures, emphasizing instead the value of acquiring cultural capital and the right kind of taste in clothes, hair-styling and cosmetics as the route to self-esteem. In contrast, the appearance of *Extreme Makeover*, perhaps the first show to routinely present surgery, including breast enlargement, liposuction, facelifts and dental implants filmed in visceral and detailed close-up, signified a radical shift in lifestyle television and in mainstream culture more generally. Indeed, the programme initially appeared in the UK only on cable and satellite channels, its whiff of disreputability (clearly linked to the emphasis on surgery) somehow confirmed by this marginal status. Yet such shows became increasingly legion during the period between 2002 and 2007, beginning to dominate cable and then terrestrial channels, especially during daytime viewing; their titles – *I Want a Famous Face* (MTV, 2005–6) and *The Swan* (Fox, 2004–) – clearly signalled the emphasis on physical transformation as the solution to women's psychological and social lack.[5]

One of the most culturally significant aspects of *Ten Years Younger*, then, has been its place in the schedules of prime-time terrestrial television, in an 8 p.m., weekday pre-watershed slot on Channel 4 that in itself suggests that the invasive makeover has become a respectable component of mainstream media culture in the UK. This is the 'lifestyle' segment of the schedule which nightly offers a raft of different but cognate hybrids of fantasy-reality television: property shows (*Location, Location, Location*, 2001–; *A Place in the Sun*, 2004–), move to the country cookery shows (*Escape to River Cottage*, 1998–; *Jamie at Home*, 2007–), and open a hotel/run a vineyard abroad (*Chateau Monty*, 2008) shows, all of which draw in their different ways on the same underlying themes of personal transformation and aspiration – the 'project of the self' – that the makeover show foregrounds in its most vivid form.

There is an additional element, too, borrowed from the conventions of the daytime talk show such as the *Jerry Springer Show* (NBC, 1991–) or *The Jeremy Kyle Show* (ITV, 2005–): the focus on the freakish, the carnivalesque and the use of ritualized humiliation. Not only does *Ten Years Younger* seek out women whose apparently dissipated lifestyle has led to what it presents as premature ageing (however that is defined), one of the compulsive pleasures of the show is the forced confrontation of the subject with her 'real', aged and abject self as defined by strangers, before she can be permitted to be made over. And as with the talk show, the policing of the female body in *Ten Years Younger* ultimately operates in order to maintain and normalize a particular set of sexual and gendered power relations.

Feel the pain...

Like its peers, *Ten Years Younger* is highly formulaic. Unlike its peers, its discursive structure is marked by an extraordinary emphasis on perdition, penitence and redemption that is as highly stylized as a hagiography of Saint Catherine.[6] Each episode is structured rigidly around scenes showing the pre-transformation subject, the transformation process itself and the climax: the post-transformation sequences in which the woman returns to her family, work colleagues or friends as a redeemed figure, both like and unlike her former self. I'll say more about this later. I want to point out first, though, how the necessity, but also the *pain*, of cosmetic surgery to transform the woman concerned is emphasized throughout each episode with the device of edited highlights of 'the story so far' that are segmented after each advertisement break. These rehearse a narrative about the bleakness of the subject's prior existence that is itself close to parable. This is then intensified by graphic images of surgery that foreground the ordeal that the penitent must undertake before the account is moved on to the next stage. In the episode featuring Pandora Ankers, for example, we are shown her grimly doling out canteen food, unable to meet the eyes of her customers because of the shame bestowed by her abjection as an unattractive woman, and then the images of her bruised and bandaged face after surgery. This sequence appears three times as each new segment of the show recaps the story. Such repetition (although it is partly determined by the show's relationship to the imperatives of commercial television) helps to construct a peculiarly Catholic narrative of confession, bodily mortification and redemption, in which Pandora's worth as a woman and her spiritual purity increases as her ordeal intensifies.

Indeed, it might be argued that the symbolic role of surgery to *Ten Years Younger* in some ways exceeds its narrative function. Pandora *must* undergo surgical procedures under anaesthetic; she *must* be rendered unconscious in order to be made anew. In this process the 'old' self dies in order for a 'new' self to be born, this time mediated by the hands of the male surgeon. It is therefore essential to the discursive logic of the show for surgery to take place, not simply so that the subject can be liposucted or rhinoplasted to a dubious physical perfection, but so that she can be – effectively – born again.

Such shows therefore offer a redemption narrative in which pain (both physical and emotional) is a necessary component of the journey the woman must undertake in order to become a better (and socially approved) version of herself. We must *see* her teeth replaced, her breasts enlarged or uplifted, her bottom sliced away and her belly sucked out, in order to verify that a necessarily painful process has taken place. The ritualized humiliation of the woman whose wilful 'neglect' of her appearance has led to her abjection is therefore a precursor to her transformation. In the course of the show she will be punished for this through the visual display of her stigmata – her wrinkles, body fat, baggy eyes and bad teeth – but finally redeemed, her sins washed away, through the benign intervention of the surgeon's hands.

Crucially, the programme deploys a (male) voiceover in order to direct the viewer to this redemptive reading of what we are seeing (this is good for the woman, she'll be a better, more confident person), while simultane-ously making some spurious points about the potential dangers of cosmetic surgery and the benefits of a healthy lifestyle, presumably so that it cannot be accused of promoting surgical procedures, although that is exactly what it does. But this voiceover also offers the meta-narrative of abjection, puri-fication and redemption in its purest form: Pandora Ankers is 'a picture of neglect'; she is 'past her sell by date' and 'a challenge' to the hairdresser who must restyle her frizzy mop. Perhaps most powerfully, the show repeatedly emphasizes the woman's abjection through her own confession: Pandora must admit her sin in order to be redeemed: 'I didn't realise; now I've been given my youth back'.

The figure of the postmodern Prometheus, the male surgeon with magi-cal transformative and healing powers, is crucial to this meta-narrative. Indeed, the highly gendered division of expertise and its relative value is clearly articulated in the way the programme's presenter and 'personal styl-ist', Nicky Hambleton Jones, is as deferential to the entirely masculine team of surgeons and dentists whose criticism of Pandora's lifestyle is a crucial component of the show's claim to educate, as she is scathing of Pandora's dodgy wardrobe (sourced at George at Asda). Hambleton Jones is cast as a 'style guru' in the publicity about the programme, but it might be bet-ter to describe her as the willing Hand Maiden to surgical intervention, since her most important function is not only to mediate between Pandora and the team of medical practitioners who are waiting to transform her but also to manage the *ideological* process whereby such procedures become naturalized.

Crucially, *Ten Years Younger* never directly addresses the social forces that might produce abjection, nor the issue of single or divorced women's rela-tive *poverty*, or their responsibility for children and families, even though the majority of its subjects are indeed middle-aged, divorced and in low-paid employment. To do so would disrupt the preferred narrative of individual moral dissipation and introduce some uncomfortable issues around economic and social inequalities that might in turn problematize the emphasis upon women's personal responsibility for their plight. Instead, the emphasis is upon the self-indulgence, lazy habits or addictions to cigarettes or alcohol which have apparently produced such a bad, scourgeable body.

At the same time, it is notable that many of *Ten Years Younger*'s subjects clearly occupy a culturally middle-class habitus, signified by their names, accents, education and life experiences. Some have a university education or its equivalent, and although occupied in low-paid jobs, are represented as having fallen on hard times through divorce, separation, bad luck or bad timing. Interestingly, not only does this tendency reinforce the programme's redemption narrative, with its tale of a 'fallen woman' restored to beauty, health and happiness through a magical intervention, it also reinforces the ideological focus on the proper class position of the woman who can and should be redeemed through such interventions. When Pandora is restored to beauty there is a sense that this is also a restoration of the proper order of things, not a turning of the world upside down.

The male gaze strikes back

The naturalization of a highly gendered division of power in *Ten Years Younger* noted above, in which male experts reconstruct, Frankenstein-like, the body of the woman, also contributes to the foregrounding of the male gaze as the measure of female self-worth as well as the show's subtext of compulsory heterosexuality. Gareth Palmer has pointed to the ways in which such shows have helped to codify what he calls the 'surveillance gaze' in contemporary culture, by forcing the subject of the makeover to confront herself as she is inscribed in 'the seemingly "objective gaze" of surveillance footage... [which] trades upon the notion that such footage offers a privileged relation to an aesthetic of "the real"' (2004, p. 183). In the case of *Ten Years Younger* this confrontation is grounded in the notion that to be surveyed by others is the only way in which the 'reality' about a woman can be properly gauged. Each programme begins and ends with the public ritual of humiliation and/or appreciation in which the woman is taken to a shopping mall or High Street for scrutiny: passers-by are asked to guess her age, the cruellest are recorded and the average of these guesses is later computed and presented to the woman. The rule is that they must add up to a shocking overestimation of her real age in order to incite the narrative.

This emphasis on the importance of others' evaluations of her, on being judged literally at face value, and on the centrality of to-be-looked-at-ness is, of course, hardly surprising in a makeover show. But the force with which it is directed at these women is chilling. How dare they neglect themselves! No wonder no man wants them! Don't they know that they must keep young and beautiful if they want to be loved? Well, they do by the end of all this, because to deny it would be to deny the premise of the programme itself, which cannot be countenanced. As Pandora is reminded: she is 52 but 'looks 59' (according, that is, to the rigged calculations based on the comments of passing strangers). What worse fate can there be in a postfeminist world in which women's corporeality, their bodies, remain so crucial to the bringing together of that fragmented set of discursive strands that produce 'me'?

Of course, for *Ten Years Younger* this scrutiny is a vital feature of the woman's necessary abjection: she is invariably assumed to be, yes, ten years *older* than she really is, and therefore the proper object of aesthetic intervention. Indeed, since women's sexual desirability to men is consistently conflated with youth or the appearance of youth in contemporary culture, the implication that a woman looks 'old' (whatever that means) is inevitably represented as damaging to her self-worth and evidence of the need for change. As Weber (2005) points out, where transformation of the 'self' is focused on the body, social censure of the kind ritually incorporated into *Ten Years Younger* functions to legitimate the need for aesthetic surgery. But this cultural imperative is inevitably reinflected as an issue of women's innately fragile self-esteem as Nicky Hambleton Jones delivers the 'truth' to her unhappy victim and then consoles her for having to face such unpalatable knowledge with the promise of a future transformed.

In the final triumphant sequence, then, Pandora is returned to the scene of her earlier humiliation and forced to re-enact the ritual of the male gaze, but this time cleansed of her physical disfigurement. It is now the job of Hambleton Jones to secure the mumbled assurances of what are usually singularly unappealing examples of British masculinity that she is now fuckable. What a relief! Imagine if all that work had been for nothing. Yet, interestingly, this happy ending is less powerful – and less troubling – than what I will call the mirror moment, which precedes it.

The mirror moment

The climax of these programmes comes in a tightly framed series of close-ups towards the end of the show. Pandora (or her equivalent) has been plucked, sucked and reconstructed, and dressed in her new finery, but she has not yet seen her 'finished' self. She is brought into a room where a covered cheval glass is standing and Nicky Hambleton Jones places her in front of it to produce what the show itself calls and the term I will advisedly deploy here – the 'reveal'[7]. Invariably, Pandora (or Joanna or Alison) stands before the (magic?) mirror that will reveal her new self, and is visibly overcome with emotion at the spectacle of her reconstructed image. We might even call this the 'tears shot' since its emphasis on the physical evidence of emotion in the form of bodily fluids – tears – is not unlike the 'money shot' of cinema pornography in its construction of tension (waiting, waiting, nearly there) and release ('oh baby, baby, you're so gorgeous'). Nicky embraces Pandora as her new best friend, and now of course the latter is worthy of that status.[8]

However, this moment is also contradictory. First, the emphasis on the mirror works to remind us of the centrality of image and of looking to the production of postfeminist femininity, in which the fractured relationship between subject and object has itself been reconstructed. Second, the outpouring of emotion signifies both the completion of the project and its *incompleteness*. The woman's tears or laughter break the boundaries of the physical self at the very moment of its construction. Having been carefully remade into a form of culturally acceptable femininity that is grounded in the smoothing out of the female body, the subject 'breaks up,' is reframed, and this disrupts the moment in important ways. Crucially, then, the woman remains unfinished, imperfect. Indeed, the figure of the reconstructed woman that appears in the mirror carries the spectre of her unfinished self. How could it not? The show has repeatedly reminded us of this spectre throughout its narrative in its compulsive return to the beginning of the story at the very moment of Pandora's redemption by replaying those images of 'before' in order to reinforce the transformation of 'after'.

Conclusion

To return finally to what I have identified as the submerged, quasi-religious discourse of ritual abjection and redemption that saturates *Ten Years Younger*, it is timely to remember that the idea of the 'perfected self' is indeed derived from Christianity, but that it is conventionally associated with the perfection of the *soul* not the body. And there are therefore two further problems here. The first is that in postmodern culture there is no soul, just the body, so any kind of perfectibility must inevitably be played out upon the flesh. The second is that if this programme is indeed mobilizing an older, half-remembered discursive formation rooted in organized religion, we should also remind ourselves that in some parts of the Christian tradition women have habitually been cast as empty vessels, without souls, and therefore as incomplete human beings. A reason for lachrymosity perhaps, but also for suspicion when it comes to ideologies of perfectibility – whatever form they take. I would therefore like to reiterate my earlier points about the limitations offered for women's agency in postfeminist culture by the spectacle of the 'unfinished', fragmented and tearful feminine self of the makeover show. The relationship this has forged with the now pervasive and pathologizing discourse of self-esteem is perhaps the most dangerous and troubling element in all of this, since it offers little that is genuinely empowering and much that reconstitutes women as hapless victims of cultural forces beyond their control. The drive towards social agency, wholeness and autonomy argued for by second-wave feminism is being drowned out by the sounds of women's bodies being rent open – to deploy an appropriately biblical turn of phrase – and remade in ways that deny the value and the reality of experience, wisdom or even of ordinary physical ageing for women. Perhaps it is time to 'make over' makeover television itself.

Notes

1. See, for example, the wide range of what is effectively free advertising for cosmetic surgery, beauty products, body shaping garments etc. which can be found when searching the official website for *Ten Years Younger*, www.channel4.com/programmes/10-years-younger

2. The extraordinarily disparate nature of this phenomenon, examples of which include gross-out comedies such as *There's Something About Mary* (1998, US, Bobby and Peter Farrelly), 'quality' British television series such as *The Virgin Queen* (2005, UK, BBC TV) and middle-brow feature films such as *Iris* (1999, UK, Richard Eyre), which include gratuitous scenes not just of an exposed and decrepit female body, but of an exposed and decrepit female body whose degenerative qualities have been *artificially constructed* through prosthesis (presumably because the 'real' bodies are themselves insufficiently disgusting) is disturbing. The fact that both *The Virgin Queen* and *Iris* present themselves as sympathetic dramatizations of old age suggests that the 'unconscious' of such texts can work against the avowed intent of the producers or authors.

3. This edition was first transmitted in December 2006.

4. Charlotte Brunsdon makes it clear that lifestyle TV has a much longer history than this since its origins lie partly in the 'hobbyist' and didactic television of the 1950s through to the 1970s in which expert gardeners, DIY-ers, cooks or dressmakers showed viewers how to make something or do a particular task. The difference lies in the emphasis on lifestyle and the transformative process.

5. A slightly different variant included *Queer Eye for the Straight Guy* (Bravo, 2003–7) and *How to Look Good Naked* (C4 2005–), both of which have helped resecure the common-sense around the apparently immutable relationship between gay men and lifestyle expertise; a trend interrogated by Andrew Gorman-Murray, who points out that such expertise is nearly always also in the service of restoring heteronormative values (2006, p. 231).

6. While it is true that *What Not to Wear* deploys a discourse of class-based bullying in which its two 'posh' presenters, Trinny Woodall and Susannah Constantine, physically poke and prod the 'unsightly' bits of their makeover subjects' bodies, the structure of the programme as a whole does not employ such an extreme form of the punitive discourse at its deepest level.

7. In the spirit of the commodification of women's bodies it seems appropriate to use a piece of jargon of this kind.

8. In spring 2009 a new series of *Ten Years Younger* began on British TV, this time with a new format in which two women were made over, with cosmetic surgery presented as an 'option' for just one participant (presumably in response to accusations that it promoted surgical procedures). And in a move that left one breathless at the audacity, Hambleton Jones was replaced as presenter on the grounds

that she looked 'too old' (and presumably couldn't be persuaded to undergo those procedures herself).

Bibliography

Bell, D. and J. Hollows (2005) 'Making Sense of Ordinary Lifestyles' in D. Bell and J. Hollows (eds), *Ordinary Lifestyles: Popular Media, Consumption and Taste* (Milton Keynes: Open University Press/McGraw-Hill International).

Brunsdon, C. (2003) 'Lifestyling Britain: The 8–9 Slot on British TV', *International Journal of Cultural Studies* 6(5): 5–23.

Dutton, K. (1995) *The Perfectible Body: The Western Ideal of Male Physical Development* (New York: Continuum).

Featherstone, M. (1991) *Consumer Culture and Postmodernism* (London, New York and Delhi: Sage Books).

Giddens, A. (1991) *Modernity and Self-Identity: Self and Society in the Late Modern Age* (Cambridge: Polity Press).

Gorman-Murray, A. (2006) 'Queering Home or Domesticating Deviance? Interrogating Gay Domesticity Through Lifestyle Television', *International Journal of Cultural Studies* 9(2): 227–47.

Harris, A. (2004) *Future Girl: Young Women in the Twenty-first Century* (London: Routledge).

Palmer, G. (2004) ' "The New You": Class and Transformation in Lifestyle Television' in S. Holmes and D. Jermyn (eds), *Understanding Reality Television* (London: Routledge).

Seidler, V. (1989) *Rediscovering Masculinity: Reason, Language and Sexuality* (London and New York: Routledge).

Weber, B. R. (2005) 'Beauty, Desire and Anxiety: The Economy of Sameness in ABD's Extreme Makeover', *Genders* 41. Available at http://www.Genders.org

Woodward, K. M. (1999) 'Introduction' in *Figuring Age: Women, Bodies, Generations* (Bloomington IN: Indiana University Press, 1999).

Part II

Negotiating Postfeminist Media Culture

6
Are You Sexy, Flirty, Or A Slut? Exploring 'Sexualization' and How Teen Girls Perform/Negotiate Digital Sexual Identity on Social Networking Sites

Jessica Ringrose

Introduction

In February 2010 The UK Home Office released a high-profile report, 'The Sexualisation of Young People'. The UK report came rather late in the international context, following on from earlier reports, including the American Psychological Association Taskforce report on the sexualization of girls (APA, 2007), and the Australian government-led research on the sexualization of children, which generated widespread debate over 'corporate paedophilia' (Rush and La Nauze, 2006).

Across these international contexts public debates over sexualization have tended to become polarized between a condemnation of sex and calls to more heavily regulate young people's use of various media, and those who critique the 'sexualization thesis' as part of a moral panic that robs children of their rights, sexuality and agency (Bray, 2008). In the UK with the release of the government report, this took the form of a dichotomy between popular support for the awareness about corporate sexualization the report generated in the media vs. stringent academic critique of the research findings, methodology and recommendations. Critique ranged from attack on a glamorous celebrity psychologist, Linda Papadopoulos leading the report (Murch, 2010) to the content itself.[1] Critics suggested the report lacked social and historical analysis of 'inequality', and had 'nothing useful to say about the ways in which children and young people might engage or participate in the contemporary media landscape, sexual or not' (Murch, 2010; Smith, 2010). It was suggested the report was simplistic, relying on an under-theorized, over-generalized buzz word, 'sexualization', that 'may distract attention from other, more fundamental – and perhaps more intractable – social problems' such as the 'inherent inequalities of a hyper capitalist society' (Buckingham and Bragg, quoted in Murch, 2010). Most significantly, by positing, rather than 'questioning' ' "sexualisation" as a driver of violence against women', the report was said to generate 'a politics of alarm' and a 'commonsense rhetoric of distress for the "lost innocence of childhood"' offering only a 'scary futurology of increasing sexualisation' (Smith, 2010).

While I do not have space to go into a more extensive review of the controversy surrounding the international or UK 'sexualization' reports, my concern is how as feminists in 'postfeminist times' (Gill, 2008), it becomes exceedingly difficult to intervene in these debates or even use the notions of 'sexualized' or 'sexualization', without being caught up in a media furore that has already overdetermined these notions (Egan and Hawkes, 2008), forcing the speaker into binary positions. On the one hand, feminists are easily reduced to 'simplistic' promoters of 'intolerant petit bourgeois alarmism', said to deflect our attention from wider issues, as Abigail Bray's (2008, p. 326) incisive analysis of the Australian public debates over 'corporate paedophilia' has illustrated. In contrast, however, one is equally in danger of being construed as lacking in moral integrity for suggesting, as many critics of the sexualization reports insist, that young people's negotiations of 'sexualization' are 'complex'. Indeed, one well known feminist academic (who shall remain unnamed) shouted at me at a recent conference when I suggested that my exploratory findings about how teen girls navigate 'sexualization' online indicated both sexual regulation *and* girls' agency and experimentation, declaring my analysis lacked political conviction because I did not situate the girls as 'at risk of being groomed for the global prostitution industry'.

In this chapter I seek to contribute to the debate on sexualization with a nuanced, feminist analysis that both takes the risks and power dynamics of 'sexualization' processes in the contemporary media context very seriously, yet tries to not oversimplify the complexity of teen girls' responses and productions within specific mediums. I draw on findings from a UK study of young people's use of the online social networking site (SNS) Bebo. In the UK, 49 per cent of those aged between 8 and 17 have an internet profile on social networking sites (SNSs) such as Bebo and Facebook, with Bebo used predominantly by the 13- to 24-year-old age group (Smithers, 2008). Children and teens' uses of SNSs have become an increasing site of public interest, with recent controversy surrounding whether sexualized imagery of girls on SNSs is placing them 'at risk' from paedophiles on the web (Mail Online, 2008). Rather than position girls simply at risk from adult sexual predators, I will suggest we need to analyse the 'postfeminist' media context, where girls are under pressures to visually display and perform a new 'compulsory' 'disciplinary technology of sexy' (Gill, 2008) in digital environments. Through analysis of online and interview data, I discuss how digital representations impact teens' relationships to themselves and others, particularly in their peer groups at school. I explore how SNSs (like other media contexts) are spaces where increasingly normalized hypersexualized and pornified discourses and visual imagery circulate rapidly. What is new or somewhat different in SNSs is the digital performance of a sexual self in these spaces. In ways like never before, social networking profiles propel public 'networked' visual and textual representations of self and others (boyd, 2008). Given feminist readings of increasing rather than decreasing levels of sexual objectification in popular media and advertising contexts (Gill, 2008), young people must continuously negotiate and make choices around which images and words to use as they construct and perform their teen sexual identities in semi-public spaces. These negotiations may illustrate both dominant tropes of hyper-sexualized femininity and masculinity, but my data also indicate young people stretch the conventional meanings of sexualized discourses, given these are already shifting in popular culture (see Attwood's analysis of shifting meanings of 'slut', 2007). In my conclusions I also briefly suggest new directions for tackling these issues in schools.

Digital sexual subjectivity

The explosion in young people's uses of social networking sites has emerged as a specific area of interest, with researchers considering how virtual spaces such as YouTube, MySpace and Facebook are commodified and marketized environments that structure the display of identity and practices of consumption, which carry both 'risks' and 'opportunities' (Livingstone, 2008, p. 459). My interest in this chapter is how the commercialized content circulating in social networking sites is gendered and sexualized in particular ways. I will explore which sexualized representations and discourses have specific value or currency in our participants' social networking sites, and how these operate for girl participants in particular, considering issues of risk and opportunity.

Suzannah Stern (2006) Stern has suggested that girls in particular are 'experimenting' with sexual 'self-commodification' online. Manago et al.'s (2008, p. 1) findings from research on college students use of MySpace in the US suggest there is 'increased pressures for female sexual objectification' on social networking sites. I will argue teens are experimenting much as they have always done with processes of developing sexual identities. However, where this differs from older forms of self-representation, is how online representation on SNSs is explicitly tied to a 'visual cyber culture' (Thomas, 2004) in particular 'networked publics' (boyd, 2008), where incitement to specific, normative forms of gendered and sexualized visual self-representation, common to the contemporary postfeminist media context, must be managed in the construction of a semi-public digital sexual subjectivity.

The idea that Western culture is being generally 'sexualized', or that more explicit sexual content is continually being 'mainstreamed' through processes like the normalization of pornographic imagery and discourses into everyday life has been widely discussed by a range of authors (Attwood, 2009; Gill, 2008; Levy, 2005; Paasonen et al., 2007). According to Paasonen et al. (2007, p. 8) 'The "sexualization of culture" refers to a fairly wide range of cultural phenomena while pornification is a more specific term pointing to the increased visibility of hardcore and soft-core pornographies, and the blurring of boundaries between the pornographic and the mainstream.' Feminist research on the rise of 'porno-chic' as part of a contemporary 'postfeminist masquerade' (McRobbie, 2009), and the 'hyper-sexualization' of women (Gill, 2008, 2009) and young girls (Bray, 2008) in media and advertising is growing, as is research investigating how girls are navigating these trends (Duits and van Zoonen, 2006).

I hope to contribute to this debate by mapping some of the discursive and visual 'conditions of possibility' (Foucault, 1982) for forging digital sexual subjectivity on the specific social networking site under study, Bebo. As Angela Thomas (2004, p. 361) describes, drawing on Jacqueline Rose's theories of the visual to explore adolescent girls' engagements online: 'certain moments of seeing, and particular visualities are central to how subjectivities and sexualities are formed'. Particular sexualized discourses and images, interpellate girls as sexualized objects, and are 'central' (Thomas, 2004) to the girls' 'performances' of sexual subjecitivties (Butler, 1993) on Bebo. Indeed, I will make the psychosocial argument that digital negotiations of their Bebo profiles, in many cases, intensify the girls' relationships to and 'investment' (Ringrose, 2008) in specific pornified symbolism, imagery and discourse. At the same time their 'experimentations' should not be viewed as sexually subjectifying them in only a negative sense, since their performances can also work to disrupt conventional meanings of sexualized discourses and images in surprising ways, as I illustrate.

The research schools and methodology

The research discussed in this paper draws on interviews and online data from a pilot study exploring young people's negotiations of social networking sites.[2] The school is an important environment to discuss social networking since research is showing that online friendship networks are typically organized around school-based peer groups (Livingstone, 2008).[3] We studied students from an English, media studies class in year 10 in Thornbury Secondary, a high achieving rural specialist college, where the level of socio-economic disadvantage was well below average; and from a year 11 media studies class at New Mills Secondary, which was in contrast

an estate school in a southern London borough, in an area of 'high deprivation'. The data included observations and group and individual interviews with 23 young people (11 boys and 12 girls, aged 14–16). After group
interviews (where we asked for permission to view their sites) we returned
for individual interviews (6 girls, 1 boy) with students whose sites raised
particular issues around gendered/sexual representation. We also studied
the online SNS profiles of many of our participants over a period of a few
months while we were carrying out the project. In addition to the sites of
participants, we considered some sites of the friend networks and romantic
interests of participants discussed in interviews and some publicly available
Bebo sites of young people in the same age range.[4]

'Skins', applications and the sexualized, commercial culture of SNSs

The social networking site Bebo is a commercial product, a brand which,
as noted, has been marketed and taken up by a specifically young target
audience (aged 13–24). Bebo was the site used predominantly by our participants, with Facebook noted by many as 'too old' (see also Willett, 2009).
Bebo profiles explicitly reference commercial culture including 'play lists'
links to favourite songs, video and TV shows clips, movies, advertisements,
music videos, sports teams, sports cars (etc.) used as part of the signifying
practices on the sites. My interest here is in outlining what type of normalized sexualized discourses and images circulate and 'constitute' (Butler,
1993) the 'virtual geography' (Papacharissi, 2009) or 'affective assemblage'
(Ringrose, 2010) of the specific localized peer online community of Bebo
under study.

One of the most important visual forms of Bebo is the 'skin', which is
the background that covers the generic site. Unlike Facebook, for instance,
Bebo's wallpaper background is integral to the visual dynamism of the site.
Thousands of skins already exist and users can update them with varying
degrees of regularity, some every day. Skins can also be modified but only
with specialized technical skills, so they are typically not authored by young
people. Skins are commodities themselves that young people find, trade or
even pay someone to make for them through Bebo networks.

A search in autumn 2008 of the website 'Top 50 Bebo Skins'[5] found a
Louis Vuitton skin to be the number one skin. Other top skins showcased
the singers Kelis and Alicia Keys, the boxer Ricky Hatton and the footballer
Michael Owen. Another top 50 skin used by students at New Mills features a
picture of Adidas shoes pressed against by a woman in stiletto heels with her
knickers around her ankles.[6] A different Adidas skin features six women clad
only in thongs, knee-high socks and volleyball shoes in a huddle with their
thong-clad butts turned to the camera. The Playboy bunny theme is popular for skins, and was used by one our participants Marie (16, New Mills),

discussed below. Jen (16, New Mills) had skin that read 'Boom chicka Wah Wah' which is a reference to a highly sexualized 2007 advertising campaign for Lynx male deodorant spray, which featured men (including Ben Affleck) attracting hundreds of (often semi-naked) women in various scenarios after applying the spray, but which also according to the urban dictionary refers to 'Music played in old porno films right after the first penetration or little bit before a blow job by the bass guitar and also used to describe someone that is very hot'.[7] Jen described finding someone through a friend that 'knows how to make skins', indicating the complex appropriation of consumer culture, since she helped in designing the skin to use this commercial slogan. Presumably Jen is using this male advertising slogan ironically to signal her own 'hotness'. Pamela (16, New Mills) told us in a group interview how her skin said 'hold me in your arms and tell me that I'm your baby girl', which she has found on someone else's Bebo profile. The skin used by Daniella (14, Thornbury), whose site is discussed in greater detail below, featured a picture of a naked Marilyn Monroe in bed. The Bebo skin used by Sam (15, Thornbury), the boy Daniella was dating (at the time), also showed a scantily clad woman who is posing in platform heels beside a Ford GT, exotic sports car (price approx. £100,000).

These skins indicate how heterosexualized dynamics in advertising and pop music are appropriated and used within the visual and textual context of the participants' sites. These skins constitute the conditions for performing *idealized* forms of teen masculinity and femininity (Nayak and Kehily, 2008) through often highly commercialized ideals of embodiment and visual display. In the cases discussed here, masculinity is epitomized in buying the consumer goods (i.e. cars and shoes) with which to gain access to the sexually commodified female body. Femininity in contrast is epitomized through approximating the sexually commodified body, performing as sexual object, and occupying the position of sexually desirable 'baby girl'. Of course these discourses can be used ironically, and illustrate experimentation with sexual identity. My suggestion is that particular discursive frames constrain the limits of experimentation to often highly regulatory and narrow formations of gendered/sexual subjectivity.

These constraints are visible through analysis of further technical applications populating the discursive milieu of Bebo sites, such as game and quiz applications which circulate widely in peer networks. Popular Bebo applications on our participants' sites included 'make a baby', which allows you to 'Make babies with your friends!' by choosing appearance, clothes and accessories, and 'Celebrity look a likes', which uses face recognition technology to help users 'Discover your celeb twin among thousands of top celebrities'. Even more popular on the girls in our studies' sites, however, are sex/romance-related quiz and interactive applications, including, 'What type of kisser are you?' and 'Kiss me', which 'lets people kiss you in various ways and places'.

The popular quiz, 'Are You Sexy, Flirty, Or A Slut?' which I have used for the title of this chapter (and which circulates widely on MySpace and Facebook also), quizzes girls on how many guys they have slept with, how short they wear their skirt, whether (penis) size is important, and whether they like strip and lap dances, among other questions. As the title suggests, it offers three subject positions: sexy, flirty, or slut; accompanied by randomized pictures mostly of girls in bras or bikinis. In one quiz result 'sexy' features a sweaty woman in towel and exercise bra. Marie (16, New Mills) got 'flirty' with a woman in exercise gear on a pole featured on her Bebo site. Here the normalization of pole dancing as a form of flirty fun is evident.[8] What is constant in the results is the nearly naked idealized female body, much like the quiz 'What Kind Of Lingerie Are You?' One possible result is 'v-string panties', with a close up of a woman's crotch wearing a yellow g-string with a diamante studded 'sexy' on it. 'What kind of girl are you' generates the response 'Eye Candy' and 'What Sexual Fantasy Are You?' creates the result 'sexy schoolgirl' with a grown woman posing – much like Britney Spears's video '...Baby one more time' – in pigtails, a kilt mini skirt, with a white shirt tied up underneath her very large breasts to expose her 'midriff' (Gill, 2009). 'What kind of sexual position are you?' enables result options such as missionary and doggy style with graphic photographic illustrations.

Whether or not the young person identifies with the stream of quizzes and results, the applications circulate widely and are part of Bebo culture: 'At the moment I've got about 31 applications sitting in my "To Do" list' (Louise, 16, New Mills). These applications are a structural process (typically created by adults) where the normalization of celebrity culture and hyper-sexualized representations of women's bodies repeat en masse through everyday interaction. Skins and applications thus shape the 'identificatory' (Butler, 1993) possibilities of crafting a digital sexual identity online.

Visual culture: 'slutty girls' and 'fat slags'

Sites are further personalized through individual profile display photos, user names and taglines. The display photo is the first thing one sees when looking at friends or doing a search through Bebo. The display photo is changed often, depending on the young person's access to a digital camera, and there are also archives of photos you can access and tag once you are on a profile. Not surprisingly, photos were a topic of considerable concern, for girls in particular, who discussed experimenting with photos, lighting and angles and how a picture could be taken with greatest visual effect. Many 'airbrushed' (Louise, 16, New Mills) their photos and there was considerable anxiety about having a bad picture posted:

Daniella (14, Thornbury): Say someone took a picture of me when I just woke up in the morning, I'd never put that on Bebo ... Because it would just be embarrassing. I need to ... have all my hair and my make-up done.

Copying and 'tagging' photos and posting comments, such as 'you're well fit', 'nice pic', 'good looking' or 'Hello Sexy' was common. As Jen (16, New Mills) suggested, the descriptive category 'sexy' was coveted yet normalized: 'saying you're sexy just means you look good'. But there was also the danger of 'rude comments' being posted such as 'fat slag', 'well ugly', 'bitch', 'slut' or 'whore', and even of Bebo profiles and display photos being 'hacked' and manipulated to make the target look 'horrible' (group interview, girls, 16, New Mills).

In relation to this highly sexualized online environment, the issue of how much 'cleavage' the teen girls should display through photos posted was hotly debated in interviews:

Daniella (14, Thornbury, group interview): I think like if you've got like say a slutty girl, she'll take a picture of her body or whatever and have it as her image ... If I came across a Bebo that's someone's got a picture of their cleavage and their body, and nothing else. And I'll think, 'Well, they obviously think too much of themselves'.

Louisa (16, New Mills, individual interview) said likewise:

If you put pictures on like that people are just going to think oh look you're like a bit of a slut or you're gagging to have sex, I had to make that choice because I thought I don't want people to see me like that.

Marie (16, New Mills, individual interview) had a strikingly similar response:

It's like you, if you go on some people's pictures you see pictures of girls in their bras, bikinis and all that ... It's like putting yourself down, it's making everyone think, oh, she's a slag ... they're trying to impress everyone. Like get all the boys thinking ... they're up for anything ... I could but ... I don't really like going round in short skirts, bikini tops and that 'cause one it's too cold and two ... I think it makes the boys think you'll do anything if you're walking around like that ... making yourself look desperate.

As these quotes illustrate, girls have to make complex 'choices' about how they will construct a sexual digital identity, with contradictory worries about how to be desirable but not 'too' slutty (see also boyd, 2008). There are tensions between sexual regulation in the peer group and the increasing normalization of (nearly) naked online display (see also Patchin and

Hinduja, 2010). Marie's quote suggests that some girls posing in bras and bikinis, creates new pressure/desires that have to be managed. Some of our participants did have the bodily properties that conformed to the hyper-sexualized images of sweaty women in exercise gear in the quiz and game applications. Heather (16, New Mills) posted a series of photos of herself in bikini on holiday on her Bebo site, and it was suggested that holiday photos were acceptable, while underwear shots were not. Yet as Gill (2008) suggests in her analysis of the disciplinary norms and particular visual criteria needed to inhabit sexually desirable and legitimately desiring femininity, some of our participants lacked the requisite physical qualities to occupy a 'sexy' subject position. Some girls like Louise (16, New Mills)[9] described 'choosing' not to put up pictures that make you look like you are 'kind of a slut' or 'gagging to have sex', but her reluctance to expose her body can also be interpreted as part of the constraints of the 'choices' around self-representation that organize the normative visual displays normalized on Bebo. Louise was overweight (she physically attacked another of our participants, Marie, earlier in the school year, when Marie was attributed with calling Louisa a 'fat slag' on MSN).[10] Louise told me, 'I don't expect comments like oh you look really sexy or fit in this picture'. While she was invested in a 'pretty' self-representation, and described airbrushing her photos and wanting to become a hair stylist in the next year when she left school, her pictures were mostly of her face taken from angles that minimized attention to her body. This is an important reminder of how the embodied 'real' (Butler, 1993) intrudes upon the possibilities of sexualized virtual self-representation on sites like Bebo, when the friend networks are members of a 'real' school community.

Playboy bunny subjectivity

Marie (16) who discussed the issue of photos of girls in 'bras and knickers' also struggled with managing a 'sexy' persona, telling me:

> I don't like walking round in bikini tops 'cause I don't like my stomach. And people say, oh, that's stupid, you've got the most skinniest stomach ever. And I was like, yeah...Like when I was 11 I used to be fat...And I used to try and walk round with my stomach breathed in, everything. I've never liked my stomach...Even now that I'm skinny.

Marie describes her reluctance to either walk around or be photographed in a bikini top because she is now too 'skinny'. But I interpret her bodily anxieties to also surround her lack of sexual development (breasts), given additional complaints about being 'small' and 'having nothing'. Marie offers an interesting example of negotiating the pornified norms of Bebo and the struggle to represent the self as 'sexy'. As mentioned her site featured the

Playboy bunny skin (a pink background with huge black Playboy bunny icon beside her user photo). Alongside the Playboy bunny skin (and her pole dancing quiz results) prominent on Marie's profile was a picture of herself in a sweatshirt and fluffy pink bunny ears (she had run the photo through an application which allows the user to change photos into a cartoon-like image). When I asked Marie about the Playboy bunny skin and the 'cartoonized' bunny photo she said she had 'loads' of pictures of the Playboy bunny in a virtual online folder and described how her mum bought the real bunny ears for herself and her 12-year-old sister; and how she also had two T-shirts with the logo. Marie also explained to me that while 'to most people' the symbol 'means like the Playboy mansion and all the girls', 'with girls it's just the bunny and girls like rabbits... just a good cartoon'.

The Playboy bunny symbol is widely used throughout the Bebo network in both skins and other applications. Marie's extensive use of the Playboy bunny merchandise both off and online, indicates the normalization, banality even, of the Playboy bunny, marketed at teen and tween girls, illustrating the trend towards 'porno-chic' for these age groups (Gill, 2008). However, in my interpretation the virtual space actually intensifies Marie's relationship to Playboy bunny symbolism and imagery. Under heightened pressures in the virtual peer environment to perform revealing bodily display (the normative conditions of fulfilling sexy in the virtual Bebo network), in the face of bodily anxieties, and not feeling able to confidently display herself in 'bras or knickers' online Marie draws explicitly on the Playboy bunny symbol, which operates in complex ways to sexualize Marie's rather non-sexual self-representation of herself in a sweatshirt. Interpellating or subjectifying (Butler, 1993) herself through the Playboy bunny motif, Marie takes on a form of digital 'bunny subjectivity'. I would posit the explicit identification with and use of the bunny symbolism helps Marie to feel sexy. In some sense calling up the meanings associated with Playboy mediates pressures of actual bodily display since Marie is fully clothed, yet the real bunny ears and virtual bunny skin references a whole host of meanings about glamour, sexiness and desirability, as well as childhood innocence. The sexualized nature of the digital bunny identity is unsurprisingly disclaimed through Marie's contradictory statement that the icon is simply an (innocent) 'good cartoon'. But she also references 'the Playboy mansion and all the (sexy) girls', thus the symbolic condensation of the Playboy bunny motif operates in contradictory and complex ways.[11]

Performing 'slut'

Girls at Thornbury High were also under similar pressures to navigate the popular media context and construct a 'sexy' digital self. In contrast, however, to Louise and Marie, Daniella (14, Thornbury),[12] who wanted to become a 'beauty therapist', was highly invested in achieving sexy depictions of her body and glamorous images of her face through the visual medium of her Bebo profile. Indeed, given her disparaging comments about 'slutty girls' who are 'up for anything' in the group interview, we were at first surprised to view Daniella's site and find that her username was actually 'Slut' and her user photo featured a plunging neckline and heavy make-up with dramatic eye-liner. Many further images on her sites featured her breasts, one of which had been put through an application to apply flashing·stars to her cleavage.

As mentioned, Daniella's skin featured a naked Marilyn Monroe in bed, with the quotations 'Its all just make believe isn't it?' and 'A wise girl kisses but doesn't love, listens but doesn't believe, and leaves before she is left'. On the one hand, this signals her site as a place of fantasy and 'experimentation' (Stern, 2006), where cynicism is used to dispel any notion of herself as feminine victim. This fantasy of sexual control is also interesting in relation to Daniella's tagline (the text immediately following her username, which recall was 'slut'), which read: 'Hi, I'm Daniella and I like it up the bum, just like your mum, and I suck dick for £5' [sic]. Daniella told me in interview that her close friend, Nicola, whose Bebo username was 'whore', wrote this tagline on Daniella's Bebo site as a 'joke' when they traded Bebo passwords one weekend. The tagline was left up on her site for some time. What is also significant is that the girls actually inscribe their friendship through these pornified discourses; as Daniella said further about her relationship with Nicola, 'I'm her slut and she's my whore', which changes the meaning of slut as a form of sexualized injury and name-calling in important ways. Feona Attwood (2007) has discussed how the popular meanings of 'slut' have shifted over time to refer increasingly in a 'jokey' way to one's sexual status, in ways that appear to resignify and reclaim slut from its injurious roots (Butler, 1993). The same sorts of shifts are evident with the term 'whore'. I have increasingly noticed 'whore' being used extensively in popular culture to mean being 'really into something', like I am a cleaning 'whore', for instance. In this way 'whore' 'sexes up' the topic under discussion, whilst also disinvesting whore from some of its conventional meanings (Attwood, 2009).

Daniella's and Nicola's usernames of slut and whore, also appear to indicate such shifts are operative within the Bebo environment, given the finding that over 25,000 Bebo users use 'slut', or have reference to 'slut' in their usernames or taglines. So to call oneself slut is not an outlying finding. Indeed a cursory look at Bebo reveals many variations on the slut username such as 'Kinky Slut', 'Lisa Mc Slut', 'Sluts on Speed', accompanied by user profile pictures of girls in their underwear, two girls straddling each other kissing (the hot lesbian fantasy) etc. Lisa Mc Slut's profile features herself in a low-cut dress with two tall cans of beer with straws in them in the back of a taxi-cab, a dense web of signifiers about alcohol and sexual availability (McRobbie, 2009). 'Whore' is also in extensive use, with even wider meanings. For instance, one of our participants' male, musically invested 'emo' friends had the username 'piano whore', indicating some of the changing connotations of the terminology. It would seem, then, that this form of 'sexed up' representation is increasingly normalized within Bebo (Attwood, 2009).[13]

Given this normalization, then, 'slut' can increasingly be called up as a 'fun' *cum* 'naughty' way of representing the self as sexually confident, experienced and knowing. In the discursive context of Bebo I have been exploring, the pornified exchange value of 'slut' is used to signal Daniella's sexiness and coolness. Although the references to slut and whore indicate pleasure and 'fun' between Daniella and Nicola, it is problematic to interpret this form of digital sexual exploration as simply empowering. For girls in particular, 'slut' and 'whore' remain complex, slippery and 'risky' signifiers to navigate.

Rosalind Gill (2008, p. 53) suggests positioning the self as always 'up for it' and the 'performance of confident sexual agency' has shifted to become a key regulative dimension or 'technology' of enacting idealized 'sexy' femininity across mainstream 'postfeminist' media and advertising, so that girls and women are '*required* to be skilled in [and take pleasure in] a variety of sexual behaviours' (my italics). An explicitly pornified dynamic is specifically illustrated in Daniella's SNS tagline: (i.e. I like it up the bum, I suck dick) and visual representations (Marilyn Monroe in bed, flashing icons applied to Daniella's breasts etc.). Daniella adeptly performs this new 'technology of sexy' through online representations enlivening a 'sexy' fantasy to be a sexually aggressive 'slut'.

But there are difficult tensions within this performance of digital sexual subjectivity and how Daniella then manages 'real life' offline identity through peer relationships. For example Daniella suggests you not only have to be perfect online but offline too:

> Popular boys in this school, you don't see them going out with girls that they would probably see as ugly...puts a lot of pressure on girls to make themselves look pretty, to make themselves just look perfect to that one boy that they really want; because otherwise, if they don't try or make an effort they're not going to want to go out with them.

It is important to consider how the visual imperative to display a sexy self on the social networking sites may potentially heighten the regime of 'perfectionism' to be performed at school as well as well intensifying a sense of abject bodily lack (Ringrose and Walkerdine, 2008), since despite her confident online displays Daniella also told me: 'I never will look at myself in the mirror and be like, oh you're really pretty, 'cos I just couldn't do that'.

What is also interesting is despite the knowing and sexually confident veneer performed digitally, Daniella worried in interviews about her relationship with Sam, saying she could not call Sam her 'boyfriend' as he had not yet asked her out (despite 'seeing each other' for six weeks). This appears to reference rather conventional heterosexualized power dynamics that position the male as the one who can seek and 'ask out', while Daniella positions herself as passively waiting. This sits in direct contradiction with Daniella's digital representation of herself as experimental, experienced, 'slut'.

I believe these contradictions in my research participants' online representations and interview narratives, lend support to Gill's (2008) thesis that the new displays of sexual confidence and expertise in constructions of sexually desirable femininity are part of a both old and new 'disciplinary technology' of sexy. Some of the newer techniques of performing digital signifiers of sexiness include citing 'porno' scripts and using sexualized imagery and symbolism online. While these techniques are not only disciplinary since they enable girls to stretch conventional boundaries around sexual representation and experiment in ways that may not be easy in face-to-face relationships (see also Livingstone, 2008), the psychosocial effects of these experiments are not solely liberating or freeing. Rather, living out a sexual identity in both digital and real-world contexts is filled with contradictions and ongoing risks of sexual regulation, particularly for girls. The precariousness of Daniella maintaining the digital sexual identity of slut was highlighted when Sam started seeing another girl, and professed his luv for her much more strongly on his Bebo site than he had with Daniella. Daniella immediately dropped the username 'slut', changing her user name to 'Daniella'. She also removed her sexually explicit tagline and swapped her revealing user photo for one of herself in school uniform with a group of friends sitting on a grassy field. She knowingly adopts a much more 'innocent' sexual digital identity within the 'sexy/flirty/slutty' Bebo continuum I have been exploring.

Conclusions

As feminists we are faced with complex issues around opportunity, experimentation and 'risk' in how teen girls are staging sexual subjectivities online in postfeminist media contexts. Some girls are performing discourses of sexy confidence online as part of a fantasy of sexually aggressive knowingness. But this is within heightened regimes of hyper-sexualized feminine visual bodily display and pornified discourses that appear to operate as 'disciplinary technologies' (Gill, 2008). The pornified discourses circulating in the Bebo networks I mapped indicated intensified, normalized forms of visual bodily objectification and textual subjectification that girls from my research were struggling to negotiate on a daily basis. Some girls found ways to (at least temporarily) creatively perform the pornified visual and discursive criteria of sexiness online, such as Marie who adopted the Playboy bunny signifiers to cite sexy, while others like Louise, who was branded a 'fat slag', could not legitimately perform 'sexy' in line with the visual criteria that constrain representation online.

Daniella offered an important case study of 'experimenting' with the boundaries of feminine sexual identity online, and she stretched the discourses of slut and whore with her close friend, Nicola, in ways that resonate with wider discursive shifts in 'sexed up' terminology (Attwood, 2009). Despite these complex manoeuvrings, sexual 'experimentation' online appeared to be in constant tension with fairly resilient, disciplinary norms of sexually appropriate conduct and heterosexualized feminine passivity in peer relationships at school. I have also been forcibly struck by what appears to be a continuing 'missing discourse of [feminine] desire' (Fine, 1988) in Daniella's and other girls' narratives. This is perhaps most pointedly illustrated in Daniella's tagline (I like it up the bum, just like your mum, and suck dick for £5), which invokes scripts derived from mainstream 'heteroporn' (Passonen et al., 2007) that describe servicing the phallus, and holds few clues about sites of genital sexual pleasure in the feminine body beyond its constitution as hole (the clitoris was not referenced in any discussion or participant website). Indeed the lack of reference to female erogenous zones was apparent across the study and constitutes a significant statement about how the contemporary pornified media contexts construct discourses of female/male sexual desire and pleasure in non-reciprocal (for girls/women), heterosexist and phallogocentric ways (see also Renold and Ringrose 2010).

In addressing some of the issues of sexual digital identity raised in this chapter, the answer is certainly not to invoke a simplistic discourse of 'protecting' girls to enable heavier sexual repression or to impose further control or surveillance on young people's use of the web, since research illustrates this would likely be unsuccessful anyway (boyd, 2008). According to dana boyd (2008, pp. 137, 138) we need to 'guide' and 'educate teens to navigate social structures that are quite unfamiliar to us'. However, it is my contention that while the online communities of social networking sites may be 'new', many discourses through which sexual commodification, sexist objectification and pornification operate are actually quite familiar, and there is a long history of critical feminist enquiry around issues such as a lack of viable discourses of desire or 'erotics' for teen girls (see also Allen, 2004). The problem is that feminist critique is out of style in postfeminist times, typically lauded as 'intolerant petit bourgeois alarmism', reactionary, anti-sex, morally backward, and steeped in victim narratives that deny women, girls or children more generally their sexual agency (Bray, 2008, p. 326; McRobbie, 2009).

I would like to end on a political note, suggesting we need to revitalize an explicitly feminist pedagogical critique around this complex, contradictory terrain of 'sexualization' and its implications for young people both online and offline (i.e. at school). In the UK, Media Studies scholars have developed teaching resources for secondary school media studies sessions exploring depictions of sex, love and relationships in the media and in advertising (Buckingham and Bragg, 2004) but have not yet adequately addressed the trends of hyper-sexualized and pornified online media environments, including SNSs. Internationally, sex and relationship education remains focused on raising awareness about the dangers of disease and pregnancy, rather than addressing sexualization and the ease and spread of sexually explicit online content, and how this might be shaping both the risks and possibilities of a discourse of 'erotics' for young people (Allen, 2004). Finding spaces to engage young people in discussions about the normalization of soft porn cultural productions like the Playboy bunny and pole dancing, as well as the perhaps harder core pornography, inspired allusions to performing anal and oral sex for money, which appeared on our teen girl participants' Bebo sites, would be a crucial staring point for helping 'guide' young people as boyd suggests. Feminist guidance would mean building up a critical literacy around the meanings and power dynamics imbued in the disciplinary technologies of sexy digital representation, which teens have to increasingly navigate. While it is crucial to take note of when and how girls stretch heterosexualized, normative injurious terms like slut and whore, we are still faced with a persistent and urgent need to find ways to talk about feminine genitalia, sexual desires and pleasures at school and beyond, as part of developing a range of alternative scripts for performing creative sexual feminine subjectivities; sexual subjectivities that hopefully will not remain so heavily bound to the phallogocentric, pornified discourses that dominated some of my research accounts.

Notes

1. I was asked to sit on the advisory committee of the UK sexualization report and therefore have some inside knowledge of the process. Government representatives suggested high-profile media figures are now specifically targeted to lead such reports, because of their media presence which is thought to generate greater awareness. The choice of Linda Papadopoulos, seen regularly on reality TV programmes such as UK's *Big Brother* and *Celebrity Fit Club*, to lead the sexualization review was similar to Tania Byron leading the 'Safer children in a digital world' review in 2008. Instead of critiquing the figurehead chosen to author the report, perhaps academic analysis might attend to how the government's increasing dependence on media-savvy experts/'academics' tells us something about the postfeminist media context itself. When women are chosen to lead on such projects, glamour and celebrity kudos appear to count as much as the content and arguments of reports. I suggest this may be more the case for women than men, given the choice of David Buckingham, an academic professor, less in the media eye, to lead on the UK 'commercialisation of childhood' report (2009).
2. The research was carried out with Rebekah Willett.
3. Young people also use the SNSs during school if they can find a proxy which allows them to circumvent the school's firewalls, as well as using them after school and on weekends to sustain contact with 'friends'.

4. There is considerable ethical debate around whether Bebo sites are public or private, in spite of whether individual profiles are publicly available. As a 'networked public' (boyd, 2008), we viewed some of the sites of our participants' peer groups. However, we are careful not to compromise the anonymity of any of the young people.
5. http://www.bebostation.com/top-rated-bebo-skins/
6. Unfortunately it was not possible to gain copyright to illustrate these images, despite the lack of certainty over whether Adidas constructs these skins or Bebo users simply appropriate the symbols and construct the skins themselves.
7. http://www.urbandictionary.com/define.php?term=Boom+chicka+Wah+Wah
8. Pole dancing as a form of 'fun' fitness for women and girls has spread in recent years, but its normalization in ever younger contexts was recently questioned by the Cardiff Council in Wales, who decided not to allow children under 16 to sign up for pole dancing fitness classes. http://www.fitness-daily.com/index. php/archives/2007/10/06/wales-council-decides-that-perhaps-pole-dancing-classes-not-appropriate-for-pre-teens/
9. At New Mills High, a predominantly working-class high school, all of the girls interviewed were entering vocational trades such as hairdressing and child care.
10. This example also points to the violent confrontational politics possible when norms of the visually ideal feminine are not met (see Ringrose, 2010, for a much fuller account of cyber-conflicts linked to SNSs).
11. For analysis of working-class girls' uses of and Playboy mansion fantasies, in ways that disrupt the conventional power dynamics of 'bunny subjectivity', see Ringrose and Renold, forthcoming.
12. The rural village surrounding Thornbury High was being gentrified, partly in response to the high league table performance of the school. Middle-class families were accessing the school, alongside long-time working-class residents. Daniella was from one of the working-class families in the village.
13. Online, social networks offer new forms of voyeurism and scopophilia, extending and democratizing some of the 'to be looked at' dynamics of celebrity culture to anyone with an SNS profile. Interestingly the practice of using a sexualized digital identity on SNSs to 'attract attention' and 'hits' to one's site has now actually been termed 'Bebo whoring' by some commentators; see http://www. sundaymercury.net/news/tm_headline=sex-attack-on-bebo-teenage-girl&meth od=full&objectid=20762793&siteid=50002-name_page.html

Bibliography

Allen, L. (2004) 'Beyond the Birds and the Bees: Constituting a Discourse of Erotics in Sexuality Education', *Gender and Education* 16(2): 151–67.

American Psychological Association (2007) *Report of the APA Task Force on the Sexualization of Girls.*

Attwood, F. (2007) 'Sluts and Riot Grrrls: Female Identity and Sexual Agency', *Journal of Gender Studies* 16(3): 231–45.

Attwood, F. (2009) 'Sexed Up: Theorizing the Sexualisation of Culture', *Sexualities* 9(1): 77–94.

boyd, d. m. (2008) 'Why Youth Social Network Sites: The Role of Networked Publics in Teenage Social Life' in D. Buckingham (ed.), *Youth, Identity, and Digital Media* (Cambridge, MA: MIT Press).

Bray, A. (2008) 'The Question of Tolerance: "Corporate Pedophilia" and Child Sexual Abuse Moral Panics', *Australian Feminist Studies* 23(57): 323–41.

Buckingham, D. (2009) *The Buckingham Report: The Impact of the Commercial World on Children's Wellbeing* (UK: DCSF).

Buckingham, D. and S. Bragg (2004) *Young People, Sex and the Media: The Facts of Life?* (Basingstoke: Palgrave Macmillan).

Butler, J. (1993) *Bodies That Matter: On the Discursive Limits of 'Sex'* (New York: Routledge).

Duits, L. and M. van Zoonen (2006) 'Headscarves and Porno-Chic: Disciplining Girls' Bodies in the European Multicultural Society', *European Journal of Women's Studies* 13(2): 103–17.

Egan, R. D. and G. Hawkes (2008) 'Endangered Girls and Incendiary Objects: Unpacking the Discourse on Sexualization', *Sexuality and Culture* 12(4): 291–311.

Fine, M. (1988) 'Sexuality, Schooling and Adolescent Females: The Missing Discourse of Desire', *Harvard Educational Review* 58(1): 29–53.

Foucault, M. (1982) 'The Subject of Power' in H. Dreyfus and P. Rabinow (eds), *Michel Foucault: Beyond Structuralism and Hermeneutics* (Brighton: Harvester).

Gill, R. (2008) 'Empowerment/Sexism: Figuring Female Sexual Agency in Contemporary Advertising', *Feminism and Psychology* 18(1): 35–60.

Gill, R. (2009) 'Supersexualize Me! Advertising and the "Midriffs"' in F. Attwood (ed.), *Mainstreaming Sex* (London: I. B. Tauris).

Levy, A. (2005) *Female Chauvinist Pigs: Women and the Rise of Raunch Culture* (London: Free Press).

Livingstone, S. (2008) 'Taking Risky Opportunities in Youthful Content Creation: Teenagers' Use of Social Networking Sites for Intimacy, Privacy and Self-Expression', *New Media & Society* 10(3): 459–77.

Manago, A.M., M. B. Graham, P. M. Greenfield and G. Salimkhan (2008) 'Self-presentation and Gender on MySpace', *Journal of Applied Developmental Psychology* 29: 446–58.

McRobbie, A. (2009) *The Aftermath of Feminism: Gender, Culture and Social Change* (London: Sage).

Murch, C. (2010) The Sexualisation of Young People: Moral Panic? Counterfire. Available at http://www.counterfire.org/index.php/features/38-opinion/4350-sex-sale-sand-morality-tales-the sexualisation-of-young-people (accessed 15 May 2010).

Nayak, A. and Kehily, M. J. (2008) *Gender, Youth and Culture, Young Masculinities and Femininities* (Basingstoke: Palgrave).

Paasonen, S., P. Nikunen and L. Saarenmaa (2007) *Pornification: Sex and Sexuality in Media Culture* (Oxford: Berg).

Papacharissi, Z. (2009) 'The Virtual Geographies of Social Networks: A Comparative Analysis of Facebook, LinkedIn and ASmallWorld', *New Media and Society* 11(1&2): 199–220.

Papadopoulous, L. (2010) *The Sexualization of Young People Review*, UK Home Office.

Patchin, J. W. and S. Hinduja (2010) 'Trends in Online Social Networking Adolescent Use of Myspace Over Time', *New Media and Society* 12(2): 197–216.

Renold, E. and J. Ringrose (2010) 'Phallic Girls? Girls' Negotiating Phallogocentric Power' in Nelson Rodriguez and John Landreau (eds), *Queer Masculinities: A Critical Reader in Education* (New York: Springer).

Ringrose, J. (2008) 'Every Time She Bends Over She Pulls Up Her Thong': Teen Girls Negotiating Discourses of Competitive, Heterosexualized Aggression', *Girlhood Studies: An Interdisciplinary Journal* 1(1): 33–59.

Ringrose, J. (2010) 'Beyond Discourse? Using Deleuze and Guattari's Schizoanalysis to Explore Affective Assemblages, Heterosexually Striated Space, and Lines of Flight Online and at School', *Educational Philosophy & Theory*. Available at https://portal. ioe.ac.uk; http://philpapers.org/rec/RINBDU

Ringrose, J. and E. Renold (forthcoming) 'Teen Girls, Working Class Femininity and Resistance: Re-theorizing Fantasy and Desire in Educational Contexts of Heterosexualized Violence, *International Journal of Inclusive Education.*

Ringrose, J. and V. Walkerdine (2008) 'Regulating the Abject: The TV Make-Over as Site of Neo-liberal Reinvention Toward Bourgeois Femininity', *Feminist Media Studies* 8(3): 227–46.

Rush, E. and A. La Nauze (2006) *Corporate Paedophilia: Sexualisation of Children in Australia* (Canberra: Australia Institute).

Smith, C. (2010) 'Corruption of the Innocent', *Times Higher Education*, 20 March.

Smithers, R. (2008) 'Bebo Named as Best Social Networking Site in Survey', *The Guardian*, Friday, 4 January.

Stern, S. (2006) 'Girls Gone Wild? I Don't Think So ...' *Spotlight: Digital Media, Learning* 15. Available at http://spotlight.macfound.org/main/entry/susannah_stern_girls_gone_wild/

Thomas, A. (2004) 'Digital Literacies of the Cybergirl', *E-learning* 1(3): 358–82.

White, E. (2002) *Fast Girls: Teenage Tribes and the Myth of the Slut* (New York: Scribner).

Willett, R. (2009) '"As Soon As You Get on Bebo You Just Go Mad": Young Consumers and the Discursive Construction of Teenagers Online', *Young Consumers: Insight and Ideas for Responsible Marketers*, 10(4): 283–96.

7
'Feminism? That's So Seventies': Girls and Young Women Discuss Femininity and Feminism in *America's Next Top Model*

Andrea L. Press

In this chapter, I examine the particular configuration of feminist and postfeminist consciousness characterizing the way many young women think and speak today. Gill (2006) has recently discussed what she terms the 'postfeminist' sensibility, a sensibility that incorporates feminist ideals, but also their rejection. McRobbie similarly discusses this paradox, wherein feminism is both assumed by the general population, and actively refuted and rejected as a belief system (McRobbie, 2009a, p. 1). In the postfeminist sensibility, feminism is rejected by those who should 'know better', and thereby the rejection itself is made 'naughty' – which, in effect, sexualizes it or makes it pleasurable; and this leads to a certain fetishization of 'anti-feminist' symbols of femininity such as an objectified sexualization of women's bodies, a militantly 'feminine' appearance, etc. There is a contradiction in the way that what are seen as the ideals of second-wave feminism – women's empowerment, autonomy, and ability to choose work, sexual and emotional lifestyles – are at the same time taken for granted, criticized, lauded and coldly rejected (McRobbie, 2007, 2009a, 2009b).

The postfeminist sensibility is related to what recent feminist scholars have been constructing as the 'third wave' of feminism – again, a feminism that has 'moved on' from what is alleged to be the second-wave emphases (too business-like a focus on equality, perhaps?), and reclaimed elements of a pre-feminist past including, importantly, an emphasis on women's sexual expression, and at the same time an emphasis on exhibiting an extreme femininity bodily, sexually and culturally.[1] Third-wave feminism is a complex term generally identified with a new version of feminism featuring these emphases, emerging[2] in the 1990s. As normally described, feminists of the third wave seek to avoid the second wave's essentialism, and maintain that the second-wave universalized the perspective of upper-middle-class, white heterosexual women.

This overthrow of second-wave feminism, in what comes to be seen as an entirely new version of feminism, makes the current feminist movement much more compatible with the neoliberal self which many have written about (Gill 2008; McRobbie, 2000, 2007). Third-wave feminism's emphasis on bodily self-expression and the ability to choose a highly sexualized lifestyle embraces the neoliberal focus on the idea that the self must be continually constructed and transformed, that it is endlessly perfectible, and that it must be continually policed to maintain this perfection. Third-wave feminism's emphasis on the desirability of women's freedom to express themselves sexually, as 'sex-objects' if they like (and invariably, they like, since this image is glamorized in an uncritical fashion), makes it naturally economically compatible with a consumer society which offers a plethora of products to a liberal self concerned with self-expression through the mode of an ever-more-perfectible appearance.

The focus on products enhancing women's bodily sexual appeal, products which bring women's bodies more firmly into the stricture of the narrow set of ideals which constitute sexual desirability in current cultural parlance, was an idea severely criticized by many second-wavers. Yet the new forms of post- and third-wave feminism criticize the second-wave resoundingly for the repressive nature of a sensibility which rejects the overt sexualization of women's bodies, and overt expressions of femininity. The postfeminist sensibility makes young women suspicious of these second-wave critiques, and at the same time, with their embrace of the constructed feminized, sexual self, much more accepting and open to notions of the liberal, perfectible self characterizing neoliberalism. Feminists today, therefore, are much more embedded in consumer society and its ideals than were feminists of a generation ago.

Entailed in this overwhelming stress on the production of sexual attractiveness is a conflation of women's social class status with conventionally attractive female bodies, faces, make-up, clothing and hair. In short, women's social class mobility is an ever-present theme, rarely explicitly referenced yet always just under the surface of the third wave's self-improvement rhetoric. There is an implicitly Cinderella-like feel to the third-wave's messages, though the Cinderella invoked has a feminist inflection. Women are promised success, glamour and happiness if only they can get the improvement script right. Prince Charming, *plus* a well-paid and glamorous career, all will follow if you can only pick out the perfect designer shoes, etc. In sum, the road to glamour is also, it is promised, the road to riches.

McRobbie (2000, 2009a) ties this social class/glamour connection to the proliferation of service sector jobs, which have certain requirements vis-à-vis appearance for women:

> Appearance and self-expression take on new importance when so many jobs are located in the service sector, at the interface with clients and

customers, and where customer service and sales require all sorts of enhanced techniques including the self-presentation skills of staff. Thus, class makes a decisive re-appearance in and through the vectors of transformed gendered individualization, with the result that class relations are themselves changed by the performative force of femininity. (2009b, p. 131)

What is striking about the situation is that while a sense of the relationship between social class and appearance is ubiquitous in current media focus on the makeover, the language of social class remains hidden even as class is constantly, if indirectly, invoked with this connection between glamour and success perennially articulated in postfeminist rhetoric and imagery.

Nowhere is the postfeminist sensibility more evident than in recent reality TV makeover shows, which focus on the minute refashioning of the female body largely through the wise use of consumer products and new lifestyle pursuits. What I primarily attempt to address here is the type of critical consciousness young women today, of various age groups and stages of development, have developed about postfeminism as an identity, and as a theoretical prism through which they come to view the world. I'm interested in how a postfeminist sensibility functions as a way of life for women coming of age in this era; how it intersects with the elements of second-wave feminism that they have absorbed alongside it; and how these belief systems impact women's relationship to social class mobility interpreted through women's attitudes towards education and career.

To illustrate these phenomena I examine young women's reactions to what is currently an extremely popular reality television show, *America's Next Top Model*. I am in the process of conducting a series of focus-groups with young teen and college-aged viewers of this show (and in the broader project, other shows as well). I offer their discussions as a template for examining the way young women think about issues of the body; of their own representations – what Laura Mulvey famously (back in the era of second-wave feminism) termed, in the context of discussing the representation of women in the classical Hollywood cinema, women's continuing 'to-be-looked-at-ness' – and how that manifests itself in the neoliberal age when the focus on the female body becomes minute, critical and aimed at constant improvement and transformation, and when this revisionary gaze is implicitly connected to promised or implied social class status.

Valerie Walkerdine (2003), Angela McRobbie (2007, 2009a), Ros Gill (2003, 2008) and others unpack the content of the relentless self-critique characteristic of the postfeminist age. They have explicated in great detail the argument I reference above, that it is the internal critical gaze, rather than outside assessment, which is most relentless for women in this new era. This is a gaze imbued with ideas of the 'perfect', all of which invoke racial, social class and sexual characteristics: as a result, it is the wealthy, white, young, heterosexual norm which this kind of policing encourages. Other identities are loathed or, in Kristeva's terms (1982), become 'abject', an entity outside the borders of one's own. Yet this process is understood popularly under the rubric of women making their own individual life 'choices', and constructing their own life-trajectories, as in the discourse of the neoliberal subject which argues that each of us is 'free' to determine our own identity and path (Beck and Beck-Gernsheim, 2002). Feminism's second-wave critique of a society which oppressed women by confining them to a limited number of social roles, or by sexually objectifying their bodies, has been transformed in the current moment. Instead, we witness a critique of those who would limit girls' and women's choices to pick these roles, to consider the objective qualities of their own bodies, and to rigorously try to transform and 'perfect' them. Perfection resides in a series of ideals which are accepted uncritically and favour the qualities of the wealthy, white, young, heterosexual subject celebrated in many media representations and advertisements. Third-wave and postfeminist rhetoric repeatedly offers women the 'freedom' to look sexy – actually, to construct their 'sexy' selves – according to these normative dimensions, or to appropriate the accoutrements of traditional femininity – e.g. pink clothes, 'girly' fashions, and a focus on homemaking and motherhood, alongside the 'accepted' second-wave idea that women should pursue a career identity.

Bev Skeggs (1997), bell hooks (2006) and others have described the contradictions this situation presents for working-class or minority women, for whom overtly sexual imagery has always been used as a part of their own 'othering' or exclusion. These contradictions exist particularly in the rhetoric of third-wave feminism, which presents a new form of 'femininity' building on pre-feminist styles and identities overtly criticized by the second wave. In third-wave feminism, for example, high heels, low-cut, revealing clothing, and retro-lingerie – gear widely criticized by second-wavers – are 'in'. The stay-at-home mom who prioritizes family over career, or the super-sexual woman who wears revealing clothing that sexualizes the female body, is newly fashionable. Second-wave feminists, in contrast, often criticized precisely these identities and styles as discriminatory towards women, or as tools of our oppression.

The styles and identities of third-wave feminism assume flesh and form in the reality makeover TV show, where overt sexuality becomes identified with decidedly positive, middle-class images. To become 'somebody' in these shows is, quite often, to be sexual, and to have the money to enhance one's sex appeal with clothing, shoes, make-up, and possibly cosmetic surgery (as, for example, in the world of *Sex and the City*). This leads to intense anxiety and confusion over the boundaries between the ideal and the vilified feminine subject (Ringrose and Walkerdine, 2008), as certainly the conventionally 'sexy' appearance was denigrated and criticized for years in the rhetoric of feminism's second wave yet is actively pursued in the third wave. I argue that these contradictory attitudes towards a conventionally sexy appearance are present for all women, middle-class and working-class, black and white, heterosexual and lesbian, young and old, as they learn the new gendered sexual scripts of the third-wave postfeminist/neoliberal era yet hear and remember the echoes of the older feminist rhetoric.

In the example of *America's Next Top Model*, hosted and created by the African American supermodel Tyra Banks, who broke through many stereotypes in her own career, we see both social class and race explicitly addressed and incorporated into the upward-mobility narrative of the show. With teens and young women in my focus-groups, I watched the recently popular images of young women learning to be supermodels featured on *America's Next Top Model*. I wondered if young women viewers, clearly the target audience for the show, were aware that this was a particular view of women, their bodies, their beauty, and their need to transcend racial and social class identities. Were they aware of, and similarly critical of, the call the show made to its contestants, and to its viewers, to treat their bodies and identities as endlessly malleable, as objects of constant critical assessment and transformative construction? Most of all I wondered if adherence to the popular versions of 'feminism' which one hears in all quarters of post-modern life – the part of second-wave rhetoric which is simply assumed, and indeed which permeates the discourse of the model on *America's Next Top Model* as well as the everyday language of women of all ages, social classes, and groups – is truly widespread. How do young women react to the ironies of the postfeminist sensibility, a sensibility rather schizophrenic in its acceptance both of women's career identities paired with the continuing foregrounding of bodily transformation and appearance? Turning to my current research on young women and their relationship to these ideas, I'd like to briefly discuss the TV show prior to presenting women's reactions.

America's Next Top Model

There's a good chance that if you turned on your television right now, an episode of *America's Next Top Model* would be airing. The show's premise is to take 'average' girls and give them the skills they need to become professional models.[3] *America's Next Top Model* is hosted by former supermodel Tyra Banks. After a series of nationwide auditions are held, potential models are selected and subsequently whisked away to a loft where they live together, with their every move unfolding before the lens of the camera in staged photo-shoots and day-to-day activities alike. Each episode chronicles the models' experiences as they complete a series of 'challenges', the first of which is typically a small-scale, informal competition that pits the girls against each other to see who has the best acting skills, who can apply make-up the fastest, or who shines the brightest personality-wise in an interview or casting call. These activities are followed by a thematically related professionalized photo-shoot.

At the end of each episode, a panel of judges headed by Banks offer their insight and critique of each girl's performance, ostensibly according to the standards of the modelling industry. The weakest model is sent home each episode, until the last model standing at the end of the cycle wins the title of 'America's Next Top Model' and the initial perquisites that come with it – a modelling contract with a top agency, a *CoverGirl* advertisement campaign, and a spread in a nationwide women's magazine. Whether in the confines of a home furnished by Tyra, on location at a shoot, or at the studio in which panel judging takes place, there's no lack of tears, tantrums or taunts on the part of the aspiring models.

Premiering in May 2003, *America's Next Top Model* has enjoyed a considerable staying power, especially amongst the 18–34 adult and 18–34 female demographics that its home network The CW targets.[4] With an average of 4 to 5 million viewers tuning in to new episodes each week and international versions of the show either currently airing or in the process of development in over 120 countries spanning the globe – from Australia and Canada to Afghanistan, Great Britain and Germany to Ghana – the show is a recognizable brand worldwide.[5] The show seems to have been constructed to appeal across a range of demographics. The cyclical nude shoot may attract the heterosexual male audience. In addition, the show offers the personality of Tyra Banks for the audience of colour, the African American former supermodel who broke many barriers for African American models by appearing on the cover of the *Sports Illustrated* swimsuit issue. There are always many contestants of colour featured on each season. The show also features gay males in the form of judges Miss J. Alexander and Jay Manuel. The contestants always come from a range of social class backgrounds, which we learn as the show delves into the life-stories of many of the young women contestants. While the show lives third-wave feminism's commitment to diversity in this way, it expressly violates second-wave critiques of the objectification of women's bodies by in effect teaching objectification as a 'science' to be learned, in the guise of teaching women the modelling profession. Young women contestants on the show are 'taught' to present themselves in a better and better light, by the standards of current media ideals, through learning the tricks of the modelling trade which teach them to use make-up, wear clothes, walk and be photographed so as to maximize the objective 'value' of their bodies by appealing as much as possible to current media ideals.

How do young women discuss these texts?

I now turn to the discussion of these shows by the young women viewers with whom I spoke. Thus far I've run[6] five focus-groups, one with pre-teen women aged 13 who were regular viewers of *America's Next Top Model*, and four with college students. The pre-teen group (the 'teeny boppers') was very small, consisting of three members only. I will identify the respondents by assigned names in the discussion section, in part because there are so few of them. The teeny bopper group consisted of three girls in the eighth grade who attended a small, private school in a Southern college town in the US. All were white and middle-class. One, Myra, was from a family with divorced parents, and she lived with her mother, a kindergarten teacher. Another, Norene, was the child of a fundamentalist Christian family: her mother was a nurse and her father a builder. The third, Johanna, was the child of two middle-class college professors.

The college student groups were for the most part white, except for the group of African American studies majors/minors. This group included two African American women, one a senior and the other a sophomore, as well as a white male and a white woman, all of whom were African American studies majors or minors. The other three groups varied in size from three to five members and included psychology, drama, media studies and political and social thought majors. Most were juniors and seniors in college. Also, most had gone to public secondary schools though one or two had gone to private secondary schools. Ages varied from 19 to 22 years old.

I caution you that all of the data here are very preliminary and presage a larger study which is planned to focus on this and several other currently popular television shows and films of different genres, all of which exhibit what Gill terms the 'postfeminist sensibility'. The data I've collected thus far indicate a pronounced trend. While both age groups show that they are intimately engaged with the show by their detailed discussions of the appearance of the aspiring models and the criticisms to which they are subjected in the course of the show, and their obvious overall enjoyment at viewing the contest, they differ in the level of self-consciousness that they display about their own relationship to the contestants and their appearance, and the level of detail with which they are prepared to discuss this issue. We could say that they differ to the degree they've entered into a neoliberal subject position – which seems to vary by developmental stage.

The teeny boppers

Pre-teen women mention how exciting they find *America's Next Top Model*. Their discussions talk about the 'exciting' photo-shoots. In a particularly poignant moment, a girl with an eating disorder wistfully fixates on who is the 'prettiest' of the contestants, saying she must be the winner. Other girls comment on the contestants' hair, their make-up, their walks. Finally each contestant's personality comes under discussion. Oh yes, personality too must be produced in the proper way for those aspiring to a top modelling position.

Nevertheless the girls are cognizant that the winner must be, ultimately, 'beautiful' in the terms of the show – the ultimate focus must be on the way she looks:

> 'If they have a lot of different poses, if they can walk, and if they're photogenic and not ugly, the girls will be judged well and might win the contest as the one with the most potential to become American's next top model.' (Norene)

Much of their discussion revolves around the bodily flaws, the ins and outs of the physical potential each contestant has to win the contest.

A second topic of intense debate amongst the teeny boppers is the 'rudeness' of the judges. Part of the show revolves around the harsh judgements made by judges about each girl, particularly as each contestant is eliminated. 'Rudeness' is an interesting focus because of its inverse relationship to the traditionally feminine quality of 'niceness'. The issue of 'rudeness' in relation to 'femininity' comes up when the pre-teens discuss the behaviour of the judges. *America's Next Top Model* provides a range of judges who display behaviour along a continuum of 'niceness' (Twiggy, former glamorous model of the 1960s) to extreme 'bitchiness' (Janice Dickerson). Tyra, the host, falls somewhere in the middle, indeed is changeable depending on the situation. It's interesting that the girls mention their shock at what they term the 'rude' behaviour of the 'bitchy' judge Janice Dickerson – almost as though in the presence of a show which is at some level *about* femininity, they must notice and criticize behaviour which flouts feminine conventions, as Dickerson's clearly does – but at some level this is the show's claim to feminism.[7] It's telling us 'we're not here to be nice, girls, we're here to produce some bitchin' competitive tough top models', an approach to a competitive career which in this case is based on the production of a perfect, constructed, commercial femininity for the photographers and, ultimately, for viewers. This is perhaps ironic as both Dickerson's extreme, nasty behaviour towards the contestants and the presentation of a modelling career as cut-throat and highly competitive, are arguably presented as versions of 'feminist' behaviour, and thereby hark back to second-wave rejections of more passive, sweet and sexual behaviours. As do many versions of the third wave, this version of feminism combines both extremes – the 'bitchy' and the sweet, the ultra-feminine with the more (some might say) 'masculine' competitiveness of a difficult and challenging career.

As Johanna noted, excusing Tyra's tough, indeed rude, behaviour,

> 'I just think that she's trying to judge the girls on what she thinks the REAL WORLD would, judge them on...I think that's helpful criticism, except for some of the stuff that Janice Dickerson says.'
>
> *Interviewer*: 'Why? Does Dickerson go too far?'

'She criticizes them on subtle things, like she just says stuff that doesn't help, like if you're ugly you can't help it, or if your eyes are too big or too small.'

When Dickerson challenges the premise that all girls can *improve* themselves and thereby enter the realm of top modelling, the girls find this offensive – it's 'not helpful' – certainly not, when the point is constant self-improvement through employing a close, critical eye oriented towards helping effect change through product use or other means of improvement. The theme of physical transformation, then, is key, as the girls note when they mention the failure of one girl who 'got sent home because she wouldn't cut her hair'. Everyone, Myra claims, knows 'you have to change your hair to look so you are more "high fashion".' According to the logic of this show, the way out of a poor or working-class background would be to change your hair, or effect other bodily transformations, most involving some kind of consumption activity.

This theme is underscored by the girls' consciousness that most of the contestants have obstacles in their lives to overcome which are larger than just their looks. Many come from lower-class or working-class backgrounds and have huge personal and family issues to overcome in their lives. Their participation in the show is presented as the factor that helps them to overcome these obstacles. The girls pick up on this, but do not have the language of social class to help them talk about it. They couch the issues in terms of 'poverty', or 'sadness'. The collective discussion, though it lacks an explicit language of social class, in fact describes some of its features, and indicates the presence of at least an incipient class-consciousness, even in these young respondents:

'They are all [i.e. the contestants] trying to be perfect, but it shows that you have to go through stuff to be able to be successful.' (Norene)
'Almost every girl they pick kind of goes through stuff... they either grow up really poor or they have a sad homelife.' (Johanna)
'Well, the people that win do.' (Myra)

Much of what the girls express here is their awareness that there are social class and other obstacles which the show represents in certain ways, and the connection that the show makes, for women, between mastering the accoutrements of femininity, and achieving upward mobility. The show makes the case that the contestants' mastering femininity, the signs and symbols necessary for a model, will help them achieve this high-powered career and thereby overcome precisely these class obstacles. And if they don't achieve the high-powered modelling career, the implication is that the girls will be better off anyway by mastering the skills of feminine appearance. The theme of *America's Next Top Model* is simply the classical Cinderella story writ large. The girls notice that, to achieve full Cinderella-like transformation (and in the absence of fairies and enchanted mice), contestants are willing to transform themselves endlessly through all kinds of expensive consumption activities and makeover processes. Girls are promised that if they achieve glamour, prosperity will follow – the two are pictured hand-in-hand. This despite the fact that many women in actuality go entirely broke and become indebted seeking the transformations required for the serious pursuit of glamour, while relatively few recoup these investments by achieving a high paying modelling career or by cashing in on their appearance in some other way (either by achieving a successful career in another appearance-based industry, or attaining marriage to a 'prince').

The show makes a stab at presenting a wide variety of physical and body images, and each show includes what's known as the 'plus-sized' model (meaning someone larger than, say, a size 0–2), at least at the beginning. The young girls, however, are not fooled by this token presence of diversity, particularly since the plus-sized models rarely win:

> 'When you look at the fashion magazines, you don't see any plus sized models, you see really skinny models. And if you look at the winners, all of them are really skinny ... the plus-sized models don't get very far in the competition.' (Myra)

The show's overt feminist rhetoric, criticizing eating disorders and including larger-sized women, does not convince the girls: winners are almost without exception impossibly skinny, beautiful and otherwise flawless, for the most part.[8] Despite the ever-present theme of transformation which promises that any girl can attain such perfection, the girls notice the flawlessness of the winners, and the unhealthy, unnatural ways in which it must be achieved. Eating disorders are a constant theme when the girls consider what is necessary to achieve model size: 'Some of them have gone through eating disorders, even though on the show they speak out against [them]' (Johanna). Though Tyra, in the discourse of the show, as one of the girls says 'really encourages the people that they are different and tells them that she loves them and that they're beautiful and that it matters on the inside and not on the outside' (Myra), in fact what the girls see in the outcome of the contests contradicts these messages. While it is difficult for them to discuss these issues outright, the girls are evidently torn by this contradiction, both in their reception of the show, and in their assessment of their own body-types and physical appearance.

The girls understand this contradiction fully well. They accept the ideals, and they *want* to be perfect according to these standards, as the following exchange indicates:

Interviewer: 'Would you want to be a top model?'

'I would because everyone likes them and they are nice and confident, photogenic and good spokesmen and relatable, if you're like perfect.' (Norene)

Of course, inherent in this idea of the 'perfect' is the white, middle-class subject that recent theorists (Kristeva, 1982; Ringrose and Walkerdine 2008) have described so eloquently. Certainly this ideal gets across to the young viewers of this show. They see, though cannot articulate, that *America's Next Top Model*'s contestants' 'problems' are related to social class issues; and they see that becoming the disciplined, white, middle-class, heterosexual subject of neoliberal consumer culture is the way 'out' of these problems – and that economic resources of the middle class are necessary for this transformation – though again, they cannot articulate these categories and judgements overtly. What is perhaps most interesting about the classed subject that is produced in *America's Next Top Model* is its particularly gendered nature. This is a specifically female subject, produced through a complicated, ritualized and internalized disciplinary regime, performed on the body and the personality (Gill, 2008, p. 152), involving consumption and transformation tailored to the particular commercial image of the female body constructed in capitalist, consumer society. Walkerdine (2003) discusses some of the pressures and complexities involved for women in particular in assuming the transfer of personal 'identities' required for social class mobility by the female subject.

The college girls

While the teeny boppers did not know what it meant when asked to say if they watched *America's Next Top Model* 'critically', most of the college girls found this a funny question:

Allison: 'Ha ha, of course, I mean, who doesn't?'

There's been a definite shift moving from ages 12 to 14, to the college girls' aged 19 to 22, in the mood or sensibility through which this show is received. While the teeny boppers found the show 'informational', the college girls receive it more overtly ironically, consonant with the fact that they've matured into middle-class television viewers, who view television ironically or at least sceptically, as the literature shows (Press 1991). However, when unpacking this aspect of their viewing, I find that their irony goes only so far – in fact, they found the show informational as well, and valued it in part for this quality.

Gill discusses the role of 'irony' in the postfeminist sensibility. She describes instances of extreme sexism in British 'lad's' magazines, in which women's breasts are rated, and compared, as allegedly constituting, by its hyper-extreme nature, the evidence that there is no longer real sexism, nor the need for feminist critique (Gill 2008, p. 160). *America's Next Top Model* operates similarly as a text, and this is displayed clearly in the way the college girls read the text. They take an attitude that is in part explained by 'now that we've passed the need for feminism, we can relax and enjoy this hyper-focus on ranking women's appearance, body parts, size, walk, etc.' After all, it's all in the interests of pursuing a successful career, which was one of feminism's most clearly stated goals for women. The irony is the fact that the extreme objectification of women's bodies that the show presents is embedded in the discourse of women's independence and career success. The rags-to-riches upward mobility through glamour storylines simply complicates the discursive structure.

In many ways the college girls echo the sentiments of the teeny boppers, carrying them even further: their level of minute examination of the bodies on view in the show, and of the self-examination they carry out on their own bodies, is even more intense, more detailed, more aware than that of the younger girls. Girls discuss in detail the way that contestants' appearances led to their losing, or winning, the competition, mentioning in turn the contestants' 'muscular bodies', 'big boobies', 'long necks – no, it's kind of wide', etc. What is ironic, however, is that their level of self-aware critique both of the show's address, and of its impact on them, is much higher as well. In one group, there was an intense discussion of the presence of the 'plus-sized' model ('by plus-sized, you mean *our* size') on the show. Girls endlessly discuss the physical characteristics of the contestants:

Allison:	'Like she's [Diane] not big she's just big…like big boobs.'
Allison:	'Bre is cute but she does not look like a model.'
Kristi:	'Her head looks really big.'
Michele:	'I think she photographs looking heavier than she does in person.'

It's interesting that these girls, all of whom attend a large public but very selective Eastern university in the US, are very critical of Tyra in a more intense way than we saw with the teeny boppers:

Allison:	'I can't stand [Tyra's ego].'
Kristi:	'Tyra's a bitch.'
Kristi:	'Man, Tyra really likes to talk about herself.'

Although the teeny boppers were also critical of Tyra's bitchiness and the 'unfeminine' nature it defined through her comments and criticisms, the college girls go further than the young girls in their criticisms of the host, one girl even commenting – rather ironically – on Tyra's own constructed identity:

Allison: 'Gee, Tyra, did you have a nose job?'

and later,

Allison: 'Tyra's nose is so funny. It's like so obviously fake.'

In comparison to the teeny boppers, the older, non-African American girls seem to have a more developed sense of their own difference from Tyra, perhaps related to her identity as an African American woman. These comments can be read in part as an attempt to draw boundaries between their own racial identity and that of Tyra's. The comments serve to draw other types of boundaries as well, such as between their own looks and Tyra's more 'fake' nose, their own dispositions and Tyra's propensity to speak about herself in an egoistic manner.

The African American girls in my sample tend to be less critical of Tyra and to focus their comments more on her successes ('she's helping ...') and her service projects aimed at lower-class black women, such as funding a camp for lower-income African American urban girls. Their tone overall is less critical – indeed, less cynical – as they receive this show and comment on its treatment of contestants, and its appeal to young women viewers, particularly from the more working-class members of this group. So, here the admiration of the bodies that the younger girls saw has transformed into a more realistic appreciation of Tyra's business acumen and success in achieving upward mobility through presenting her body, and beauty, in a commercially viable way.

What was perhaps most sad in my discussions with the white middle-class college girls was just *how* aware they were of the way the show's spectacle was encouraging them to develop an endlessly critical sensibility about their own bodies and appearance, and just *how* aware they were as well that the level of critique they were encouraged to develop was unreasonable, indeed, entirely unrealistic ('the girls told their weights – I'm the same height as that contestant, if I weighed what she weighed – 35 pounds less than what I weigh – I couldn't walk'). They overtly mention their worry about the show's impact on 'younger' girls, presumably those more vulnerable than themselves. In addition, the college girls are more critical than the young girls about how the show systematically breaks down the self-esteem of its contestants.

Ironically, perhaps, this very cruelty is part of the appeal. The intensity of the college girls' attention to the show's details revealed the extent of their buy-in. They bought it, and they felt it, and the show was succeeding (along with the other cultural pressures which it so well expressed) in making them ultra-critical of themselves. Interestingly once again, this issue is discussed quite differently by my African American respondents, who seem less critical of the low weights necessary for models to make it. They remark uncritically that a girl in the profession of modelling would need to be thin, in contrast to the comments of the non-African American respondents above. When asked whether college life encouraged girls to develop eating disorders, they disagree with this, and find that college life encourages healthy behaviours like eating well and exercising in a healthy manner. There is a way that, partially protected by their culture from the body-weight pressures the white girls experience, they focus in a more clear-eyed manner on the commercial requirements of modelling, what is necessary for success – and mobility – through this route.

Some scholars trace the origin of critical media theory to the Frankfurt School (Horkheimer, 2002; Horkheimer and Adorno, 2002). As Horkheimer and Adorno ended their famous essay on the 'Culture Industry' by saying 'the ultimate triumph' of the ad for mouthwash is that consumers see through the ad yet buy the mouthwash anyway (1972, p. 222), these girls – the non-African American respondents – are buying the mouthwash. Goldman (1992) continues in this vein by arguing that more current ads draw us in by hailing audiences as knowing and sophisticated consumers – they flatter us with the notion that we can 'see through' attempts to manipulate us.

Certainly the white college girls exemplify this audience to a 't' – they both see through the attempted manipulations, *and* they buy in fully. This differed from the African American respondents. They did not engage in the same minute critique of their bodies, nor did they display an overtly critical sensibility when discussing their bodies. One girl in fact repeatedly referred to girls being 'small like me', though in fact she was no smaller or thinner than many of the other girls in the study.[9]

Conclusion

Our popular media culture floods us with images of the endless possibilities for consumption to which particularly we as women are called to attend. Much of this consumption is directed towards the transformation of our bodies and every aspect of our appearance, and our personalities as well, as necessary to achieve the appearance of the 'top models' portrayed in this show. The postfeminist neoliberal sensibility promises us that we can take charge of these appeals, and of this transformative work, picking and choosing what we actively desire, and resisting and rejecting the rest. It promises that successful transformation is possible, and that improvement, even perfection, is possible for all, with enough work, enough information, and the wise choice of lifestyle and products.

Yet even cursory discussions with girls and young women show that the forms of coercion embedded in these media appeals are not particularly hidden or subtle. Why has the feminist critique failed in its attempts to inform about these issues, to tease out the coercive from the critical subjectivity? Adorno and his buddies may be laughing in their graves at the claims of postfeminism and the third wave that young women are newly 'liberated' from the shackles of an ideologically coercive past. Interviews with young women indicate that these new calls which hail women to the endless work of self-perfection are experienced as coercive and dominating, but nevertheless do not generate any form of collective resistance.[10]

Early feminist media scholars once discussed the 'domestication and de-politicization' of feminism on television and in popular film. Yet these theories stopped short of describing the extent to which such a contradictory understanding of second-wave feminist critique could be incorporated into the self-concept, and self-understanding, of young women. This happened to such a degree that, together with our culture's backlash against feminism, feminism's ideals face true eradication at the cultural, and personal, level, replaced by the increasingly fierce levels of coercion and surveillance represented in new third-wave and postfeminist images and ideas.

Notes

1. See //en.wikipedia.org/wiki/Third_Wave_feminism for a good introduction to third-wave feminism. The term 'third-wave' is often traced to an essay written by Rebecca Walker entitled 'Becoming the Third Wave' in *Ms.* magazine, January/February 1992. She coined this term in the context of speaking about the multiple contradictions of the Anita Hill/Clarence Thomas hearings for feminists in the 1990s. In particular she claimed that she was a 'third-wave' feminist, rather than a 'postfeminist', thereby asserting that there was still a need for feminism, though a new version that transcended some of the issues plaguing second wave feminism, in particular the exclusion of women of colour and lesbian women. The essay was reprinted in Ryan (2001, Reprinted, pp. 78–80). See also Dicker and Piepmeier (2003), Gillis et al. (2004), Reger (2005) and Walker (1995) for further discussions of third-wave feminism.
2. See //en.wikipedia.org/wiki/Third_Wave_feminism#cite_note_14
3. I am indebted in this discussion of the show to my former undergraduate student, Danielle Blundell, who also organized the first group of college-aged students who watched and discussed *America's Next Top Model* and on whom I report here. I am also indebted to my graduate student Niva Shooshy for her help in organizing other groups of college students, and for discussions about her parallel research with Israeli audiences.
4. 'AMERICA'S NEXT TOP MODEL' AND 'ONE TREE HILL' PROPEL THE CW TO FIRST ON WEDNESDAY IN WOMEN 18–34 'TOP MODEL' AND 'ONE TREE HILL' LIFT CW STATIONS TO FIRST OR SECOND IN 8 OF TOP 10 MARKETS WITH KEY DEMOS'. The CW press release, posted on 28 Sept. 2006. See http://www.thefuton-critic.com/news.aspx?id=20060928cw01 [accessed 27 Feb. 2008].
5. *'Afghanistan's Next Top Model'.* Available at http://abcnews.go.com/International/popup?id=3674253 [accessed 27 Feb. 2008].
6. One of the college focus-groups was run by my undergraduate student Danielle Blundell.

7. Fairclough (2008) discussed how the word 'bitch' is used variously in postfeminist culture, both to celebrate women who are confident and self-assured, and to continually denigrate them. Here again we see a little of both, with Janice's personality explicitly juxtaposed to Twiggy's, and Tyra falling somewhere in the middle, able to impersonate both the 'bitch' and the supportive, 'nice' woman, feminine in traditional ways.
8. Though in one season the plus-sized model did win.
9. In fact, the literature about girls and eating disorders has indicated that distorted body-size perception is not as common amongst African-American girls in the US. See for example Neumark-Sztainer et al. (2002) and White et al. (2003).
10. I am grateful to this volume's editors for highlighting this point for me.

Bibliography

Beck, U. and E. Beck-Gernsheim (2002) *Individualization* (Thousand Oaks: Sage).

Dicker, R. and A. Piepmeier (eds) (2003) *Catching a Wave: Reclaiming Feminism for the 21st Century* (Boston: Northeastern University Press).

Douglas, S. (2004) *The Mommy Myth: The Idealization of Motherhood and How It Has Undermined Women* (New York: Free Press).

Fairclough, K. (2008) 'Fame Is a Losing Game', *Genders* 48: 1–13.

Gill, R. (2003) 'From Sexual Objectification to Sexual Subjectification: The Resexualization of Women's Bodies in the Media', *Feminist Media Studies* 3(1), March: 100–5.

Gill, R. (2008) 'Postfeminist Media Culture: Elements of a Sensibility', *European Journal of Cultural Studies* 10: 147–66.

Gill, R. and E. Herdieckerhoff (2006) 'Rewriting the Romance: New Femininities in Chick Lit?', *Feminist Media Studies* 6(4): 487–504.

Gillis, S., G. Howie and R. Munford (eds) (2004) *Third-Wave Feminism: A Critical Exploration* (Basingstoke: Palgrave Macmillan).

Glucksmann, M. A. (2005) 'Shifting Boundaries and Interconnections: Extending the "Total Social Organization of Labour"' in J. Parry, R. Taylor, L. Pettinger and M. Glucksmann (eds), *A New Sociology of Work?* (Oxford: Blackwell).

Glucksmann, M. A. (2009) 'Call Configurations: Varieties of Call Centre and Divisions of Labour', *Work, Employment and Society* 18(4): 795–811.

Goldman, R. (1992) *Reading Ads Socially* (London and New York: Routledge).

Hemmings, C. (2005) 'Invoking Affect: Cultural Theory and the Ontological Turn', *Cultural Studies* 19(5): 548–67.

Hemmings, C. (2009) 'Telling Feminist Stories', *Feminist Theory* 6(2): 115–39.

hooks, b. (2006) *Outlaw Culture: Resisting Representations* (New York: Routledge).

Horkheimer, M. (2002) *Critical Theory: Selected Essays*, trans. Matthew J. O'Connell and Others. (New York: Continuum). (Translation copyright 1972).

Horkheimer, M. and Adorno, T. (2002) *Dialectic of Enlightenment*, trans. Edmund Jephcott (New York: Continuum).

Kristeva, J. (1982) *Powers of Horror: An Essay on Abjection*, trans. Leon S. Roudiez (New York: Columbia University Press).

McRobbie, A. (2000) 'Feminism and the Third Way', *Feminist Review* 64: 97–112.

McRobbie, A. (2004) 'Postfeminism and Popular Culture', *Feminist Media Studies* 4(3): 255–64.

McRobbie, A. (2007) 'Top Girls? Young Women and the Post-Feminist Sexual Contract', *Cultural Studies* 21(4–5), July/September: 718–37.

McRobbie, A. (2008) 'Pornographic Permutations', *The Communication Review* 11(3): 111.

McRobbie, A. (2009a) *The Aftermath of Feminism* (London: Sage).

McRobbie, A. (2009b) 'A Response to Susie Orbach: On Generation and Femininity', *Studies in Gender and Sexuality* 9: 239–45.

Neumark-Sztainer, D., J. Croll, M. Story, P. J. Hannan, S. A. French and C. Perry (2002) 'Ethnic/Racial Differences in Weight-Related Concerns and Behaviors among Adolescent Girls and Boys: Findings from Project EAT', *Journal of Psychosomatic Research* 53(5): 963–74.

Orbach, S. (2009) 'Chinks in the Merged Attachment: Generational Bequests to Contemporary Teenage Girls', *Studies in Gender and Sexuality* 9: 215–32.

Press, A. L. (1991) *Women Watching Television: Gender, Class and Generation in the American Television Experience* (Philadelphia: University of Pennsylvania Press).

Press, A. and T. Liebes (2003) 'Feminism and Hollywood: Whatever Happened to the Golden Age?' in J. Curran and N. Couldry (eds), *Contesting Media Power* (Boulder, CO: Rowman and Littlefield).

Reger, J. (ed.) (2005) *Different Wavelengths: Studies of the Contemporary Women's Movement* (New York: Taylor and Francis).

Ringrose, J. and V. Walkerdine (2008) 'Regulating the Abject: The TV Make-Over as Site of Neo-Liberal Reinvention Towards Bourgeois Femininity', *Feminist Media Studies* 8(3): September: 227–46.

Ryan, B. (ed.) (2001) *Identity Politics in the Women's Movement* (New York and London: NYU Press).

Skeggs, B. (1997) *Formations of Class and Gender* (London: Sage).

Tasker, Y. and D. Negra (2007) *Interrogating Postfeminism: Gender and the Politics of Popular Culture* (Durham: Duke University Press).

Walker, R. (1992) 'Becoming the Third Wave', ms., January/February.

Walker, R. (1995) *To Be Real: Telling the Truth and Changing the Face of Feminism* (New York: Anchor Press).

Walkerdine, V. (2003) 'Reclassifying Upward Mobility: Femininity and the Neo-Liberal Subject', *Gender and Education* 15(3): 237–48.

White, M. A., J. R. Kohlmaier, P. Varnado-Sullivan and D. A. Williamson (2003) 'Racial/Ethnic Differences in Weight Concerns: Protective and Risk Factors for the Development of eating Disorders and Obesity Among Adolescent Females', *Eat Weight Disorders* 8(1): 20–5.

8
Media 'Sluts': 'Tween' Girls' Negotiations of Postfeminist Sexual Subjectivities in Popular Culture

Sue Jackson and Tiina Vares

In recent years 'tween'[1] girls in Anglo-American societies have emerged from relative obscurity to become the focus of public and academic scrutiny. The gaze directed at them is a particularized and often anxious one, grounded in notions that these girls might be growing up too fast, more specifically that they are precociously sexualized. Concerns about 'tween' girls' sexualization have largely made their way into the media and public domains through a growing collection of popular culture texts such as *The Lolita Effect* (Durham, 2008), *What's Happening to Our Girls* (Hamilton, 2007) and *So Sexy So Soon* (Levy and Kilbourne, 2008) as well as through various reports (e.g. *APA Task Force Report on the Sexualisation of Girls, Corporate Paedophilia*). However unintentionally, these texts strike an alarmist chord that produces *all* girls as 'in trouble' and create a flurry of media response. Somewhat paradoxically, as Gill (2007) points out, media generate concerns and perhaps revive moral panics about girls' sexuality while also being cast as the source of girls' assumed premature sexualization.

Postfeminist popular culture provides a rich source of 'girlie, hyper-sexualised' representations (Renolds and Ringrose, 2008) that underpin anxieties, concerns and 'panics' about the sexualization of girls. 'Sexy' clothing embodies hyper-sexualized, hyper-feminine meanings of post-feminist media subjectivities, for example the constitution of women as both (hetero)sexually desiring and (hetero)sexually desirable (Gill, 2007). Concerns about the premature sexualization of girls frequently cohere around clothing, particularly the direct marketing to girls of body-revealing attire, adult underwear such as G-strings, and clothing emblazoned with adult sexual messages (Lamb and Brown, 2006). Concern also mobilizes around anxieties that girls will aspire to and emulate the 'girlie', 'sexy' clothing styles depicted in magazines and worn by their favourite female celebrities. Problematically, notions that girls are sexualized in these uncomplicated, direct ways by the media assume girls to be a homogeneous group.

Moreover, sexualization claims appear to appropriate a simple media-effects model that positions girls as uncritical media victims (see also Egan and Hawke, 2007). Importantly, we do not take issue with the argument that girls now have to negotiate a social landscape that more specifically and expressly addresses them as sexual subjects. However, we contend that it is timely to explore such an important issue from the perspective of girls themselves to find out about *how* they manage it. In this chapter we present some initial work from a three-year research project in which we are investigating how pre-teen New Zealand girls make sense of the popular culture they engage with. Contrary to the notion that girls passively and uncritically absorb and emulate media representations, we show how girls use various discursive strategies to negotiate the 'hyper-sexualized' femininities media make available to them. Focusing on girls' talk about sexual significations of celebrities' (un)dress, we examine in particular girls' use of the 'slut' figure to reject the sexualized representations of female celebrities with whom they engage. First, however, we examine in more depth some of the literature addressing meanings of sexuality mobilized in clothing, in particular the notion of 'sexy' clothing as a signifier of postfeminist subjectivities.

'Sexy' clothing

A sexually empowered, confident, fun-loving subject (Machin and Thornborrow, 2003; McRobbie, 2009) inhabits the postfeminist wardrobe where, for example, T-shirts variously proclaim a bold sexual desire or allude to the (sexy) body underneath (Gill, 2007) and the thong conveys a 'naughty' but liberated sexuality borrowed from mainstreamed pornographic chic (McNair, 2002). As Attwood (2005, p. 402) observes, the selling of sex to women via fashion and sex toys falls 'somewhere between the acceptable and the forbidden, the fully dressed and the naked'. Choosing and buying a 'sexy' product, such as a thong, provides, in a consumer sense, a means of producing self as confident and sexy (within constraints of class and ethnicity). The promotion and availability of adult 'sexy' clothing such as G-strings, bras, tight fitting crop-tops, short skirts and tiny shorts for young girls is, as mentioned earlier, a particular feature of premature sexualization concerns (e.g. Lamb and Brown, 2006). As with young women, T-Shirts, underwear and night wear provide a message board for girls' heterosexuality, to overtly produce girls in sexual ways with T-shirt captions such as 'Sassy Kitty', 'Recess Flirt' and 'Hello, my name is Hottie' and 'Little Slut' on underpants (Lamb and Brown, 2006). The similarities in the sexualized marketing of products for girls and adult women construct the advertising strategy dubbed Kids Getting Older Younger (Cook and Kaiser, 2004), a strategy designed to engage with girls' desires to appear older and more sophisticated and women's desires to appear younger and 'girlie'. In this consumer culture, pre-teen girls come to 'know that looking sexy is cool' or 'hot' and makes them 'cute' and desirable to boys (Lamb and Brown, 2006).

Popular culture provides a significant site for girls to become familiar with notions of being 'sexy', 'cute' and 'hot'. In magazines for pre-teen girls, for example, girls are instructed on ways to present themselves as desirable and attractive (to boys) through 'hot' outfits, tamed hair and kiss-worthy lips (Griffin, 2004). Through fashion and make-up features, girls learn that at 'any age they can have fun being sexy' (Lamb and Brown, 2006). Observing the 'sea-change' in pre-teen girls' magazines, McRobbie (2008, p. 545) comments that they 'produce sexuality as both thinkable and recognisable through fashion items such as crop tops, thongs, low-rider jeans, tiny bikinis and provocative T-shirts'. For pre-teen girls, pop music is a highly significant part of their everyday lives (Baker, 2004) and pop music celebrities are accordingly a widely accessed resource for constructing identity (Boden, 2006). Television, magazines, the internet and music DVDs all provide pre-teen girls with access to pop music icons. It is in this celebrity sphere that we perhaps see the most graphic expressions of what has been called 'porno-chic' (see McNair, 2002) and, more critically, 'raunch culture' (Levy, 2005). Both of these terms refer to the mainstreaming of pornographic representations. While McNair adopts a celebratory stance, Levy critically views it as the repackaging of sexist objectification in the guise of sexual empowerment. Meanings of 'raunch culture' around 'being sexy' are made readily available to girls in visual celebrity pop music culture. In many music videos, for example, body exposure (e.g. bra tops and brief shorts or very short skirts, tight body-fit dresses) is accompanied by acts of sexual simulation, self-touching, sexual poses and so on.

Although 'raunch' is celebrated in postfeminist popular culture, in girls' lived worlds meanings of wearing clothes that border the 'dressed' and 'undressed' are often produced by a more regulatory socio-cultural eye. As Chris Griffin (2005) observes, whereas a postfeminist discourse constructs a 'sassy girl' subject who offers 'the potential to experiment with sexualized practices such as the adoption of revealing clothing', inhabiting a 'sassy girl' subjectivity carries potential risks in 'signifying sluttiness rather than sassiness'. Awareness of such risks is suggested by research with girls whose accounts point to significations of short skirts, tightly fitting clothing and the ubiquitous thong as denoting a 'tart' or 'slut' subjectivity (e.g. Gleeson and Frith, 2004; Malson et al., 2002; Renolds and Ringrose, 2008). Attwood (2007) notes the lengthy classed and gendered history of the term 'slut' in the regulation of, mainly, working-class women and girls' sexuality. However, she also points to more subversive and disruptive uses of the term in recent history such as the Riot Grrls' inscription of 'slut' on their bodies and texts such as *Macho Sluts* that (re)claim 'slut' as a positive sexuality. Girls in our study, however, more often employed the term within its regulatory meanings when discussing the clothing of female celebrities. In the remainder of the chapter we explore the ways in which girls in our 'tween' popular culture project discursively constitute and negotiate the performance of 'hyper-sexualized femininity' through the figure of the slut.

'Girls, "tween" popular culture and everyday life': the research project

The material in this chapter is drawn from the first phase of the three-year project 'Girls, "tween" popular culture and everyday life', currently in its second year. Our participants are 71 girls who in 2008 were recruited from three primary and two intermediate schools in two metropolitan sites in New Zealand: Christchurch (35 girls) and Wellington (36 girls). In 2008 approximately half of the girls were in Year 7 (10–11-year-olds) and half in Year 8 (12–13-year-olds). Girls identified themselves as coming from diverse ethnic and socio-economic backgrounds.

The project uses focus-group interviews and media video. The process involves an initial focus-group discussion of girls' perspectives around the popular culture that they engage with, followed by individual media video diaries (filmed at home) that provide more in-depth accounts about girls' everyday engagement with popular culture. Girls film their media diaries for about ten minutes each day for one month and then gather for a second group discussion that traverses reflections and experiences related to the media diaries. In order to explore potential changes in girls' engagement with popular culture, the research process is repeated in the second year of the project. Guidelines are provided to help girls with filming ideas and to ensure that ethical requirements are adhered to (e.g. around filming).

In this chapter we reflect primarily on focus-group material from the first year of the project (2008). However, we also incorporate some media video diary material produced in the same year to illustrate how this method enabled more reflexive kinds of accounts. Working within a feminist poststructural theoretical framework (see Weedon, 1987) our analyses use a thematic-discursive approach, also referred to as thematic decomposition (see Stenner, 1993). This poststructuralist framework enables us to treat our participants' material as simultaneously productive of notions about sexuality and produced by discourses in circulation in their lived worlds. Our focus in this chapter is on how girls' discursively negotiate the representations of sexuality embodied in the clothing modes of popular culture celebrities they engage with. More specifically we examine how the girls use the 'slut' subjectivity to manage celebrity sexual representation. As an important caveat to our analysis, the discursive constructions of the slut produced in girls' talk are viewed as highly specific to the context of being invited by adult researchers to discuss popular culture and girlhood.

The 'slut' and girls' negotiation of celebrity (un)dress

The 'slut' emerged as a dominant figure in girls' talk about the dress of popular celebrities. Girls across our groups uniformly constructed 'slutty' modes of dress as signified by 'mini skirts', 'low tops', 'bikini' or 'underwear' styles (i.e. midriff baring), and clothes revealing most of the legs: in short any 'skimpy' form of clothing that exposed too much body. A complete absence of clothing, as in nakedness or semi-nakedness, similarly constituted being a 'slut'. Girls' accounts held such representations to be ubiquitous in 'tween' popular culture, resonating with 'porno-chic' (McNair, 2002), 'raunch culture' (Levy, 2005) and a sexual postfeminist sensibility (Gill, 2007). The figure of the 'slut' provided the girls with a discursive strategy to negotiate conflicting discourses of girlhood, for example tensions between 'good' and 'bad' girl femininity/sexuality (Walkerdine, 1990). To illustrate, we examine some of the girls' talk about the Pussycat Dolls and Miley Cyrus both of whom evoked strong opinions.

The Pussycat Dolls

This five piece American girl-band dates back to 1995 when it was a burlesque dance group but was reinvented as a music group in 2003. The Dolls' dominant mode of dress adopts the 'underwear' style described by girls, with crop-tops, bikini-tops, tight fitting short dresses, short 'shorts' and high boots. Such (un)dress has clear connections with both their burlesque billing and with a sexualized postfeminist sensibility (Gill, 2007). However, girls in our study rejected the Dolls' postfeminist 'porno-chic' styled appearances and mobilized the 'slut' figure to constitute the girl-band as morally bereft. The following extract from a group of 12–13-year-old Intermediate girls illustrates this:

Melissa:	'Have you guys seen that Pussycat Dolls, um, that new song?' (Several: 'Yeah, yeah'). 'Their outfits are like, ew.'
Renee:	'They're like – yeah.' (Melissa makes hissing sound like either cat or ripping fabric)
Barhere:	'Put some clothes on.'
Amanda (Interviewer):	'So, you're sort of like, negative on the music videos ...'
Renee:	'Yes, they dress so, like –'
Lisbeth:	Well, some of them are okay but now they're just dressing like, really, like
Renee:	'Slutty.'
Lisbeth:	'Yes, that's the word.'
Charity:	'Idiots.'
Melissa:	'And you know, you know perverts and stuff.' *(giggles, everyone laughs)*

Amanda:	'Oh, yeah, *lots* of them!'
Melissa:	'They, they, they watch those things and they go, "oh, my god", and then they're like'
Barhere:	'It's just like, eww!'
Melissa:	'It's like, it's like, ew!'

The expression 'ew' conveys the girls' sense of disgust with the way that the Pussycat Dolls and other pop stars like them dress. In struggling to find the word to describe the representation, Lisbeth is helped out by Renee who provides the group with the term 'slutty' as a fitting ('yes that's the word') description. Historically, the term 'slut' has long been used by women against women, commonly by way of maintaining or enforcing sexual norms (Attwood, 2007). Attwood notes that for teenage girls in particular, the term is used as a way of branding and excluding other girls, and in this instance the 'slut' provides a strategy for the girls to carefully separate their own subjectivity from the 'sluts' they watch. Such separation may assume particular importance for girls in the context of adult/parental concerns that girls will emulate the sexual dress of pop celebrities. Signalling her awareness of parental concerns, Lindsey (Year 8, Primary), for example, commented, 'it comes back to that whole like, slutty sort of thing, like they don't want us to look at them and stuff, and if we look like that too ...' Both Lindsey's comment and the initial girls' talk about the Pussycat Dolls orient to meanings of the 'slut' around appearance and displays of flesh rather than (hetero) sexual behaviours. However, in the Pussycat Dolls discussion the heterosexual meanings of 'slutty' dress become more apparent through the subsequent mention of 'perverts' which situates the exposed bodies of female pop music icons like the Pussycat Dolls as objects of a sexually deviant gaze. Melissa recognizes the pleasure in the pervert's gaze, her 'oh my god' uttered as an expression of the gazer's lust, not disgust. On the other hand, the notion of a perverted gaze draws disgust from both Melissa and Barhere who give prolonged emphasis to their 'ew' responses. We found 'ew' to be a fairly common way in which girls expressed their disgust with 'skimpy' clothing's signification of sexuality norm violation (i.e. overstepping the boundaries of how much body exposure was deemed appropriate). In addition to disgust, distancing from the 'slut' is also discursively achieved in the girls' talk here through dismissal as an idiotic performance. In other groups too, girls similarly dismissed 'slutty' dress as 'stupid' or 'weird', both of which position them as more smart and sensible than those adopting such styles of dress.

In the video diaries we similarly found examples of girls invoking 'ew' in disgust with what they were viewing on television channel pop music videos. However, the diaries enable us to explore the more embodied and non-verbal responses as evident in this transcript and action description from Amber's video diary:

> 'I don't exactly like the Pussycat Dolls, but... *(A holds the earphone in front of her, twitching it to punctuate her statement.)* I do like – this song. .... I'm not really a fan of actual Pussycat Dolls *(raises earphones, plugs them in again so we can hear the song playing)* but um I, I do like this song, but um, *(sniffs)* I did watch, for a little while, um, who wants to be the next Pussycat Doll or something like that, and, Aisha, I think it was Aisha won, so she's in the Pussycat Dolls, but some of the stuff, man, it's so hard-out, *(makes contemptuous face)* real like, strippy-dippy, it's really gross.' *(wrinkles nose)*

Amber, an 11-year-old Intermediate girl, uses a number of strategies that work to distance her from the Pussycat Dolls throughout her narrative. First, she positions herself as 'not really a fan' and an irregular viewer of their performances. As was fairly typical of other girls, she makes the distinction between liking the song and not liking the girl-band. Finally Amber's disgust signals her disapproval of and distancing from the girl-band's modes of 'strippy-dippy' dress, articulated both verbally in 'really gross' and expressed non-verbally in her 'contemptuous face' and wrinkling her nose.

We found that the elision of 'slutty' clothing with other forms of conveying sexual meaning (e.g. body movement, sexual simulation, self-touching) did not feature in discussion groups, but it did emerge in the occasional girl's video diary. Of particular note, at times when girls did comment about what they were watching it was more likely to be in moments of self-eroticization than in a heterosexual context. Renee (age 13, Intermediate), for example, expressly wanted to draw our focus to an act of self-touching in the Pussycat Dolls video:

> 'See, look, they're like wearing, sort of like, slutty clothes. Wait, and see, she does something soon, I'll show you (singing along) Get it- when I grow up, I wanna be famous, I wanna be a star, I wanna be in movies/ When I grow up-see, look [Points at screen but the action is indiscernible to us] See? She like grabs herself.'

The act of self-eroticism is made noteworthy by Renee's pointing it out to us and inviting us to participate in the audience gaze. In contrast to Renee's enthusiasm for showing us the incident, Alicia vocalized her disgust with a loud 'ew!' at a scene in a Lady Gaga video where the popstar, clad in the clothing style termed 'slutty' by girls, is writhing sexually in a paddling pool. Conversely, however, Alicia made no response to a simulated sexual scene featuring Lady Gaga in between two men. In similar vein, when Lene was watching Katie Perry's video 'I Kissed a Girl', which connotes 'lipstick' lesbianism, she drew our attention to the 'pretty yuck' 's- word' (slutty) 'stuff they're wearing' and not the sexual meanings being produced in the activities of the two women. Significantly, in our view, both Lene and Alicia's disgust responses focus on performances of sexuality constituted outside of normative heterosexuality. One way of reading 'ew' in this instance is that it allows the girls to position themselves as heterosexual. Positioning self as heterosexual assumes particular importance in girls' everyday lives where in Western societies, unlike in popular culture, their sexuality continues to be policed and regulated within constraining heteronormativity (Harris et al., 2000).

Miley Cyrus

While the Pussycat Dolls were constituted as 'slutty' because of their 'skimpy' outfits, Miley's construction as a 'slut' related to a photographic image in *Vanity Fair* (June, 2008). In this representation she was depicted draped in a bed sheet, her back and shoulders bared. The photo-shoot generated considerable discussion amongst the girls across our groups, invariably initiated by them and not by us. Disagreement and debate sometimes characterized girls' discussions; some girls considered the pressure exerted on media stars to seek publicity, others expressed disgust with her appearing 'naked', and a considerably less voiced perspective did not see her photo-shoot as in any way problematic. Although Miley was not actually naked, girls nonetheless described her as such and, uniformly, it was the matter of Miley's nakedness that constructed her as a 'slut'. An extract from one of the Year 8 Intermediate groups (all age 13 except Erica) illustrates:

Erica:	'I don't like Miley Cyrus, anybody' *(inaudible)*
Group:	'Nooooooo'
Alisi:	'Ew, I heard that she, I heard that she took her clothes off'
A:	*'Nobody likes her!'*
Selena:	'Yeah, she did'
Alisi:	'And she was like, and she was like'
Erica:	'She took pictures, she took pictures and sent them to Nick Jonas, I'm like'
Alisi:	'And then her Dad was really mad at her'
Vanessa:	'She's trying to, she's trying to fit in, like'
Alisi:	'She wants to be Rihanna, Rihanna and that'
Vanessa:	'She's just trying to be a slut like everyone else'

As with the Pussycat Dolls, disgust is again mobilized around the (over) exposed body in Alisi's 'ew' about Miley's disrobing. Together the girls exchange information about Miley that assumes a flavour of celebrity gossip in which girls contribute random pieces of knowledge to the discussion. As a general observation, we obtained a sense of celebrity knowledge (whatever its status) working as a kind of cultural currency amongst the girls. Erica's 'currency exchange' here is the information about the cell phone pictures Miley reportedly sent to her boyfriend in which she is not naked but posed rolling up her top to expose her midriff. Both Erica and Alisi's information works to support Vanessa's subsequent construction of Miley as a 'slut'. Moreover, Vanessa appears to show her broad knowledge of celebrity culture in identifying 'being a slut' as the celebrity norm that Miley is aspiring to. Girls' constitution of Miley as a 'slut' may be read as a moment of both resistance and regulation: resistance to the 'hyper-sexualized femininity' endemic in postfeminist popular culture and regulation through a discourse of 'good girl' femininity. Fairclough (2008) observes such regulation of female celebrities (e.g. Britney Spears, Paris Hilton, Lindsay Lohan) through a 'Bitch Culture' discourse that denigrates and misrepresents the women and constructs them as fallen 'bad girls'. She illuminates 'the paradox' that celebrities like Miley are caught in; on the one hand 'encouraged to imitate plastic female stereotypes of postfeminist sexuality' and on the other 'condemned as behaving in morally reprehensible ways'. 'Bitch Culture' discourse provides girls, such as those in our study, with a highly accessible moral discourse that is readily mobilized to account for displays of (postfeminist) sexuality considered to have crossed a normative boundary.

However, girls' moral denigration of Miley as a 'slut' was multilayered and more complex than her state of (un)dress. Miley's character Hannah Montana in the Disney channel television series of the same name featured as a significant foil against which her denigration as a 'slut' could be understood. In the television series, Hannah Montana is an icon of idealized 'good girl' femininity and girls in our study uniformly constructed Cyrus's performance in the part as providing a 'role model' for younger girls. Her 'naked' pose in 'real life' accordingly signified a violation of that status, deeming her to be, in some girls' perspectives, a 'bad influence' on young fans. This construction of Cyrus is illustrated in the following discussion amongst a group of 11-year-old girls (Primary, Year 7).

Cayla: 'For the photo shoot she had a sheet over her and it looked like she only had a sheet she was actually wearing clothes – it was for this teen magazine and everybody said it was really bad and she was only like fifteen and it was a really bad influence on other girls.'

Daria: 'Yeah it went to a *Playboy* magazine and everything.'

Tiina: 'So why has it been a bad influence?'

Unknown: 'It was for this famous New York magazine.'

Cayla: 'Because like she was only like, she was like posing she was kinda like naked with a sheet but she had clothes on underneath.'

Unknown: 'But it looked like she was naked.'

Cayla: 'And she was all posing and stuff.'

The girls' negotiation around Miley's construction as a 'bad girl' is punctuated with tensions and uncertainty. Cayla gives her impression, more than once, of Miley 'actually wearing clothes' underneath the sheet which holds the possibility of redemption if nakedness underlines her degeneration into a 'slut'. On the other hand, it is unclear whether looking naked is equivalent to being naked and accordingly subject to the same regulatory practices of moral reprehension. Nor is it clear that the girls themselves construct Miley as a 'bad girl' who is a 'bad influence' on 'other girls'. Tiina's question asking why Miley is a bad influence goes unanswered. Perhaps the only hint in the girls' talk about the underlying transgression that constructs Miley as a 'bad girl' is Daria's perception of the photo being sent to *Playboy* magazine which alludes to the possibility of it as being sexually risqué, and potentially transgressive or 'bad'. Cayla attributes the 'bad girl' construction to others – 'everybody said' – and it is unclear whether the reference to Miley being 'only 15' and a 'bad influence' is her own opinion or a continuation of what 'everybody said'. Here the regulatory, policing eye of the 'other' ('everybody' and/or perhaps Cayla) deems Cyrus to have violated not only a femininity norm but also an age appropriate norm. Despite rhetoric of Girl Power sexual freedoms, in practice girls' sexuality continues to be under surveillance and regulated (Griffin, 2005). The elision of Miley's young age and her 'bad influence' is also a salient one from the perspective that much of the public outrage following publication of the photograph oriented to Cyrus's particular appeal to and connection with young audiences as a young actress herself. Lindsey (12, Primary School Group) articulates this construction of Miley as a 'bad influence' in the context of her function as a 'role model' for girls (as her Hannah Montana character):

'The thing is, you know, the big thing about Miley Cyrus is that she's like, supposedly the role model because she's set such good examples in the past, you know, and so, to get that – you know. It's not really fair on her. If that's what she wanted to do, then, you know, she does what she wants to do. But if she's being exampled as the role model that's probably not the wisest choice.'

Lindsey's comment demonstrates an awareness of the limits of choice in a postfeminist Girl Power discourse: Miley should be able to do what she wants to but she is constrained by expectations of conformity with notions of 'good girl' femininity (Walkerdine, 1990). In posing 'naked', Miley is seen to have abdicated her responsibility of being a 'role model' for girls and casts her as the 'good girl' turned 'bad'. We want to emphasize the strength of this particular 'good girl' femininity discourse in girls' discussions of Miley's photo-shoot and its significance in underscoring her constitution as a 'slut'. However, such framing of her also needs to be understood in the context of the extensive, largely negative, publicity that the photo-shoot received in which moral discourses and the rhetoric of 'Bitch Culture' circulated widely. For young female celebrities like Miley it seems that any celebration of 'post-feminist' freedom in sexual body display readily slides into their 'downfall', to be cast as 'sluts' or 'fame-whores' (Fairclough, 2008).

Conclusion

In this chapter we have explored the ways in which girls' talk about (un) dress codes of the female celebrities they engage with works as a site for the production and negotiation of subjectivities. Girls' constructions of the Pussycat Dolls and Miley Cyrus as 'sluts', signified through clothing that implicitly or explicitly exposed too much of their bodies, simultaneously allowed girls to position themselves as 'other'. In other words, 'good girl' femininity was not compromised by enjoying the music or watching 'slutty' celebrities. Disgust worked as a strategy for girls' careful negotiation of the 'slut'. We found some resonance here with Susan Miller's (2004) psychological theorization of disgust as inhabiting the border between notions of self as 'good' and notions of self as 'bad'. Where that disgust cohered around acts of auto eroticism and girl–girl sexual performance rather than hetero-sexuality, it enabled girls to position self as heterosexual. Like disgust, moral condemnation similarly enabled girls to mark out the border between self and 'slut'. Posing in a bed sheet for a magazine violated not only 'good girl' femininity but also role model expectations ('bad influence') and age norms for body exposure. However, we do not wish to imply that girls made use of discursive distancing strategies – disgust and moral condemnation – in a straightforward, uncomplicated way. To the contrary, there were sometimes conflicting, contradictory accounts, elusive notions and hedged opinions. Such variation and tension are a reminder that 'bad' girls may not always be condemned as such, and that the 'slutty' representation in one video may be countered in a recuperation move in another context (see Bell, 2008).

Nonetheless at the point of time when the discussions took place, the constitution of the 'slut' appeared to have a strong hold in girls' accounts of celebrity style and (un)dress. Girls' mobilization of the 'slut' is particularly interesting in the context of anxieties about girls aspiring to emulate sexual styles and behaviour depicted in popular culture. Rather than making meanings of the celebrity's representations within a postfeminist discourse of fun-loving, sexually empowered freedom (Gill, 2007), girls, to the contrary, rejected such meanings through invoking the 'slut'. In doing so they harness a regulatory arm of policing conventional 'good girl' femininity (i.e. the 'slut') to disrupt some of the sexuality meanings produced in post-feminist discourse. In their research with 'tweenage' and teen girls Renolds and Ringrose (2008) similarly found this binary of the 'good girl' and the 'othered' 'slut' functioning to resist 'hyper-feminine, hyper-sexualized embodiments' (as in girls' clothing). The knotty intertwining of resistance and regulation presents a challenge for feminist researchers and theorists. On the one hand, the notion of girls' critical engagement with postfeminist media and rejection of postfeminist sexuality performances can be seen as encouraging and positive; a foil to the idea that girls are easily influenced by popular culture and aspire to emulate its celebrities. On the other hand, if old gender binaries are resurrected to enable such resistance, the 'line of flight' (Renolds and Ringrose, 2008) is problematic. For those of us who work with girls, the challenge is to encourage and assist them to critique the postfeminist media subject in ways that do not rely on the gender binary.

Acknowledgements

We wish to acknowledge the Royal Society of New Zealand Marsden Fund for the financial support of the research project 'Girls, "tween" popular culture and everyday life'.

Note

1. We use quotes around the term 'tween' to denote its construction by North American marketers in the 1980s 'as an ambiguous, age-delineated marketing and merchandising category' (Cook and Kaiser, 2004) that is so broad (7–14) as to be relatively meaningless. In references to our own material we use the term 'pre-teen' that, while still a construction, is more specific to our 11–13-year-old girls. Additionally, it avoids the sometimes sensationalized meanings surrounding the term 'tween'.

Bibliography

American Psychological Association, Task Force on the Sexualization of Girls (2007) Report of the APA Task Force on the Sexualization of Girls (Washington, DC: American Psychological Association). Available at www.apa.org/pi/wpo/sexualization.html

Attwood, I. (2005) 'Fashion and Passion: Marketing Sex to Women', *Sexualities* 8(4): 392–406.

Attwood, F. (2007) 'Sluts and Riot Grrrls: Female Identity and Sexual Agency', *Journal of Gender Studies* 16: 233–7.

Baker, S. (2004) 'Pop in(to) the Bedroom: Popular Music in Pre-Teen Girls' Bedroom Culture', *European Journal of Cultural Studies* 7: 75–93.

Bell, E. (2008) ' "From Bad Girl to Mad Girl": British Female Celebrity, Reality Products and the Pathologisation of Pop-Feminism', *Genders OnLine Journal* 48.

Boden, S. (2006) 'Dedicated Followers of Fashion? The Influence of Popular Culture on Children's Social Identities', *Media Culture & Society* 28: 289–98.

Cook, D. and S. Kaiser (2004) ' "Betwixt and Be Tween": Age Ambiguity and the Sexualisation of the Female Consuming Subject', *Journal of Consumer Culture* 4: 203–27.

Durham, M. G. (2008) *The Lolita Effect* (Woodstock, NY: Overlook Press).

Egan, R. D. and G. Hawke (2008) 'Girls' Sexuality and the Strange Carnalities of Advertisements: Deconstructing the Discourse of Corporate Paedophilia', *Australian Feminist Studies* 23: 307–22.

Fairclough, K. (2008) 'Fame Is a Losing Game: Celebrity Gossip Blogging, Bitch Culture and Postfeminism', *Genders OnLine Journal* 48.

Gill, R. (2007) 'Postfeminist Media Culture: Elements of a Sensibility', *European Journal of Cultural Studies* 10: 147–66.

Gleeson, K. and H. Frith (2004) 'Pretty in Pink: Young Women Presenting Mature Sexual Identities' in Anita Harris (ed.), *All About the Girl: Culture, Power and Identity* (London: Routledge).

Griffin, C. (2004) 'Good Girls, Bad Girls: Anglocentricism and Diversity in the Constitution of Contemporary Girlhood' in A. Harris (ed.), *All About the Girl: Culture, Power and Identity* (London: Routledge).

Griffin, C. (2005) 'Impossible Spaces? Femininity as an Empty Category', *ESRC Research Seminar Series: New Femininities*. Available at www.lse.uk/collections/newfemininities

Hamilton, M. (2007) *What's Happening to our Girls?* (Camberwell, Victoria: Viking, Penguin).

Harris, A., S. Aapola and M. Gonick (2000) 'Doing it Differently: Young Women Managing Heterosexuality in Australia, Finland and Canada', *Journal of Youth Studies* 3: 373–88.

Lamb, S. and L. Brown (2006) *Packaging Girlhood* (New York: St. Martin's Press).

Levy, A. (2005) *Female Chauvinist Pigs: Women and the Rise of Raunch Culture* (New York: Free Press).

Levy, D. and J. Kilbourne (2008) *So Sexy So Soon: The New Sexualised Childhood and What Parents Can Do to Protect their Kids* (New York: Random House).

Machin, D. and J. Thornborrow (2003) 'Branding and Discourse: The Case of *Cosmopolitan*', *Discourse & Society* 14: 453–71.

Malson, H., Marshall H. and A. Woollett (2002) 'Talking of Taste: A Discourse Analytic Exploration of Young Women's Gendered and Racialised Subjectivities in British Urban, Multicultural Contexts', *Feminism & Psychology* 12: 469–90.

McNair, B. (2002) *Striptease Culture: Sex, Media and the Democratisation of Desire* (London: Routledge).

McRobbie, A. (2008) 'Young Women and Consumer Culture', *Cultural Studies* 22: 531–50.

McRobbie, A. (2009) *The Aftermath of Feminism: Gender, Culture and Social Change* (London: Sage).

Miller, S. (2004) *Disgust: The Gatekeeper Emotion* (Mahwah, NJ: Analytic Press).

Projansky, S. (2007) 'Mass Magazine Cover Girls: Some Reflections on Postfeminist Girls and Postfeminism's Daughters' in Y. Tasker and D. Negra (eds), *Interrogating Postfeminism: Gender and the Politics of Popular Culture* (Durham and London: Duke University Press).

Renolds, E. and J. Ringrose (2008) 'Regulation and Rupture: Mapping Tween and Teenage Girls' Resistance to the Heterosexual Matrix', *Feminist Theory* 9: 313–38.

Rush, E. and A. Nauze (2006) *Corporate Paedophilia: Sexualisation of Children in Australia*. Discussion Paper No. 90. Available at www.tai.org.au/documents/downloads/DP90.pdf

Stenner, P. (1993) 'Discoursing Jealousy' in E. Burman and I. Parker (eds), *Discourse Analytic Research: Repertoires and Readings of Texts in Action* (London: Routledge).

Walkerdine, V. (1990) *Schoolgirl Fictions* (London: Verso).

Weedon, C. (1987) *Feminist and Poststructuralist Theory* (Oxford: Basil Blackwell).

9
Is 'the Missy' a New Femininity?

JongMi Kim

Introduction

In the early 1990s, a new term emerged to refer to young married women in Korea. The term is *'Missy'*, which means a young married woman who dresses like and presents herself as an unmarried woman. Married women have begun to identify themselves with the term instead of the traditional title, *'Adjumma'*[1] because they do not want to take on the traditionally associated images and lifestyle implied by this title, especially ageing and dowdiness. The novel term *Missy* originated from a small advertising campaign to promote a department store in the early 1990s. It rapidly became widespread in different components of the Korean media and has been redefined to refer to young and attractive married women who want to look like unmarried women and share their lifestyle and attitudes. This has caused huge controversy amongst social commentators and feminist scholars, who argue about how to understand this explosive concept.

In order to examine whether *Missy* can be understood as a form of new femininity, I will first describe the origins and prevalence of the concept *'Missy'* in the media and how the rapid spread of this figure became a subject of controversy amongst social scientists, including feminist scholars in South Korea. Moreover, I will analyse my own empirical interview data[2] to discuss precisely how women aged between 20 and 40 really construct their femininities using the concept of the *Missy* derived from the media and adapted to their own experiences and preferences.

Emergence of the *Missy*

In 1994, a small-scale advertising campaign for one of the major department stores in Seoul made a great cultural impact in South Korea. In the advertisement, copywriters invented a novel term, *Missy*. It is a combined term, which means 'married women who look unmarried'. In the advertisement, the main slogan was 'I am a *Missy*, the *Missy* is different'. It has been widely used and rapidly came to represent an alternative lifestyle for women. Even the copywriter was surprised at the speed with which this term took on a social meaning and the way in which it has come to evoke a specific image of women and femininity (Lee, 2002, p. 149).

This new figure was not only the product of a marketing campaign but was also related to the general conditions underpinning the emergence of a new concept of femininity, influenced by globalized images of femininity and by changing economic conditions. In South Korea, the concept of married femininity changed as the number of working women increased with industrialization during the 1970s and 1980s. During this period, there was a general tendency for women to have more opportunity to undertake higher education and pursue their own career. The *Missy* refers to young married women who were born in the 1960s, and grew up in the 1970s under the military dictatorship. Because of industrialization and huge labour migration from rural areas to big cities like Seoul, most of them lived in urban settings and grew up in nuclear families. This generation received from 10.37 years (women) to 11.78 years (men) of education on average (Kang, 1996, p. 594). When this generation became young adults in the 1980s, many of them supported and became involved in the democratic movement against the military regime. From this experience, the whole generation tended to be somehow more socially sensitive and active than any other generation in the South Korean history (Moon, 2005, pp. 102–3).

The initial response from society to the advertising campaign which invented the term *Missy* was very enthusiastic. Consumers, in particular young housewives, embraced the concept and identified themselves with the term. The prevailing image of the *Missy* was immediately absorbed by the mass media, as much as it had been promoted and influenced by media in the first place. The widespread popularity of the new image in media representation in the 1990s accelerated in film and television drama. The genres of Western melodrama and romantic films were being recycled and translated into the South Korean cultural context, with the *Missy* as one key translated image from Western images of femininity.

For example, the figure of the *Missy* became more popular and a subject of controversy when a television drama, *The Lover* (*Aein*, director: Changsoon Lee, MBC, 1996), was broadcast in September 1996. It was about an extramarital love story of two successful professionals in their mid-thirties. The drama had an enormous impact on society. The audience rating reached 36.3 per cent in October 1996 (Kim, 1996). Thousands of husbands made enquiries at the telephone office to check their wives' call list to see if they were having affairs (Lee, 2003). The actress who had the role of the heroine in the drama, Sin-Hye Hwang, became another icon of the *Missy*. In addition, the motto of the drama, 'beautiful immorality' became a very popular phrase at the time.

Since *The Lover* first raised the issue of the extramarital affair, many films and dramas have flourished. The difference between *The Lover* and the post-*Lover* films and dramas is perhaps that the sexual relations and discourses are more openly implicated and described in later projects. The director of *The Lover* made the extramarital affair a romantic fantasy but did not depict sexual relations. However, the post-*Lover* films and dramas put the sexual relationship at the centre. Furthermore, the *Missy* is always located in the central stage of the extramarital affair and, as such, liberal sexual attitudes have become the main property of the *Missy*. Lee So-Hee pointed out that the story of the extramarital affair has experimented with the possibility of recognizing a new morality governing middle-aged wives' subjective sexuality and individuality. The social discourse around these kinds of films and drama show that female sexuality in modern Korea conflicts with the Confucian ideas of fidelity and chastity (Lee, 2002, pp. 157–8). In this context of media representation, it is easy to suggest that the concept of the *Missy* has replaced the old concept of the wives, or *Adjumma*, as the one with which married women identify themselves.

Other films have further built upon this tendency to increasingly provide spaces for women's desires and characters and scenarios within which they can identify themselves as the *Missy* and arguably as reflecting certain aspects of globalized images of femininity. In the previous media representations, women having an extramarital affair (or love affair) used to end up being tragically killed or committing suicide. Moreover, the woman who is seeking fulfilment of her sexual desire was described as a kind of hybrid monster. As So-Young Kim, the feminist film critic describes, in the post-*Aeln* period, the image of women has radically shifted and the mass media attempt to represent women's voices (Kim, 1998). The common theme of those films and dramas is that they are beginning to show female sexual desires, more confidence and self-awareness.

The *Missy* representations in these films and TV dramas contribute to the popularity of *Missy* as an alternative lifestyle for women. The connotations of these film and drama images are that heroines are self-confident, career oriented and desirable lovers. Young women have taken up these images and used them in the process of constructing their own alternative identities, coming to refer to themselves as *Missy*, reworking and replacing the image of *Adjumma*. Given the increasing significance of this image, it is, therefore, perhaps opportune to examine the process of its emergence, as I attempt to do below.

Controversy over the *Missy*: media masquerade or real subject?

The Missy as a pseudo-reality of commercialism

Since her emergence as a powerful new figure, the *Missy* has been a subject of debate amongst social scientists and feminists in South Korea reflecting varying opinions regarding the many pros and cons of the real – or otherwise – entity of the specific group of women – the *Missies*. Many comment that the concept of the *Missy* is an illusory entity only driven by the dominant force of consumerism since it was invented and promoted solely for the purpose of commercial advertising. Hence, critics of the *Missy* claim that it is a fabricated concept, which creates more powerful images of 'superwomen': progressive and modern characters, rejecting old and traditional conservative ideas, and influenced both by a changing Korean social context and by global media images and consumerism. This critical position can be found in the argument of a leading feminist in South Korea, Young-Ja Lee (2000). In her analysis of the phenomenon of the *Missy*, she argues that the *Missy* is an illusory and pseudo reality, which was encouraged by the mass media. Women are exposed repeatedly to the concept through advertisements and mass media representations. According to her analysis, 'at the moment of the advertised image turning into real character, nobody can make sense of whether the *Missy* is a commercial by-product or voluntarily constituted genuine entity' (Lee, 2000, p. 60).

This type of criticism is reminiscent of similar arguments around the construction of new femininity in Western contexts, resonating particularly with the 'yummy mummy'. It is argued that new femininity emphasizes self-surveillance, monitoring and discipline. Moreover, criticism of new femininity not only focuses on individualism, choice and empowerment, but also emphasizes consumerism and the commodification of difference (Gill and Arthurs, 2006; McRobbie, 2006). This important contribution from the West reveals how and where feminism is attempting to understand consumption and new femininity within the processes of global capitalism and is similar to how the *Missy* has been understood as new femininity in the South Korean context of globalization. In particular, understandings and criticisms of the concept of the *Missy* by feminists have centred on this aspect of consumerism and commodification of difference, rather than an actual assessment of the restrictions facing married women in South Korea. However, this critical view of the *Missy* is perhaps only based on two-dimensional feminist ideas, in which young women as mass consumers are seen simply as the dopes or victims of consumerism with functional needs and no desires of their own. Such views ignore the process of the active transformation of women. From this perspective, the *Missy* is not thought to be seeking and constructing her identity actively. Indeed, if one followed this type of critical analysis, the women's subject position would probably disappear. Instead, the subject formation seems only to be regarded as an object oppressed by commercialism and the patriarchal system and this contributes to the phenomenon that women's subject formation in global capitalism is often overlooked.

In this chapter, the study of cultural practice requires studying 'macrological alliances' and the 'micrologies' of women's subject positions in order to understand that their position can be actively transformed, rather than being merely an object of oppression by consumer forces. The practice as *Missy* can perhaps best be seen as a meeting point where multiple factors constitutes the subject-cultural practice and their inherent temporalities. Of course, the *Missy* was originally formulated and encouraged by the support of consumerism and mass media. In addition, it is perhaps valid to state that the image of the career oriented and 'unmarried-look-a-like' housewives was initially just an illusion. However, if we entirely accept South Korean feminists' criticisms (Cho, 2002; Lee, 2000) and the Western feminists' criticism (Gill and Arthurs; McRobbie, 2006) of women's position within global capitalism, then there would be no possibility of the actor committing to, or participating in, her own transformation of identity. In practice, the images of the *Missy* portrayed by commercialism and mass media may open up women's imagination to the possibilities of building a new identity that expresses their desires and self-realization. According to Kaplan (1995), 'it would be difficult to find subjects not interpellated in the world making activity of consumption ... [we need] studies of corporate practices, site of consumption and subject formation ... without account for agency, resistance, subjectivity ... without constructing narratives of oppositional binaries' (p. 61). Similarly, I would argue that the practices of *Missy* are perhaps constituted culturally and mediated by women's own active social relations. As I will attempt to show, it seems clear that the women are well aware of the situations in which they are positioned and are choosing their identity based on self-realization as well as cooperating with consumerism.

Therefore, it seems that thus far feminist analysis of the *Missy* phenomenon has overlooked the possibility of women's subject formation in constructing their identities. With the deficiencies of these main competing critiques of the *Missy* discussed above, it would be helpful therefore at this point to return to my empirical data and the revelations of young women themselves to discover if a more convincing explanation can be found in their own voices.

Is *Missy* a new femininity?

In the series of interviews with 101 women aged between 20 and 40, I raised the issue of the *Missy* in several lines of questioning relating to who the *Missy* is, what the definition of *Missy* is, and how informants identify themselves with *Missy*. Most married women who I interviewed clearly expressed their desire to be *Missy*. One of the informants remarked, 'I would love to be a *Missy* and I would love to be seen as a *Missy*.'

As seen, the central definition of *Missy* refers to married women who want to look like unmarried women (*Agassi*). Although their marital status is that of married women who expect to perform all the duties conducted inside and outside of their house, in a sense, they still want to be considered as unmarried women. In other words, the *Missy* transcends the marital status boundary from married to unmarried women, as an attractive, sexy and youthful identity.

At a glance, the *Missy* can be a technique of visual knowledge identified in dress and body codes. The visual technique is perhaps the best way of a woman masquerading as unmarried. As such, the *Missy* can be regarded visually as an 'unmarried woman' by adopting or assuming her style. On this point, the visual technique of the *Missies'* appearance seems to demonstrate how such masquerading brings into play contingent, complex and negative identification to *Adjumma*, as revealed in the informant's revelation below.

If the *Missy* is an identity that contains the desire to masquerade as unmarried women (*Agassi*), why is marital disguising a significant desire for young women in the contemporary South Korean context? It may be because, young women reject the traditional image of the 'wise mother and good wife', represented by the *Adjumma*. *Adjumma* was the universalized concept used to refer to married women as the signifier. However, the concept, *Adjumma*, has been associated with a long list of expected codes of conduct for women, which are only accomplished by sacrificing herself in favour of her family. Thus, the image has become unattractive for a generation that wants to embrace women's desires and the pursuit of self-realization. In the contemporary context which incorporates influences from a changing consumer society and from a globalized media context, the image of married women that they now wish to portray encompasses their desire to prolong self-realization and development, as they did before marriage. The newly created concept of the *Missy* for women in the late 20s and 30s age group is similar to that of the *Agassi* who may have more freedom and power to control their own lives.

The meaning of *Missy* is articulated in the meanings the informants attach to the practices involved. When most informants talk about the *Missy*, their descriptions sketch the abstract visual images of the *Missy* (fashion, appearance, style and age) which perhaps reflect, and are reflected by, consumer and media images, then move to describing the image of *Adjumma*, and finally returning to the *Missy* to define it as a counterpart to, and rebellious of, the concept of *Adjumma*.

Indeed, the *Missy* has been presented as embodying confidence and, as noted earlier, as putting their energy into self-cultivation/their appearance/ improvement of their own life. The following interview shows clearly what young Korean women think about the *Missy*:

HE: 'I think I am a *Missy* because I am investing a lot of energy for my inner and external development to have my own satisfaction. For *Missy*, her weight of life is more centred on herself rather than husband or children.'

Q: 'What is difference between the *Adjumma* and *Missy*?'

HE: 'I think the *Adjumma* is someone who is loose and careless about her life, only thinking about her husband and child. Unlike *Adjumma*, the *Missy* is keeping up tensions in everyday life.'

Q: 'What does it mean, tension?'

HE: 'Well ... tension, I think, is the motivation to develop my life.'

(Full-time housewife, age 34)

As can be seen, the informant points out what the *Missy* means from her point of view, which includes one of the main definitions that the *Missy* is more focused on her own development rather than family affairs or rearing children. However, despite the prevalence of the image in the media, it seems not possible to define it without comparison with the concept of *Adjumma*. From the extract, it is noticeable that there is a precise difference between the *Missy* and *Adjumma*, namely tensions in everyday life. The informant thinks that the *Adjumma* is careless and not interested in taking care of herself, whereas the *Missy* is always maintaining her consciousness in terms of motivating her life. Thus, if the *Missy* can be seen as opposed or in opposition to the *Adjumma* discourse, it is in the process of making visible the fractured identities of old femininities.

By contrast, the informant in the following interview is usually identified as a *Missy* but sometimes she identifies herself with *Adjumma* when she behaves 'wrongly':

S: 'I never had been called *Adjumma* till that moment; people usually called me a *Missy* even when I had my second son, Joonyoung. One day, I was stuck in a terrible traffic jam on my way back home. So I tried to change my direction, and drove my car into a private car park although I was aware that I should not. At that moment, one guy shouted at me "*Adjumma!* You should not park your car here". I was thinking at the moment, yes, that's right, I am *Adjumma*.'

(Full-time housewife, age 37)

The appearance of this informant may be that of a *Missy*, as she identifies herself, but her identity can shift between *Adjumma* and *Missy* in different instances. The informant allowed the man to call her *Adjumma* when she noticed that she broke a rule in the parking lot. Therefore, in her construction, the *Adjumma* image seems to be closely related to negative behaviour not just a negative appearance, while the *Missy* image is associated with the positive and active side of her everyday life. This can read in the same way as other historical examples of 'passing' – as the forming of identity marked by permeable boundaries; i.e. the anxiety of being 'misread' or 'correctly read'. The informant above does not want to be an *Adjumma*. However, although the images can be seen as oppositional, in real practice, both identities are intermingled and coexist, showing that the two concepts are situation-dependent. As an unresolved identity of competing femininities, the *Missy* refers to imagined identities compounded with uncertainty, insecurity and anxiety. Thus, the *Missy* identities are competing by which it can be seen that new femininities have not yet arrived and have not been fully realized but rather are represented in a competing and conflicting image. When most informants talk about the *Missy*, their descriptions sketch the abstract visual images of the *Missy*, move to describing the images of *Adjumma*, and finally return to the *Missy* to define it as a counterpart of *Adjumma*.

In fact, the whole process of struggling to define new identities starts with the crisis of the old images of married women as a result of global transformations and new images of femininity. The old images of married women cannot fulfil what women desire and accomplish. The existing concept and images of married women with *Adjumma* have been too uniform and fixed to offer a solution to the crisis. At this point, the action they take is mimicking the unmarried women who are categorized as *Agassi* and masquerading as unmarried. Indeed, in this instance, what women appear to want is to be gazed at by the other in an 'intentional misrecognition' between married and unmarried women.

The in-and-out-ness of the *Missy*

One intriguing point I found emerging in my interviews is that although informants retain the name of the *Missy* to express their identities, the actual identity formation is not exactly what many social scientists have described nor precisely that portrayed by the media. Rather, they are constructing the formation itself by approximating the given package of the *Missy* and withdrawing from it. This in-and-out-ness of the *Missy* identity shows the complexity with which the informants are struggling and contesting with married femininities in contemporary society. Furthermore, it should be noted that this in-and-out-ness seems to be totally based on locally contingent contexts. There is no simple informants' reading of *Missy* representation in the media and the informants tactically use the resources including given packages of the *Missy* and *Adjumma* images in order to constitute their identities.

For example, the following interview observes that informants endorse, hesitate and refuse some facets of the *Missy*. Some informants reject aspects of the *Missy* and contextualize her within their own perspective.

IK: 'I don't think I am a *Missy*.'
Q: 'Why do you think you are not?'
IK: 'I am not following that trendy way.'
Q: 'You don't follow ... ?'
IK: 'I am not interested in decorating my appearance.'

Q: 'Do you think the *Missy* is all about appearance?'
IK: 'Yes, probably, about appearance. I don't like to stay home looking humble without any make-up. I really want to wear make-up when I am home and go to the supermarket. I never wear humble clothes.'
Q: 'You mean you think you are the *Missy*, don't you?'
IK: 'I think that when I am working... maybe having a lover.' *[laughing]*
Q: 'Do you think it is better to be the *Missy*?'
DY: 'Yes, I think I should decorate myself very well when I go out.'
Q: 'What do you think?'
SB: 'I never decorate myself. Those who are trendy are progressive like that although I am so far from interested in being the *Missy*.'
(Full-time housewives, ages 27–33)

The focus-group above shows interesting reactions to the concept of *Missy* from each informant: the informant IK clearly shows her ambivalent attitude towards the concept, although she is consciously mocking it. She is cautious and hesitating to commit to the *Missy* concept fully because she is aware of its superficial character. However, her ambivalence towards the image is also revealed: she is stepping in and out of the boundary of the *Missy* by remarking that she does not like to be seen as following the trendy way but actually she expresses her desire to have an attractive appearance. By contrast, informant DY reinscribes the *Missy* as being about appearance. Furthermore, the informant SB does not identify herself at all as *Missy*. The informants' discussion as to whether or not they identify with the *Missy* is competing. They do not want to accept the given image of *Missy* in terms of being purely about appearance. The informants seem aware of criticisms of the *Missy* as a consumer dope. From the interview, it is interesting to see that the *Missy* does not seem to provide a clear negotiation point for the formation of identities. In fact, the characteristic of appearance is probably not providing a negotiation point. This may be partly because people are consciously aware of the origin of the concept, which was, has been, and still is closely associated with consumerism. However, as informant IK and SB revealed cautiously, they still have desires to resurface their self-identities and desires, which are still latent and are only reluctantly exposed, if at all, in the interview. In that sense, the *Missy* does not represent a safe and settled boundary. Rather, it is what they want to be, without having any safe harbour.

Without a safe harbour, the discourse of the *Missy* reaches an ambivalent position. The informants interact within the *Missy* discourse. According to the informants, the contents of the *Missy* are 'self-cultivating' and 'keeping tight'. The *Missy* has a self-centred lifestyle, rather than a victim of self-sacrifice, and she invests in her own development. The following extract shows how the informants can put on and take off the *Missy*, each reinventing the concept from their own point of view, and contextualizing it from their own position.

Q: 'Do you think you are *Missy*? Or are you identifiable with *Missy*? Do you think people recognize you as a *Missy*? With regard to your previous discussion, you don't seem to want to be called *Missy*.'

DW: 'I would love to be called the *Missy*. Sometimes, I am suspicious about the concept of *Missy*. I can imagine *Missy*'s house would be messy and untidy. She is focusing on herself only, while she is not doing proper domestic work. The domestic work may not be her priority. She could escape from all domestic obligations. She is only taking care of her appearance and her improvement. Selfish woman!'

(Full-time housewife, age 39)

The informant above clearly also has ambivalent feelings about *Missy*. She likes to be called *Missy*, but she shows her anxiety and prioritizes the domestic work as her obligation. She therefore seems to be struggling and oscillating between a self-sacrificing character as old identity and a selfish woman as new identity. For her, the *Missy* image is described as only taking care of herself and neglecting her domestic work. What the informant imagines being the *Missy* image may be too selfish for her to identify with. In her remarks, the boundaries between her personal and family boundaries are separated and the separation seems to cause some struggle and hesitations. In this sense, she is still stepping in and out of boundaries.

Conclusion

This chapter has explored the emergence of the figure of the *Missy* in Korean media. Whilst emerging from an advertising campaign the *Missy* has captured the imagination of Korean society and become a site of contested identification for many women in their 30s. Such women do not unthinkingly adapt this identity as passive dopes, but rather take it up, negotiate it and resist it.

Thus, the *Missy* is here the fantasy of ability – or a technique to become without adopting or taking on signifiers of the subordinated other – *Missy* therefore becomes a mechanism for reconstituting or reproducing the other as the 'not-*Adjumma*' from within, rather than beyond, the structure of the *Adjumma*. If *Missy* is coming out in antagonism to *Adjumma*, we can then possibly regard the emergence of the concept *Missy* as not an entirely alternative concept to pre-existing terms that refer to feminine identities in South Korea, although many women attempt to identify themselves with the *Missy* category. However, on the other hand, the image of *Missy* is not firmly harboured to any existing categories like *Adjumma* or *Agassi*, meaning that it is not possible to find any secure ground to explain the new identity formation such as economic class or political preference. *Missy* could, therefore, be a product of consumerism, of transformation of *Adjumma* or a representation of new femininity. None of these is clear. However, what is clear is that for informants *Missy* is an imagined, unsettled and unfixed term, one that is under construction and not one which is simply imposed as a ready-made package by the media and consumerism.

Therefore, I suggest that within the multitude and shifting images described here the informants' desire was not in the first place merely the product of Western mass media, but in fact emerged from their own negotiation with their positions in their own context. Finally, this in-and-out-ness of the *Missy* identity shows the complexity of how the informants are struggling and contesting with married femininities in South Korea. This can most clearly be seen in the way the interview data reveal that informants endorse, hesitate and refuse some factors of the *Missy*. Furthermore, as shown, the open discourse of their newly expressed desires is accompanied by their negotiation of marital life. This desire is still undecided, is perhaps never going to be decided, and is based on their imagination. It can be said that it is a 'space of dream' or 'paradoxical space' – never settled or defined. In other words, the *Missy* could be best understood as a conjuncture of conflicting desire and new femininity, continually in the process of transformation.

Notes

1. The conventional category used to refer to housewives in South Korea is *Adjumma*. Literally, *Adjumma* means a distant female relative, usually older and married. It is, however, used in a more general fashion as a convenient title for any older female, usually past her thirties and presumed to be married with children. Nevertheless, this general meaning referring to married and old women has changed significantly in recent years. In particular, through the industrialization process since the 1960s, the meaning of the term gradually shifted from being a positive and general term to one that is negative and derogatory. The term, *Adjumma*, now often connotes "audacious", "unconsidered", "unashamed" and "ignorant" femininities. Even their appearances can be seen to be typified as such, often represented with short, permed hair, tattooed eyebrows and clown-like make-up.
2. This empirical research was conducted in South Korea between 1999 and 2000. During my fieldwork, I interviewed 101 women in 21 group interviews and individual interviews.

Bibliography

Cho, H. (2002) 'Living with Conflicting Subjectivities: Mother, Motherly Wife, and Sexy Woman in the Transition from Colonial-Modern to Postmodern Korea' in L. Kendall (ed.), *Under Construction: The Gendering of Modernity, Class and Consumption in the Republic of Korea* (Honolulu: University of Hawaii Press).

Gill, R. and J. Arthurs (2006) 'Editor's Introduction: New Femininities?', *Feminist Media Studies* 6(4): 443–51.

Kang, I.-S. (1996) *The Challenged Generation: The Fifties in South Korea* (in Korean) (Seoul: Tonga Ilbosa).

Kaplan, C. (1995) 'A World without Boundaries: The Body Shop's Trans/national Geography', *Social Text* 43: 45–66.

Kim, H.-R. (1996) 'Missy Looks Become Common', (in Korean) *News Review* (20 January): 30–1.

Kim, S.-Y. (1998) 'Questions of Women's Film: The Maid, Madame Freedom, and Women' in C. Choi (ed.), *Post-Colonial Classics of Korean Cinema* (Irvine, CA: Korean Film Festival Committee at the University of California, Irvine).

Lee, J. H. (2003) 'Pleasure Seekers Stand on the Edge: Review of Love Affair Films', (in Korean), *Hankyoreh* 21(467), 17 July. Available at http://www.hani.co.kr/section-021 015000/2003/07/021015000200307090467023.html [accessed 20 July 2003].

Lee, S.-H. (2002) 'The Concept of Female Sexuality in Korean Popular Culture' in L. Kendall (ed.), *Under Construction: The Gendering Modernity, Class and Consumption in the Republic of Korea* (Honolulu: University of Hawaii Press).

Lee, Y.-J. (2000) *Men and Women in Consumer-Capitalist Society*, (in Korean) (Seoul: Nanam Publishers).

Lynch, M. (1985) *Art and Artifact in Laboratory Science: A Study of Shop Work and Shop Talk in a Research Laboratory* (London: Routledge & Kegan Paul).

McRobbie, A. (2006) 'Young Women's Illegal Rage', paper presented at the conference, World Girl in Global Frame (Goldsmiths College, University of London).

Moon, S. (2005) *Militarised Modernity and Gendered Citizenship in South Korea* (Durham: Duke University Press).

Part III
Textual Complications

10

Of Displaced Desires: Interrogating 'New' Sexualities and 'New' Spaces in Indian Diasporic Cinema

Brinda Bose

> [W]ith the close-up, space expands; with slow motion, movement is extended. The enlargement of a snapshot does not render more precise what in any case was visible, though unclear: it reveals entirely new formations of the subject.
>
> Walter Benjamin, 'The Work of Art in the Age of Mechanical Reproduction' (1969, p. 236)

Cinema, extending (or reconfiguring, if one will) the still photograph, offers a new point of departure for a discussion on ways in which space and movement function in the representation of images. If Benjamin is talking, here, of the close-up shot as a technical innovation that transforms what we see and how we see it, I will attempt to read the cinematic apparatus itself as a 'close-up', that identifies particular moments in time and space and places them in a narrative of images, not necessarily rendering them 'more precise' but revealing, instead, 'entirely new formations of the subject'. Anna Friedberg has used Benjamin's formulation to understand the role of cinema in postmodernity (1991, p. 419); I will look at cinema as a postmodernist intervention in the diasporic condition – so caught in complexities of time, space and motion – and attempt to read patterns of changing sexualities in the context of such shifting gazes and spaces.

In the Indian context, I believe it is useful to study the affects and effects of the modernizing impulse on 'new' sexualities in 'new' urban/diasporic/globalized spaces both as they are read and represented in cinema as well as in how the cinema itself participates in the production of certain understandings – and enactments – of social changes and transitions. The city – and by imaginative extension, the diasporic/globalized space – has occupied an ambivalent position in the Indian nationalist imaginary throughout the process of nation-building since India achieved independence in 1947, often a confrontational as well as a contemplative site that

161

signifies 'modernity' and its concurrent promise as well as its ills, in relation to the traditional ethics of a very old culture. Non-normative sexualities, which have always occupied a liminal space in socio-political configurations, make this site one of both empowerment through transgression and containment through regulation. The 'new' (or newer) Indian cinemas, I suggest, become a critical site for the mapping of a convergence of anxieties about urbanity/globality/modernity/sexuality, making the cinematic text itself a cultural, sociological and intellectual intervention in this process of the making, breaking or shifting of identities in post-independence India. Indian diasporic cinema plays a unique role in this process; it may be said to constitute the 'Other' which indigenous Indian cinema both talks to and positions as a point of reference, the insider/outsider figure whose interventions are significant and need to be engaged with.

In considering some of the better-known work of two Indian diasporic filmmakers, Mira Nair and Gurinder Chadha, I will attempt here to frame questions of the anxieties around urbanity, globality and sexuality along the axes that diaspora offers, particularly in contexts of 'home' – as a site of memory, longing, nostalgia, desire – by tracking four films along a trajectory of insider/outsider commentary over about fifteen years (1991–2007) that focus on the Indian diasporic space in the United States and in England, and both read and reveal it as a contested site for 'home'-grown predicaments. In the course of this exploration, I would like to suggest that the Indian diasporic film has slowly been transitioning to a state in which it both engages with, and represents, a perception of diasporic life that increasingly relegates nostalgia about 'home' to a gesture that is significant mainly for its ritualistic function, and not as an impetus for staggering change. This transition is enacted by, and embodied in, the lives of the second generation of diasporic Indians who are obviously comfortably assimilated in what is, to all intents and purposes, their homeland, distant (both in real and metaphoric terms) from their 'roots' which speak to them eloquently but not always effectively through their parents, for whom, however, 'home' is necessarily synonymous with an overwhelming longing to return to it.

Stuart Hall has usefully identified the 'New World' of the diasporic location as one constituted of 'a narrative of displacement', recreating therefore the desire to return to 'lost origins'; 'And yet', he says, this 'return to the beginning' is like the imaginary in Lacan – it can neither be fulfilled nor requited, and hence is the beginning of the symbolic, of representation, the infinitely renewable source of desire, memory, myth, search, discovery – in short, the reservoir of our cinematic narratives (1990, pp. 235–6). It is generally accepted that an 'endless desire to return to lost origins' lies at the heart of the diasporic experience of living away from one's homeland. However, in the aftermath of globalization, and the subsequent shrinking of the globe by enhanced exchanges and transmission, what was once distant and unattainable is now fairly easily available, if genuinely desired. The new diasporic identity, in process of formation, has changed to assimilate within it not the true longing for a return to roots but much more forcefully a sheer desire/need for nostalgia; as second-generation South Asians settle more comfortably in Britain, for example, they begin to recognize the exercise of memory as the only means of keeping in touch with that part of their hybrid, hyphenated identity that is far away. Cinema, as Hall astutely notes, serves this need particularly well in providing a 'reservoir of...narratives' that one can both dip into as well as create afresh.

Diasporic South Asian cinema gestures to that Lacanian 'imaginary' of the desire for the 'other' that can be neither fulfilled nor requited. In a general context, the gendered/sexual identity of the diasporic sub-continental has been a particularly difficult terrain to negotiate, given the rather strict inherited 'traditions' of culture that have been held up against the influx of Western 'permissiveness' within the diasporic space. Negotiations have hinged on the question of whether identity in this third space, so to speak, is to be true to origins (thereby validating a pure nostalgia) or to the adopted culture (thus allowing one to assimilate more easily into the New World) or – most difficult of all – try to construct a self that acknowledges both. Narrative cinema like Gurinder Chadha's *Bhaji on the Beach* (1993) has attempted to negotiate conflicting South Asian sexual identities in a diasporic space in Britain that is ever more embattled by the decreasing distance between original and adopted homelands since the global communication explosion of the late twentieth century. The cinema of Mira Nair has represented the vast, and vastly multicultural, spaces of the USA, earlier in *Mississippi Masala* (1991) and more recently in *The Namesake* (2007). Gurinder Chadha's later reprise of diasporic generational conflict in Britain in the successful *Bend it Like Beckham* (2002) marks an evolution in the understanding of diasporic identity caught in the inevitability of assimilation. Increasingly, as the longing for traditions recedes, that emptied space within the diasporic psyche appears to be occupied by a guilty need/desire for nostalgia that at once validates one's 'origins' and distances it effectively.

Hall has posed certain key questions about cultural identity, diaspora and representation, suggesting that 'Perhaps instead of thinking of identity as an already accomplished fact, we should think, instead, of identity as a "production", which is never complete, always in process, and always constituted within, not outside, representation' (1990, p. 222). Thinking of identity itself as 'production' can be useful in considering the cinema that attempts to recreate, represent, and 'fix' diasporic identity – a 'fixing' that is as much to do with capturing as it is to do with finding a remedy – because our task, clearly, is not just to identify this cultural identity but also to interrogate the process of its production.

To return to Benjamin, however, the camera that closes in upon diasporic experience, in the cinema that attempts to understand this (dis)located space, may be said to reproduce its realities in a particular mode that then offers entirely new formations of the subject. Sexualities, especially in contexts of desiring and transgression, assume a metonymic function in the representation of diasporic desiring of various tones and colours in these films. In fact, not only does sexual desire and transgression here stand in for other kinds of desires and transgressions in this 'transgressed' place, but it also enacts an argument with the pressures of (cultural) tradition that are always at war within diasporic individuals who thrive on nostalgia for a faraway homeland and yet are not averse to embracing what may be the opportunities offered by a more liberating space – liberating not simply because it is located in the West, but because its inhabitants are dislocated and therefore oddly freed from some of the constraints of that very 'home' that they are nostalgic about.

Hall also talks of the 'the eye that records and tells', therefore doing so 'in context' of its own situation, location, position. It is this position that determines how cultural identity will be represented. It may be defined in terms of 'one shared culture, a sort of collective... [reflecting] the common historical experiences and shared cultural codes which provide us, as "one people", with stable, unchanging and continuous frames of reference and meaning, beneath the shifting divisions and vicissitudes of our actual history' (1990, p. 223). Alternatively, the enunciated cultural identity may recognize Derridean *difference*, a matter of 'becoming' rather than 'being', acknowledging ruptures and discontinuities, belonging to the future as well as the past (Hall 1990, p. 225).

It is neither particularly revelatory nor revolutionary to say that noteworthy diasporic cinema most often belongs to the latter category, not only recognizing ruptures and discontinuities but locating themselves at those (dis)junctures, and articulating their difficulty in representing a utopic oneness that some misplaced loyalty may demand of them. What is more interesting, however, is to consider how these moments of confrontation – between traditional oneness and radical fragmentation – use nostalgia to effectively further distance the past from the present, the act of remembering itself being transformed into an act of homage. Nostalgia becomes the safety-hatch into which new-generation diasporic South Asians ritualistically disappear when they feel the need to salute their origins, emerging all the more convinced that what they have fought to achieve is infinitely more desirable to possess. These filmmakers participate very consciously in this process of myth-making, where memory/nostalgia is the myth upon which dislocated diasporic identity rests. Dislocation, after all, is both artistically and politically enabling, and nostalgia becomes the key signifier in a text that likes to see unfulfilled desire/longing locked in an unbreakable metaphoric relationship with the notion of diaspora.

The concept of diaspora places the discourse of 'home' and 'dispersion' in creative tension, inscribing a homing desire while simultaneously critiquing discourses of fixed origins (Brah, 1996, pp. 190–3). In the context of gender identity in the South Asian diaspora, it also places in creative tension the discourses of nostalgia and freedom, where the former represents not just the safety of tradition but also satisfies the need to 'desire' that which has been lost or left behind, while freedom signifies the sexual possibilities that the new world enticingly offers.

Gurinder Chadha's *Bhaji on the Beach* (1993) uses 'Bollywood' as a fantasy trope while it explores – and exposes – gendered identity politics in a South Asian community in contemporary Britain. The film records a day in the life of a group of immigrant Indian women in Birmingham, whose disparate existences are thrown together during a trip to the beach organized by the Saheli Women's Centre (a battered women's shelter that is itself a product of the impact of Western feminism upon the South Asian community in Britain). Even as the group – ranging from teenagers to grandmothers – are determined to force the mood of gaiety unfurled by a rollicking Punjabi version of Cliff Richards's 'Summer Holiday' playing in their minibus, Chadha touches upon their individual lives complicated by issues of arranged marriages, interracial alliances, racism, sexism and violence against women set against the backdrop of various 'Western' liberalizing tendencies and influences.

Bhaji on the Beach focuses mainly on the plight of two women: a young mother who has taken shelter at the Centre along with her small son after being physically abused by her husband, and a seventeen-year-old who, on the verge of fulfilling her parents' ambitions for her by going to medical school, discovers that she is pregnant by her black boyfriend and finds her world crashing about her ears as she contemplates the effect that this news will have on her family. What was planned as an innocent, and innocuous, trip to Blackpool on the festive Illuminations night turns nightmarish as the news of her pregnancy becomes known to the elder women in the group who react with expected outrage, while Ginder – the young mother – discovers her husband Ranjit to be in pursuit of them, apparently with the evil intention of abducting their son. Some comic relief is provided by the plight of Asha, a middle-aged wife and mother prone to 'visions' in the Bollywoodian mode every time she is confronted by nascent feminist existentialist angst related to her consistently subservient role in her family's life. The gallantly romantic attentions of a quaint Englishman as he plies her with ice-cream and welcome masculine appreciation momentarily turns her head, but even as she emerges from the fantasy to reject it, it provides her with the confidence in herself as a woman that Chadha clearly considers a necessity in the process of gendered identity formation amongst South Asian immigrants.

The central dilemma that Chadha identifies in her film is the psychological battle that each woman faces, not merely in the specific problems presented by unwanted pregnancies, marital violence and menopausal angst, but more critically in dealing with them through cultural barriers created by gender/sexual taboos that have been imported from the homeland. No easy solution appears to be in sight, either to reconcile the group to their tradition-bound heritage or to free them into lives more stereotypically 'Western'/liberal, but the real significant outcome of the day lies as much in the group's ability to foil Ranjit's intention of terrorizing Ginder and their son by rallying together against him, as it lies in the young pregnant teenager staying behind in the comforting arms of her boyfriend, who has also pursued her to Blackpool, as they pledge to 'handle' their crisis together.

Rather than debating the question of how true – or not – Chadha's representation of the plight of Indian immigrant women in Britain facing conflicts in their gendered/sexual identities is, it may be more interesting to consider the film in the context of a monitored cultural 'production', and the repercussions that such a text would expect to have on its primary target audience, the South Asian community across the world. In the Report of the Commission (chaired by Bhikhu Parekh) on the Future of Multi-Ethnic Britain, published in 2000, a statement on the 'changing' nature of communities that can no longer be insulated from each other concludes: 'Increasingly, people have the capacity to manoeuvre between distinct areas of life and to be "cross-cultural navigators". Hybrid cultural forms have emerged, especially in music and the arts. In this context, does "Britishness" have a future? Or have devolution, globalization and the new cultural diversity undermined it irretrievably?' (2000, p. xv). We may assume that the questions posed in the report are rhetorical. It is not just that the people inhabiting Britain have become 'cross-cultural navigators', however; the hybrid cultural forms emergent from this society also bear this characteristic, almost like a responsibility.

South Asian immigrant cinema, for example, has constantly tried to mediate between (Eastern) tradition and (Western) permissiveness in its struggle to represent – and come to terms with – changing sexual mores in its hybrid society. Chadha's *Bhaji on the Beach* is a case in point: it feels the need to validate a very 'Indian' sense of community even while it must endorse a more 'liberated' lifestyle that signifies progress as well as amalgamation with the adopted country. Jigna Desai, in her reading of the film through the tropes of what she calls 'Homesickness and Motion Sickness', suggests that 'Chadha's film offers the possibility that if home is fiction, it can be written and rewritten' (2004, p. 146), and astutely infers that her protagonists never prescribe the 'return-home theory as a cure for homesickness' even while they 'perpetuate constructions of home that nonetheless reproduce home as a space of surety and safety, of fixed identity and culture, following the binary logic of anticolonial nationalism' (2004, p. 146). Indeed, it appears to me that the bonded female community of South Asians that Chadha celebrates in the film is her one consistent gesture to the nostalgic mode, while her endorsement of new sexual and/or gender identities in *Bhaji* is more confidently an acceptance of the possibilities embedded in

Western liberated feminisms available to South Asian women in their new homes. As Gayatri Spivak has said of the location of the diasporic woman in transnationalism, 'Her entire energy must be spent upon successful transplantation or insertion into the new state ... She is the site of global public culture privatized ... She may also be the victim of an exacerbated and violent patriarchy which operates in the name of the old nation as well' (1997, p. 251). Clearly, there is a need to relegate nostalgia for the homeland to a safe spot from which it can emanate feelings of comfort without impinging its harsher realities upon the present (dis)location.

Mira Nair's *Mississippi Masala* (1991) may be grouped with South Asian diasporic films of the early phase, though it took the debate away to a whole new territory across the ocean, to America. Colourful and energetic, the film is, basically, a romanticized celebration of the multicultural possibilities of the USA in which Mina, a young woman of Indian origin, falls in love with Demetrius, an African American, and despite a Romeo-and-Juliet-like threat of family disapproval, is able to push the boundaries of restrictions upon her private choice enough to break out of her close-knit anti-black/racist South Asian community and walk into the sunset with her black lover for a new uncharted future together, both loosened from their respective ethnic roots. The film embodies, in essence, the Great American Immigrant Dream of love across racial barriers, and has generally been critically acclaimed as both a celebration of melting-pot America and a repudiation of South Asian racism against blacks, where Mina's defiance of her family's horror at her choice of Demetrius is seen as a progressive-minded refusal to perpetuate a nationalist nostalgia in the film. However, as Jigna Desai has pointed out, the film 'turns to mobility and the heterosexual mixed-race romance as a resolution to displacement and exclusion' (2004, p. 73), and we cannot afford to ignore some of these escapist modes of resolution that make the film uncritically jubilant about multicultural America. What is actually more interesting in the film is that Mina and Demetrius are both products of the dislocation of races from before their own time: Mina is Ugandan-born, and her Indian parents migrated westwards to America when they were driven out of Uganda during the violent dictatorship of Idi Amin, and Demetrius is of African descent but has never been to Africa. As Desai says, 'This disassociation prevents any simple constructions of essentialist belonging, thus problematizing the ethnonational terms of identity within the film because Mina and her family "originate" not from the expected homeland but from Demetrius' supposed homeland' (2004, p. 76). The notions of belonging, exile and nostalgia are therefore impossibly complicated by such movements across continents, and the pertinent point here is that for each of the protagonists in such a story (not just Mina and Demetrius but their parents and relatives and friends as well), 'home' is a different location, whether imaginary or real. Therefore, when Mina and Demetrius finally waltz off into an unmarked, unidentified stretch of America to carve out their own place in the sun, the aplomb with which they can take that decision is as much to do with the fact that they mainly need to contend with an inherited nostalgia for their ethnic roots that they only partially sympathize with, as it is to do with the great promise of individualism that America offers them.

The question of sexual and/or gender identities, as always, becomes far more complicated when one looks at homosexuality. Bhikhu Parekh in his report on Britain writes: 'Racism exacerbates, and is exacerbated by, sexism – they reinforce each other in vicious circles and spirals, and intertwine to the extent that it is impossible to disentangle them... Sexual rivalries in sexist and patriarchal contexts exacerbate fears and fantasies among white people about the supposed sexuality, promiscuity and fecundity of people believed to be racially different' (2000, p. 67). Immigrants who are homosexuals face multiple discriminations: those of racism and sexism as well as those of patriarchy, conservatism and homophobia, and find themselves in exile in many more ways than the average heterosexual immigrant. Notions of home, exile and belonging are of course lodged as a holy triumvirate in the very idea of diaspora, in which an ubiquitous sense of belonging is a free-floating signifier between the twin teasers of nostalgia for the native land and desire to possess (and be possessed by) the adopted one. For the immigrant homosexual, it may be said, this elusive sense of belonging remains a free-floater, unable to attach itself to either past or present location.

The Great American Dream of freedom and individuality has, in fact, emerged as a sustained trope in South Asian diasporic cinema, including those emerging out of England. Gurinder Chadha's commercially successful *Bend it Like Beckham* (2002), about a young British Punjabi girl Jesminder (Jess), whose dream of playing competitive soccer is fuelled by her closest friend, the tomboyish (or butch?) Juliette (Jules) and their young Irish coach Joe, is overtly a cross-racial heterosexual love story pegged on a winning formula of the joie-de-vivre of sports matched with the comedic elements of a South Asian family adjusting to changing socio-cultural parameters as their children grow up more British than Indian. In an interview about the film, director Gurinder Chadha says that she wanted to give her audience 'the nuts and bolts of integration. That's what it's about, the process of being second generation or third generation Indian, very specifically in London. And no one really has done anything to show how you do balance, not only culture, but also gender and sexuality. By focusing on these two characters, you get a strong picture on the constraints but also the processes that allow them to be who they are' (Chadha, 2003). It is significant, perhaps, that Jess not only fights a plucky battle in London with her loving but traditional and over-protective Sikh family to become who she is, but also has to finally fly out further westwards to America to pursue her ultimate dream and passion to train in soccer. Again, it is worth pondering where Jess's nostalgia for her homeland will be located: presumably, if anywhere, then in London, where she has left behind her immediate family, and where she grew up and learnt to be who she is. The site of nostalgia will therefore be dislocated from her ancestral roots, and one suspects that such a dislocation from the 'originary' will be relatively painless.

What is even more interesting about *Bend it*, however, is that despite Chadha's brave talk of chronicling how one can balance changing attitudes to gender and sexuality, the film skirts, flirts with, but finally refuses to confront a relationship of homoeroticism, if not homosexuality, between the two young women, Jess and Jules, as they come of age in London. Despite the wicked, wild promise of their very natural and engaging friendship that constantly borders on the lesbian, Chadha is always quick to pull in the reins and re-establish, time and again, that all of it is innocently, exuberantly girlish – and the ultimate proof of that is provided in the rivalry for their male coach's attention that the friends anguish over. For they are both not only in love with Beckham, but also apparently in love with their coach Joe, and almost sacrifice their friendship to this desire for heteronormativity. As Jigna Desai suggests, films such as *Bend it* 'attempt to disrupt South Asian gender normativities of heterosexuality through challenging the dominant gendered ideologies such as female chastity and virginity, multiracial romance, and arranged marriages' (2004, p. 214) thereby inserting a notion of feminist agency as a marker of the freedoms imbibed in the diasporic homeland, but insist simultaneously upon the impossibility of 'an Asian queerness' (2004, p. 214). Even more cleverly, as Desai points out, 'the film proposes that the viewer would accept a same-sex relationship between Jess and Jules but does not have to because the viewer is already always in the know about the platonic nature of their relationship. Hence, the film does not have to deny the possibility, but merely to disavow its accuracy' (2004, p. 215). Gayatri Gopinath contends, in fact, that the film 'renders its brand of liberal feminism palatable through a strategic containment of queer female sexuality' and that it also 'predicates its assertion of girl power on the containment of the specter of lesbianism that women's sports inevitably conjure up' (2007, pp. 128–9). It may be said, therefore, that in *Bend it*, the cinematic apparatus constructs a vision of possible new diasporic sexualities only to deconstruct it, but in the deliberate destruction of any transgressive potential for the young girls a sort of transformation is suggested, a sliding from traditional to progressive and back again that clears a space for speculation and suspicion. Though an empathic camera closely tracks this speculative space for non-normative sexualities in the diaspora, it fails, of course, to sustain its promise and momentum and tapers off into a tame endorsement of heteronormativity.

Anne Friedberg traces the transformation of the production of the mobilized cinematic gaze from modernity to postmodernity, from the public sphere to a 'spatial and temporal displacement [that] has become fully integrated into everyday life, extending beyond high art and the public sphere ... to mass culture and the private realm' (1991, p. 420). It could be said, however, that the state of diasporic displacement is symptomatic of the postmodern (and perhaps postcolonial) condition, and the cinematic gaze that probes and dissects it for public consumption produces consciously the split realities of its representation on celluloid. In representing 'new' (read 'liberal', perhaps) sexualities in this 'new' (transgressed, dislocated, free-floating) space of the Indian diaspora in the West, contemporary diasporic cinema flirts with, but refuses to commit to, radical stances and actions that would completely destroy its status quo so delicately created and maintained through the trope of nostalgia for the homeland.

Mira Nair's film based on the novel of the same title by Jhumpa Lahiri, *The Namesake* (2007), enters a new space in dislocated nostalgias by embodying a representation of the filmmaker's own memories of homelands, real, inherited or adopted. Some of the statements that Mira Nair has made in her interviews about the filmmaking process for *The Namesake* reveal this intense relationship between the real and imagined: 'I wanted to make a Bengali film in America; I love those early films of Satyajit Ray – the economy, the courtship, the charm. So that type of sweetness, and then with the clang and coolness of Manhattan. It's a completely New York movie in some ways but with people who look like me in the centre' (Nair, 2007). Nair says of Calcutta, a city that informs the film even when it moves around the streets of New York: 'Calcutta is incredibly layered; layers of history in that city. And it's a city that's devoted to politics and art, the mix of it…It's always bristling with some kind of life. I love that city…I grew up in that city. It was a wonderful banquet for me to try and capture that.' Answering a question on her personal investment in the story, Nair says candidly, 'Of course. It was like total possession. I can't tell you. And because I know how precious it is to be inspired, I really follow that inspiration. It doesn't happen often that you have this wave of "I have to make this. I was born to do this." '

Obviously, Nair's identification with the story being told in the film is total, despite the fact that none of the actual stories of its individual protagonists may be hers – what she identifies with as her 'possession' is the epicentre of the nostalgia, as it were; the rumblings of feeling and belonging in an emotional register for the city of one's past that must then necessarily be expressed through a certain fracturing of the artistic consciousness, perhaps what T. S. Eliot called so precisely 'the objective correlative', or the subtle shifting of registers in order to cope with the sheer overwhelming rush of mixed memories and desires. An intimately crafted, touching film with some remarkable portrayals of first-generation and second-generation South Asian life caught in frenetic New York, *The Namesake* is significant not merely for the stories it tells of the universal immigrant experience in juggling past with present, but for being a film that operates at a primordial, mythic level, sublimating the filmmaker's eye into the film's 'I', becoming not merely a film about nostalgia but both literally and metaphorically an artifice that enacts the very nostalgia it speaks of.

In the eye of the storm – as well as the calm – of *The Namesake*, therefore, is not so much the young man Gogol Ganguli (who is thus christened by his erudite father after his favourite writer Nikolai Gogol) – the second-generation immigrant son of overwhelmingly Bengali parents Ashima and Ashoke who lived out their married life in New York, resident aliens in so many senses of the term – but his mother Ashima, who embodies in the film the clash of cultures that remains at the very essence of our understanding of diasporic existence. As Ashima struggles to engender an identity, a skin that she can be comfortable in as she negotiates multiple, bewildering choices in the proverbial land of plenty, the cinematic gaze lingers on her with a kind of sensuousness that makes her emblematic of both the trauma and the promise of processes of transformation. The camera produces – and reproduces – Ashima as she grows from a luscious young woman at home in Calcutta waiting for her marriage to be arranged, to a shy but equally luscious bride who learns to housekeep in a tiny Manhattan apartment with a husband she hardly knows to begin with, to, finally, a mature but still luscious widow and mother of grown children who decides to return to her roots in her homeland to find solace when she is left all alone in the 'lonely country' that is the diaspora abroad. In many ways, in her sustained lusciousness lies her story: Ashima exudes a quiet allure and makes of New York a home with friends and family for decades, but like a homing pigeon she heads back to Calcutta to settle in middle age. Yet she emerges – produced by the cinematic apparatus as it tracks her movements across continents, back and forth, propelled by memory and nostalgia, visions and re-visions – as a probable face of new (and/or evolved) diasporic femininities, sensual, complex, difficult, even recalcitrant. Her desires are continually displaced, even as spaces and sexualities across the diaspora continually reconfigure themselves.

One may want to see Ashima's imaging by Mira Nair, using Indian actor Tabu (known for her understated but potent sensuality), as a deliberate assertion of the changed/changing face of female sexuality in the relatively 'new' space of the Indian diaspora as it has begun to define itself in counterpoint to the 'new' globalized spaces of home, and therefore read in this statement an enactment of the politics of diaspora filmmaking rather than see it as a representation of the 'reality' of diasporic women's lives, arguable as any such single reality will certainly be. In a late sequence in *The Namesake* in which Ashima, after she has chosen to primarily relocate to Calcutta (now Kolkata), is pictured in a song recital on a terrace one balmy evening, her appearance – with flowing hair, colourful sari and sensuous, if full, curves – is clearly meant to indicate how America has shaped her sensibility, how the diaspora has contributed to her 'making', as it were. Ashima is able to choose to return to her roots when she feels that her life in America has become lonely, but is able to re-establish herself in this world she had long left on exactly her own terms. Not only is the retention of her 'lusciousness', despite her dis/re-location, an affirmation of the sensuous being she grew into in the New World, but it appears as if her return itself is a vindication of that being, a wild and passionate pursuit of a sudden, almost wanton longing to be home again now that life in the diaspora no longer fulfils her desires. Here, then, is a highly imaginative displacement of sorts – that relates sexuality to its locations – offering perhaps another turn for 'new' femininities in 'new' spaces.

Bibliography

Benjamin, W. (1969) 'The Work of Art in the Age of Mechanical Reproduction', in trans. H. Zohn and H. Arendt (ed.), *Illuminations* (New York: Schocken).

Brah, A. (1996) *Cartographies of Diaspora: Contesting Identities* (London and New York: Routledge).

Chadha, G. (2003) Interview with Gurinder Chadha. Available at http://www.popmatters.com/film/interviews/chadha-gurinder-030403.shtml [accessed 2 March 2010].

Desai, J. (2004) *Beyond Bollywood: The Cultural Politics of South Asian Diasporic Film* (New York and London: Routledge).

Foster, G. A. (1997) *Women Filmmakers of the African and Asian Diaspora: Decolonizing the Gaze, Locating Subjectivity* (Carbondale and Edwardsville: Southern Illinois University Press).

Friedberg, A. (1991) 'Les Flaneurs du Mal (l): Cinema and the Postmodern Condition', *PMLA* 106(3): 419–31.

Gopinath, G. (2007) *Impossible Desires: Queer Diasporas and South Asian Public Cultures* (Calcutta: Seagull Books).

Hall, S. (1990) 'Cultural Identity and Diaspora', in J. Rutherford (ed.), *Identity: Community, Culture, Difference* (London: Lawrence and Wishart).

Kaplan, E. A. (2000) 'An Interview with Pratibha Parmar', *Quarterly Review of Film and Video*, 17(2): 85–105.

Laurie, N., C. Dwyer, S. Holloway and F. Smith (1999) *Geographies of New Femininities* (New York: Longman, Pearson Education Limited).

Nair, M. (2007) Mira Nair. Available at http://motherjones.com/media/2007/03/mira-nair?page=3 [accessed 2 March 2010].

Parekh, B. (2000) *The Future of Multi-Ethnic Britain* (London: Profile Books).

Spivak, G. C. (1997) 'Diasporas Old and New: Women in the Transnational World' in A. Kumar (ed.), *Class Issues: Pedagogy, Cultural Studies and the Public Sphere* (New York: New York University Press).

11
Notes on Some Scandals: The Politics of Shame in *Vers le Sud*

Sadie Wearing

This chapter is primarily a reading of the 2003 film *Vers le Sud*, which follows the stories of three middle-aged female tourists in 1970s Haiti who have sex with much younger, male, islanders in return for presents, clothing, jewellery and money. This narrative trope, of a sexual encounter between an 'older' (comparatively socially privileged) woman and a younger man, has a rich cinematic history and I will be drawing on this history in part to ask, what are the particular contours of this story as it is being told *now*, in comparison with the iconic versions presented by Douglas Sirk's, *All that Heaven Allows* (1955) and Fassbinder's *Ali, Fear Eats the Soul* (1974)? In the context of this edited collection's focus on new femininities, what might the retelling of this story have to tell us about new *older* femininities, particularly how older women's sexuality is currently being negotiated and how this relates to questions of power? Other recent films have also used this motif, including *The Roman Spring of Mrs Stone* (dir. Robert Allan Ackerman, 2003) and *The Mother* (dir. Roger Michell, 2003) and I am interested in how these films touch upon wider questions of how women's ageing bodies are subject to very specific forms of visibility and shame that link to issues of race and class. I will be arguing that, in comparison to the earlier films, recent versions offer a highly ambivalent account of women's 'new' sexual longevity, an account which emphasizes both the illegitimacy but also the tenacity of the taboo surrounding mature women's sexuality in that shame ultimately 'sticks' (Ahmed, 2004, pp. 92–3) as a bad feeling attaching to the (relatively[1]) older woman, a bad feeling that invites a dis-identification from the audience.

If, as I have discussed elsewhere (Wearing, 2007) increasing attention and visibility is being paid to sexuality in the figure of the older woman in popular culture I am interested here in, broadly speaking, identifying and examining the cultural politics[2] of the affects which surround this figure, particularly shame. It has been possible recently to chart in a range of popular cultural texts how older women's bodies are subject to increasing scrutiny, discipline and sexualization through, for example, increasingly ubiquitous 'makeover' narratives which offer the fantasy of a permanent 'ageless' present for the body. These texts can be read as thoroughly implicated in contemporary phenomena such as the normalization of cosmetic surgery in the context of an imperative to rejuvenate the (female) body where the shaming of the ageing body inaugurates a narrative of its rehabilitation into what Katz and Marshall have called 'sexual functionality and fitness' (Katz and Marshall, 2009). Diane Negra has identified another of the affective dimensions of this as she suggests that 'in a cluster of recent popular film representations, the story of ageing uncertainly but inexorably out of youth is marked by a deep and sustained melancholy' (Negra, 2009, p. 77). In the films under discussion here shame and melancholy are understood to be operating both at a narrative level (all of them contain scenes which rely for their intelligibility on the cultural proximity of shame to older women's sexuality) but also, at a less easily identifiable level, these affects can be understood in terms of what Sianne Ngai calls 'tone', 'a cultural object's affective bearing, orientation, or "set toward" the world' (Ngai, 2005, p. 29).

In this chapter, then, I look to some of cinema's antecedents to this narrative trope to explore how the theme of intergenerational sexual encounters works repeatedly to reveal these as inevitably, but ambiguously, 'scandalous'. On the one hand, these narratives may suggest a relaxation of the taboo neatly summed up in Simone de Beauvoir's widely quoted assessment of cultural attitudes towards older people's sexuality as considered 'repulsive' (de Beauvoir, 1972, p. 3) or invisible. On the other hand, the particular generational configuration gives rise to the playing out of ongoing cultural anxieties over ageing and female transgression. Recent film narratives centring on 'transgenerational' couples provide an interesting insight into a 'postfeminist' cultural landscape wherein contradictory ideological pressures are exposed in the embodiment of the sexualized 'older woman'. Scandal marks the female ageing body as transgressive, shamed and/or melancholic. Karen Stone, the central character in *The Roman Spring of Mrs Stone*, is ultimately annihilated by this shaming. In another recent example, May, the 'older woman' in *The Mother* anticipates it but remains caught in its logic, however in Cantet's film the transnational negotiation of this narrative explicitly invokes such shaming, only to question its purchase, specifically on the female body. I'm interested here in opening up the questions that this instability raises, both within the film narratives themselves but also in the possible mobility of this embodied affect, shame, to the film's audience. As Sara Ahmed points out 'shame as an emotion requires a witness' (Ahmed, 2004, p. 106); this is a point I shall return to in my analysis by asking what are the politics of witnessing the shame attached to the privileged middle-aged white female body engaged in intimate sexual acts with a younger, poorer man who is also differentially positioned through racial, class or national affiliations?

I believe these narratives repay close analysis since they offer a complex series of explorations of questions of age in relation to class, 'race' and sexuality[3] through their dissection of transgenerational and transcultural encounters. The aim here, then, is to try to explore some of the ways in which affects generated by cinema's structures of viewing correspond to, but also complicate, 'interested' readings of films, by which I mean those readings that aim to highlight the specificity of representational regimes which circumscribe the cultural imaginary around questions of ageing bodies, and ageing female bodies in particular, whilst remaining attentive to the other axes of difference, exclusion and power that the films explore. The results, I suggest, are ambiguous with intergenerational sexual desire revealed as implicated in complex networks of power and affect. I want to suggest here that paying attention to the affective dimensions of the representations of older femininities here alerts us to the ways shame regulates, with varying amounts of success, transgenerational sexual conduct and intimacy through troubling the potential for sympathy and identification with the female protagonist. As I will show, this is something of a shift from some earlier cinematic versions of this encounter[4] where the emphasis is on the narrowness and rigidity of the social and sexual norms that victimize the lovers and thereby expose wider economic inequalities and class and race hierarchies. The analysis which follows contrasts this with the more recent variations of this cinematic trope and suggests that whilst they similarly invite a response which is attentive to the emphasis on complex dynamics of power, that attention ought also be given to the newly inflected shame narratives which are produced around the feminine subjects represented here.

Narratives of shame and shaming

The films under discussion here are diverse in terms of genre, distribution, nationality, political affiliation and so on but they share narrative and formal preoccupations with the sexuality of 'older' women and all link this preoccupation to the exposure of the complexity of social power and forms of oppression. Mostly, they tend ultimately to reveal the limits of ageing women's social power even when they occupy an otherwise privileged position. One obvious point to begin analysis of these films with is that, as the recent adaptation of Zoe Heller's novel, *Notes on a Scandal* rather unsubtly hammers home, intergenerational sex (in popular fictions) is indeed, precisely 'scandalous' and marks a transgression which usually, though not inevitably, invites ridicule and 'shame' to be heaped upon the female protagonist. For example, in *Notes on a Scandal* the 'older woman' (Sheba Hart) is both tabloid and (implied) sexual prey as a result of her 'obsession' with a fifteen-year-old schoolboy. May, the eponymous central protagonist of *The Mother* is both sexually humiliated by her younger lover and beaten up by her daughter in that film's denouement; in the recent remake of Tennessee

Williams's *The Roman Spring of Mrs Stone* the ageing Broadway star Karen Stone ends the film apparently inviting her own murder at the hands of a young, lascivious vagrant. In the earlier films too, *All that Heaven Allows* and *Ali Fear Eats the Soul*, the endings are famously muted, equivocally restoring the lovers to each other but, notoriously at a cost; as Mulvey puts it in both: 'the man falls victim to the stress of the relationship and ends an invalid, with the woman at his bedside' (Mulvey, 1989, pp. 46–7). The narratives can frequently, therefore, be read as somewhat punitive. In all of these films, moreover, the questions of class and differentials of social power are linked to the ambiguous social and sexual positioning of the younger man. Age is only one of the elements that separates the 'lovers' in these films,[5] and broadly speaking the audience's sympathies are either with the 'couple' against the unfeeling world, or with the woman. Arguably the social and economic differences between the couple in all of the aforementioned films are, in part, ameliorated by the discourse of love and romance, sexual curiosity and compassion or obsession. In Cantet's film *Vers le Sud* (*Heading South*) the economic and racial privilege of the older woman which defines the 'relationship' offers no such amelioration, rather, it is literally a transaction. The white, professional, North American and European middle-aged women who travel to Haiti pay the young islanders for sex, and this transaction is emblematic of the broader exploitations that the islanders suffer. The bodies of the men are subject to a range of humiliations, confinements and exhibitions as they are argued over, photographed, dressed and undressed and put at intolerable political risk by the women who appear wilfully oblivious to the dangers and complexities of 1970s Haiti under the control of 'Baby Doc' Duvalier. The ensuing complex dissection of enmeshed racial, sexual and geopolitical, postcolonial and generational politics explored by the film does not leave the female protagonists immune to this narrative's usual, dismal, outcome. One of the three central characters, Ellen (played by Charlotte Rampling) a middle-aged tourist who 'pay[s] young men to love her', ends the film chastized and bereft, exiled back to an unwelcoming 'home'. In this film, however, the highest possible price for transgression is paid by the young man, Legba, and his islander lover who both end the film naked and dead on the beach. How complicit the blindness and greed of the white women are in this death is a question that the film is scrupulous to leave to the viewer to judge. One character in this film, however, Brenda, significantly evades the fate that seems so frequently to befall those cinematic characters who breach the generational sexual divide and it is her story that I want to concentrate on here.

Brenda

Brenda's story links female sexuality and second-wave feminist discourses of empowerment and she can be read as representing a particularly unsettling version of white, affluent, postfeminist femininity. Unlike the two earlier films which deploy the grammar of melodrama to elicit sympathy (good feelings) for their protagonists Cantet's film stages its narrative through a much more ambiguously affective dissection of transgressive desire.

If we turn to readings of the earlier films it is possible to contrast the production of affect across these ostensibly similar narratives. Mulvey's reading of Sirk and Fassbinder draws attention to the distanciation effect they both produce; she suggests that 'both brought to the cinema a sense of theatrical distanciation (drama as spectacle) that works against the tendency of film to absorb the spectator into itself' (Mulvey, 1989, p. 46). For Brecht this is of course a political act, to instil in the audience the discipline of thinking politically about the scene played out (and in broad terms emphasizing a hierarchy of the mind over the body and its affects or emotions). A consideration of the affective dimension of cinema, however, was understood by Fassbinder to be crucial; he is quoted as insisting: 'With Brecht you see the emotions and you reflect upon them as you witness them but you never feel them...I think I go further than he did in that I let the audience *feel and think*' (Fassbinder, quoted in Chaudhuri, 2005, p. 648).

Cantet's film has similarly ambivalent affective qualities with the audience compelled to both feel and think, thus deconstructing this alleged contradiction. In this Cantet's film can be likened to Steven Shaviro's discussion of another Fassbinder film *Querelle*, where he argues that 'the alienation effect does not free the audience from involvement in the spectacle, but itself functions as a new mode of complicity. For Fassbinder, questions about cinematic form are always also, quite directly, questions about subjectivity, sexuality and power and vice versa' (Shaviro, 1993, p. 163). This can be very directly related to *Vers le Sud*. The film's narrative is repeatedly 'interrupted' by what appear to be 'interviews', or perhaps the theatrical term 'soliloquies' is more apt.[6] These scenes are under-motivated in purely narrative terms – their status within the diegesis of the film is ambiguous, we never know to whom the characters are addressing their thoughts and reflections but the scene is apparently one of a kind of benign interrogation, or confession. One of these scenes takes the frail-looking Brenda as its subject; we have seen Brenda arrive at the island, a rich American tourist alone in a luxury hotel where she reacquaints herself with the young islander Legba. In the scene in question Brenda tells the story of her previous relations with Legba, the scene takes place in her hotel room, she is on the bed wearing only underwear and a loose blouse. In forensic detail she describes how she and her husband 'sort of adopted' the boy who 'didn't look a day over 15' and explains how she first had sex with him:[7]

> I edged my hand over and placed it on his chest. Legba opened his eyes and immediately closed them again that encouraged me and I moved my hand down his body. Such soft young skin, he was motionless and I slid two fingers into his bathing suit and touched his cock. Almost

immediately it started getting hard ... I looked around to see that nobody was coming and I threw myself on him. I literally threw myself on him. It was so violent I couldn't help but scream I think I never stopped screaming. It was my first orgasm. I was forty five.

As in the Fassbinder film here the 'distanciation' effect of the camera and the 'excess' of the length of the shot, ensures that the spectator is encouraged to acknowledge the staging (the effect) of this confession. But this staging does not encourage a cerebral, disembodied critical position; instead it provokes a visceral, gut-wrenching sensation which might be named as shame. This is a very difficult scene to watch; it is physically uncomfortable in ways that call for attention to the affective dimension of cinema such as those encouraged by the work of Steven Shaviro and Vivian Sobchack, amongst others (Shaviro, 1993; Sobchack, 2004). But it is also worth noting that this scene partly functions as a 'confession' and as Foucault reminds us:

> The confession was, and still remains, the general standard governing the production of the true discourse on sex ... it is no longer a question simply of saying what was done – the sexual act – and how it was done; but of reconstructing, in and around the act, the thoughts that recapitulated it, the obsessions that accompanied it, the images, desires, modulations, and quality of pleasure that animated it. For the first time no doubt, a society has taken upon itself to solicit and hear the imparting of individual pleasures. (Foucault, 1990, p. 63)

So what is the deployment of this sexual confession 'doing' – performing – here? The scene, I suggest, offers Brenda's sexual confession in ways that make a 'spectacle' of the complex dynamic of scopic exploitation, for Brenda is 'framed' here – as the venetian blinds' slats that resemble bars on her luxurious hotel room window testify, as she gazes on the object of her desire from the inside. She is framed then as both exploiter and exploited, as victimized by bourgeois codes of feminine sexual repression, the analysis of which has frequently invoked confessional modes (Radstone, 2007), *and* as blithely and shockingly predatory, bribing a semi-starving boy for her sexual gratification. While her vulnerability is highlighted through her apparently unwitting exposure of both her desire and her body (through the camera's slow but inexorable closing in on her) nevertheless the 'deployment' of this sexual narrative is ambiguous at best. Brenda's gestures in this scene are, in keeping with the film's wider preoccupations, both defiant (her eyes repeatedly meet rather than evade the camera) and only briefly and with ambiguous motivation do her bodily gestures evoke the affect which I'm suggesting is most consistently associated with intergenerational sexuality – shame.

A little later in the film Brenda is once again caught in a scopic regime which reveals both her narcissistic self-absorption and (or related to) her invulnerability to the controlling gaze of others. At a dance held at the hotel her partner, Legba, is visibly dismayed at her inability to conform, literally, to the correct deportment of white femininity 'of a certain age' and implicitly, to the established conventions of the (female) sex tourist and (male) sex worker exchange. Brenda's desires are marked in this scene as excessive and like her attempt to exclusively colonize the black body (Legba she is told 'belongs to everybody') are punished with a humiliation that she is clearly only very partially aware of, her myopic self-absorption shielding her from the disapproving and amused gaze of the tourists and islanders alike. Brenda's narcissism and desire for 'the other' are mutually implicated ('I loved the way he looked at me', she says), but the irony here is that she is oblivious to the 'spectacle' that she is making of herself. Brenda's humiliation is only partially apparent to her and whilst she does indeed risk censure her class, race and economic privilege successfully both blinds and protects her.

The differences between Brenda's fate and those of other characters is telling: while Legba ends the film naked and dead on the beach, Ellen, with whom Brenda has grudgingly negotiated for the young man's time and attention, is left grief stricken (literally immobilized and isolated in a final shot of her at the airport). Brenda's 'shamelessness' by contrast enables her to avoid this fate and continue her journey through the Caribbean, the 'heading south' of the film's title, with the implicit suggestion of further islands and islanders to be exploited. The final shots of the film are of Brenda on a boat speeding away from Haiti, calm and serene (affect-less), her voiceover informing the audience that she intends to keep travelling: 'I want nothing to do with men from the north'. It is Brenda's face which fills the frame at the end of film – the tropes of female empowerment and emancipation through travel are clearly in play here but the colonizing implications of such individual 'emancipation' are also exposed: with the wind and sun highlighting her blonde whiteness she muses on the as yet undiscovered pleasures of the Caribbean – 'such lovely names I wanna know them all'. Brenda who has always hated being looked at ends the film turning away from the camera, her desiring and consuming gaze triumphant.

Reading shame

Brenda's dislike of being looked at is congruent with an analytics of the power of the gaze as constituting in the most oppressive possible ways a subjectivity in the control of the other, as Fanon's 'Look, a negro!' definitively testifies (Fanon, 1986, p. 109). However Brenda's dislike might also be read as related to her failure or refusal to be 'shamed'. This resistance, in this context, produces, politically, the inverse of Fanon's insight. Here, the embodiment of the affect of shame is less about individual negotiations of gendered and racialized subjectivity, rather it is a product precisely of Brenda's failure to be properly 'affected': she displays no grief at Legba's death and her acquisitive and oblivious (literally she cannot see what her privileged status means for others) gaze triumphs over any possibility of remorse or even attachment. To explain this a little more clearly I want to turn here to Eve Sedgwick's discussion of the relations between shame and sociality. Sedgwick utilizes Michel Franz Basch's description of the origins of the 'shame humiliation response' which takes its recognizable form – 'eyes down head averted' – in infants when the mutual gaze between caregiver and infant is disrupted. The caregiver's failure to respond to the child's gaze is quite precisely a loss of sociality; thus Sedgwick suggests:

> Shame floods into being as a moment, a disruptive moment in a cir-cuit of identity- constituting identificatory communication. Indeed like a stigma shame is itself a form of communication. Blazons of shame, the fallen face with eyes down and head averted – and, to a lesser extent, the blush are semaphores of trouble and at the same time of a desire to recon-stitute the interpersonal bridge. (Sedgwick, 2003, p. 36)

Brenda's lack of shame then might relate to her own emancipatory project, in her voicing of a refusal to be subject to the controlling gaze of patriarchy, emblematized by her ex-husband – 'I always hated the way he looked at me' – but her pleasure in the 'way he [meaning the now dead Legba] looked at me' suggests that the costs of this emancipation are paid elsewhere, for while she might indeed love the way Legba looked at her the audience are privy to the far more critical gaze he actually affords her.

Whilst a number of characters might be seen in the film to attempt to 'shame' Brenda, by definition shame can only be properly so called if it is precisely recognized and thus embodied as Sara Ahmed puts it:

> Shame as an emotion requires a witness... it is the imagined view of the other that is taken on by a subject in relation to itself.... in shame I am the object as well as the subject of the feeling. Such an argument cru-cially suggests that shame requires an identification with the other who, as witness, returns the subject to itself... In shame, I expose to myself that I am a failure through the gaze of an ideal other. (Ahmed, 2004, p. 106)

So, here, while the film's complex negotiation of the postcolonial scene explicitly invokes shame the 'affect' has only an ambiguous purchase on this 'shamed' body. As Eve Sedgwick and Jacqueline Rose have both argued shame is both profoundly individual and profoundly social (Rose, 2004; Sedgwick, 2003), it is both contagious or mobile[8] and related to performance, to identity, to development – in remaining narcissistically self-absorbed and without 'shame' Brenda can continue to 'travel' to appropriate, to buy young bodies. But is this shaming whilst not performative within the diegesis of the film – it is not 'taken up' by the recipient in the way that the author

(Legba) intended – nevertheless, does shame travel somewhere here? And is it recognizable to scholars interested in 'age'? Critics of 'stereotypical' representations of ageing will be alert to the 'ageism' of shaming in relation to questions of intergenerational sex and might even be tempted to, in a paranoid reading, feel (affect again) somewhat uncomfortable at reiteration of shaming and, specifically, age, in a cultural landscape that so frequently renders female sexuality, in de Beauvoir's words 'revolting' or invisible. Which is only to say that, of course, there are familiar limits to such 'interested' readings, limits which debates within feminism and gender studies have long been accustomed to exposing. By rendering identification with this character profoundly, politically problematic Cantet's film is very different from say, Sirk's, as it is her very shamelessness which under other circumstances critics of the narrow range of representations of ageing femininity might wish to applaud. As Laura Mulvey writes in relation to Sirk's heroine, Cary, in *All that Heaven Allows*, 'she has no heroic or exhibitionist qualities and the gaze and gossip of the town cause her agonies of embarrassment. The camera takes in the prurient voyeurism which turns the sexual association of a middle aged woman with a younger man into an act of public indecency' (Mulvey, 1989, p. 43). This then is a successful act of 'shaming' – ironically, however, it is one in which as Mulvey's reading amply shows the audience sympathy stays with Cary, the social exclusions which render her relationship 'indecent' are demonstrably cruel. Shame, then on the townsfolk and we as viewers remain innocent and un-implicated and crucially un-'affected' the shame which attaches diegetically insulates the audience from feeling its affect. In Cantet's film, by contrast, the shame which *fails* to attach diegetically might be seen to perform an analogous function of illuminating the complexity of social privilege and exclusion; shame then appears to act here (and in film more generally) in ways that are suggested by Sedgwick in relation to shame's potential for an activist politics:

> Shame and identity remain in very dynamic relation to one another, at once deconstituting and foundational, because shame is both peculiarly contagious and peculiarly individuating. One of the strangest features of shame, but perhaps the one that offers the most conceptual leverage for political projects, is the way bad treatment of someone else, bad treatment by someone else, someone else's embarrassment, stigma, debility, bad smell, or strange behaviour, seemingly having nothing to do with me, can so readily flood me – assuming I'm a shame-prone person – with this sensation whose very suffusiveness seems to delineate my precise, individual outlines in the most isolating way imaginable. That's the double movement shame makes: toward painful individuation, toward uncontrollable relationality. (Sedgwick, 2003, p. 36–7)

I want to suggest then that while Brenda is a character with whom the audience is invited to 'disidentify', she is exposed as a ruthless and acquisitive colonizer whose narcissistic investment in her own victimization renders her oblivious to the devastating effects of her actions on others, nevertheless her 'bad treatment of someone else' is precisely how the film produces its desired 'affective' response in the audience; shame is operating here then not only at both a diegetic and an extra diegetic level but also operating in contradictory ways, since it is precisely the failure of the character to 'feel' shame that might be understood to provoke the audience's discomforted, embodied response, a response which in turn opens up the space for considering the layered politics of affect in negotiating film narrative from an 'interested' perspective. This reading then would be in keeping with the much more overt cultural politics of shame which are discussed by Sara Ahmed who notes that 'the expression of shame is a political action, which is not yet finished as it depends on how it gets "taken up"' (Ahmed, 2004, p. 120). So whilst shame is evaded by Brenda it maintains a political potential but one which on the one hand can be understood as progressive – the (post) colonial politics of this scene are clear – but might also be understood as restating the legitimacy of norms of sexual desire and conduct which do not cross racial or generational lines. For, as Ahmed also notes:

> The story of moral development is bound up with the reproduction of social norms, in particular with norms of sexual conduct. Shame can work as a deterrent: in order to avoid shame, subjects must enter the 'contract' of the social bond, by seeking to approximate a social ideal. Shame can also be experienced as *the affective cost of not following the scripts of normative existence.* (Ahmed, 2004, pp. 106–7 italics in original)

A recent remake of the Tennessee Williams novella, The *Roman Spring of Mrs Stone* likewise can be read in terms of an enactment of an oscillation between stressing humiliation and sympathy for its lead female character. Like *Vers le Sud, The Roman Spring of Mrs Stone* is both an adaptation and a period piece; it is an adaptation of Tennessee Williams' novella and a remake of a version which starred Vivien Leigh as an ageing Broadway star widowed and forlorn in Rome. As in *Vers le Sud* there are two central female leads involved in both tourism and the procurement and enjoyment of young men. One, the Contessa (Anne Bancroft) supplies the young man to the other more sympathetic character, Karen Stone (Helen Mirren). Similarly to Sirk's film the social privilege of Karen Stone shields and imprisons her in luxurious but coldly lit (dominated by blue) interiors (Mulvey, 1989, p. 42). Like Brenda, the character is located in the liminal space of the tourist and in the liminal temporality of so called 'middle age'.

Also like Brenda, for a considerable portion of the narrative at least, sexual gratification successfully cushions her from attempts to shame her. For a considerable period of the film a combination of passion, self-awareness and (paradoxically enough) self-loathing allow her to evade 'shame'. But this avoidance is ultimately proven to be only a temporary reprieve and in the final shots of the film she invites the young vagrant who has been following her throughout the film into her apartment where, it is implied, he stabs her to death. This follows the betrayal of a young Italian gigolo, who turns on her taunting her with the literal shaming narrative of a tabloid 'scandal'. Her humiliation is further compounded by the Contessa (who has played the role of procurer): she is 'ridiculous', she has 'descended to the depths...to an abyss'.

As in Sedgwick's designation of shame as foundational in terms of the development of identity, it interrupts a primary narcissism (also demonstrably social) for Karen, in contrast to Brenda whose narcissism precisely protects her from shame (supreme self-absorption as resistance to the gaze that would define her). In this film Karen is protected from 'shame/humiliation' by her explicit acknowledgement of the (prior) narcissistic wounds of ageing – her gaze into the mirror is very different from Brenda's. Her alienation from her own youthful, beautiful self – 'I had them once' – appears to be exactly what she mourns as she 'drifts' through Rome, properly melancholic. This response to the loss of youth accords with what Margaret Gullette identifies as the primary narrative of ageing in Western culture, the story of decline, and she argues that it is precisely through the endless reiteration of this story of decline that we are all 'aged by culture'. Recent theorizations of ageing and subjectivity have also taken as their starting point the reflection in the mirror that inaugurates a reassessment of the self (Woodward, 1991, pp. 53–71) but Helene Moglen's recent work offers a rather more optimistic model which draws on psychoanalytic understandings of the processes of mourning and melancholia to suggest the possibility that 'the melancholic longings of ageing are transformed into a productive process', a process she names as 'transageing'. Moglen argues for the dynamism of the processes of mourning the loss of the youthful body but she does make a distinction which may be of relevance here:

This form of mourning changes our understanding of the relation of consciousness to time and to the fluid, fluctuating, enriching presence of absence. To remain mired in the past is to deny the alluring mystery of present and future. That allure persists until the body does finally overwhelm the mind – during exceptional illness, for example, or in cases of 'deep age' and approaching death – when loss becomes irreparable. Then the horizon flattens and dimensionality disappears. (Moglen, 2008, p. 306)

One question that remains, then, is how far the stories that are repeatedly told of the 'dangers' to women (political, familial or in terms of identity) of transgenerational desire, how far these stories may also hinder the possibilities for 'transageing' in part through their deployment of affective regimes dominated by shame and melancholy? The fact that the women in these films are socially ostracized, physically punished or suffer other humiliations can be read as a critique of the prurience of 'the social' whilst simultaneously enacting the abjection/disgust it appears to critique in relation to older women's sexuality (having it both ways perhaps). Of interest in this regard is also Theresa Brennan's account of the ways that 'being aged' through the images which 'involve dictates about what the not-young are no longer capable of doing or being', results in a projection, in psychoanalytic terms, of 'rigidity and entropy' which 'ages' the recipient (Brennan, 1999, p. 138).

The final point that I want to make here in relation to these films' treatment of the congruence between age and shame relates to 'masculinity', for whilst Karen and Brenda are ambiguously and differently 'shame-less' (a designation which of course, performs a shaming function as in the speech act 'you shameless hussy', which though not strictly performative nevertheless often attempts to produce that which it names, i.e. shame) Paulo, Karen's younger lover, is hypersensitive to shame. Not only is he grievously insulted by the sniggering which accompanies the couple in public but his hypersensitivity to slights to his masculinity – a trait which he shares with Darren the younger man in *The Mother* and to a lesser extent Legba, and of course the eponymous hero of Fassbinder's film, Ali – seems to be precisely the 'risk' for masculinity which accompanies intergenerational sexual encounters. Here, in addition, this is linked to the films' postwar Italian milieu; it is a 'racial' or national shame and inverts the youth/age paradigm from the bodies of the lovers to the two national contexts from which they speak. Ancient Rome is impervious to the conquests of the arriviste Americans and the final speech of the film has the fascist Contessa moving seamlessly from a tirade against Karen Stone's sexual scandal to a condemnation of American wartime aggression: 'Do you think you can bomb us and kill our children and tell us how to behave?'

Conclusion

In contrasting ways then, all these films link the mobile affect, shame, whether diegetically or in the reception of the film, to questions of how intergenerational sexual encounters might be read in proximity to questions of race, class and nation. What I have tried to open up here then is that 'reading age' in the experience of watching and critiquing film does not preclude attention to the other '"other" question' (Bhabha, 1992) and that this might not only be thought, considered, evaluated and other scholarly things, but also, felt. This might matter because in contrast to the earlier films discussed the 'new femininities' explored here offer versions of intergeneration intimacy which stress the exploitative and the narcissistic – aspects of the representational regime of femininity which are of course far from 'new'. What does seem to be new in the narratives discussed here is the specific way that the management of shame is implicated in broader questions of race, class and postcolonial dynamics. Whilst earlier versions of this story offered a narrative overcoming class and race difference through a dissection of the politics of shame whereby it is the injustice of norms of sexual conduct which are under scrutiny, more recent versions of this narrative, particularly *Vers le Sud*, quite properly and painfully expose the ruthless, shameless, injustice of economic privilege and inequality – a by-product of which is perhaps to reinforce those repudiations of transgenerational racial and class desire which the earlier films equivocally celebrated.

Notes

1. One of the striking things about *Vers le Sud*, however, is how conventionally beautiful and indeed how 'youthful' the female protagonists are; the women in this film are in their 40s and early 50s whilst *The Mother* and *The Roman Spring of Mrs Stone* both explore relationships between women in their 60s and men in their 20s and 30s.
2. In using this term I am drawing on a range of recent work which has explored the 'cultural politics' of emotions and affects (Ahmed, 2004; Berlant, 2004; Probyn, 2005; Rose, 2004; Sedgwick, 2003).
3. These films have a history of inviting such analysis, Thomas Elsaessers's and Laura Mulvey's readings of Douglas Sirk's *All that Heaven Allows* and Fassbinder's *Ali Fear Eats the Soul*, for example, explore the ways in which the central couple in these films are positioned as 'outsiders' and how, in keeping with melodrama's preoccupations, these relationships expose 'irreconcilable social and sexual dilemmas', the ways that 'patriarchy victimizes men', the ambiguous theme of 'the continued sexuality of mothers' and, particularly with reference to the latter film, the complex dynamics of 'race' and, in the former, 'class' (Mulvey, 1989, p. 43). As Shohini Chaudhuri's reading of *Ali* emphasizes, these are films which have inspired film theorists to reconsider the analytics of the gaze in relation to gender, race and class. Kaja Silverman's reading exemplifies this in its exposing the controlling, racist and the objectifying 'gazes' of Fassbinder's film (Chaudhuri, 2005, pp. 650–1).
4. An exception here is *The Graduate* (dir. Mike Nichols, 1967) which was also recreated as a successful West End and Broadway revival directed by Sam Mendes from 2000–3. This narrative is extremely condemnatory of the suburban seductress, Mrs Robinson. However, significantly for my argument in this film the lovers are separated only by age; they are closely matched in terms of their shared race, class and economic privilege.
5. A crude summary could note that class dominates the 'difference' between the lovers in *All that Heaven Allows* and *Notes on a Scandal*; in *Ali Fear Eats the Soul*, the younger man's status as an Arab immigrant is contrasted with the older Emmi's white, (relatively) secure economic positionality; in *The Roman Spring of Mrs Stone* the younger man is 'native' to the older woman's 'tourist' but also occupies a

marginal social identity as a paid lover in contrast to Mrs Stone's wealth and celebrity; in *The Mother* the younger man again is economically marginalized, a craftsman in contrast to May's family's urban 'sophistication'.
6. The film is an adaptation of short stories by the Haitian writer Dany Laferrière.
7. I am deliberately avoiding the use of more emotive terms here, since these, such as 'seduced' or 'abused', are precisely, I am arguing, left by the staging of this scene for the viewer to establish.
8. A completely unscientific survey of responses to the film suggests I am not the only member of the audience who quite literally experiences, in an uncomfortably embodied way, shame during Brenda's confession to the camera.

Bibliography

Ahmed, S. (2004) *The Cultural Politics of Emotion* (Edinburgh: Edinburgh University Press).

Beauvoir, S. de (1972) *Old Age*, trans. Patrick O'Brian (London: André Deutsch).

Berlant, L. (2004) *Compassion: The Culture and Politics of an Emotion* (New York and London: Routledge).

Bhabha, H. K. (1992) 'The Other Question: The Stereotype and Colonial Discourse', in *The Sexual Subject a Screen Reader in Sexuality* (London: Routledge).

Brennan, T. (1999) 'Social Physics: Inertia, Energy and Aging', in K. Woodward (ed.), *Figuring Age: Women Bodies, Generations* (Bloomington: Indiana University Press).

Chaudhuri, S. (2005) 'Ali: Fear Eats the Soul: An Anatomy of Racism' in J. Geiger and R. L. Rutsky (eds), *Film Analysis* (New York and London: W. W. Norton and Company).

Fanon, F. (1986) *Black Skin, White Masks* (London: Pluto Press).

Foucault, M. (1990) *The History of Sexuality, Volume One* (Harmondsworth: Penguin).

Gill, R. (2007) *Gender and the Media* (Cambridge: Polity Press).

Katz, S. and B. Marshall (2003) 'New Sex for Old: Lifestyle, Consumerism, and the Ethics of Aging Well', *Journal of Aging Studies* 17: 3–16.

McRobbie, A. (2004) 'Notes on What Not to Wear and Post-feminist Symbolic Violence' in L. Adkins and B. Skeggs (eds), *Feminism after Bourdieu* (Oxford: Blackwell/The Sociological Review).

Moglen, H. (2008) 'Ageing and Transageing: Transgenerational Hauntings of the Self', *Studies in Gender and Sexuality* 9: 297–311.

Mulvey, L. (1989) *Visual and Other Pleasures* (Basingstoke: Macmillan).

Negra, D. (2009) *What a Girl Wants? Fantasizing the Reclamation of Self in Postfeminism* (Abingdon: Routledge).

Ngai, S. (2005) *Ugly Feelings* (Cambridge, MA: Harvard University Press).

Probyn, E. (2005) *Blush: Faces of Shame* (Minneapolis: University of Minnesota Press).

Radstone, S. (2007) *The Sexual Politics of Time* (Abingdon: Routledge).

Rose, J. (2004) *On Not Being Able to Sleep: Psychoanalysis and the Modern World* (London: Vintage).

Rose, N. (2001) 'The Politics of Life Itself', *Theory, Culture, Society* 18(6): 1–30.

Sedgwick, E. K. (2003) *Touching Feeling: Affect, Pedagogy, Performativity* (Durham: Duke University Press).

Shaviro, S. (1993) *The Cinematic Body* (Minneapolis: University of Minnesota Press).

Sobchack, V. (2004) *Carnal Thoughts: Embodiment and Moving Image Culture* (Berkeley: University of California Press).

Wearing, S. (2007) 'Subjects of Rejuvenation: Aging in Postfeminist Culture' in D. Negra and Y. Tasker (eds), *Interrogating Postfeminism* (Durham: Duke University Press).

Woodward, K. (1988) 'Youthfulness as a Masquerade', *Discourse* 11(1): 119–42.

Woodward, K. (1991) *Aging and its Discontents: Freud and Other Fictions* (Bloomington: Indiana University Press).

12
The Limits of Cross-Cultural Analogy: Muslim Veiling and 'Western' Fashion and Beauty Practices

Carolyn Pedwell

Drawing commonalities between embodied practices understood to be rooted in different cultural contexts has become prevalent in a range of feminist literatures. One analogy increasingly drawn is that between Muslim veiling[1] and so-called Western fashion and beauty practices.[2] Nancy Hirschmann suggests, for example, that Western feminists need to ask themselves whether 'the veil' is more oppressive than 'Western fashion' trends such as Wonderbras, mini skirts and blue jeans (1998, p. 361). Similarly, Sheila Jeffreys (2005) argues that beauty practices prevalent in 'the West' such as make-up, dieting and cosmetic surgery should be understood as 'harmful cultural practices' comparable to 'non-Western' practices as female genital mutilation and veiling. Linda Duits and Liesbet van Zoonen claim that both girls wearing headscarves and those dressed in 'porno-chic' are 'submitted to the meta-narratives of dominant discourse' which define their everyday practices as inappropriate and deny them the power to define their own action (2006, p. 103). These types of comparisons are now increasingly echoed within mainstream media discourse. For instance, in an article exploring veiling practices in the UK in *The Observer* Andrew Anthony argues that 'the veil and the bra top are really two sides of the same coin' (2005, p. 17). The premature recognition of female sexuality implicated by the veiling of girls as young as seven or eight 'is every bit as significant, and disturbing, as dressing a child in a high-street approximation of Britney Spears, all bare midriff and attitude' (p. 17).

Those who make links between Muslim veiling and 'Western' fashion and beauty practices clearly differ in their social locations and political agendas. Most, however, frame their comparisons with a concern to interrogate cultural essentialism, ethnocentrism and racism. These authors seek to deconstruct the binary of the 'liberated, uncovered Western woman' and the 'oppressed, veiled Muslim woman' that dualistic representations of Muslim veiling and 'Western' fashion and beauty practices often depend on and mobilize (Ahmed, 1992; Göle, 1996; Pedwell, 2008a, 2010). Through illustrating the ways in which particular practices involve similar discourses, motivations and rationales, these analogies interrogate the geopolitical relations of power through which such practices are represented as hierarchically discrete and query how the term 'culture' is employed differentially on the basis of axes such as race, nation and religion. Moreover, providing a counter-discourse to postfeminist perspectives which associate the open display of the female body with empowerment and sexual agency (MacDonald, 2006), they illustrate the ways in which women's and girl's bodies function *across* cultural contexts as carriers for wider political, economic and nationalistic imperatives. In the context of the analysis of 'new femininities' with which this collection engages, cross-cultural analogy represents a framework for thinking through apparently divergent gendered identities in contemporary multicultural and transnational contexts.

In this chapter, I want to examine how these cross-cultural analogies work. My analysis focuses on two recent Western feminist texts that draw links between Muslim veiling and 'Western' fashion and beauty practices: Sheila Jeffreys's *Beauty and Misogyny: Harmful Cultural Practices in the West* (2005) and Linda Duits and Liesbet van Zoonen's 'Headscarves and Porno-Chic: Disciplining Girls' Bodies in the European Multicultural Society' (2006). Jeffreys argues that while veiling and make-up are often seen as opposites, they are in fact analogous in that both mark women as subordinate, revealing their 'lack of entitlement' in patriarchal cultures (2005, p. 38). She explains that her book was motivated by a 'growing impatience' with the 'Western bias' of the United Nations' conceptual categories which interpret practices common in 'the West' as 'emanating from consumer "choice" from "science" and "medicine" or "fashion"', rather than culture, which 'may be seen as something reactionary that exists in the non-West' (p. 35). Through calling attention to the gendered oppression involved in beauty practices common in Western industrial contexts, Jeffreys contests Western-centric notions of personal choice and individual agency and emphasizes that 'the personal is political' (p. 10). Focusing on the Dutch context, Duits and van Zoonen object to the fact that public debates about girls' wearing of headscarves on the one hand and forms of 'porno-chic' such as belly shirts and visible G-strings on the other have been conducted separately as if they bear no relation to one another. This, the authors argue, obscures the fact that both debates are 'held together by the regulation of female sexuality' (2006, p. 103) and, in both, 'girls are denied their agency and autonomy' (p. 104). In drawing links between veiling and porno-chic, Duits and van Zoonen highlight the ways in which women's and girls' bodies become the 'metonymic location' for contemporary social dilemmas across cultural, ethnic and religious boundaries (p. 104). Concentrating on issues of intersectionality, cultural difference and agency, I will argue that, despite their significant differences, Jeffreys's and Duits and van Zoonen's analyses produce some common effects which tell us more about what cross-cultural analogies *do* in feminist theory, as well as their *limitations* as an anti-cultural essentialist tool.

Analogy, intersectionality and cultural difference

An analogy is defined as 'a person or thing that is like or comparable to another' (*OED*, 2001, p. 27). As the emphasis is on likeness, analogies must impose what I have termed a 'metric of commensurability' to make (at least) two entities comparable within a single discursive framework. In different ways, Jeffreys and Duits and van Zoonen both employ a metric of gender/sexuality to translate Muslim veiling and 'Western' fashion and beauty practices into a common theoretical and political language. Duits and van Zoonen's phrasing makes this process particularly clear: although debates about the veil and porno-chic 'are conducted independently from each other', they argue, 'they are part of a *single hegemonic discourse* about women's sexuality that transcends these partitions' (2006, p. 104, italics mine). My interest here is in examining what is at stake in imposing gendered metrics to make these practices commensurable. In addressing this question, it is important to acknowledge that analogies are performative. Following Judith Butler's understanding of performativity as 'that reiterative power of discourse to produce the phenomena that it regulates and constrains' (Butler, 1993, p. 2), I use the term 'performative' to underscore that analogies do not simply describe but rather actively *produce* the embodied practices that they draw together. Through the repeated acts of translation involved in constructing gendered commensurability among practices, analogies enable particular ways of reading these practices and the relations of power in which they are embedded, while disallowing others.

Within Jeffreys's text, veiling and make-up are produced as commensurable through translating make-up into the logic in which veiling has been commonly understood. If make-up has been widely conceived as being about women's choice and even as a sign of their liberation *against* readings of the veil as a symbol of women's oppression, Jeffreys's analogy overcomes this separation by framing both as practices that confirm women's subordinate status as objects of male sexual desire within patriarchal systems. While the expectation that 'respectable women in Islamic culture' will 'cover their heads and bodies so that men are not sexually tempted' may seem opposed to the expectation in the West that women will 'dress and makeup in such a way that men are sexually tempted', she argues, 'there can be seen to be a connection' (2005, p. 37): through both veiling and make-up, 'women are required to fulfil men's needs in public places and do not have the freedoms that men possess' (p. 44). Jeffreys's analogy therefore constructs both veiling and make-up as defined fundamentally by their patriarchal meanings and effects. Duits and van Zoonen's analogy functions, in turn, through making veiling intelligible within the logic of sexual regulation and decency through which porno-chic has been widely addressed. As the authors argue, in associating the veil with issues of gender inequality, multicultural excess and the separation of church from state *and not* the concerns of sexuality and decency through which porno-chic has been defined, public debates in European societies obscure the fact that 'a basic religious motive for covering the head and the face is tied in with sexuality and unwanted encounters' (2006, p. 108). Within Dutch society, they argue, both girls wearing head-scarves and those dressed in porno-chic are produced as outliers within an acceptable continuum of female decency. While the former are constructed as 'too decent' the latter are judged as 'not decent enough'. Within Western consumer culture, both are caught between a postfeminist rhetoric in which 'the overt presentation of sexuality' is figured as a maker of 'liberation from repressive societal codes' and a feminist critique which labels this an 'illusion' which 'joins seamlessly with the commercial interests of individualism and capitalism' (p. 112). Thus, although Duits and van Zoonen frame their analysis as one concerned with the discourses through which veiling and porno-chic are understood, rather than one about the character of the practices themselves, their analogy, like Jeffreys's, nonetheless produces a particular understanding of the meanings of these practices. Veiling and porno-chic become defined predominantly through their relationship to gendered norms of sexuality and decency. The authors make this clear in a rejoinder to their earlier text: 'It is obvious that both styles are obsessed with girls' bodies and sexuality: Muslim styles aim to protect girls' bodies from the public eye, consumer capitalist styles seeking to expose them to the public eye' (Duits and van Zoonen, 2007, p. 263).

Like these authors, I feel that gender and sexuality are crucial in these embodied practices, and this makes feminist analysis particularly important in this context. Furthermore, the gendered narratives Jeffreys and Duits and van Zoonen employ reveal salient links between particular forms of practice that are not often identified within the mainstream and are actively effaced by binary constructions that pose Muslim veiling and 'Western' fashion and beauty practices as fundamentally distinct. I want to argue, however, that, in both texts, the translations involved in making these practices commensurable result in two key effects that I understand as problematic. Firstly, in separating hierarchies of gender/sexuality from other relations of power, these analogies encounter difficulties in representing these practices as constituted through multiple and intersecting axes of differentiation. Secondly, in translating one embodied practice into the metric through which the other has been commonly understood, without interrogating the relations of power which underscore this metric, both gendered analogies are susceptible to slipping back into articulations of essentialist cultural difference.

With respect to the first point, in mobilizing a narrative of universal patriarchy to link Muslim veiling and 'Western' beauty practices, Jeffreys's analogy figures gendered relations of power as both ontologically prior to and separable from other systems of domination. This prevents her from theorizing the intersection of multiple axes of power as central to the diverse meanings of the varied forms which veiling and beauty practices take. For example, while Jeffreys makes brief reference to feminist analyses of the ways in which veiling may enable Muslim women to 'alleviate the harms suffered by women as a result of male dominance' (2005, p. 39), she does not consider the ways in which veiling and beauty practices may also, in very different ways, serve as adaptive strategies which respond to other oppressive systems, such as racism and cultural exclusion. In her study of Muslim women living in Canada, for instance, Homa Hoodfar (2003) observes that veiling has played a crucial role in helping some Muslim women adapt to Canadian society in the face of cultural difference, exclusion and racism. Other theorists have explored how claims to beauty that reproduce particular gendered norms have simultaneously provided a basis for anti-racist political agency. Maxine Leeds Craig suggests that in the context of a late nineteenth-century racist and classist aesthetics which portrayed black and working-class female bodies as grotesque, ugly and licentious against constructions of white, middle- and upper-class female bodies as classical, beautiful and virtuous, black women in Europe and North American 'proclaimed the beauty of black women in ways that simultaneously proclaimed their virtue' (2006, p. 170). Claiming gendered norms of beauty was a risky strategy for black women, 'who as women and blacks were already primarily seen as bodies', yet also a necessary one: 'black women had to claim beauty or...be annihilated' (p. 174). Jeffreys also does not consider the connections between veiling, anti-colonialism and a resistance to 'Western' values, which have been linked to indigenous patriarchies in particular contexts, but cannot simply be reduced to a linear logic of gender oppression (Ahmed, 1992; El Guindi, 2003; Göle, 1996).

Duits and van Zoonen's analogy also poses problems for representing intersectionality. By arguing that veiling has been addressed predominantly in relation to multiculturalism and porno-chic primarily in relation to decency, but that both should be understood in relation to decency, the structure of their analogy functions to split off discourses of decency (associated predominantly with gender/sexuality) from those of multiculturalism (associated predominantly with culture/race/nation). It consequently becomes difficult to analyse how sexualized discourses of decency are often co-constituted by racialized constructions of culture and nation. In her study of debates concerning girls wearing headscarves in French schools, for instance, Joan Scott argues that, in being judged as 'too decent', the veil became constructed as a sign of Muslim sexual aberrance (i.e. one that prevented the 'normal' interaction between the sexes central to 'proper' sexual maturation and identity development), which in turn became a marker of Muslim cultural difference and exclusion from the French ideal of secularism. As she contends, 'sexuality was the measure of difference, of the distance Muslims had to traverse if they were to become fully French' (2007, p. 166). Duits and van Zoonen's analogy also makes it difficult to represent how the postfeminist and neoliberal discourses within which they understand porno-chic to be embedded are not only gendered and sexualized, but also highly racialized and classed. Indeed, the skin-showing female body idealized by postfeminist rhetoric as a marker of women's sexual empowerment, is routinely a white, middle-class female body. Other (racialized) female bodies continue to be aberrantly sexualized within these forms of representation (Gill, 2006). From this perspective, porno-chic would need to be theorized as associated not only with decency discourses structured by norms of gender and sexuality but also by social, cultural and economic relations of power ordered by norms of race. To be clear, my argument here is not that Duits and van Zoonen fail to acknowledge the importance of race, nation and cultural difference in the context of their article. Indeed the racialized hierarchies implicated in certain ways of analysing veiling and porno-chic represent a starting point for these authors. My contention is that after identifying the relevance of race, culture and nation as they interact with gender and sexuality in the development and meaning of particular practices, they then go on to use an analogical framework for representing the links and similarities between veiling and porno-chic which does not seem capable of articulating these intersections in any sustained way. Moreover, while they raise the relevance of issues of race, cultural difference and nation in regards to veiling in their text, they do not acknowledge that such issues are also relevant to porno-chic. In implying that veiling is 'raced' and that porno-chic is not, this move may keep intact the problematic racialized binaries that they claim to want to disrupt (Pedwell, 2007, 2010).

If Duits and van Zoonen translate veiling into the metric of porno-chic without examining the racialized hierarchies ordering this metric, Jeffreys translates make-up into the logic of veiling without interrogating the essentialist narratives which underscore this logic. In including 'Western' beauty practices alongside 'non-Western' practices within the United Nations' category of 'harmful cultural practices' she unambiguously assumes that a variety of 'non-Western' practices, such as veiling, are fundamentally patriarchal and harmful to women and simply seeks to have 'Western' practices measured by the same yardstick. She also reinforces a divide between 'Western' and 'non-Western' practices that downplays the ways in which these practices clearly cross-over national and cultural contexts. Thus, while Jeffreys frames her analysis as one motivated by anti-cultural essentialist imperatives, one might argue that her analogy reifies ethnocentrism and essentialism by taking the oppressive nature of 'non-Western' practices for granted. This presents problems for theorizing the cultural cross-over, intermixture and reappropriation that characterizes girls' and women's embodied practices within a range of geopolitical contexts (Bhachu, 2004). Similarly, while Duits and van Zoonen acknowledge that 'girls' decisions to wear a headscarf have also become a particular way of making Islamic fashion statements' (Kilicaby and Binkark, 2000 cited in Duits and van Zoonen, 2006, p. 113), their dualistic categorization of girls as either 'G string girls' or 'headscarf girls' (p. 113) would seem to render unintelligible a range of subjects who may straddle or exceed these boundaries. The Muslim girl who considers herself both 'Islamic' and 'Western' and who may experiment with mixing make-up, elements of 'porno-chic' and particular aspects of Islamic dress as a way to negotiate her diasporic identity, seek a sense of cultural belonging in a Western industrialized context, or indeed to call attention to the specific difficulties in doing this, provides just one example.

Analogies and agency

I now want to think more carefully about the understandings of agency these two analyses express. Jeffreys suggests that the primary concern of feminist analysis should be to identify and remedy women's experiences of gender oppression, whether or not girls and women understand themselves to be oppressed. Indeed, she quite plainly rejects discourses of autonomous choice employed by girls and women to explain their sartorial choices, arguing that while 'both the veil and makeup are often seen as voluntary behaviours by women, taken up by choice and to express agency', there is considerable evidence that both practices are caused by 'the pressures arising from male dominance' (2005, p. 38). By contrast, while Duits and van Zoonen acknowledge that girls often do not critically interrogate their understandings of their sartorial choices 'as a matter of individual freedom', their main concern is that girls' own perspectives are being excluded from debates about both veiling and porno-chic through patriarchal discourses that figure them as victims without agency. From this perspective, Jeffreys' rejection of accounts of 'individual choice' and 'personal expression' might be read as an example of the very silencing of girls' voices that Duits and van Zoonen object to. Yet, without downplaying these differences, I want to argue that the texts also convey a similar conception of what agency *is* and *how it operates*. That is, both understand agency as something that has been *denied* to girls and women and thus something that might be *given back* to them. For Jeffreys, women's agency has been denied by cultures which compel them to veil or wear make-up as markers of their sexual difference and subordination. Feminist analysis should play a role in restoring women's agency by urging governments to enact effective societal changes which enable women to 'have access to the privilege possessed by men of not having to be concerned for appearance and being able to go out in public barefaced and bareheaded' (2005, p. 38). For Duits and van Zoonen, girls' agency has been denied within both public debate and feminist rhetoric which figure 'girls as "docile bodies" on which power – of Islam, capitalism or "men" is inscribed, and from which (thus) no independent rational contribution can be expected' (2006, p. 114). Feminist research can remedy this agency deficit by 'giving girls a voice' (p. 115). In figuring agency as that which has been *denied to girls* but might be restored through feminist action, both texts construe the capacity for agency as coming *after* the constitution of the subject, rather than that which the subject is constituted *through*. This conceptualization of agency has particular consequences for how the relationships between culture, embodied subjectivity and agency are theorized. That is, in separating embodied subjects from the contexts in which they are produced, it figures 'the meaning and sense of agency' as something which can be 'fixed in advance' rather than that which emerges only through an analysis of the particular contexts and 'concepts that enable specific modes of being, responsibility, and effectivity' (Mahmood, 2005, p. 14).

In suggesting that feminist empowerment may be achieved through enabling women to choose to present a 'visible' or 'open' face and body, Jeffreys' argument implies that women's embodied actions can be delineated into binary categories of patriarchal oppression (wearing the veil or make-up) and feminist resistance (appearing bareheaded and barefaced). She thus installs one particular conception of embodiment as the universal feminist ideal. This makes it difficult for Jeffreys to analyse the ways in which gendered norms are 'performed, inhabited and experienced' differently in different contexts, with varying implications for women's agency (Mahmood, 2005, p. 22). For example, in her study of women active in the Islamic mosque movement in Egypt, Saba Mahmood suggests that agential capacity for these subjects 'is entailed not only in those acts that resist the norms but also in multiple ways in which one inhabits norms' (p. 15). The task of realizing piety placed women of the mosque movement 'in conflict with several structures of authority' and yet, she argues, 'the *rationale*' for these conflicts was not predicated upon, and therefore cannot be understood only by reference to, arguments for gender equality or resistance to male authority. Nor can these women's practices be read as a reinscription of traditional roles, since the women's mosque movement has 'significantly reconfigured the gendered practice of Islamic pedagogy and the social institution of mosques' (p. 15). Furthermore, in portraying both the veil and make-up as 'masks' that might be discarded to enable women to 'show themselves as the real and equal citizens that they should be in theory' (Jeffreys, 2005, p. 38), Jeffreys figures veiling and various fashion and beauty practices as both superficial and separate from women's interior subjectivity and authentic agential capacity. This prevents her from analysing the ways in which embodied practice, subjectivity and agency often develop simultaneously, in and through one another, rather than independently of one another.

Unlike Jeffreys, Duits and van Zoonen do not employ a binary of patriarchal oppression/feminist resistance to assess Muslim veiling or 'Western' fashion and beauty practices. This is in part because they acknowledge that the meanings of these practices are diverse, but also because they aim specifically to critique 'top-down discourses' which impose meanings on girls' clothing choices that do not take account of the opinions of girls themselves. Yet, while the authors spend the first part of the article interrogating the essentializing and objectifying ways in which girls' sartorial choices are constructed through public discourses, this critical concern with the relationships among gender, discourse and power does not appear to be carried through to latter part of the piece. Indeed, Duits and van Zoonen's concluding argument that feminist analysis should, above all, concentrate on 'giving women a voice' (2006, p. 11), and their insistence that this imperative need not be qualified, would seem to eschew critical analysis of the complex relations of power which produce girls' 'speech acts'. Left unaddressed by their analysis are the key questions of how, in this context, we can understand the relations of power which condition 'who can speak' (and be heard) and what kinds of hierarchies are mobilized in the act of 'giving voice' (Spivak, 1988). Rosalind Gill has argued that Duits and van Zoonen's analysis conveys little sense of the cultural contexts in which girls and young women's sartorial choices are exercised: 'In the desire to respect girls' choices', she suggests, 'any notion of cultural influence seems to have been evacuated entirely' (2007, p. 73). I think Gill makes an important point, but I also want to make a slightly different one. That is, that the authors may need to think further, not only about the kinds of subjects and voices that the cultural and political contexts they are concerned with engender, but also the kinds of subjects *their own discourse* (re)produces and 'gives voice' to. If we understand cross-cultural analogies to be performative, then it follows that Duits and van Zoonen's analogy actively *constitutes* not only the embodied practices that they render commensurate, but also the imagined subjects of these practices. In linking veiling and porno-chic through a gendered narrative of sexual regulation, their cross-cultural analogy draws on and reiterates some familiar narratives of gender/sexuality, cultural identity and agency to render particular subject positions intelligible (Butler, 1993). An intelligible subject within their analogy is arguably one who may be defined as either (but not both) a 'G-string girl' or a 'headscarf girl' (who is understood to be synonymous with a 'Muslim girl'); who is in a position which enables her to 'use a discourse of individual agency to defend [her] sartorial choices'; and whose articulations of individual choice and personal expression resonate within a framework in which veiling and porno-chic are understood to reflect norms of gender, sexuality and decency (Duits and van Zoonen, 2006, p. 113). By contrast, those embodied subjectivities and voices who do not meet these discursive criteria (e.g. those subjects who disrupt these categories of feminine cultural identity, who remain silent or who do not mobilize dominant conceptions of individual choice and agency, or who understand their practices in ways that do not privilege gendered norms or sexual regulation) are rendered unintelligible. My point here is that, in figuring agency as that which has been denied to girls and may be *restored* to them through making their voices heard in feminist research, Duits and van Zoonen neglect to address the ways in which 'giving voice' is *itself* a power-imbued process – which they (along with a complex range of other actors and forces) play a role in shaping – and through which a particular subject 'with agency' is constituted (Spivak, 1988).

Conclusion

My discussion has examined some of the limitations of cross-cultural analogy as a feminist tool for addressing cultural essentialism. Theorists who link Muslim veiling and 'Western' fashion and beauty practices seek to disrupt essentialist discourses which represent these practices as fundamentally different and discrete. Yet, as illustrated through my analysis of Jeffreys' and Duits and van Zoonen's texts, analogies which link 'Western' and 'Muslim' embodied practices through a metric of gender/sexuality often function to replace problematic (racialized) difference with problematic (gendered) sameness. While cultural essentialism, ethnocentrism and racism are cited as a key concern by many authors, their analogies seem to proceed by dropping race and cultural difference out of the picture. When posed as an end-point to anti-essentialist analysis, these analogies may therefore *defer*, rather than tackle head on, analysis of the ways in which cultural essentialism and racism intersect with gendered and sexualized processes of domination to constitute embodied practices and cultural groups as fundamentally distinct. Because cross-cultural analogies often cover over, rather than interrogate, essentialist articulations of racialized cultural difference, these distinctions are liable to re-emerge problematically to reinstate oppositional categories and prevent analysis of cultural cross-cover, intermixture and reappropriation. Moreover, feminist analogies which construct cross-cultural commonalities between embodied practices via a narrative of 'restoring agency' often position agential capacity as both knowable in advance and separable from embodied subjectivity. This can prevent analysis of the specific processes through which different forms of agency are constituted and inhabited, as well as examination of the relations of power involved in discursive acts of 'giving voice'. Understanding feminist cross-cultural analogies as *performative* rhetorical devices may enable greater critical attention to be paid to the ways in which they mobilize existing narratives of gender/sexuality, culture and agency to (re)produce particular forms of knowledge and subjectivity, which are linked to a range of potential theoretical, social and political implications and effects.[3]

Notes

1. 'Veiling' is an English word used to refer to a very wide array of women's Islamic dress around the world. As such, while the term 'veiling' has wide currency in Western industrialized nations, it problematically homogenizes a diverse collection of practices. As Fadwa El Guindi (1999) points out, there is no one Arabic term equivalent to the English 'veil'.
2. I employ terms such as 'Western' and 'non-Western', 'Muslim' and 'non-Muslim' to indicate the types of distinctions made in the literature I am analysing. The generalizations they imply, however, are often troubling. Labelling Muslim veiling 'non-Western' obscures the wide practice of veiling in Western industrialized countries by women who may consider themselves both 'Muslim' and 'Western'. In turn, identifying practices such as make-up or the contemporary 'porno-chic' style as 'Western' obscures the extent to which they are practised by a diverse range of subjects all over the world. Thus, while I use these labels for analytical clarity, my objective is to highlight the ways in which they continue to be problematic.
3. Elsewhere I argue that rather than illustrating how embodied practices are *fundamentally similar*, we might more fruitfully examine how they are constructed relationally *in and through one another*. To this end, I develop a relational web approach that focuses on unravelling the multiple binary threads linking various practices in a wider representational economy. Thinking through relational webs, I suggest, enables us to unpack how, rather than being 'absolutely unrelated, polarised, or analogous', embodied practices such as Muslim veiling and 'Western' fashion and beauty practices 'are discursive constructs that come to matter in contextually specific ways and in relation to other discursive formation' (Sullivan 2009: 282–3) (see Pedwell, 2008b, 2010).

Bibliography

Ahmed, L. (1992) *Women and Gender in Islam: Historical Roots of Modern Debate* (New Haven and London: Yale University Press).

Anthony, A. (2005) 'The Big Cover Up', *The Observer*, 20 November.

Bhachu, P. (2004) *Dangerous Designs: Asian Women Fashion the Diaspora Economies* (London: Routledge).

Butler, J. (1993) *Bodies that Matter: On the Discursive Limits of 'Sex'* (London: Routledge).

Craig, M. L. (2006) 'Race, Beauty and the Tangled Knot of Guilty Pleasure', *Feminist Theory* 7: 159–77.

Duits, L. and L. van Zoonen (2006) 'Headscarves and Porno-Chic: Disciplining Girls' Bodies in the European Multicultural Society', *European Journal of Women's Studies* 13(2): 103–17.

Duits, L. and L. van Zoonen (2007) 'Who's Afraid of Female Agency? A Rejoinder to Gill', *European Journal of Women's Studies* 14(2): 161–70.

El Guindi, F. (1999) *Veil: Modesty, Privacy and Resistance* (Oxford: Berg).

El Guindi, F. (2003) 'Veiling Resistance' in R. Lewis and S. Mills (eds), *Feminist Postcolonial Theory: A Reader* (Edinburgh: Edinburgh University Press).

Gill, R. (2006) *Gender and the Media* (Cambridge: Polity Press).

Gill, R. (2007) 'Critical Respect: The Difficulties and Dilemmas of Agency and "Choice" for Feminism: A Reply to Duits and van Zoonen', *European Journal of Women's Studies* 14(1): 69–80.

Göle, N. (1996) *The Forbidden Modern: Civilization and Veiling* (Ann Arbor: University of Michigan Press).

Hirschmann, N. J. (1998) 'Western Feminism, Eastern Veiling and the Question of Free Agency', *Constellations* 5(3): 345–68.

Hoodfar, H. (2003) 'More Than Clothing: Veiling as an Adaptive Strategy' in S. S. Alvi, H. Hoodfar and S. McDonough (eds), *The Muslim Veil in North America: Issues and Debates* (Toronto: Women's Press).

Jeffreys, S. (2005) *Beauty and Misogyny: Harmful Cultural Practices in the West* (London: Routledge).

Macdonald, M. (2006) 'Muslim Women and the Veil: Problems of Image and Voice in Media Representations', *Feminist Media Studies* 6(1): 7–23.

Mahmood, S. (2005) *The Politics of Piety: The Islamic Revival and the Feminist Subject* (Princeton: Princeton University Press).

Oxford University Press (2001) *Oxford English Dictionary* (Oxford: Oxford University Press).

Pedwell, C. (2007) 'Theorising "African" Female Genital Cutting and "Western" Body Modification: A Critique of the Continuum and Analogue Approaches', *Feminist Review* 86 (July): 45–66.

Pedwell, C. (2008a) 'Intersections and Entanglements: Tracing "the Anorexic" and "the Veiled Woman"' in E. Olesky et al. (eds), *Gender and Citizenship in a Multicultural Context* (Oxford: Peter Lang).

Pedwell, C. (2008b) 'Weaving Relations Webs: Theorizing Cultural Difference and Embodied Practice', *Feminist Theory* 9(1): 87–107.

Pedwell, C. (2010) *Feminism, Culture and Embodied Practice: The Rhetorics of Comparison* (London: Routledge).

Scott, J. (2007) *The Politics of the Veil* (Princeton: Princeton University Press).

Spivak, G. C. (1988) 'Can the Subaltern Speak?' in C. Nelson and L. Grossberg (eds), *Marxism and the Interpretation of Culture* (Basingstoke: Macmillan).

Sullivan, N. (2009) 'Transsomatechnics and the Matter of "Genital Modifications"', *Australian Feminist Studies* 24(60): 275–86.

Part IV

New Femininities:
Agency and/as Making Do

13
Through the Looking Glass? Sexual Agency and Subjectification Online
Feona Attwood

Discourses of sexual agency have been seen as central to the development of new femininities, part of a broader shift in which older markers of femininity such as homemaking skills and maternal instincts have been joined by those of image creation, body work and sexual desire. This chapter examines debates about women's sexual oppression and agency, with particular reference to their objectification and subjectification in popular cultural forms. It considers how useful these debates are in the contemporary Western context where media and communication technologies are developing very rapidly, offering women unprecedented access to new forms of cultural production, most obviously online in blogs, chat rooms and communities. It situates these technologies in the broader cultural context of sexualization and shifts in the way visibility and celebrity, sexual display and agency are conceived. It asks how these developments impact on the representation of women's sexuality and what opportunities they provide for women to become involved in constructing and presenting their sexual selves. Focusing particularly on alternative pornography, it asks how we can develop an understanding of sexual agency in this context and how cultural and technological developments potentially make space for the representation of new constructions of sexuality and femininity.

Agency – 'as if'

A concern with women's objectification has long been central to feminist debates about representation and is probably even more central to popular perceptions of feminism where it is taken to indicate both anti-sexism and a presumption of feminist distaste for sex and bodily display. However, beyond the assertion that objectification turns female subjects into objects of sight and that this involves a power relation in which women are subordinated, there has been comparatively little in the way of a sustained theoretical discussion of objectification. Although the real focus of debates about objectification has been the genre of pornography, it is Laura Mulvey's groundbreaking work on narrative cinema that remains the most coherent articulation of this position. Mulvey argues that here, in the playing out of male fears and desires, women are made to *'connote to-be-looked-at-ness'* (1989, p. 19), 'turned...into objects of display...Yet, in a real sense, women are not there at all.' They are 'simply the scenery on to which men project their own fantasies' (1987, p. 131).

Mulvey's theory and the kind of textual analysis which supports it remains a useful and interesting explanation of cultural anxieties around women's bodies, though it becomes less persuasive the more widely it is applied. Certainly, it remains the case that women's bodies are over-exposed in the representational systems of modern and late modern cultures, and this requires explanation. Claims that women are encouraged to internalize the gaze of real or imagined observers (Berger, 1972) are also persuasive. However, explaining bodily display merely as an index of male fantasy or of female discomfort is too simplistic to be of real use.

This is particularly so in a context in which the exposure of the body – male and female – seems to be increasingly central to forms of popular representation and to individual self-expression. The question of bodily display and objectification needs further investigation, and following a period during which earlier feminist critiques became deeply unfashionable, the debate about women's sexual objectification has been revived by some feminist theorists. For some, the objectification of women has acquired new significance, becoming a means of recruiting women to an acceptance of their continued objectified status in popular culture.

According to Rosalind Gill, this involves a 'deliberate *re-sexualisation* and *re-commodification* of bodies' which, although it relies on depictions of women as 'knowing, active and desiring', actually marks a shift from 'an *external male judging gaze to a self-policing narcissistic gaze*' (2003, p. 104). This form of 'sexual subjectification' is 'objectification in new and even more pernicious guise' (2003, p. 105). It is part of the development of a post-feminist sensibility 'organized around notions of choice, empowerment, self-surveillance, and sexual difference, and articulated in an ironic and knowing register' (2007b, p. 271). The 'possession of a "sexy body"...is presented as women's key (if not sole) source of identity' (2007b, p. 255), in line with a broader sexualization of culture, the reassertion of sexual difference and the use of irony and knowingness to express 'sexist or homophobic sentiments' (2007b, p. 267).

In Gill's formulation, the kind of agency promised by the display of the sexy body only appears to offer a strong and positive subject position to women, whilst actually positioning them as an object for others, and indeed, for themselves. In the process, women are reduced to their bodies and subjected to impossible standards of acceptability which are likely to cause enormous anxiety and stimulate endless self-monitoring. Here 'agency' involves an injunction to constantly remake the self in ways which do nothing to benefit women. Nonetheless, women are asked to act *as if* this is freely chosen and *as if* they are agents. But while it is true that popular media continue to be overpopulated by sexualized images of women's naked or scantily clad bodies, these need not always signify as Gill argues they do.

This question of agency has been taken up in a debate between Gill and Linda Duits and Liesbet van Zoonen, focusing on discussions of 'headscarf' and 'porno-chic' girls; both groups whose clothing decisions regularly come under scrutiny and regulation. These discussions, Duits and van Zoonen argue, work as the location for particular social dilemmas about religion or sexual decency (2006, p. 107). In the articulation of those dilemmas, 'both conservative and liberal discourses end up denying the female subjects their agency' – and girls' voices are left out of the debate (2006, p. 114). Duits and van Zoonen argue that in such a context, particularly when girls themselves draw on a discourse of agency to defend themselves, feminist researchers must treat girls as 'capable and responsible agents' whose forms of self-presentation must be understood as 'speech acts' which need to be interpreted (2006, p. 115). For Gill, any interpretation of those acts must be made 'in the context of the norm of sexualized self-presentation' if we are to understand how social ideals become 'internalized and made our own' (2007a, pp. 72–6). Yet, as Duits and van Zoonen note, this is to close down an analysis of the variety of cultural practices that can be observed in women's contemporary engagements with bodily display. Just as it may not be the case that these are always characterized by a 'postfeminist sensibility', neither is it true that all girls dress in porno-chic style, as the existence of 'headscarf girls' clearly demonstrates (2007, p. 164), and even where they do it is not clear what the meanings of this style are for those who adopt them.

There are a number of factors that underpin this potential plurality of meanings. First, the visibility of feminist discourse in public and popular culture has worked to challenge the norm of women's sexual passivity and compliance, making it possible to imagine sex as a source of strength and independence. Second, a move towards sexualization at all levels of popular culture has fused notions of a strong confident self with body display, self-pleasure and erotic gazing. Looking and being looked at no longer necessarily signify powerlessness, as they do in the accounts given by Berger and Mulvey. Men are increasingly objects of erotic gazing (Bordo, 1999; MacKinnon, 1997), while new figures of male and female metrosexuality have worked to associate stylish sexiness with cultural capital. Third, the developing centrality of the celebrity body in Western cultures has inflected images of women's bodies in new ways. This has a particular impact on the potential significance of the displayed female body where visibility is associated with success and admiration. Fourth, the meanings of nudity are shifting, as Ruth Barcan notes, working variously to satirize, heroicize or celebrify their subjects, and both as ways of claiming and rejecting glamour (2004, p. 212). The range of meanings indicated by the naked body on display is multiplied in this context. Fifth, opportunities for image-work and media making are increasingly accessible to women in new forms of sexual representation such as D.I.Y, alternative or independent pornography. As a consequence, the potential for more diverse presentations of femininity and female sexuality has dramatically increased and issues of self-presentation have assumed new importance alongside older models of representation.

One offline example – the emergence of neo-burlesque performance – is interesting in this context. Neo-burlesque revives an earlier tradition of erotic performance associated with and dominated by women, notably in the 1870s and 1930s, and combining 'satire and sexiness' (Willson, 2007, p. 38). In its current incarnation, burlesque performance often demonstrates an alternative stance associated with sex and music subcultures as well as with female and gay male audiences, and it has been seen as representing fertile ground for playing with the norms and ideals of sexy femininity. As Jacki Willson notes, the fascination with display and visibility, evident in debates about the veiling and unveiling of women, is played out here, just as it is in the clothing practices of 'headscarf' and 'porno-chic' girls. But what is also significant is the way that the 'tease' of burlesque allows performers to take control of the performance environment (Willson, 2007, p. 167). As Debra Ferreday shows, the construction of the vintage feminine 'look' associated with neo-burlesque (2008, pp. 56–7) also challenges practices of femininity which are 'grounded in shame', focused on 'erasure' and 'disguise', and which conceal both the labour and the anxiety that they involve. In contrast, vintage femininity is shame-less, foregrounds an alternative D.I.Y approach and resists 'the notion that feminism and femininity are mutually exclusive, and that the enthusiastic pleasure taken in feminine identity is inherently problematic'. As Ferreday argues, it is easy enough to see these performances as evidence of women's lack of agency, based on the argument that they are 'capable of being (mis)read as a reproduction of normative heterosexuality' (2008, p. 53), or that they may be assimilated into the mainstream. But this ignores any sense of 'the locatedness of feminine identity and performances which would account for women's lived experiences of femininity' (2008, p. 61). What is also important here is that whilst it may be useful to ask why particular aesthetics, sensibilities or practices become popular in specific contexts, we need not collapse analyses of these phenomena into statements about women's absolute freedom, or insist that they have none whatsoever.

Life on screen

Online, women have also played key and often dominant roles in new practices of sexual and bodily display. Although public discussions of online

sexuality have frequently focused on sexual deviance, addiction, degradation and danger, the internet also offers unprecedented freedom to create,
distribute and access a much more diverse and interesting set of sexual representations and practices than have previously been available. It also provides a new context for the consumption of sexually explicit texts. As Zabet
Patterson has argued, new forms of online interactive pornography may
shift the 'nature of the relationship between viewer and woman-as-spectacle'
(2004, p. 110), collapsing the distance between the subject and object and
between passivity and activity (2004, p. 117). This is intensified because of
the way in which the computer has been constructed as a 'private space *within*
a public environment' that 'opens out onto a larger space of the Internet, a
space which is itself importantly both public and private' (2004, p. 120).

The particular form of viewing experience constructed in this context suggests something rather different from the voyeuristic relationship generally
assumed to exist between porn model and viewer. The sense of participation in which subject and object, private and public, appear to be collapsed
is echoed elsewhere in the contemporary 'explosion' of reality genres and
the keeping of online webcams and journals which 'frequently articulate
a public space of privacy' (Kitzmann, 2004, p. 122) and where media use
is increasingly seen as an 'individual creative activity' in which people
interact with images rather than passively consuming them (Kitzmann,
2004, p. 45).

The widespread use of mobile technologies, preoccupation with lifestyle, celebrity and body work, a fascination with constructing 'reality',
and developing technologies for living life 'on screen' provide the context
for online displays of women's bodies. These take a variety of forms. In
an early piece of writing Marj Kibby (1997) noted that the way women
were choosing to present themselves online was highly context-specific.
For example, in televideo sex, a form of sexual encounter that depends
on making the body visible through webcam use, bodily display is clearly
necessary. Yet women's sexual performances involved quite specific forms
of display; for example, they tended to 'depict themselves through a shot
of their breasts', rather than through the display of their faces or genitals as
men did. In contrast, in textually based multi-user domains, women often
downplayed their sexuality. However, on home pages many women chose
to 'emphasise their sexuality as an integral part of their identity', often
including 'an identifiable, full-length "glamour" portrait'. Kibby argued
that although the internet offers the possibility of creating a genderless
self, there are particular contexts of computer-mediated communication
where women appeared to be insisting on 'their right to present a sense of
self constituted, at least in part, through their experience of inhabiting a
gendered, sexed body'.

More recently, Michelle White has noted how 'camgirls' use online spaces
to represent themselves, documenting their everyday lives through live

broadcast images and blogs. These often also work to restructure relations of looking, challenging simple notions of woman-as-object (2003). At a formal level, women's image is presented as 'unfinished and incomplete', whilst the spectator's own reflection in the screen works to undercut spectatorial distance; the webcam spectator is 'too close to see' (2003, p. 20) in a detached or voyeuristic way. Women cam operators often ironize voyeuristic gazing too, by using images such as fishbowls or images of themselves as powerful gazers. White argues that these women connote 'to be looked-at-ness' (2003, p. 22) in a very ambivalent way, engaging with that position not only by controlling the ways in which they make themselves visible, but also by developing rules around viewing relations and by reflecting upon these. Many women report feeling 'safe and even comfortable while they are being watched', and are supported by fans against harassment (2006, p. 71). Their experiences suggest that 'the controlled forms of visibility, which they choose, provide a much more empowering position than submitting to traditional forms of the gaze' (2006, p. 72).

In addition, camgirls' sites are not simply about display and gazing but about women as users of technology, builders of communities, and, crucially, as communicators. Women webcam operators are a significant part of the camgirl audience and are encouraged in their practice by other operators (White, 2006, p. 73). Treating the work of women webcam operators and other online producers as a significant form of cultural production is important as part of acknowledging the vital role that women play in technological aspects of culture. From this point of view, women's webcams 'offer a setting in which to emphasize women's employment of the Internet and a means to rethink other aspects of their cultural representation' (White, 2006, p. 84).

Another arena for women's engagement with display is in the proliferation of alternative porn sites. 'Altporn' can be dated to around 2000 with the emergence of sites such as Blue Blood, Gothic Sluts, NakkidNerds and Super Cult, and the appearance of the most well-known site, SuicideGirls in 2001. These often combine sexual display with alternative styles of presentation, as well as incorporating the features of online communities such as blogs, cams, chat rooms and message boards. Some sites are concerned with particular subcultures such as goth or hippie; altporn.net listed around 40 such sites in its Altporn History Timeline in 2007.[1] Traffic ratings for January 2008 showed over 200,000 visitors per month for the most popular site, SuicideGirls, with other sites visited by anywhere between around 700 and 170,000 visitors per month.[2] Other alternative porn sites draw on countercultural politics. Fuck for Forest is an 'erotic non-profit eco organization' which relies on members' donated images and uses porn to 'save the forests'. A number of other sites are also notable for their alternative takes on presenting sexuality. Beautiful Agony features images of the faces of women (and some men) as they orgasm, while sites such as No Fauxxx and Bella Vendetta draw on sex and gender politics from sex-radical and queer perspectives.

Many of these sites are dominated or run by women. All challenge some of the established aesthetics and address of much mainstream pornography. In addition, some operate as spaces where many feminist critiques of pornography – that porn subordinates women, or makes them passive or objectified, or subjects them to conventional standards of beauty or norms of femininity, or that porn excludes women both as producers and consumers – are taken on, often quite explicitly. As Shoshana Magnet has argued (2007), even SuicideGirls, the most commercial of altporn sites, eroticizes 'deviant' femininity in the form of tattoos and piercings, disrupts conventional beauty ideals and presents its models as active and intelligent. Pin-up display is combined with models' journal entries dealing with a range of issues ranging from sexual harassment to schoolwork. Discussion groups on feminism and women's sexuality within the site help to foreground women's pleasure and knowledge. Women are envisaged not as the passive object of a gaze when they display their bodies, but as actors, artists and sometimes activists.

'Furry Girl' is one of the new female 'porn professionals' participating in the wave of new and alternative takes on sexual representation. She runs her own site, furrygirl.com, plus three others: vegporn.com provides 'alternative erotica and sex-positive culture for herbivores and those who love them', featuring vegans and vegetarians 'of all shapes and sizes' as well as restaurant reviews, interviews and naked vegan recipes; thesensualvegan.com features 'quality adult vegan products'; and eroticred.com is a site for 'homemade...menstruation porn created by a variety of hot models of all shapes and styles on their periods!' The purpose of this site is to show that menstruation is 'a healthy, interesting, and fun part of the lives of all female-bodied folk'. However, as Furry Girl notes, this focus has proved problematic. Although 'photos of women being throat-fucked and pissed on' are commonplace elsewhere in the porn industry, 'adult industry types' responded to the idea that menstruation can be sexy as 'very disturbing', 'unacceptable' and 'offensive'.

Furry Girl's 'furriness' refers to her preference for not removing body hair and furrygirl.com is 'an evolving collection of amateur porn created by a real gal with a hairy pussy, hairy pits, and hairy legs'. Furry Girl is a 'true do-it-yourself amateur', making and controlling all aspects of her self-representation and offering 'a more intimate experience' than 'any flashy corporate site'. In addition to looking at her weekly photos and videos, members can email her, read her journal and Twitter updates, post on the members' message board, and chat to her in her weekly cam shows. In addition members can request picture sets and videos, or pay extra for custom work or private cam shows.

Furry Girl's engagement with her audience is located somewhere between the fully commercial and the gift economies that characterize many social networking sites and online communities. Some content is free, but members pay a monthly fee of $20 to gain access to more content and more interaction. Like camgirl sites, furrygirl.com is a space that contains different levels of privacy and publicity. Thus, while the site invites spectators 'into the bedroom of a naughty all-natural gal', it also sets clear limits to what is accessible and acceptable: 'I simply don't have the time to email photos to everyone', 'my site is not a dating ad, and I'm not looking for people to have sex with through it', 'I do not not sell/license my content and I am not looking for "photographers" to "work with"', 'And don't ask me about my "real name", my lips are sealed.' In order to contact Furry Girl, correspondents must agree with the following statements:

* 'I am NOT emailing to ask if I can fuck Furry Girl or be in photos with her.'
* 'I am NOT emailing to ask Furry Girl about modeling for my amateur photo projects.'
* 'I do NOT expect a reply for at least a month for non-urgent questions.' (I get lots of email!)

Like other alternative porn models, Furry Girl combines bodily display with the presentation of a unique self, expressed through personal information about her life and tastes. Her site bio contains information about her personal details ('I live with a little gray cat named Mr. Mouse... I'm interested in just about everything, from sex to gardening to history to film to medicine... I'm an avid reader. I've been vegan for almost 9 years... I love travel... I'm happily child-free... I'm also an atheist'); physical statistics ('perky A cup... very long natural brown hair that comes to my waist'); sexual orientation ('I'm a poly slut and I usually end up sleeping with my friends, not random strangers... I like boys and girls, as well as people that don't fit into male-or-female boxes. I love all sorts of genderqueer/pansexual/crossdressing/kinky types, especially drag kings and guys who like to play with me when I'm wearing my strap-on'); and sexual tastes and turn-ons ('just about anything, as long as it's safe, sane, consensual and hot... smart people who excel at whatever they are passionate about... People with good reading and writing skills').

Clearly, Furry Girl presents herself as 'to-be-looked-at' and certainly, as a sex worker, she is sexualized and commodified. Yet it is hard to see why she has no agency; indeed, rather than reduce herself to an objectified 'sexy body', she insists that her body should be understood as part of an individual identity, even within the confines of a commercial transaction. Her refusal of conventional porn styles in favour of constructing a persona that emphasizes the unvarnished body, active desire and pleasure in performing can be read as a D.I.Y. mode of self-presentation which is proud and shameless and which attempts to give new meaning to bodily display and sex commerce.

Here, sexual display is both personalized and politicized. As well as her commitment to veganism and the celebration of menstruation, Furry Girl has a clear sense of the ethics and politics of porn presentation. In her view, alternative porn should emphasize its performers' pleasure, allow them 'to express themselves and have a say in how they are presented', portray them 'as multidimensional beings, with interests other than sex', and be 'an expression of the people who make it'. It should defy conventions of beauty, body type and style, challenge 'stereotypes and negative attitudes about race, size, gender, and sexual orientation', and uphold 'the idea of safe, sane, and consensual sex play' (in Watson, 2006).

Agency – 'making do'

The construction of sexual agency and ethics expressed in camgirl and alternative porn sites invites a reconsideration of women's bodily display online. Foucault's notion of technologies of the self (1988) and Butler's theory of performativity (1990) are perhaps most pertinent for developing this.

In Foucault's work, the idea of 'technologies of the self' is part of an attempt to formulate a view of subjectivity that explains how individuals must draw on available discourses, and yet can act autonomously. Butler is also concerned with the production of subjectivity 'within the processes of signification that construct the self' where the subject is constructed performatively through the repetition of given signs and norms. Agency is 'located within the possibility of a variation on that repetition of norms' (Butler, 1990, p. 145) and conceptualized in terms of a 'taking up of tools' 'where the very "taking up" is enabled by the tools lying there' (Butler, 1990, p. 145). According to Barvosa-Carter, the choice of one set of tools over another 'gives the self a reflexive space, a critical distance, and a competing perspective...with which it can see anew, critique and potentially vary its own identity performances' (2001, p. 127).

From this perspective, agency can be seen as the self-reflexive adoption of a specific discourse, and we can extend this to the kinds of 'speech acts' which particular sartorial choices, displays of nakedness, and uses of media technologies might indicate. A similar formulation is used by Foucault to conceptualize ethics as 'the considered form that freedom takes when it is informed by reflection' (in Rabinow, 1997, p. 284) and an ethical sensibility as 'a process of constant experimentation and reappraisal, in which new experiences are integrated, and reflection helps determine future actions' (in Albury, 2003, p. 207). These conceptions of agency and ethics do not appeal to absolute categories of good and evil or liberation and control, but take account of context and circumstance.

As Dennis Waskul has noted (2003, p. 126), discussions of online bodily display need to be attentive to the 'varied dynamics of the relationships between bodies, selves, and the situated contexts in which both are located'. The significance of the body and its relation to the self is not fixed; instead the body 'is something that is read, interpreted, presented, concealed, and made meaningful in an ongoing negotiated process of communication and situated social interactions' (Waskul, 2003, p. 127). Waskul concludes that increasingly we can see the construction of 'a body-as-*performance* relationship' (2004, p. 31), both in terms of the specific context of online display and the broader social context in which 'what it means to be associated with a body has clearly been altered'. This is evident in a whole range of practices which image the body, emphasizing the 'malleability of body presentations' and their significance in indicating personhood (Waskul, 2003, p. 93).

In the examples I have discussed, women engage with and negotiate modes of bodily display, using them to perform a sexual self. They take up a range of technological, aesthetic and communicative tools in the relatively safe spaces of rehearsal and ritual, play and performance that they inhabit. They are not always or only sexual, though they claim the right to be so in some contexts. Camgirls present themselves as cultural producers, challenging the representation of women as technologically inept and as passive sexual objects. They take on the power relations of looking, defying objectification and experimenting with ways of refusing, commanding and controlling the spectators' gaze. Similarly, altporn producers play with models of deviant and alternative femininity, often foregrounding the politics of sex and gender and rearticulating what it means to be on display. Discussions of new femininities have often focused on how, in late modern societies, women's sexual agency is foregrounded but ultimately denied, and how new cultural forms and preoccupations become part of this process. Yet cultural and technological shifts also open up a space for the presentation of new feminine sexualities. It is hard to see these merely as compliant responses to male desire, fantasy or fear, as Mulvey's account suggests, or simply as forms of the anxious self-policing by which Gill suggests contemporary femininity is often reduced to the production of a 'sexy body'. Instead, camgirls and altporn producers often insist on the presentation of a sexual self which is firmly located within the context of their lives, relationships and politics. Here, agency is always a form of 'making do', but it is also one which exceeds the limitations within which it is necessarily produced, becoming a new way of doing femininity and making culture.

Acknowledgement

I would like to acknowledge the support of the AHRC in funding a period of study leave which enabled me to research women's online sexual self-presentation.

Notes

1. http://altporn.net/category/features/traffic-study/page/3/ [accessed 12 February 2009].
2. http://altporn.net/category/features/traffic-study/ [accessed 12 February 2009].

Bibliography

Albury, K. (2003) 'The Ethics of Porn on the Net' in C. Lumby and E. Probyn (eds), *Remote Control: New Media, New Ethics* (Cambridge: Cambridge University Press).
altporn.net, http://altporn.net/ [accessed 24 November 2008].
Barcan, R. (2004) *Nudity: A Cultural Anatomy* (Oxford amd New York: Berg).
Barvosa-Carter, E. (2001) 'Strange Tempest: Agency, Poststructuralism, and the Shape of Feminist Politics', *International Journal of Sexuality and Gender Studies* 6(1/2): 123–37.
Beautiful Agony, www.beautifulagony.com [accessed 24 November 2008].
Bella Vendetta, http://bellavendetta.com [accessed 24 November 2008].
Berger, J. (1972) *Ways of Seeing* (London: Penguin).
Bordo, S. (1999) 'Beauty (Re)Discovers the Male Body', in *The Male Body: A New Look at Men in Public and in Private* (New York: Farrar, Straus & Giroux).
Butler, J. (1990) *Gender Trouble: Feminism and the Subversion of Identity* (London: Sage).
Duits, L. and L. van Zoonen (2006) 'Headscarves and Porno-Chic: Disciplining Girls' Bodies in the European Multicultural Society', *European Journal of Women's Studies* 13(2): 103–17.
Duits, L. and L. van Zoonen (2007) 'Who's Afraid of Female Agency? A Rejoinder to Gill', *European Journal of Women's Studies* 14(2): 161–70.
Erotic Red, www.eroticred.com [accessed 24 November 2008].
Ferreday, D. (2008) 'Showing the Girl: The New Burlesque', *Feminist Theory* 9(1): 47–65.
Foucault, M. (1988) 'Technologies of the Self' in L. H. Martin et al. (eds), *Technologies of the Self: A Seminar with Michel Foucault* (Amherst: University of Massachusetts Press).
Fuck for Forest, www.fuckforforest.com [accessed 24 November 2008].
Furry Girl, www.furrygirl.com [accessed 24 November 2008].
Gill, R. (2003) 'From Sexual Objectification to Sexual Subjectification: The Resexualisation of Women's Bodies in the Media', *Feminist Media Studies* 3(1): 100–6.
Gill, R. (2007a) 'Critical Respect: The Difficulties and Dilemmas of Agency and "Choice" for Feminism', *European Journal of Women's Studies* 14(1): 69–80.
Gill, R. (2007b) *Gender and the Media* (Cambridge: Polity Press).
Gothic Sluts, www.gothicsluts.com [accessed 24 November 2008].
Hippie Goddess, www.hippiegoddess.com [accessed 24 November 2008].
I Shot Myself, www.ishotmyself.com [accessed 24 November 2008].
Kibby, M. (1997) 'Babes on the Web: Sex, Identity and the Home Page', *Media International Australia* 84: 39–45. Available at http://www.newcastle.edu.au/discipline/socio-anthrop/staff/kibbyma [accessed 16 April 2005].
Kitzmann, A. (2004) *Saved From Oblivion: Documenting the Daily from Diaries to Web Cams* (New York: Peter Lang).

MacKinnon, K. (1997) 'A Decade of Outing the Male Object', in *Uneasy Pleasures: The Male as Erotic Object* (London and Cranbury: Cygnus Arts/Fairleigh Dickinson University Press).

Magnet, S. (2007) 'Feminist Sexualities, Race and the Internet: An Investigation of suicidegirls.com', *New Media & Society* 9: 577–602.

Mulvey, L. (1987) 'You Don't Know What Is Happening, Do You, Mr. Jones?' in R. Parker and G. Pollock (eds), *Framing Feminism: Art and the Women's Movement, 1970–1985* (London: Pandora).

Mulvey, L. (1989) 'Visual Pleasure and Narrative Cinema', in *Visual and Other Pleasures* (Bloomington and Indianapolis: Indiana University Press).

No Fauxxx, www.nofauxxx.com [accessed 24 November 2008].

Patterson, Z. (2004) 'Going On-line: Consuming Pornography in the Digital Era' in L. Williams (ed.), *Porn Studies* (Durham and London: Duke University Press).

Rabinow, P. (ed.) (1997) *Ethics: Subjectivity and Truth* (New York: The New Press).

The Sensual Vegan, www.thesensualvegan.com [accessed 24 November 2008].

Suicide Girls, www.suicidegirls.com [accessed 24 November 2008].

VegPorn, www.vegporn.com [accessed 24 November 2008].

Waskul, D. D. (2003) *Self-Games and Body-Play: Personhood in Online Chat and Cybersex* (New York: Peter Lang).

Waskul, D. D., Douglass, M., and Edgley, C. (2004) 'Outercourse: Body and Self in Text Cybersex' in D. D. Waskul (ed.), *net.seXXX: Readings on Sex, Pornography, and the Internet* (New York: Peter Lang).

Watson, P. (2006) 'Alternaporn: We Sing the Body Politic'. Available at http://www.lazaruscorporation.co.uk/v4/articles/alternaporn.php [accessed 23 November 2006].

White, M. (2003) 'Too Close to See: Men, Women, and Webcams', *New Media & Society* 5(1): 7–28.

White, M. (2006) *The Body and the Screen: Theories of Internet Spectatorship* (Cambridge, MA: MIT Press).

Willson, J. (2007) *The Happy Stripper: Pleasures and Politics of the New Burlesque* (London: I. B. Tauris).

14
Reckoning with Prostitutes: Performing Thai Femininity

Jin Haritaworn

> We, the Mail Order Brides/M.O.B., are a trio of young Filipina-American artists engaged in (wedded to) a collaborative process of cultural investigation. We have taken our name in response to the common misrepresentation that Filipina women make ideal *(read: submissive, obedient)* brides, a myth born from the unfortunate economic reality that makes women and their labor the Philippines' leading export. It has not escaped our attention that, acronymically speaking, '<u>M</u>ail <u>O</u>rder <u>B</u>rides' abbreviates down to a more sinister series of initials which inform the darker subtext of our connivings and conspiring.
>
> (Mail Order Brides, 'Artists' Statement',
> cited in Velasco, 2008, p. 15, emphasis in original)

A few months ago, I came across the San Francisco-based 'Mail-Order Brides/M.O.B.' through the work of an American colleague, Gina Velasco (2008). It was my first encounter with a cultural activism that thoroughly refuses the sexual conservatism of a diasporic collectivity which is first and foremost imagined as the source of cheap 'maids' and 'brides'.[1] Rather than expressing moral outrage about, or attempting to disprove, the relentless stereotyping of Filipinas and the nation they come to negatively symbolize, the M.O.B.s tackle the figure of the mail-order bride head-on in ironic performances. Velasco shows how the queer ensemble use 'parody', 'humour', 'feminist camp' and 'ethnic/national drag' (Velasco, 2008, pp. 15ff.) in order to interrupt a circulation of bodies and images which continually returns those assigned female[2] and Filipina to their moral and economic place.[3] The M.O.B.s' info-mercial *Always a Bridesmaid, Never a Bride*, for example, launches a multi-layered critique of the ways in which Filipina femininity becomes the constitutive outside of respectable femininity: excluded from the domestic realm as wife, the Filipina is nevertheless reintroduced as maid: 'cheap', underpaid, sexually available. In their performances, photographs, karaoke videos and art installations, the ensemble challenge the truths of the mail-order bride discourse by sticking the labels 'maid' and 'bride' onto their own bodies. They empty the stereotype by filling it so amply it bursts at the seams.[4]

As multiply dis/located subjects, the M.O.B.s complicate single-issue notions of agency, performativity and femininity. They contest the intimate investments in normalcy, assimilation and respectability, by both mainstream society and by diasporic, feminist and queer counter-publics that variously resist, mimic and rework its gendered, racial and sexual double standards. This is reflected in the 'stages' they choose for their 'mobbing': from same-sex marriage ceremonies and 'karaoke bars to the local Chinatown parade in downtown Oakland' (Velasco, 2008, p. 16). Few normativities remain safe: the self-fulfilling trope of the 'bride' in the Western media, the heteronormativity of an increasingly assimilationist gay movement, and the complicities of the Philippine state in the global commodification of Filipinas' intimate labour (ibid.).

The ensemble complicate any singular notions of new femininities. Feminist theorists have rightly problematized simple dichotomies of female sexual subjecthood vs. objectification, and the role that the capitalist media play in shaping and constraining the discursive field within which young women (and, one might add, trans people who are female-assigned or feminine-presenting) lay ownership to their bodies and sexualities (Gill, 2003). This is further complicated for those whose exclusion from sexual agency occurs at a more categorical level, where to be sexual means to be always already abject, *prostituted*.[5] For many Southeast Asians, to enter into sexuality paradoxically means *to leave the realm of desire and the desirable*. For the figure of the 'Filipina' or the 'Thai woman' is desirable only from a problematic position; a voiceless object to be bought, sold and 'trafficked' between white and brown men (as well as our own patriarchal families). For the 'female' Southeast Asian subject, therefore, sexual agency occurs in a different discursive realm, which calls for different engagements, resistances and subversions. These include by necessity not only the state, market and media, but also Western feminism itself, with its material and ideological investment in the 'trafficked victim', and its historical complicities in the rescue, objectification, patronage and 'protection' of female subaltern bodies and sexualities (Agustín, 2007; Doezema, 2001; Kapur, 2005).

Inspired by the M.O.B.s, I attempt to map this discursive realm from my own transnational entry point, of Thai 'mixed race'[6] and second generationality. Drawing on interviews with people in Britain and Germany who, like me, were raised in 'mixed' Thai/'interracial' families, I argue that racism threads itself through the sexual and gender negotiations of those who grew up under the sign of 'prostitution', largely in the absence of alternative repertoires. If these negotiations are constrained by a white, heteronormative lens which automatically reassigns them to the realms of 'the victim' and 'the prostitute' (a misrecognition which as I will show next also pervades

Western feminist and queer scholarship), the question of sexual agency, for Thai as well as other female and sexual subalterns, is nevertheless not one we can afford to dismiss.

'Trafficking' and 'performativity'

The M.O.B.s are so remarkable and refreshing because their unruly agency denaturalizes the doxic, largely unchallenged view of Southeast femininity as always already 'trafficked' and incapable of sexual agency. In the Thai case, we are used to viewing trafficking as a continuation of imperialism and warfare in the region, whose landmarks include the Rest&Recreation programme that returned American soldiers to life, after taking those of other Asians nearby; the sex tourism developed in the infrastructure of R&R under the guidance of the World Bank; and the colonial legacies of concubinage and prostitution that preceded American imperialism in the region (Bishop and Robinson, 1998; Levine, 2000).

While important in its anti-colonial analysis, this narrative nevertheless often reproduces the hegemonic discourse on Thai femininity in problematic ways. 'Thai woman' (and other discursively 'prostituted' femininities) is only ever thinkable as 'trafficked', 'prostituted', interracially coupled, and 'bride'.

> The mail-order bride industry is essentially a form of trafficking, [Sheila Jeffreys] maintains [in her new book *The Industrial Vagina*], with many of the women who are advertised on marriage agency websites later being sold into prostitution by their husbands. The majority of men who access these services are white and from wealthy countries, and their brides come from cultures where the female stereotype is subservient and docile. (Bindel, 2008, n.p.)

There is a slippage in this statement between agency-arranged marriages, interracial relationships, sexual violence and slavery. However, people who are abused, sell sex, meet their partner through an agency, or meet them in an office, often attach different meanings to these intimate events (see Ruenkaew, 2003). Many of my interviewees laboured hard in order to represent their families as the products of romantic love or, in its mixed-race variation, the 'love that knows no colour'. Their anti-racist critique of violent readings of their families, which were automatically assumed to be the result of prostitution, sex tourism or agency arrangements, often had a moral timbre, as sex workers were blamed for giving Thai people and the Thai nation a 'bad name'. In fact, interviewees who could not or would not present their genealogies in opposition to sex work complained about the discrimination that they experienced at the hands of other diasporic Thais. The *lack* of distinction between 'Thai' and 'prostitute' in the Orientalist discourse is thus *productive* of distinctions and hierarchies in Thai diasporic space, which besides their class violence also serve to circumscribe female sexual agency (see Skeggs, 1997).

While ostensibly describing a universal, binaried divide between male perpetrators and female victims, the feminist trafficking discourse nevertheless produces its own exclusions. 'Prostituted' women from 'other', implicitly more 'traditional', cultures appear as hyperbolic figures of female victimization, whose suffering is self-evident and not in need of further explanation or conceptualization. Like other affective performances (Ahmed, 2004), this narrative of pain and injury has its own sociality. It produces differences between those described as injured and those positioned as witnesses who must intervene (see Doezema, 2001). If the 'brides' are 'from cultures where the female stereotype is subservient and docile', it takes emancipated 'feminists' (presumably from 'modern' cultures) to rescue them. Jeffreys and Bindel almost literally repeat the patriarchal colonial view of subaltern women as 'ideal *(read: submissive, obedient)* brides' (M.O.B.s). While adopting anti-colonial discourse, they show themselves untouched by a postcolonial feminism which rejects and critiques Western feminist strategies to enter into agency by fixing subaltern women as passive, backward objects that cannot act but must be acted upon (e.g. Mohanty, 1988).[7]

Migrant sex work and sex tourism are complex topics that deserve more detailed discussion (see Agustín, 2007; Doezema, 2001). My point here is that we need to scandalize the dominant representation of Southeast Asian femininities as always already prostituted in its own right, and need to do so without reinscribing either/or dichotomies between feminist/victim, good girl/whore, positive/negative image. This forces us to examine new femininities, as not only about objectification as female, but also about distinctions between different femininities, some of which occur in feminist texts and contexts themselves. Looking at performativity in such a framework would mean opening our allied gaze to different kinds of performances, involving settings, stages, talents and plots that may not always be immediately apparent or transparent to us. It would mean expanding our performative repertoire, from one that contests distinctions between 'male' and 'female' (Butler, 1991), to one that takes on moral, racial and economic distinctions as well. In other words, we should put the drag queen in conversation with other ironic, parodic, subversive figures, such as the ladyboy or, indeed, the prostitute her/himself.

Such an invitation goes against the grain of a feminist history which has 'rendered ghostly' (Gordon, 1997, p. 18) not only prostitutes but other sexually and gender-excessive figures, such as the butch lesbian, the bisexual femme, or the woman who dares to name her experiences of child sexual abuse alongside her lesbianism or sadomasochism (Allison, 1984). As a result of the 'sex wars' between 'radical' (anti-porn, anti-SM, etc.) feminists and 'sex radical' (sex positive, often 'queer') feminists, sex and gender, including transgressive acts and objects such as drag, pornography and other sexual services and commodities, have been recovered as sites of pleasure rather than merely danger (Vance, 1984). More often than not, however, the sex-radical subject is implicitly white. Even in sex worker rights activism, the migrant sex worker often remains coterminous with the 'trafficked victim', who constitutes the limit of sex worker agency and subjectivity (Doezema, 2001).

How may we conjure the Thai prostitute back? What kind of performances would it take to transform the power which this figure holds over our imaginations, our identities, our desires (or repression thereof), and our choices to orient ourselves towards, or away from, the people, objects haunted by her (Gordon, 1997)? Butler's (1991) notion of people, things and places is helpful here, as it helps us understand how hegemonic gender identities ('woman', 'respectable') are rendered 'natural' through endless repetition (see Skeggs, 1997). She also invites us to notice different kinds of performances which, often in the deprivileged, unofficial spaces of the intimate, the subcultural, the playful and dramatic, subvert these categories; not by disproving them as 'negative representations' but by exposing, often mockingly, the power relations which produced them. Yet here, too, people of colour appear as the limit. Butler's essay 'Gender is Burning' (1993) was a response to feminist critiques that saw her concept of gender as performance as voluntaristic, celebratory and power evasive. In it Butler concedes that there are indeed limits to drag, and illustrates this with a discussion of the house scene in New York, the subject of Jenny Livingston's film *Paris is Burning*. As Jay Prosser (1998) notes, Butler's focus on the working-class, African American and Latino/a, transsexual subjects of the film, in particular the two trans women Octavia St. Laurent and Venus Xtravaganza, problematically particularizes them. Prosser scandalizes how Butler fails to mourn Xtravaganza's violent death during the making of the film, and invents her instead as the constitutive outside of subversive performance, whose investment in femininity and economic survival is dysfunctional and complicit with the symbolic order. As with the trafficking discourse, feminine-presenting people of colour here appear as victims without agency, or with a problematic agency that smacks of 'false consciousness'. Again, they appear as the limit – of drag, and indeed of performativity itself.

In the remainder of this chapter, I will explore how performativity may be pushed beyond these limits. If in dominant representations, people of Thai descent do not perform, but just are, the people whom I interviewed often resisted and messed with this expectation. In the following, I will illustrate some of the ways in which my interviewees performed their racialized genders and sexualities, often in (disowned, reclaimed, extended) kinship with the figure of the Thai prostitute. While interviewees could critique it, disprove it or subvert it, they could never quite get away from its haunting presence (Gordon, 1997).

Performing Thai femininity

Neither could I. My research was avowedly not about prostitution. I resented the prostitute's one-sided domination of all things Thai. Like the 'persistent and troubling ghosts in the house' described by Avery Gordon, she nevertheless kept coming back with a vengeance. Gordon coins the term 'haunting' to describe

> how that which appears to be not there is often a seething presence, acting on and often meddling with taken-for-granted realities... The ghost is not simply a dead or a missing person, but a social figure, and investigating it can lead to that dense site where history and subjectivity make social life. The ghost or the apparition is one form by which something lost, or barely visible, or seemingly not there to our supposedly well-trained eyes, makes itself known or apparent to us, in its own way, or course. (Gordon, 1997, p. 8)

The prostitute crept into every single conversation I had with my twenty-two interviewees of Thai descent, most of whom had mixed, but not always part-white, parentage. Sometimes conjured consciously, at other times noisily haunting our dialogue, she made her appearance variously: during discussions of others' views of our parentage, border control practices, media texts on Thailand, or staring reactions to our families during Sunday strolls in the park.[8]

Jin: 'What kind of stereotypes have you come across in German people about Thainess or Thai people and Thailand itself?'
Watcharin: 'Well, that Thais are especially nice and friendly or laugh a lot. And that they are really good, like at servicing, serving in restaurants or *(laughs)*, whatever, stewardesses and stuff, that is always much appreciated. Um, and then stereotypes or certain ideas that Asian women are somewhat loose or at least you think that an Asian woman could also be a prostitute, yes, this idea exists very, very strongly in the German frame of mind. Um, and that Asian men aren't real men anyway, there is also always this idea you see.'

'Watcharin Thong', an interviewee of Thai and German parentage in his late twenties whose name, along with all others, I have anonymized, links the sexualization of Thai femininity with a colonial division of labour that constructs Asians as naturally suited for providing sexual and other reproductive services to white people. While Southeast Asian women are identified with prostitution, Asian men, too, are feminized and 'not real men'. The stereotypes which Watcharin critiques carry remnants of an eighteenth- and nineteenth-century ideology of bourgeois respectability, which constructed the sovereign subject in opposition to the racialized, feminized and sexualized (Mosse, 1997; Said, 1978).

If Thai people are 'naturally' adept at sex work, restaurant work and air hostessing, these activities are nevertheless not on the same moral playing field. Most of my interviewees located them at radically different proximities to respectability.[9] The popularity of *Thai food* with British and German people was often highlighted as a 'positive' force, which counteracted 'negative' stereotypes about *Thai sex*. This evaluation mirrors media representations of Thainess around the time of the interviews, which foregrounded Thai food and Thai sex as meaningful to multicultural society (Haritaworn, 2002). If Thai food bestowed positive meanings to its consumer (in the figure of the sophisticated urbanite), Thai sex was located at the opposite end of the value/pathology continuum (Skeggs, 2004). Thus, white men who are depicted as going for Thai women are working-class, often older, disabled, or otherwise unattractive, and always unable to deal with emancipated (i.e. white) women and gender relations in the modern West. Their consumption of Otherness is not interpreted as an expression of their membership in the cosmopolitan community, but rather of their lagging behind it. It locates them more closely with a premodern culture that (in contrast to its interracially commercialized cuisine), can never be in any hybridity with Britishness.

While evaluated very differently, ethnic food and ethnic sex are nevertheless located in a shared symbolic and economic field. As products for consumption, the labour that produces them is similarly feminized, immaterial, undervalued and informalized (Agustín, 2007; Hardt, 2007; Hochschild, 1983). In Thai migrations to the West, which occurred in larger waves after official recruitment had already stopped, these forms of labour present very real alternatives for surviving a racist labour market that de-classes, dequalifies and underdocuments migrants (Erel, 2003). Thai community spaces such as the Buddhist temple in Wimbledon (London), and the refectory of the Technische Universität Berlin which is regularly hired for Thai festivals, are sites of conviviality between Thai sex workers, interracial families of various gendered and classed make-ups, and Thais working in restaurants or elsewhere. These are also the sites that I visited between 2001 and 2003 in order to recruit participants.

'Anita Thawisin' was the middle-class daughter of a Thai man and a British woman.[10] She was in her mid-twenties when I interviewed her. As a white teenager, she had topped up her pocket money by waitressing in the up-market restaurant of her father 'Soemsak Thawisin', whom I also interviewed. Anita described the restaurant as a complicated space. On the one hand, it was a familial site of cultural reproduction where she was exposed to Thai culture and the influence of older Thai women.[11] While describing the other restaurant workers as family members, she also referred to them as 'mail-order brides' in 'pretty unhealthy relationships', who frequently needed help from her parents. Anita thus partly repeated the rescue discourse on Thai femininities and intimacies. At the same time, she found herself caught in the same gaze in the restaurant:

> I think with the guests, that was the point when I realized that my Thainess was questioned a bit more. Because they saw me as a Thai woman, as a Thai waitress, so that I always, never really...I was never really aware how.. kind of Thai I look until I was in a costume like that and.. people talk to you like you're stupid and.. can't speak English, even though it's *clear*, it's obvious you can speak English, but people...like, they always talk to you as if you.. you're just...and they made comments, too. You know, the kind of comments, kind of, to do with Thai women. [JH asks what kind of comments] I can't remember the details, it's a long time ago. Hm, but yes, rude things, when people tried grabbing one of the girls or.. made certain comments, yes, insinuations.. simply things that cross the borders of respect.

In her father's restaurant, Anita becomes a 'Thai woman' in more ways than one. By dressing up as a 'Thai woman' and assuming a position of hospitality, she is seen to invite sexual and racial harassment. It does not matter that her father prides himself in running an exclusive restaurant whose hospitality is symbolized by the Thai silk dresses worn by all waitresses. In donning the traditional costume of 'Thai women', Anita fails to embody the postcolonial respectability which this figure symbolized to the Siamese modernizers, who invented it in close hybridity with the binaried gender/sex system introduced by the Europeans (Fishel, 1999).[12] Instead, she unwittingly invites the ghost of the 'Thai prostitute' to make its presence known in this exoticized space, designed as it is to satisfy angry white people's desire to 'eat the Other' (hooks, 1992). Anita's failure to perform respectable Thai femininity intelligibly illustrates the near impossibility of disrupting the prostituting gaze on the feminized Thai body. In the transnational space, you cannot perform 'Thai woman' without being possessed by the 'Thai prostitute'.

Anita's account disappoints hopes in the 'ambiguous' body, in which performativity theorists, too, have invested heavily (see Haritaworn, 2009). The point where her body is recognized as Thai also gives rise to its sexual harassment. The label 'Thai woman/prostitute' sticks on it in such a way that attempts to distinguish between moral and immoral, prostituted and non-prostituted become not just violent but futile. If a sex worker can easily be imagined as non-Thai, the reverse requires far more labour. To be a Thai female means to be already prostituted.

The essentialism with which Anita's multiracialized body is mis/recognized thus fails to fulfil performativist hopes in the subversive in between. Such expectations are also complicated by my rereading of another interview. 'Bee Sornrabiab' was a young person then in their[13] late teens. Born in Thailand to two Thai parents, Bee migrated to Berlin as a child when their mother got married (and later separated) from a white German man, with whom Bee was living at the time of the interview. Bee identified through the Thai gender identity 'tom', which together with its feminine equivalent 'dee' (borrowed and adapted from the English 'tomboy' and 'lady' respectively) has become the subject of much recent anthropological interest (e.g. Wilson, 2004). Bee expressed their alliance to feminine women of Thai parentage and gave a strong critique of the ways in which these are hailed as 'only good for the one thing'. While serving as a witness to their feminine-presenting friends, Bee is interpellated by the same violent gaze. In the following, they describe the circumstances that ultimately resulted in their leaving school without any qualifications:

> 'I was thirteen or fourteen, and the boys were so stupid. I was already a tomboy after all. And the boys bullied me, saying dumb things like "What's your mother's profession?" and stuff, and that's then how it started. *[Describes explaining the bullying to teachers and social workers, who did not intervene.]* I'm like "Thanks a lot, you can't help me either. I can't just sit there when one of them whispers from behind 'Hey. When are you gonna give me that massage?'"* That's what was happening, it was really quite bad.'

The white boys in this account refer Bee back into a femininity that is neither 'normal' nor 'privileged'. Bee describes how teachers and social workers refuse to support them against the harassers. Deviating from an already abjected womanhood, Bee is twice disentitled to the 'female' privileges of patriarchal protection. First, as a female-assigned person of Thai descent, they appear to invite harassment rather than chivalry. This harassment further takes on a punitive character as Bee's gender nonconformity appears to refuse their 'natural' place at the service of white men and boys.

Bee's story points to the double standards of the trafficking discourse, which presents its subjects (white feminists, the state) as protectors of Southeast Asians. In the bullying encounter, Bee is forced back into the role of the 'prostituted victim,' but one that *does not deserve protection*. Ironically, the very trafficking discourse which is meant to save victimized Thai women produces the conditions that force Bee to leave school with no qualifications, and no support from the authorities to whom they turn for help.

Bee's account also complicates interpretations of female masculinity as subversive of sexism and heterosexism. Kimberley Chang and L. H. M. Ling (1999), for example, in their otherwise brilliant comment on the colonial continuities through which global elites entitle themselves to the cheap affective labour of migrant Filipinas, suggest 'the tomboy' as a technology of resistance to the sexual harassment of the

Filipina body. While it is true that some people experience or even fashion their gender in direct opposition to societal norms and expectations, reducing gender nonconformity to a function of racism, sexism and classism ignores the ways in which individuals seek to express and determine their own bodies, biographies and desires in ways that feel authentic to them. Furthermore, Bee's narrative complicates such a voluntaristic model. Their deviation from a heterosexual hyper-femininity to which white men claim free and unfettered sexual access does not protect them from being hailed as the Thai woman/prostitute. Rather, Bee's reference back into their 'natural' position as an interracialized object of sex – and sexual disgust – occurs with a force that constitutes its own kind of violence.

Performing the Thai prostitute

Interviewees were not one-sidedly defined by the prostitute discourse. They used countless strategies to contest their Othering – from returning the gaze and talking back, to performing respectability, to passing (including as generically Eurasian or of colour), to messing with the colonial discourse more directly. 'Luzia Heinen', a Berliner then in her late twenties, described how when she was younger, she and her friends at school had made fun of people's attempts to dissect their racialized bodies.

Luzia: 'Most find it interesting, quite positive.'
Jin: 'Yes. And what do they find interesting?'
L: 'That you have access to another culture. "And do you still speak Thai?" And I go "Nah, not really" *(both laugh)*. I also know a lot of people from binational ... I have this friend who's half-Malaysian, she doesn't speak Malay, either, and a friend who's half-Filipino, she speaks no Tagalog. And of course I've been out and about with them, and that's how it's always like ... But we also tried to pass ourselves off as something we weren't.'
J: 'How so?'
L: 'Oh, dunno, we told people we were sisters *(J laughs)* living in France and um ... dunno, loving the same man or having an affair with the same man, who is however married and, um, somehow ... well, whatever, what you tell random people.'

Luzia and her friends exert agency by playfully inhabiting exoticizing stereotypes of Asian women. Their role-play evokes strong colonial images in me – a white man who is married (presumably to a white woman) but has a few 'Oriental concubines' on the side. However, the girls are not passive objects in this encounter. Their performance is hybrid: the Same in a body that looks Other, they expose the colonial discourse as a narcissistic fantasy and disappoint its desire for authentic, exotic, erotic Otherness (Bhabha,

1994). They hold a mirror in the voyeur's face and reflect back his gaze, which purports to see everything but sees nothing.

The girls' impersonation of 'Oriental' femininity nevertheless enables them to emerge as active subjects. Sex remains unspoken, yet their sociality is clearly a pleasurable, active and (homo)erotic one. It is horizontal, collective, meant for each other as much as the onlooker, who is replaced in this performance to be the spectator in the back row. Their action is not overtly political, yet it powerfully reclaims the female-assigned Southeast Asian body from the flat script of the mail-order bride discourse.

The word 'concubine' remains unsaid in this encounter. Luzia's remains a 'respectable' narrative, which stubbornly ignores the hauntings in the room.[14] In fact, even 'Thai' is absent from the performance. If doing recognizably Thai femininity automatically prostitutes a subject (to the point where, like Anita, she appears to *invite* her own violent objectification), the subject of erotic performances will face particular pressure to confine their Thainess to the background.

Is it surprising that none of my female interviewees made any direct attempts at 'mobbing'? The absence of more direct subversions of 'Thai' femininity must be contextualized with my sampling strategies, which did not foreground sexuality, let alone sex work, as criteria.[15] Of course, transgressive sexual strategies are not exclusive to 'queer' populations.[16] It may nevertheless not be a coincidence that the one interviewee who tackled the prostitute head-on, 'Phil Taylor', positioned himself within a gay (male) subculture.

> 'I don't deny it, I laugh about it, I joke about it. I just say *(puts on a camp voice)* "Oh gawd!" You know, like my friends will say "Oh, yeah, Phil and his podium dancing." I say *(camp voice)*: "Yeah, I got it from my mother, she was a whore." *(We laugh)* And it's okay, because...and they're quite shocked the fact that I've just said that. But yet because I, I've accepted it, and I haven't got any qualms about...that side of it, I'm not embarrassed any more, I'm old enough to be able to choose my friends, to be able to accommodate that background.'

This is how Phil related to me how he negotiated the fact that his mother used to be a sex worker with his gay friends. I am interested in his choice of a queer grammar, and a queer setting, to engage with the haunting figure of a Thai. His striking of a queer register is intelligible to his friends and myself as queer witnesses, who hear his narrative as a familiar journey from shame to pride. His choice of a queer space is also meaningful. As a gay man, his performance of excessive femininity and table dancing could easily pass for Camp rather than Whore, and does not automatically invite sexual harassment or a spoilt reputation. Male-assigned and identified, and often read as white, the prostitute does not stick to Phil's body in the same way. Nevertheless, Phil's conjuring of her, back into a queer biography and diasporic imagination from which she was disowned, and which she haunted, constitutes no small feat. By entering into her kinship, her genealogy; by stepping into her inheritance, *which becomes his background*; by offering her his body even *(excessive, exhibitionist, uber-feminine, mixed, fag, whore)*, Phil not only reclaims his body from the fearful clutches of compulsive respectability but appeases the ghost herself, re/membering and restoring her, to a community which more often than not labours hard to leave her behind.

Conclusion

What does it take for different feminized subjects (female, gay, Asian, etc.), who are located at different distances from respectability, to reclaim a pathologized body and identity? When my interviewees of Thai descent discussed their gender identities, or even just their genealogies, the ghost of the Thai prostitute was never far away. Inspired by Avery Gordon's call that we engage with our ghosts directly and respectfully, I have suggested that we pay attention to the prostitute's 'seething presence', even and especially in narratives that run from her or try to will her away. This is necessary for two reasons. First, to bring home those excluded from Thai diasporic, queer and feminist spaces, and who were lost to us. Second, to restore sexual agency to female-assigned people of Thai descent, even and especially in contexts that reflect our genders or feminine-prestenting sexualities back to us distorted, that can see no significance in our rise from the ashes. The prostitute – as ghost, as ancestor, as organic performer, as subaltern subject – is thus a force we had better learn to reckon with.

Notes

1. Since writing this, I have had the pleasure to become 'acquainted' with independent filmmaker Michael Shaowanasai's *The Adventure of Iron Pussy* series. Staged in Bangkok's sex tourist mile Patpong, it undertakes a similar project of subverting sexual/colonial tropes of Thainess, albeit from a gay male perspective. See the last section of this chapter on the question of gender positioning and sexual agency.
2. The term 'female-assigned' comes from transgender and transsexual activism and opens up the possibility of bodily self-determination and subjective identification beyond an externally assigned gender binary. This is important in our discussion of the 'Thai prostitute', which interpellates not only those who comfortably fit the category 'Thai woman', but also other female-assigned or female or feminine-identified positionings, including female-assigned people who present masculine (who may identify as butch, transmen or *tom*), and male-assigned people who present feminine (MTFs, transwomen or *kathoey*). Thus, like the 'Thai woman'

the 'Thai ladyboy' is always already prostituted, as the controversy around a Tiger Beer advert in November 2008 showed (Sweeney, 2008).

3. I am indebted to Sara Ahmed's (2004) idea that affect sticks to some bodies more than others.

4. http://wofflehouse.com/mob/always-a-bridesmaid/ (accessed 1 March 2009).

5. In critiquing the discursive 'prostitution' of Thainess in the transnational imagination, I am aware of the tightrope I am walking, between challenging racist stereotypes and reinscribing a diasporic nationalism founded in respectability, sex-work phobia, and gender, sexual and class oppression. More work is clearly needed which explores these questions from the perspective of those who have done sex work themselves.

6. I cite the contested terminology of 'mixed race' in order to draw critical attention to the ideologies and practices of stock and descent through which many bodies and identities continue to be constituted, a process which I, following Fanon, describe as dissection (Haritaworn, 2009). I occasionally use the term 'multiracialization' to highlight the hierarchical forces and processes through which the minds and bodies of people of differentially racialized parentage become constituted as 'ambiguous', 'confused' and 'unwholesome'.

7. Laura Agustín (2007) describes the rise of the rescue industry, which recreates the problems it purports to address. Thus, government responses to abolitionist feminist lobbying have largely consisted in protectionist practices which control female emigration and immigration. Migration by legal means has become ever harder, and both female and male migrants are now largely restricted to informal working conditions which make them vulnerable to exploitation and abuse.

8. Elsewhere (Haritaworn, 2008), I write myself into the co-produced narratives more directly, by discussing my own changing political and personal positionings towards my research subject/s.

9. I thank Beverley Skeggs for reminding me, during the Markets and Sexualities workshop at Kent University, 25 February 2009, that no one 'has' respectability, but rather that it is performed from various locations of distance and proximity to the ideal.

10. For a labour analysis of Anita's account, see Haritaworn (2002).

11. This 'familial' representation obscures the class and citizenship divisions in the restaurant, which was of course primarily a site of capitalist production and consumption.

12. These, ironically, contrasted with the Siamese ones, which the Europeans saw as unattractively androgynous (e.g. Jackson, 2003).

13. I use the pronoun 'they' for Bee. 'They' is often used in queer and transgender subcultures when people do not know which pronouns a person prefers, or wish to acknowledge their disidentification from their assigned gender status.

14. Some of the women in my sample were also able to perform themselves in proximity with other generically exoticized femininities, such as the 'beautiful Eurasian' (Haritaworn, 2007).

15. I had initially attempted to interview several generations of each family in order to examine how Thainess is reproduced intergenerationally.

16. Radical queer commentators have indeed noted the increasingly assimilationist trend in gay politics and communities (Sycamore, 2004).

Bibliography

Agustín, L. (2007) *Sex at the Margins* (London: Zed).

Ahmed, S. (2004) *The Cultural Politics of Emotion* (Edinburgh: Edinburgh University Press).

Allison, D. (1984) 'Public Silence, Private Terror' in C. Vance (ed.), *Pleasure and Danger* (New York: HarperCollins).

Bhabha, H. (1994) 'Of Mimicry and Man', in *The Location of Culture* (London and New York: Routledge).

Bindel, J. (2008) 'Marriage Is a Form of Prostitution', *The Guardian* (12 November). Available at http://www.guardian.co.uk/lifeandstyle/2008/nov/12/women-prostitution-marriage-sex-trade [accessed 1 February 2009].

Binnie, J. and B. Skeggs (2006) 'Cosmopolitan Knowledge and Production and Consumption of Sexualized Space: Manchester's Gay Village' in J. Binnie et al. (eds), *Cosmopolitan Urbanism* (London and New York: Routledge).

Bishop, R. and L. Robinson (1998) *Night Market* (London and New York: Routledge).

Butler, J. (1991) *Gender Trouble* (London and New York: Routledge).

Butler, J. (1993) 'Gender Is Burning', in *Bodies that Matter* (London and New York: Routledge).

Chang, K. and L. H. M. Ling (1999) 'Globalization and its Intimate Other', *Gender and Global Restructuring* 1(2): 27–43.

Doezema, J. (2001) 'Ouch! Western Feminists' "Wounded Attachment" to the "Third World Prostitute"', *Feminist Review* 67: 16–38.

Erel, U. (2003) 'Skilled Migrant Women and Citizenship Practices' in M. Morokvasic et al. (eds), *On the Move! Gender and Migration* (Opladen: Leske & Budrich).

Fishel, T. (1999) 'Romances of the Sixth Reign: Gender, Sexuality, and Siamese Nationalism' in P. Jackson and N. Cook (eds), *Genders & Sexualities in Modern Thailand* (Chiangmai: Silkworm).

Gill, R. (2003) 'From Sexual Objectification to Sexual Subjectification: The Resexualisation of Women's Bodies in the Media', *Feminist Media Studies* 3(1): 100–6.

Gordon, A. (1997) *Ghostly Matters* (Minneapolis: University of Minnesota Press).

Hardt, M. (2007) 'Foreword' in P. Clough (ed.), *The Affective Turn* (Durham: Duke University Press).

Haritaworn, J. (2002) 'Der ethnisierte Arbeitsplatz als Ort paradoxer Identifikation' in M. Castro Varela and D. Clayton (eds), *Migration, Gender, Arbeitsmarkt. Neue Beitraege zu Frauen und Globalisierung* (Koenigstein am Taunus: Ulrike Helmer Verlag).

Haritaworn, J. (2007) 'Beautiful Beasts: Ambivalence and Distinction in the Gender Identity Negotiations of Multiracialised Women of Thai Descent', *Women's Studies International Forum* 30(5): 391–403.

Haritaworn, J. (2008) 'Shifting Positionalities: Reflections on a Queer/Trans of Colour Methodology', *Sociological Research Online*, 13(1). Available at http://www.socresonline.org.uk

Haritaworn, J. (2009) 'Hybrid Border Crossers? Towards a Radical Socialisation of "Mixed Race"', *Journal of Ethnic and Migration Studies* 35(1): 59–78.

Hochschild, A. (1983) *The Managed Heart* (Berkeley: University of California Press).

hooks, b. (1992) 'Eating the Other', in *Black Looks* (Boston: South End Press).

Jackson, J. (2003) 'Performative Genders, Perverse Desires: A Bio-History of Thailand's Same-Sex and Transgender Cultures', *Intersections* 9. Available at http://intersections.anu.edu.au/issue9/jackson.html [accessed 14 June 2009].

Kapur, R. (2005) *Erotic Justice: Law and the New Politics of Postcolonialism* (London: Glass House Press).

Levine, P. (2000) 'Orientalist Sociology and the Creation of Colonial Sexualities', *Feminist Review* 65(1): 5–21.

Mohanty, C. T. (1988) 'Under Western Eyes', *Feminist Review* 30: 61–88.

Mosse, G. (1997) *Nationalism and Sexuality* (New York: Howard Fertig).

Parker, D. (1994) 'Encounters across the Counter: Young Chinese People in Britain', *New Community* 20(4): 621–34.

Prosser, J. (1998) *Second Skins* (New York: Columbia University Press).

Ruenkaew, P. (2003) *Heirat nach Deutschland* (Frankfurt am Main: Campus).

Said, E. (1978) *Orientalism* (London: Penguin).

Skeggs, B. (1997) *Becoming Respectable* (London: Sage).

Skeggs, B. (2004) 'Uneasy Alignments, Resourcing Respectable Subjectivity', *GLQ: A Journal of Lesbian and Gay Studies* 10(2): 291–8.

Sweeney, M. (2008) 'Easy, Tiger! Newspaper Beer Ads Banned Over Pics of Thai Ladyboy', *The Guardian* (28 November). Available at http://www.guardian.co.uk/media/2008/nov/26/tiger-beer-ladyboy [accessed 1 February 2009].

Sycamore, M. (2004) *That's Revolting! Queer Strategies for Resisting Assimilation* (Brooklyn: Soft Skull Press).

Vance, C. (ed.) (1984) *Pleasure and Danger* (NY: HarperCollins).

Velasco, G. (2008) 'Representing the Filipina "Mail-Order Bride"', in 'Figures of Transnational Belonging' (University of California Santa Cruz: Unpublished PhD thesis).

Wilson, A. (2004) *The Intimate Economies of Bangkok* (Berkeley: University of California Press).

15
Migrant Women Challenging Stereotypical Views on Femininities and Family

Umut Erel

'Muslim' migrants (whether as an ascribed or self-chosen identity) and even Muslim citizens are currently constructed as a key figure of threatening Otherness to European values (cf. Bourne, 2007). Whether through explicit policies or through implicit symbolic representations, migrants are required to position themselves vis-à-vis shared values in order to prove they can be legitimate members of the society they live in. Increasingly, gender equality and sexual liberalism stand in as measures for migrants' ability to positively identify with the wider freedoms that 'European values' are associated with (cf. Haritaworn et al., 2008).

As gendered and racialized Others, the figure of the migrant woman of Muslim background is central to debates on social cohesion and citizenship in Europe. As we are witnessing a shift from multiculturalism to social cohesion agendas, European governments emphasize the importance of shared values as the basis for citizenship. Citizenship in this account is a privilege that must be earned by migrants. Non-migrant citizens on the other hand are incited to police the appropriate hurdles on the pathway to integration and citizenship for migrants. Thus, those who are formally citizens can perform this subject position as 'citizen' by policing whether or not migrants exhibit the correct 'shared' European values. The renewed emphasis on the importance of citizenship as a shared identity aims at transcending the pluralist orientation that was supposedly fostered by multiculturalism. However, presenting citizenship as a privilege that migrants must win has two effects: first, it reinscribes a universalist, egalitarian and democratic orientation as the property of national or European identity. Secondly, it channels debates on citizenship away from questions of rights-claiming and democratizing participation to policing the boundaries of who can and cannot be admitted.

This chapter intervenes in these debates, using life stories of migrant women from Turkey in Britain and Germany.[1] It shows how some migrant women's self-presentations challenge heteronormative ethnicized representations of femininities. By making visible the counter-hegemonic articulations of migrant women's femininity the chapter shows how migrant women are able to exercise sexual agency, making themselves, if not under conditions of their own choice. While for many of them the migration project was motivated by the wish to escape particular forms of gendered control and enable a wider choice of gendered lifestyles, it would be wrong to assume that after migration they experienced a paradise of gender equality. On the contrary, the stereotypical representations of migrant women as particularly oppressed by cultural norms and the men of 'their' ethnic group contribute to new dynamics of gendered and ethnicized subjectification (cf. Gutierrez Rodriguez, 1999; Lutz n.d.; Morokvasic et al., 2003). The juxtaposition of European values of gender equality on the one hand and migrants from so-called Muslim countries as embodying female oppression on the other is constituted by racialized notions of tradition and modernity. These notions pervade theoretical frameworks for understanding changing relationships and personal identities. Engaging migrant women as subjects with agency opens the way for mobilizing sexual citizenship not as a measure for the ability of migrants to integrate, but as a device for widening and deepening the basis and content of rights to sexual identities and relationships.

Migrant women's sexual identities: beyond the modernity–tradition dichotomy

Until recently, migrants from Turkey constituted the largest national minority group in Europe before 2004 accession. In Germany 'Turkishness' forms a highly salient ethnic and racialized category that encompasses first-generation migrants and those born in Germany. Ethnic differentiation within the group of migrants from Turkey is also often eclipsed in public representations. While migrants from Turkey are not central to public discourses on ethnic minorities in Britain, some of the features of the discourses outlined here are applied to Muslim families in Britain, a label under which migrants from Turkey are often classified (cf. Küçükcan, 1999). Ethnic minority families from so-called Muslim countries are often conceptualized as embodying a close-knit, traditional family. In this view, the main site of oppression of women is the family, which is backward and patriarchal (cf. Lutz, n.d.; Otyakmaz, 1995; Waltz, 1996). Gender has been a central element in representations of migrant women for decades; while the themes have been changing and in recent years the themes of young men's crime rate, forced marriage, the wearing of headscarves, and so-called honour killings have been highlighted, the gender issue has been a constant (cf. Huth-Hildebrandt, 2002). Indeed, gender relations are often a polarizing device in debates on migration and social cohesion.

Debates on migrant families from Turkey often converge around a general belief that they are characterized by strong family ties and responsibilities as well as patriarchal structures. This reproduces a racialized dichotomy of modernity vs. tradition: European societies are seen as modern, characterized by individualization, fragmentation of stable relationships and forms of belonging, increasing speed of change and the pluralization of cultural options as well as a sharpening of social inequalities and a decline in economic opportunity (cf. Heitmeyer et al., 1997). While the nuclear family is one of the central social institutions challenged by modernization, these challenges are viewed as containing positive opportunities such as an increasing realization of democratic and egalitarian family relations (Beck and Beck-Gernsheim, 1998; Giddens, 1992). Within such discussions of the modernization of family relations, migrant families' experiences are not considered and tacitly assumed as residues of tradition (cf. Klesse, 2007a, 2007b). The very notions of modernity and tradition are in themselves racialized (Bhatt, 1997; Goldberg, 1993).

Giddens's and Beck and Beck-Gernsheim's models focus on heterosexual relationships. Where reference to lesbian, gay or bisexual relationships is made, this tends to idealize them as even more democratic, since gender inequalities do not have to be negotiated within these (cf. Klesse 2007a, 2007b). This is a problematic reduction of power relations to gender. Weeks et al. (2001) who focus on intimate relations of 'non-heterosexuals' seem to replicate this by downplaying the significance of power relations within gay and lesbian relationships as well as communities. Thus, the authors argue for the centrality of 'non-heterosexual community knowledges' for formulating and claiming relational rights. While critiquing how power relations can limit the accessibility of these resistant community knowledges, it is important to challenge the marginalization of racialized subjects in the production of these community knowledges and spaces (cf. Held and Leach, 2008). Who contributes their experiences and epistemologies? Whose stories are heard, institutionalized and multiplied as 'community knowledge'? Whose stories are marginalized as supplementary in accounts of democratizing sexual identities, relationships and cultures? Both the heterosexual and the non-heterosexual discussions of 'pure relationships', 'post-familial' (Beck and Beck-Gernsheim, 1990) families or 'families of choice' (Weeks et al., 2001) rely on an analytical framework of modernity vs. tradition that is implicitly racialized even when it remains apparently silent on ethnicity and 'race'. The intimate lives of migrants and ethnic minorities of Muslim background are often constructed as rigidly traditional, constraining women's autonomy and thus an impediment to the integration of migrant families to a supposedly democratic egalitarian ideal of gender and family relations among European societies. My main concern here is to point out the inadequacies of a view of migrant sexual identities and intimate relations as the embodiment of stability and tradition as a stereotype that exerts both repulsion and attraction. The problem is not how empirically verifiable the stereotype is but that it *fixes* a singular reality (Bhabha, 1994). This does not mean that migrant women from countries with a Muslim majority are not subjected to restrictive gender practices. However, the stereotype fixes migrant women to the figure of victim of gendered oppression: this gendered oppression is explained as a consequence of cultural or religious aspects of Islam. The problem with this stereotype is that it does not take account of the agency and the struggles of migrant women. The stereotype homogenizes gender relations and gender ideals, overemphasizing the explanatory power of 'Muslim' culture and religion. Thus, there are of course a range of counter-hegemonic gender relations and identifications among migrants, both before and after migration. Furthermore, the stereotype is instrumental to dichotomizing Western versus 'Muslim' groups. Thus, the figure of the oppressed migrant woman from Turkey is discursively employed to maintain ethnicized boundaries. The focus on 'Muslim' *culture* to explain the position of migrant women furthermore neglects the role of structural and material factors: migration regimes and labour market incorporation along gendered and ethnicized lines shape access to gendered and sexual relations and identities. The stereotype is not simply problematic because it relies on false facts; it creates a dichotomizing structure of Orientalist knowledge. The stereotype erases the diversity and complexity of gender and sexual relations and identities and most importantly the agency of migrant women. The life stories presented here put forward alternative views on how migrant women's constructions of femininity challenge such notions of traditional families of Turkish background.

Sexual identities and personal status

The group of women whose life stories I have elicited are specific in that most women are single or divorced, and the sample included lesbian and bisexual migrant women. This is particularly significant as sexuality is rarely discussed in the literature on migrant women, thus contributing to the invisibility of lesbian and bisexual migrant women and reinforcing heterosexual normativity. Social science literature views single and divorced women of Turkish background as exceptions and largely ignores them (for exceptions, cf. Erdem, 2000; Liversage, 2009). Rather than simply constituting an empirical gap, I suggest that this is a structural absence reinforcing the stereotype. For example, Küçükcan's (1999) study on Turkish migrants in Britain, theorizing the family as the ethnic community's core social organization, makes no reference to female-headed households or divorce in his study. In contrast to these normalizing representations, I am interested here in how some interviewees' life stories articulate particular forms of femininities that rarely find voice in accounts of migrant women from Turkey (cf. Gutierrez Rodriguez, 1999; Lutz, 1991). Through thematizing their choices of being single, or childless or in a relationship with a woman, the interviewees here challenge gendered, ethnicized normative femininities.

In the next section I discuss the self-presentations of some migrant women regarding their sexual identification. I argue for a more complex approach to the intersection of ethnicity, migration and sexuality that takes internal differentiations, overlapping and multiple identifications into account. Finally I discuss how the concept of intimate citizenship can be utilized to understand migrant women's sexual identifications.

Dilek: 'Because I am against this system I am also against marriage'

Dilek's narrative emphasizes the normativity of heterosexual marriage and motherhood and the marginalization of other choices, particularly in Turkey. Dilek is a 40-year-old researcher in Britain. In her life story, she elaborates the theme of striving for individuation. This, to her, means gaining the economic and social independence to be able to live alone. She worked for seven years as a researcher in Istanbul, where she was unable to afford living by herself and had to share accommodation with her sister. For many years she saw migration abroad as 'a fantastic dream', that she hoped would enable her to try out a different gendered lifestyle. This has even influenced her choice of a job, as her employer promised the opportunity to go abroad. In this sense, Dilek invested many years in her migration project. Dilek presents her choice to be single as partly political resistant, and partly as articulating her radical notion of individuality:

D: 'One thing, the marriage institution is one of the important institutions that helps the survival of the capitalist system, the nuclear family... therefore I think the institution of marriage needs to be torn down, I think this system will not collapse unless marriage disappears. I believe that the capitalist system is based on this and will continue with it. Because I am against this system I am also against marriage. But moreover, I am against two people's long term relationship. *(laughs)*

U: *(laughs)*

D: 'For example I am not thinking of living with someone, either. People's personalities begin resembling each other when they start living together. They do not create separate ideas, but only one idea. You begin resembling each other after a while and also to pressure each other. I have experienced this even when living with my sister. [...] For example although I say these things, when I live with someone – probably it has to do with being an older sister – I am so responsible, like a mother I begin to think about what my sisters do, if they have eaten dinner even. [...] So it's not only the institution of marriage I reject, but also living with someone, and that seems very strange to people and therefore they do not accept you.'

Dilek delineates her ideal of autonomy from notions of maternal care and views any cohabiting arrangement, not just in a couple relationship, as a restriction of her individuation. Gilligan (1982) theorized notions of care and autonomy as highly gender-specific. According to her, girls' gender-specific development and their identification with their mothers' gender identity leads to a stronger orientation towards relationality and care rather than autonomy. Women therefore develop a different form of subjectivity based on the ethics of care. Relatedness, dialogue, compromise and the ability to link justice and care are at the basis of Gilligan's notion of an ethics of care. Dilek's desire to develop a more autonomous self can be read as resistance to normative femininities. This contains contradictions, as Dilek ironically notes her own care about whether her sister has regular meals. The impediments to realizing Dilek's ideal of autonomy are, however, not only psychological or social, but, in this case, first and foremost economic. The dichotomization of femininity as caring and masculinity as autonomous is of course not Dilek's personal problem but a pervasive social construct, and possibilities of individually subverting this are limited. The tension between autonomy and responsibility and care cannot be fully resolved, as both aspects coexist in constructions of subjectivity.

In Turkey Dilek felt ostracized in many social contexts as a single woman. Thus she recounts about her relationship with her colleagues in Turkey:

D: 'Because they look at you and think "she's still not married, if only she found a husband and got married, then we could become closer friends". This is the way they think. Whenever they start a friendship, it is always with family ties. No woman, even if she works, makes a move independently of her husband. Therefore, all friendships develop in this way. My relations with my married sister are also limited. Because she has children she makes friends with people with children, or with her husband's friends.'

Dilek's experience indicates how deeply ingrained an ideal of femininity she challenges by trying to shift the emphasis of her sense of subjectivity from care and responsibility towards autonomy. Thus, she criticizes hegemonic family-centred forms of sociality as excluding single women.[2] How deeply Dilek's self-presentation challenges the hegemony of the heterosexual marriage and/or family ideal can be glimpsed from the incomprehension her views are met with:

'Anyway if you say [that you never thought of marriage], they don't talk to you. If you reject marriage, and if I say this, it seems very strange to them, and they annoy you and you annoy them.'

The ideal of marriage and family is thus constructed as the horizon of what is thinkable and communicable. Dilek's formulation of her own ideal of autonomy that goes beyond this horizon leads to a breakdown of communication. If we take communication to be at the basis of community, Dilek's outspokenness in positioning herself outside of the hegemonic frame of communicability can be interpreted as a resistant subjectivity challenging the heterosexually normative modes of community in which female subjectivity is inscribed. When Dilek finally realized her 'fantastic dreams' of migrating to Britain, she could test out her ideal of living alone in practice. Being able to afford living alone was something Dilek finally savoured. At the time of interview, she had been living in the UK for two years. She enjoyed the opportunity to live by herself. Yet, she also became aware of problems of social isolation which she had not faced in this way in Turkey.

Nâlan: 'I never thought of marriage as inevitable'

At the time of interview, Nâlan was in her early forties and a single mother of a 17-year-old son living in the UK. She relates a range of negotiations of female sexual subjectivity. As a young, financially independent woman in the late 1960s and early 1970s in Istanbul, she rejected marriage for personal and political reasons:

> N: I read another book. That is Wilhelm Reich's book called 'The sexual revolution'. [...] After that we made sexual revolutions in our life. Therefore, we always thought of marriage as myth, dependence. Therefore, actually I would have left home even earlier. But in Turkey if you are not yet 18 years old, the police can take you back home. That is why I stayed at home until I was 18.'

When she began living with her boyfriend, she experienced strong social pressure both from her family and others. Thus, they were required to present a marriage certificate to rent a flat or when going on holidays: 'in these situations, women were humiliated very much' since it is the woman who is marked with the 'whore stigma' (Pheterson, 1990). After a few years, she yielded to the pressure and got married 'as a formality'. However, she felt that the institutionalization of the relationship impacted on her subjectivity, through assimilating her into the hegemonic forms of love relationships. Although Nâlan's decision to marry was taken instrumentally, she was subjectified in the terms of these normalizing practices. Thus, the 'formality' of marriage is not independent of, but co-constitutes her subjectivity. The interplay of agency and subjectification is also expressed in Nâlan's account of becoming a mother. She bore her son during a period when she and her husband were politically persecuted after the military coup d'état of 1980 and went into hiding. While Nâlan does not expand on the difficulties of mothering in such a situation, she points out the positive effects of having a child in this period. She felt very isolated, since contacts with their political friends were very limited.

'Of course, in this situation to have a child gave us something to do. Because the child takes up all your time [...] And [...] because of having a child we appeared more like a normal family, that is what made life a bit easier.'

Although for Nâlan the identities of political activist and mother were both central to her notion of self, the role of mother supported an appearance of social and political inconspicuousness. When she decided to divorce her husband, this new status of divorcee led to new forms of social control:

'But because I was alone, my brothers who hadn't been around until then started coming to my house. [...] On the other hand, [her husband's] parents [...] became all nervous. No one wanted us to separate. They were more afraid that as a single woman something could happen to me. And second, their honour ... as a separated woman, a divorced woman on her own at home, your boyfriends will come. They were totally ... they didn't accept it. And I was a young woman, 29 years old when I separated from my husband. I realized this, when my brother threw a male friend of mine out, [...] He came and called me a prostitute and threw my friend out. That's when I realized that life is not going to be easy' *(laughs)*.

Her brothers' social control reveals a paradox: while the presumed reason for controlling her social and sexual life is to prevent her loss of reputation, it is precisely their own intervention that labels her a 'prostitute'. This social control was not only exercised by her family: Nâlan gives an example of walking late at night with a male friend. When a police man controlled their papers and saw that they were not married, he threatened to arrest them. Nâlan's narrative articulates the different forms of sexual subjectification she experienced through different life stages and marital statuses – as a single woman, as a married mother and as a divorced single mother. She developed new strategies of resistance against each of these forms of subjectification. Her decision to migrate was based on the hope that she could escape the gendered control she experienced as a divorcee. For this migration project she relied on the support of her political networks from left-wing and women's movement activism. Despite this, at least during the first years of her migration project Nâlan experienced an increased gendered vulnerability to sexist and racist harassment in the workplace. It was only with gaining a secure residence status, improving her language knowledge and gaining access to more skilled work that she could overcome these problems. Thus, while the wish to broaden a choice of gendered lifestyles or escape restrictions of choice of sexual identities and relationships can be an important motivation for migration, such wider choices are not always available in the context of migration. Especially migration regulations, gender and ethnically hierarchized labour markets and gendered racisms are factors that produce gendered and ethnicized oppressions and vulnerabilities in the countries of migration.

Melahat: conceptualizing lesbian love

Through internal rural–urban migration and remigration, Melahat, in her mid-thirties and living in the UK, experienced different gender roles. Thus, her own gender identity was questioned in the village: as she had grown up in the city and had not learned the female gendered skills of the village, she was seen to be working 'like a man'. In this sense, the villagers used not sexual desire or behaviour but her role in the gendered division of labour as a marker to ascribe her a (partial) gender identity. Her family tried to pressure Melahat into a marriage while she was still very young and even planned this without consulting her. Melahat emphasizes that her reasons for not wanting to marry were purely emotional, not political. But she resisted so forcefully, 'continuously in such a militant way', that her family gave up on this plan. Melahat recounts that one of the main reasons for her refusal to get married was that during this time, she had a love relationship with a woman in the small town. At the time she was not aware of the concept of lesbian love, and simply thought that she was 'experiencing something unique that no one else experienced'. She does not expand on this, except to point out that the separation from her lover caused her a lot of suffering. She could not share this experience with anyone. As she could not concentrate on her work, either, she got herself into debt and decided to leave the village to go to a big city. Although within a few years Melahat had established herself economically, her continuing suffering from this failed love relationship and her sense of being 'different' motivated her to migrate again, this time to the UK.

> *U:*   'What were your expectations when you came here [...]?'
> *M:*   'Well, let me tell you this, I didn't have any expectations actually.'
> *U:*   'Hum.'
> *M:*   'My expectation was first to gain some distance from that society because of my relationship.'
> *U:*   'Hum.'
> *M:*   'My relationship or better, I couldn't even imagine that such a relationship could exist. I didn't know. I experienced it without knowing.'
> *U:*   'Hum.'

M: 'I came here and realized that this was a relationship.'
U: 'That it is a relationship that can be called a relationship.'
M: 'Yeah.'
U: 'Before it seemed more like a close friendship ...'
M: 'Something like that. I experienced it somehow differently but probably I was mad that I live like this and so on. I thought that only I live like this.'
U: 'Hum.'
M: 'Ah, I don't know ... (pause)
U: 'You didn't have any expectations from here, it was more about getting out ...'
M: 'Hum. A liberation, liberation.'

Melahat articulates how the lack of a concept of lesbian made it difficult to make sense of her relationship. Migration to a new society necessitates and enables a new positioning of the self, including in the area of sexuality. In this way, migration can trigger a process of coming out, even to oneself (Kuntsman, 2000). During the interview Melahat did not talk about coming out or about sexuality explicitly. Instead, she talked about encountering open or covert homophobia in community organizations, at the workplace and in personal relations. Weeks et al. (2001) argue that ethnic minority people are faced with a particular constellation of risk at the interface of racism and homophobia:

> Members of minority ethnic communities frequently have to balance their loyalty to their communities of origin, which provide support against racism, however 'traditional' their values, with attempts to explore their sexual desires and identities. ... as such, black non-heterosexuals often experience further dimensions of risk in terms of navigating everyday life. (Weeks et al., 2001, p. 186)

While it is important that the authors address the intersectionality of racism and homophobia, the argument contains some problematic assumptions. First, there is an implicit dichotomization of ethnic minorities with 'traditional' values and 'non-heterosexuals' as predominantly 'white'. This is part of the modernity difference hypothesis that assumes a racialized geography of modernity. They furthermore essentialize the notion that black people have a loyalty to 'their' ethnic community. The problematic omission is that there are, of course, also ethnic minority 'non-heterosexual' communities. Moreover, ethnic minority people construct differentiated notions of community on the basis of ethnicity but also other commonalities and values (cf. Manalansan, 2006). They view identification and belonging in the tension of homophobia and racism as more complex. Their families and friendships with ethnic minority people and groups are not only a support against racism, but some of them also support them in their sexual life-styles. Moreover, they experience homophobia from both ethnic minorities and the ethnically dominant population. Their own strategies of building friendships and intimacy frequently cross ethnic boundaries, often as a conscious decision for diversity. Thus, homophobia should not be viewed as ethnically bounded. The experience of multiple forms of exclusion and domination requires and engenders 'partial identifications' (Parker, 1995) of ethnic minority lesbian, bisexual and transgendered people, requiring a higher degree of self-reflexivity and identity work than for ethnic major-ity people whose community knowledge and worldviews are normalized within gay, lesbian, bisexual and transgender subcultures.

Transnational sexual citizenship rights

The life stories discussed here challenge the ethnicization of notions of (late) modern versus traditional intimate and sexual identities and family relations. The chapter presented a range of ways in which migrant women negotiate and challenge heteronormative and family-centred female sub-jectivities. Over their life course, they articulated changing alternative or resistant modes of femininity as single by choice, 'sexual revolutionary', divorcee, single mother or lesbian. The complex sexual identities and rela-tionships contradict a stereotypical fixing of migrant families and femi-ninities as stable, traditional and oppressive. Indeed, while the women did experience and narrate instances of gendered oppression, their own resist-ant articulations of femininity themselves disrupt a homogenized idea of 'Turkish migrants' as defined by gender relations labelled 'traditional'. The stories here have focused on pre-migration experiences, emphasizing how migrant women have challenged gendered restrictions. The wish to access alternative modes of gendered lifestyle is a strong element in migration moti-vations for women from a range of different countries (Kofman et al., 2000; Manalansan, 2006). The idea that a wider range of gendered lifestyles is accessible in European countries than in Turkey is widespread. Indeed, some of the migrant women interviewed here refer to this idea when reflecting about their migration decision, though in other contexts of their life story they do not reproduce such clear distinctions of 'here' and 'there'. Migration to Germany and the UK indeed offered the women economic and social opportunities to live independently of marriage or natal families. However, my concern here is to deconstruct the stereotypical fixation of migration as a unilinear journey of modernization and gendered and sexual emancipa-tion. If we look only at socially predominant discourses of female sexuality in Europe and Turkey we miss out on other aspects structuring and shaping migrant women's access and ability to live a variety of gendered and sexual identities. Gendered racialized discourses have cast migrant women from Turkey as oppressed by gendered norms and patriarchal family structures.

Yet, these are not simply neutral assessments, instead these discourses co-constitute the range of forms of recognition and misrecognition the migrant women are faced with. In interpersonal relations, this active misrecognition can be felt as undermining one's self identification in gendered, sexual and ethnic terms and, of course, beyond these (cf. Erel, 2007). As another interviewee, Nilgün, put it, she felt these ascriptions were 'dis-abling' (Erel, 2003), indeed these misrecognitions of migrant women's counter-hegemonic gender and sexual projects contribute to the invisibility of queers of colour and migrants' ways of creating new forms of intimacy and family. Moreover, these discourses affect not only interpersonal relationships, but also institutionalized forms of recognition. Encounters with welfare officials, migration officials, teachers and employers are shaped by these discourses, as well as migration and employment policy. The economic incorporation of migrant women often deskills them, in particular if they are undocumented or if their immigration status limits their access to particular jobs and social rights (Kofman and Raghuram, 2005). This then leads to the prevalence of migrant women in low-paid, ethnically and gender segregated jobs, often in the informal economy where they may experience enhanced gendered and ethnic vulnerability to exploitation and harassment (e.g. OSCE, 2009; Piper, 2008). Indeed, class positioning as mediated through migration trajectories and status is an important factor shaping migrant women's access to gendered and sexual choices. Yet, these aspects that structure and co-construct migrant women's gendered and sexual identities are overlooked in debates based on stereotypical representations of migrant women as embedded in 'tradition'. Stereotypical representations of migrant women as victimized in gendered power relationships in the migrant family play a strategic role in obscuring the workings of gendered racism.

The discussion of the migrant women's life stories has touched upon two aspects of what Richardson (2000) defines as the three subsets of sexual rights: 'conduct-based rights claims, identity-based rights claims and claims that are relationship based' (2000, p. 107). As migration is one way of realizing choice in sexual identities, our understanding of sexual rights should take account of this, challenging heterosexist assumptions of migration and integration policy. Many citizenship rights are grounded in notions of heterosexual coupledom, which is taken as normative. For migrants, the regulatory potential of these heteronormative and often ethnocentric notions are often exacerbated explicitly or implicitly as they become conditions for attaining residence rights or formal citizenship (such as family formation and reunification regulations) although formally the 2004 Civil Partnerships Act now recognizes same-sex partners.

The life stories presented here were elicited in 1999. Since then, we have witnessed restructuring of the arenas of citizenship, migration and integration policy in both Germany and Britain. Indeed, both countries have begun to emphasize the need for migrants to be useful to be admitted.

This is enshrined in the Zuwanderungsgesetz in Germany and the British Managed Migration Policy. Current governmental discourse, both in the UK and Germany contrasts the notion of social cohesion built around common values to multiculturalist ideas of celebrating difference. Multiculturalism in this sense, and indeed implicitly the notion of multiethnicity, is presented as undermining social cohesion. One problem with the professed shift from multiculturalism to a social cohesion (UK) or integration agenda (Germany) is that many of the egalitarian impulses of multiculturalism are abandoned, too. Whether multiculturalism has been an institutionalized policy (as it has been for decades in the UK) or a frame of reference for alternative social projects (as in the German context since the 1980s), after 11 September 2001, it has increasingly been blamed for ethnic minorities supposedly leading 'parallel lives' in many European countries. This in turn has been seen as a prime reason for the radicalization of some Muslim young men. Ethnic minorities and migrants, especially Muslims in Europe have come under increasing pressure to prove they are willing and able to integrate.

One of the key discursive strands in the delegitimization of multiculturalism has been the argument that multiculturalism is too tolerant of ethnic minority groups' cultural practices that are assumed to be oppressive of women. Black and ethnic minority feminists have long critiqued such articulations of multiculturalism that empower the authoritarian, patriarchal – supposedly most culturally distant – social forces as representative of ethnic minority cultures. They argue that this disregards internal divisions, and importantly leaves intact a claim of ethnic minority leaders, lacking any democratic legitimacy, to control 'their' women (Patel, 1997; Sahgal and Yuval-Davis, 1992). Yet, the current mainstream critique of multiculturalism as detrimental to ethnic minority women does not build on this critical, anti-racist feminist tradition (Patel, 2008). Instead this 'peril of multiculturalism for women' (Bilge, 2008) discourse reproduces elements of the version of multiculturalism it supposedly critiques. First, it is based on a cultural determinism that views ethnic minorities, and in particular women, as overdetermined by 'their' culture. Second, it essentializes ethnic minority groups' cultures as homogeneous and always based on women's oppression. Third, it dichotomizes this with a construct of 'Western' liberal culture on the other hand. Lastly, it presents ethnic minorities, and in particular ethnic minority women, as victims without agency who cannot either interpret 'their' culture differently or act differently from its assumed tenets. Indeed, a narrow notion of social cohesion as currently promoted in Europe attacks not only anti-racist struggles, but also black feminist struggles.

A recent example for this is the (failed) attempt by a local London council to withdraw funding from a long-established organization, Southall Black Sisters, with the argument that their services for black and ethnic minority women suffering from domestic violence were 'divisive and discriminatory' and therefore was not conducive to social cohesion (cf. Patel, 2008). While the life stories presented here have been elicited previous to the shift from multiculturalism to social cohesion and managed migration, the methodological emphasis on migrant women's self-presentations of challenging heteronormative ethnicized representations of femininities remains highly relevant. Indeed, current debates on migration and integration often dichotomize women's interests and the interests of migrant groups. In this context, making visible the counter-hegemonic articulations of migrant women's femininity is one way of challenging this discursive dichotomization.

Notes

1. It is based on a study on skilled and educated migrant women from Turkey in Britain and Germany (Erel, 2009).
2. This is echoed by other interview partners.

Bibliography

Apitzsch, U. (1996) 'Frauen in der Migration', *Frauen in der Einen Welt* 1: 9–25.

Beck, U. and E. Beck-Gernsheim (1998) *The Normal Chaos of Love* (Cambridge: Polity Press).

Beck-Gernsheim, E. (1998) 'On the Way to a Post-Familial Family: From a Community of Need to Elective Affinities', *Theory, Culture, and Society*, Special Issue on Love and Eroticism 15(3/4): 53–70.

Bhabha, H. K. (1994) *The Location of Culture* (London: Routledge).

Bhatt, C. (1997) *Liberation and Purity: Race, New Religious Movements and the Ethics of Postmodernity* (London: UCL Press).

Bilge, S. (2008) 'Between Gender and Cultural Equality' in E. F. Isin (ed.), *Recasting the Social in Citizenship* (Toronto: University of Toronto Press).

Bourne, J. (2007) *In Defence of Multiculturalism*. IRR Briefing Paper no. 2

Erdem, E. (2000) "Mapping Women's Migration: A Case Study of the Economic Dimensions of Female Migration from Turkey to Germany', paper presented at the conference Assimilation – Diasporization – Representation: Historical Perspectives on Immigrants and Host Societies Migration History (Humboldt Universität Berlin, 27–29 October).

Erel, U. (2003) "Gendered and Racialized Experiences of Citizenship in the Life Stories of Women of Turkish Background in Germany', in J. Andall (ed.), *Gender and Ethnicity in Contemporary Europe* (Oxford: Berg).

Erel, U. (2007) 'Constructing Meaningful Lives: Biographical Methods in Research on Migrant Women', *Sociological Research Online*, 12(4). Available at http://www.socresonline.org.uk/12/4/5.html

Erel, U. (2009) *Migrant Women Transforming Citizenship: Lifestories from Germany and Britain* (Aldershot: Ashgate).

Giddens, A. (1992) *The Transformation of Intimacy: Sexuality, Love and Eroticism in Modern Societies* (Cambridge: Polity Press).

Gilligan, C. (1982) *In a Different Voice* (Cambridge, MA: Harvard University Press).

Goldberg, D. T. (1993) *Racist Culture: Philosophy and the Politics of Meaning* (Oxford: Blackwell).

Gültekin, N. (2003) *Bildung, Autonomie, Tradition und Migration. Doppelperspektivit biographischer Prozesse junger Frauen aus der Türkei* (Opladen: Leske & Budrich).

Gutierrez Rodriguez, E. (1999) *Intellektuelle Migrantinnen – Subjektivitäten im Zeitalter von Globalisierung. Eine postkoloniale dekonstruktive Analyse von Biographien im Spannungsverhältnis von Ethnisierung und Vergeschlechtlichung* (Opladen: Leske & Budrich).

Haritaworn, J., E. Erdem and T. Tauqir (2008) 'Gay Imperialism: Gender and Sexuality Discourse in the War on Terror' in A. Kuntsman and E. Miyake (eds), *Out of Place: Interrogating Silences in Queerness/Raciality* (York: Raw Nerve Books).

Heitmeyer, W., J. Müller and H. Schröder (1997) *Verlockender Fundamentalismus* (Frankfurt am Main: Suhrkamp).

Held, N. and T. Leach (2008) ' "What Are You Doing Here?" The "Look" and (Non) Belongings of Racialised Bodies in Sexualised Space' in A. Kuntsman and E. Miyake (eds), *Out of Place: Interrogating Silences in Queerness/Raciality* (York: Raw Nerve Books).

Huth-Hildebrandt, C. (2002) 'Der Blick auf die fremde Frau' in E. Rohr and M.M. Jansen (eds) *Grenzgägerinnen: Frauen auf der Flucht, im Exil und in der Migration* (Giessen: Psychosozialer Verlag).

Klesse, C. (2007a) 'Gender, Sexuality, and Race in Post/modernisation Theories on the Intimate' in A. Cervantes-Carson and N. Rumsfeld (eds), *The Sexual Politics of Desire and Belonging: Interdisciplinary Readings on Sex and Sexuality* (Tijnmuiden: Rodopi).

Klesse, C. (2007b) *The Spectre of Promiscuity: Gay Male and Bisexual Non-Monogamies and Polyamories* (Aldershot: Ashgate).

Kofman, E. and P. Raghuram (2005) 'Gender and Skilled Migrants: Into and Beyond the Work Place', *Geoforum* 36(2):149–54.

Kofman, E., A. Phizacklea, P. Raghuram and R. Sales (2000) *Gender and International Migration in Europe: Employment, Welfare and Politics* (London: Routledge).

Küçükcan, T. (1999) *Politics of Ethnicity, Identity and Religion: Turkish Muslims in Britain* (Aldershot: Ashgate).

Kuntsman, A. (2000) *Migration and Sexuality*, Lecture at the International Women's University Hanover, Project Area Migration.

Kymlicka, W. (1995) *Multicultural Citizenship: A Liberal Theory of Minority Rights* (Oxford: Oxford University Press).

Liversage, A. (2009) 'Turkish Divorces in Denmark: Investigating Gender and Power Across Transnational Spaces', ESA, 3 September, Lisbon.

Lutz, H. (1991) *Welten verbinden. Türkische Sozialarbeiterinnen in den Niederlanden und in der Bundesrepublik Deutschland* (Frankfurt: Verlag für interkulturelle Kommunikation).

Lutz, H. (n.d.) *Migrant Women from So-called Muslim Countries*, University of Amsterdam: Occasional Papers, Institute of Social Science.

Manalansan, M. L., IV (2006) 'Queer Intersections: Sexuality and Gender in Migration Studies', *IMR* 40(1): 224–49.

Morokvasic, M., U. Erel and K. Shinozaki (eds) (2003) *Crossing Borders and Shifting Boundaries: Gender on the Move* (Opladen: Leske & Budrich).

OSCE (2009) *Guide on Gender-Sensitive Labour Migration.* Available at www.osce.org/publications/eea/2009/05/37689_1289_en.pdf [accessed 24 November 2009].

Otyakmaz, B. Ö. (1995) *Auf allen Stühlen. Das Selbstverständnis junger türkischer Migrantinnen in Deutschland* (Köln: ISP Verlag).

Parker, D. (1995) *Through Different Eyes* (Aldershot: Avebury).

Patel, P. (1997) 'Third Wave Feminism and Black Women's Activism' in H. S. Mizra (ed.), *Black British Feminism: A Reader* (New York and London: Routledge).

Patel, P. (2008) *Defending Secular Spaces*, 4 August. Available at http://www.newstatesman.com/uk-politics/2008/08/religious-state-secular [accessed 7 October 2008].

Pheterson, G. (1990) *Hurenstigma. Wie man aus Frauen Huren macht* (Hamburg:Galgenberg).

Piper, N. (2008) 'International Migration and Gendered Axes of Stratification' in N. Piper (ed.), *New Perspectives on Gender and Migration: Livelihood, Rights and Entitlements* (London: Routledge).

Rex, J. (1994) 'Ethnic Mobilisation in Multi-cultural Societies' in J. Rex and B. Drury (eds), *Ethnic Mobilisation in a Multi-cultural Europe* (Aldershot: Avebury).

Richardson, D. (2000) 'Constructing Sexual Citizenship: Theorizing Sexual Rights', *Critical Social Policy* 20: 105–35.

Sahgal, G. and N. Yuval-Davis (eds) (1992) *Refusing Holy Orders: Women and Fundamentalism in Britain* (London: Virago).

Waltz, V. (1996) 'Toleranz fängt beim Kopftuch erst an. Zur Verhinderung von Chancengleichheit durch gesellschaftliche Verhältnisse' in W. Heitmeyer and R. Dollase (eds), *Die bedrängte Toleranz* (Frankfurt: Suhrkamp).

Weeks, J., B. Heaphy and C. Donovan (2001) *Same Sex Intimacies: Families of Choice and Other Life Experiments* (London: Routledge).

Yuval-Davis, N. (1997) *Gender and Nation* (London: Sage).

16
Negotiating Sexual Citizenship: Lesbians and Reproductive Health Care

Róisín Ryan-Flood

Introduction

This chapter explores lesbian women's experiences of reproductive health care and the extent to which such health care is characterized by heteronormativity at different spatial scales. A growing number of lesbian women are embarking on parenthood in the context of an openly lesbian lifestyle. Recent changes in 'intimate citizenship' (Plummer, 2003) include the separation of sexuality and reproduction, and the achievements of the lesbian, gay and bisexual rights movement. These changes have influenced reproductive decision-making among lesbian women, for whom a lesbian identity and motherhood may no longer appear incompatible. Although lesbians have always been parents – from previous heterosexual relationships – the new generation of lesbians who become parents after coming out is a decidedly new development. This pioneering generation of lesbian parents therefore constitute a new figure within the broader domain of new femininities and one whose experiences are profoundly affected by the wider context of sexual citizenship. However, the reproductive pathways of lesbian parenthood remain relatively unexplored in the academic literature, particularly outside the UK and US. This chapter will argue that lesbian experiences of reproductive health care reflect processes of social exclusion, with reference to lesbian parenthood in Sweden and Ireland. This exclusion occurs in relation to inequitable sexual citizenship, such as legislation that denies them access to assisted conception for example. These discriminatory processes may force some lesbian women with sufficient financial resources to explore transnational options in reproductive technologies. Lesbian women without the necessary financial capital are therefore doubly excluded. Discrimination is also experienced in relation to homophobia from medical staff during prenatal and antenatal care.

Geographies of sexuality have addressed the mutually constitutive nature of identity and space. Sexual identity is not simply a private issue, as the legal regulation of sexual practices, relationships and possibilities illustrates. Multiple strategies render 'public' space heteronormative, including contexts where parenting may be enacted, such as hospitals, schools and neighbourhoods. Parenthood is supported within clearly heteronormative parameters. The prohibition of services such as assisted insemination for lesbians in many countries is indicative of the highly regulated nature of this realm and forces some lesbians to seek supportive services beyond national boundaries. Lesbians who embark on parenthood, like heterosexual parents, encounter new social networks and institutional spaces. Becoming a lesbian parent also necessitates coming out in new spaces and presents particular dilemmas. This chapter draws on interviews with 68 lesbian parents in Sweden and Ireland. All participants embarked on parenthood after coming out. The lack of awareness among service providers about lesbian parenting and homophobic attitudes were detrimental to participants in this study, who were unsure of a supportive response in health-care provision as a result. This uncertainty provided a stressful edge to everyday life. The discursive constructions of space within the research illustrate the heteronormative understandings of 'the family' pervading reproductive health care spaces.

Lesbian parents and reproductive health care

Recent theories of sexual citizenship have often expressed scepticism at the emphasis on 'family based approaches' within the wider literature. For example, Binnie and Bell (2000) suggest that a concern with partnership and parenthood in sexual citizenship theory forces a heteronormative familial practices perspective, obscuring the radical potential of queer subjectivities and lives. Similarly, Halberstam suggests that 'Queer uses of time and space develop in opposition to the institutions of family, heterosexuality, and reproduction, and queer subcultures develop as alternatives to kinship-based notions of community' (2003, p. 1). While these points are helpful reminders of the potential of queer intimacies to challenge hegemonic norms, they also reinforce the binary of queer intimacies versus heteronormative parenthood, excluding the complicated realities of lesbian parents, who may be both subversive and normative in different ways. The ability to transgress is often a signifier of privilege. Lesbian parents face complex choices about how to protect their children and family from homophobic discrimination, while simultaneously they may wish to pass on values of tolerance and diversity that they experience as a result of living a queer life. The rather disparaging attitude to lesbian motherhood in some queer theory can also be seen as a reflection of androcentrism.

Theory and research about lesbian parenthood often falls within a assimilation/transgression binary, emphasizing either the normative dimensions of these families, or their potential for radical challenges to heteronormative practices. On the one hand, an entire generation of research has indicated that children of lesbian and gay parents develop along normative psychological lines (Stacey and Biblarz, 2001). This research has played a significant role in combating negative assumptions about the well-being of children in these families. Decades of research illustrate that a lesbian identity is in no way incompatible with the ability to be an effective and nurturing parent. The overwhelming emphasis in research therefore has traditionally been on the children in these families. Stacey and Biblarz (2001) argue that the concern with emphasizing the normative dimensions of childhood development in lesbian and gay parent families has obscured how these families may be different in a positive way. For example, the children often report feeling more aware and tolerant of diversity compared to their peers raised in conventional families. More recent work has begun to explore the experiences of lesbian parents themselves (Agigian, 2006; Dunne 1998a, 1998b; O'Sullivan, 2004). Some of this work suggests that these families may offer a potential for egalitarian family practices. For example, Dunne's (1998a) research suggests that lesbian parents are more likely to share childcare and housework equitably, which she attributes to the possibility of practising intimate relationships freer from some of the confines of dichotomous gender role expectations. In this chapter, I consciously choose to approach the experiences of lesbians within reproductive health care without recourse to a sameness/ difference perspective. In other words, my concern here is not whether lesbian parents either subvert or reinforce heteronormative spatiality. Rather, I explore the ways in which their paths to parenthood illustrate the heteronormative ideologies underpinning wider reproductive health care and lesbian parents' efforts to negotiate this.

The majority of published work on lesbian parenthood continues to originate from North America and the UK. Research on sexuality and space has often focused on the queer commercial scene, neglecting more 'everyday' spaces, particularly in relation to parenthood. As Knopp (1998, p. 172) has noted, there is a need for more work on a greater variety of queer experiences. This chapter explores a rather different terrain – the everyday spaces of reproductive health care in two European states and how lesbian participants negotiate them. Their endeavours illustrate the heteronormative construction of diverse spaces and the ways in which spatial identities can be destabilized by lesbian parents.

Sexual citizenship in Sweden and Ireland

Lesbian women have experienced significant constraints with regard to parenthood possibilities in both countries. Although Sweden has initiated some important legislative reforms regarding queer equality, at the time that this research was carried out, lesbians and gay men faced particular difficulties in relation to parenthood. Sweden introduced registered partnerships for same sex couples in 1995[1] (recently changed in 2009 to a gender neutral category of marriage).[2] However, the partnership laws specifically prohibited any parenting possibilities, including adoption and access to assisted conception. Lesbian and gay parenthood subsequently became the major terrain for queer equality struggles in recent years and has been a source of tremendous political and popular debate. The Swedish government published a commission report in 2001, the findings of which concluded that having lesbian or gay parents was in no way detrimental to children (SOU, 2001, p. 10). The laws on adoption were changed in 2003, so that adoption, including second-parent adoption, is now possible for lesbian and gay couples. However, problems remain with the way that this new legislation has been formulated, as it is based on a heteronormative vision of kinship as consisting of two parents (see Ryan-Flood, 2005, 2009b).[3] The law was also later changed to allow lesbians to access assisted reproduction services in Sweden,[4] although these changes were not in place at the time of fieldwork. However, these services are only available to women who are cohabiting or married (whether heterosexual or lesbian).

Lesbian parenthood has had a far lower profile in Ireland, where the regulation of new reproductive technologies (NRTs) has traditionally been left to the discretion of medical practitioners. The potential legal and ethical implications of NRTs were ignored in normative discourses that depicted them as a resource for heterosexual married couples with fertility difficulties. Thus, the introduction of NRTs in Ireland did not precipitate a public crisis. McDonnell (1999) notes that the pronounced absence of public debate about NRTs has meant that public discourse has not been influential in their regulation. There is no law prohibiting lesbians from access to assisted conception services; however, most service providers currently only treat heterosexual couples. A private clinic previously openly advertised its services to lesbian women. It is possible that the liberal market policies of Ireland (and Britain) facilitate access to private services, unlike in a social democratic society such as Sweden, as appears to have been the case in Finland, where private clinics have made their services available to single and lesbian women. However, as it can be difficult to locate a supportive clinic, Irish women seeking donor insemination often travel abroad to avail themselves of this service, typically to Britain. Adoption is restricted to heterosexual couples and single (presumably heterosexual) women. Fostering has, however, been possible for Irish lesbians. Indeed, local health boards have advertised for foster carers in Irish queer publications. The impetus for this was the chronic shortage of foster carers in Ireland, rather than an endorsement of lesbian parenthood. Nonetheless, it has meant that local health boards have been forced to acknowledge that lesbian sexuality is not incompatible with parenthood. Although lesbian parents in the two countries have experienced similar levels of exclusion at a policy level, the differing levels of visibility with regard to lesbian parenthood reflect different political moments. Civil partnerships for same sex couples came into effect in Ireland in December 2009. This legislation did not encompass parenting possibilities. It does appear however to have resulted in increased visibility for lesbian parenthood and acted as a rallying call to the lesbian and gay equality movement in Ireland, in the way that similar legislation did in Sweden over a decade earlier.

The path to parenthood: consequences of spatial exclusion

As lesbians were unable to access assisted conception services easily in Sweden and Ireland, fertility clinics and other places of service provision were coded as heteronormative spaces and new reproductive technologies (NRTs) became part of heteronormative imaginaries.[5] There were numerous consequences of this exclusion, most obviously that lesbian participants were forced to travel abroad for these services. In addition, some participants were deterred by the prohibitive cost and effort of this endeavour and opted to become co-parents instead. Susanne, a Swedish participant, did attempt to identify the source of her inability to conceive with a basic infertility investigation. She and the donor – a gay male friend – informed doctors that they were attempting to conceive together. While they did not lie outright and say they were a heterosexual couple, they did not reveal that they were gay. The prospect of lying to medical staff, in combination with the invasive nature of further fertility treatment, made Susanne decide not to persist any further with her efforts. Eventually her partner became the biological mother of their child:

> 'We had these clinical examinations and I did some x-rays and anyway the next step was an operation, laparoscopy and that's quite, to me it's quite a large step and we somehow stopped there and we were talking, discussing and I felt that my drive [...] wasn't big enough for that step [...] and also there's legal difficulties in Sweden anyway, you're not allowed to do IVF, it's difficult to say now afterwards whether I'd have gone through the whole programme if it had been legalised [...] Maybe I might have, but we were kind of lying every time that we entered the clinic and eh I don't know.' (Susanne, Swedish participant)

During fieldwork, I also interviewed an Irish lesbian, Bridget, who had attempted to become pregnant, but eventually gave up after several years of unsuccessful inseminations and has remained childless.[6] She was unwilling to seek a medical consultation, as she assumed doctors would be unhelpful towards a lesbian in her situation. As a result of medical policy that confines services to heterosexual couples, both these women were unable to undergo intra-uterine insemination (IUI). This is a simple procedure performed by medical staff, which involves the placing of semen closer to the cervix and thus maximizes the chance of conception. Like Susanne, Bridget was also concerned that fertility treatment would involve invasive procedures. Clearly, their experiences are not isolated cases. In addition to those participants in this study who experienced fertility problems, there are probably many other Irish and Swedish lesbians who have been unable to conceive and denied the possibility of adoption or affordable fertility treatment. This group of women – lesbians who are unsuccessful in their attempts to become pregnant and/or parents – is a largely hidden population. Their efforts are invisible, unless they manage to adopt or become parents with a partner.[7] I also interviewed a number of women who had opted to pose as heterosexual in order to access assisted fertility services. Their experiences provided a shocking illustration of the intense stress and discomfort associated with being forced back into the closet in order to receive the appropriate medical treatment (see Ryan-Flood, 2009a).

In this context of exclusion from reproductive services and technologies, home insemination constitutes a form of resistance. However, for those participants who chose the clearly 'low-tech' route of home insemination with a known donor, the restricted possibilities for medical consultation and advice also occasionally created difficult scenarios. Although the 'turkey baster' is a recurrent feature of alternative insemination in popular culture,[8] it is in fact a rather awkward size for this purpose. A smaller syringe is more appropriate given the relative volume of semen involved. Participants in this study typically used a needleless syringe for insemination. Occasionally straws and a speculum were also deployed to optimize the possibility of conception. While there is a considerable literature on alternative insemination (e.g. Mohler and Frazer, 2002; Pepper, 1999; Pies, 1988) and participants were aware of how to perform this straightforward procedure, accessing the materials necessary – such as syringes – occasionally proved difficult. A lack of familiarity with the utensils themselves and how to obtain them resulted in uncomfortable situations for several participants. As it was not possible to ask their doctor openly for information – who would possibly not be familiar with lesbian home insemination in any case – they were forced to rely on word of mouth or helpful friends for advice. This occasionally caused some difficulties.

For example, Katarina, a Swedish participant, ran into difficulties when attempting to find a syringe for insemination. She was aware that appropriate ones were available for free at local pharmacies. Unable to disclose the fact that she wished to obtain a syringe for the purpose of insemination, Katarina was forced to provide an alternative reason for the purchase. She therefore told the pharmacist that she needed one to give her child an injection (the most common reason for obtaining a free syringe). However, she did not realize that the syringes came in different forms. The pharmacist asked what medicine her child was taking, in order to determine the correct type. Katarina then replied 'I don't know', at which point she understandably felt extremely foolish. She emailed me afterwards to describe the incident:

> 'I said "I don't know" when she asked me what type of syringe I wanted. They are free at the pharmacy but they have different kinds and that made me [feel] really embarrassed and confused because I didn't know that. I felt so stupid when she asked because it's a syringe to give a child medicine and she asked me what medicine I should give my child. And I don't know?!??? I didn't [...] tell her the whole story but she solved my problem by saying "you better try the basic one" and it turned out to be right.' (Katarina, Swedish participant)

This example illustrates how lesbian parenting remains to some degree an 'underground' activity, in that participants cannot be entirely open about their plans to become parents in all contexts, regardless of whether they actually require medical help or not. The denial of basic medical consultation and information resulted in numerous stressful situations that could not be anticipated by participants. It therefore exposes their vulnerability in contexts where appropriate services are restricted to heterosexuals. This exclusion occurs across various modalities of space, manifested in diverse contexts such as pharmacies and in the imagined spaces of NRTs.

Transnational journeys

Some participants opted to travel abroad for assisted reproduction services, such as donor insemination and IVF, which were not available to lesbians in Sweden at the time and were difficult for lesbians to access in Ireland. This was a significant financial undertaking, involving costly procedures such as artificial insemination and in-vitro fertilization, as well as travel and accommodation. For most participants, the costs involved were prohibitive and beyond their means. A small number of participants did, however, seek these services in countries such as England, Denmark and Finland.

The case of Katarina and Elisabet is particularly illuminating. They initially attempted to conceive with a known donor. After a period of unsuccessful home inseminations, he decided to move abroad but remained committed to being a donor. He therefore deposited sperm with a sperm bank in neighbouring Denmark. Katarina travelled to Denmark every month for insemination. However, the donor's sperm had reacted badly to the freezing process and after a year of unsuccessful attempts to become pregnant, they decided to opt for an anonymous donor with a high sperm count. They were uncomfortable, however, with a completely anonymous donor, as was the only available option in Denmark at that time. So Katarina asked the Danish clinic to import sperm from the Sperm Bank of California (SBC), which offered a 'donor identity disclosure' option, whereby resulting children could receive the donor's contact information when they turned eighteen. So the SBC sent sperm to Denmark and Katarina continued to travel there for inseminations. When no pregnancy resulted, they decided to try IVF. However, it was not possible for lesbians to get IVF in Denmark at that time, but it was possible in nearby Finland. So the SBC sperm was sent from Denmark to Finland, where Katarina travelled for IVF, eventually giving birth after a second IVF attempt. During her second round of IVF, the staff at the Finnish clinic informed her that there was some political debate in Finland at that time about whether lesbians should be able to access assisted reproduction services, so if this round did not work, they might not be able to do another one. Should this scenario arise, they suggested that Katarina have the donor sperm shipped to Russia, as it would be possible to continue with IVF there. Katarina later emailed me about this situation:

> 'Isn't this totally stupid. These little sperms have to travel around the whole world and me too before they will get into me ...' (Katarina, Swedish participant)

In this instance, the lesbian reproductive network involves five countries: Sweden, where the lesbian couple live, Denmark where they travel for insemination, the US where the sperm originates, Finland where IVF is performed, and potentially Russia, should the regulations in Finland change. This highlights the potential for transnational networking among lesbians attempting to conceive and the various agencies and services who are willing to assist them. The transnational routes to pregnancy and the networking among the various clinics in different countries which have to collaborate in relation to shipping sperm for example, are entirely overlooked in wider literature about reproductive health care, and lesbian parenthood. It is of course only possible for those lesbians who have sufficient financial resources to undertake the procedures. Katarina and Elisabet referred several times during the interview to the loans they had taken out and the financial sacrifices they had made in order to fund the treatments. The transnational networking involved highlights how important the notion of borders remains for lesbians excluded from assisted reproduction services within national boundaries.

Educating the 'caring professions'

In addition to problems encountered in becoming pregnant due to exclusionary practices, many participants reported numerous difficulties with staff in prenatal and antenatal care. Uncertainty about the consequences of disclosure regarding their sexuality was a cause of concern. Numerous interviewees described feeling stressed about outing themselves to potentially unsupportive staff. On the whole, participants found members of 'caring professions' to be sympathetic and helpful. However, midwives and doctors often had little or no experience of dealing with lesbian parents and participants frequently found themselves in the position of educating personnel, both as to the type of treatment that they required and in terms of correcting problematic assumptions about their families. Participants reported feeling somewhat drained by this aspect of their encounters with service providers, in addition to facing the challenge of embarking on parenthood. One Irish participant, Evelyn, resented having to challenge her midwife's ideas about family forms and father-absence within their family, particularly as they pertained to her son. The midwife in question ostensibly attempted to be cognizant of diversity in family forms, but nonetheless made reference to 'fathering and mothering' at the end of their prenatal course, without acknowledging that not all families consist of a father and a mother:

> 'She [midwife] [...] would work hard at being very politically correct but she did a bit of a wobbly at the end of it, where she forgot, at the course, talking about fathering and mothering and whatever. She rang up out of the blue [...] and the next thing was something about and who is going to play the fathering role in our relationship and I was like, what, you know, where are you getting off. So we kind of, I had to bring her through all of that, you know, which I resented having to do [...] She had never met Cormac [son] [...] and she had decided that he needed a lot of controlling or whatever, kind of fatherly heaviness or whatever. But anyway so [...] that certainly rubbed up the wrong way in terms of having to deal with her issues around our family.' (Evelyn, Irish participant)

The difficulties of participating in prenatal courses as a lesbian couple, or single lesbian expectant mother, were a feature of several participant accounts. Course providers often assumed that all participants were heterosexual. Although they reported some awareness of issues pertaining to lone mothers, lesbian parents appeared to be a relatively unknown phenomenon. This lack of support exacerbated participants' concern about the possibility of exposure to homophobia, not only from course providers, but also from the other people attending the courses.

Participants also reported similar difficulties among midwives and other medical personnel in terms of a lack of familiarity and awareness of their family form. They were often the first lesbian expectant parents that staff had encountered. Again, the issue of educating staff arose. For example, in the following excerpt Eimear, a co-parent, describes how she is treated differently by their doctor in relation to their child:

E: 'Our doctor was a bit dismissive, Dr. O'Reilly just didn't consider me and still doesn't really consider me as the other parent.'
R: 'You feel there's a difference?'
E: 'Oh yeah, yeah.'
S: 'And I'd agree there, there is, would be a difference in the way she treats us, without a doubt.'
E: 'I'd just insist on going in each time and attending and being a part of it. But she doesn't respond to me, like she asks Sorcha everything.'
S: 'Yeah.' (Eimear and Sorcha, Irish participants)

The treatment of co-parents ranged from dismissiveness, to a complete lack of understanding of her place within this family. For example, Elin, a Swedish co-parent describes what happened when she took her young son to hospital without her partner Ylva:

E: 'When I was with the smallest, when he was six months old I went to the hospital.'
R: 'And what happened?'
E: 'They asked for the parent. [...] I think they thought that I was with Ylva's ex-husband or something, that I was together with him.' (Elin, Swedish co-parent)

Saffron (1999) notes the importance of awareness of lesbian clients' needs on the part of midwives and other service providers. Although lesbian parents in the two countries also established spaces specific to lesbian parents – such as support groups for example – instances of service provision specifically oriented towards lesbian parents were extremely rare. In Stockholm, there is one midwife who is recommended by the national organization for LGBT equality, RFSL,[9] as someone working in this area who has particular expertise regarding lesbian parents. However, this remains exceptional.

Assumption of heterosexuality

The conflation of pregnancy with a heterosexual identity in myriad contexts was a recurring feature of Swedish and Irish accounts. This illustrates the role of space in shaping identity – for example, a woman giving birth in a hospital is assumed to be heterosexual. Thus, specific spaces inform readings of identity. For many participants, the recurring assumption of heterosexuality was depressing and served to make them more aware of their marginalization and therefore vulnerability in society. Mairéad, an Irish participant, was a single mother who found hospital questions about her 'husband' or 'boyfriend' – never 'girlfriend' – tiresome:

> 'At the hospital they were saying do you want to call your husband. I said I don't have a husband, do you want to call your boyfriend, I don't have a boyfriend [...] and if they had of said do you have a girlfriend, but there was just that and I think I was feeling very vulnerable, I was in pain so I was very like oh bother all of this bother all the straight people like all these questions, questions, questions [...] because I'd had nine months of this you know and em and I was tired of it you know, tired of it all.' (Mairéad, Irish participant)

These questions could also be experienced as alienating by solo heterosexual mothers, but it is interesting that for Mairéad acknowledgement of her lesbian identity was important. As pregnancy was so strongly associated with heterosexuality, biological mothers in both countries experienced a negation of their lesbian identity in many spaces as a pregnant woman. Unlike co-parents, whose lesbian identity becomes apparent in the assertion of parenthood (which is itself continually contested), biological mothers in this study found that their sexuality was rendered invisible by pregnancy. Stina, a Swedish participant, experienced feelings of frustration similar to those articulated by Mairéad regarding the assumption of heterosexuality because of her impending motherhood:

> 'But it was also that people seeing me as pregnant thought I was heterosexual once again. So all these people who didn't know me, okay I couldn't go in the streets screaming I'm a pregnant lesbian but it was disturbing [...] and I wanted people to know that also a lesbian can be a pregnant woman, so when I got the opportunity I always told people in some way that I was lesbian too, that was very important to me. (Stina, Swedish participant)

If the biological mother was automatically categorized as heterosexual, her partner – the co-parent – was often assumed to be a helpful friend or relative. Participants who did not wish either to lie about their sexual identity and relationship, or marginalize the role of co-parents, were forced to continually challenge this interpretation of themselves as heterosexual. Podmore (2001) argues that it is not always possible for lesbians to express diverse aspects of their identity in an integrated way, for example queer spaces may not be inclusive of ethnic diversity and heteronormative spaces are exclusionary on the grounds of sexuality. Thus, lesbians from ethnic minorities may suppress various aspects of their identity in different spaces. Similarly, lesbian parents in this study struggled for recognition of themselves as lesbians and parents. Swedish participants tended to be more direct and open when communicating with hospital staff and expect both partners to be treated as equal parents, whereas Irish participants emphasized the importance of equal access, such as extended visiting hours, rather than acknowledgement of their relationship or parental role.

The confusion about understanding that participants and their children represented a lesbian family form illustrates the ways that families are invariably interpreted through a heteronormative lens. For example, the supportive midwife of the Swedish couple, Katarina and Elisabet, recorded that Elisabet (the co-parent) was a 'mother' in their medical records. Minutes after Katarina gave birth, a new nurse on duty asked her if Elisabet was 'the mother'. Katarina was nonplussed by this question and asked her to clarify. In an interesting attribution of motherhood to biogenetic substance, the nurse then explained that she thought Elisabet was the egg donor. She had read their records and interpreted the reference to Elisabet as a 'mother' in this way. Despite having just endured a protracted and difficult birth, Katarina had to come out to the nurse and explain that she and her partner were a lesbian couple who had conceived a child by insemination.

The failure to acknowledge co-parents could be a source of pain to couples in both countries. This was a common theme of participant accounts regarding medical emergencies, including miscarriage. In these distressing circumstances, hospital staff often appeared unaware or unwilling to acknowledge their status as lesbian couples. Participants themselves did not always feel capable of illuminating staff on this point, in what was a medical emergency scenario. This exacerbated an already emotionally difficult situation:

'My experience in the hospital wasn't great at all in terms of Maeve's [partner] involvement when I was miscarrying, they didn't really understand or accept or whatever the fact that she was my partner. I don't think they quite got it [...] so that was very hard.' (Gráinne, Irish participant)

'When we went to the hospital [...] especially one older male doctor [...] we told him that we were both mothers but he didn't want to see me like a mother, he wanted to see me like Margareta's [partner] friend. And we didn't take that discussion then but it doesn't feel good [...] I will have to fight in some situations I think. (Linnea, Swedish participant)

Swedish couples were more likely to press for an acknowledgement of their partnership status, as illustrated by Linnea's comment 'I will have to fight', above. In contrast, Irish participants tended to 'choose their battles', occasionally prioritizing a helpful and less stressful service over communicating their lesbian identity. For example, an Irish couple, Caoimhe and Aisling, chose not to mention their lesbian identity in the context of a hospital childbirth. While Caoimhe was present throughout the birth, she was ostensibly there as the 'birthing partner', rather than co-parent:

> 'In the hospital I was [...] her birthing partner, I wasn't her partner do you know what I mean or I wasn't the mother or the husband or whatever, I was just her birthing partner and they didn't know our relationship so every now and again you just for peace's sake you just say nothing but that doesn't make me feel that I'm less because you know like instead of getting involved in a situation that you don't want to be slightly embarrassed or you don't want Aisling [partner] to be embarrassed or you know you just go with the flow you say look I'm a friend I'm here to help her with the baby so but that didn't make me feel less excited or part of it because when I was ringing my friends they were all congratulating me. These were nurses I just wanted them to do a job, I didn't need them to recognise me.' (Caoimhe, Irish participant)

In this sense, Irish participants' accounts of their interactions with relevant personnel appeared to be characterized by a greater degree of self-conscious distancing on the part of participants, than seemed to be the case among their Swedish counterparts. This was a strategy that Irish participants adopted in order to deal with a heteronormative context that was potentially unsupportive at a time when their main priority was to access a particular service. In this particular case, as Caoimhe indicates in the above quote, her personal understanding of herself as a parent was not undermined, as she received sufficient validation from friends and family – in other words her parental identity was made visible and supported in alternative spaces and contexts.

Homophobic discrimination and heteronormative expectations

In addition to a lack of awareness of lesbian parenting in general, participants who were open about their identity as lesbians occasionally encountered active criticism of their life choices. For example, the midwife who attended Maeve, an Irish participant, during childbirth communicated her disapproval regarding Maeve's family form. The birth was unusually long and there were complications. The midwife was unsupportive of Maeve in this context as a result of her homophobic opinions:

> 'I felt there was one [midwife] that was a bit moralistic [...] she was giving out to me about pushing [...] I'd been pushing for hours and I was getting very tired [...] no matter what I was doing I couldn't push him out [...] she [midwife] was tired and stressed but there was a touch, just a touch moralistic about it, this shouldn't be happening anyway, you know lesbians.' (Maeve, Irish participant)

Several participants found nursing staff at hospital behaved in overtly homophobic ways after the birth. For example, a Swedish participant, Gunilla, had difficulties breastfeeding and many nurses were uncomfortable being alone with her, so were reluctant to help. Another participant described how she felt excluded by midwives:

'I just felt that they, it wasn't okay with them when I was there [...] because I felt like no one there knew me and no one wanted to help me except one midwife who wanted to help me before I left and then I gave her a hug and said goodbye when we were leaving and some person had told her "how could you hug her she's a lesbian". So it wasn't only my feelings.' (Magdalena, Swedish participant)

In addition to the general lack of awareness and prejudice that participants encountered, there were countless instances in which particular spaces were clearly inscribed in heteronormative ways. For example, hospital hours gave special privileges to visiting fathers, rather than co-parents. Although all participants who gave birth in hospital were able to negotiate the same access for co-parents, the prospect of having to do so was a source of anxiety prior to giving birth. Participants were concerned that they would encounter homophobia and resistance in response to their efforts to ensure that co-parents had the same hospital visitor hours automatically awarded fathers. Furthermore, in a Swedish context, hospital policy conferred donors with special privileges that birth mothers did not always find appropriate or desirable. Åsa, a Swedish participant, recalled that the donor visited her every day when she was in hospital and was insensitive to the fact that she wanted more time and space for herself and her partner. As he was the father, he was entitled to these lengthy visits, despite the fact that she had not had a relationship with him:

'He didn't announce, it was just suddenly he'd stand there in the door and I was trying to sleep and I was bleeding and the milk was...and I just came in and sat down for hours and talked about other things, his private life and...I didn't have the strength, he wasn't that close to us. He was the father to her [child] but he wasn't that close to me, he wasn't my husband. [...] But because he was the father to her he was always welcome and [...] you [partner] should be the one who is always welcome and he should have this special time of the day when visitors come. [...] The hospital didn't do wrong but it made a little bit of a problem because it was a very strange family, they didn't know how to deal with it. They tried to be nice.' (Åsa, Swedish participant)

Another problem encountered in hospitals concerned recognition of partners as next-of-kin. There is no formal recognition of lesbian and gay partnerships in Ireland, thus all lesbians and gay men in relationships are vulnerable to exclusion from the decision-making process regarding their partners in situations such as medical emergencies. This occasionally featured in participants' accounts. For Irish participants, there was no possibility of being recognized as their partner's next of kin. One couple attempted to redress this, albeit unsuccessfully:

> G: 'You tried to put me down as your next of kin as well but there was difficulty with that.'
> M: 'There was a difficulty with that, wasn't there? And I wouldn't give them another name. That bit at the end, we refused to give them a name. Because legally you're not recognized as next of kin, so I refused to give them a name.' (Gráinne and Maeve, Irish participants)

In Sweden, due to legal recognition of cohabiting or 'sambo' relationships and registered partnerships, for those couples who had children after the introduction of these laws in 1988 and 1995 respectively, co-parents could be identified as next of kin. Nonetheless, one Swedish couple in a registered partnership reported that medical staff did not keep the co-parent informed of her partner's condition after she was rushed to hospital with complications and given a Caesarean section. Fathers are allowed to attend this operation, but staff did not offer her this option. In addition, she was not asked if she would like to touch their child, who was placed in an incubator in intensive care. She was in a state of shock as a result of her partner and child's illnesses and the emergency nature of the operation, thus it did not occur to her at the time that physical contact with their child might be possible. The treatment she received highlights her vulnerability as a parent in a context where she was not legally recognized. Even when, as in Sweden, partnership status was legally recognized, the heterosexual nuclear family model is so ingrained that co-parents could nonetheless be excluded from important scenarios, such as attendance at the birth of a child by Caesarean section.

While participants reported many instances where medical and other staff were supportive and open, the fear of encountering homophobic reactions in a variety of contexts, including hospitals, was experienced as stressful. Clearly, participants did occasionally experience overt hostility and discrimination. However, encounters with institutions were more generally characterized by a lack of awareness concerning lesbian parent families. Thus participants were forced to educate staff – an onerous task – while simultaneously seeking their services.

Conclusion

The ways in which lesbians continually struggled to assert their intersectional identities as both lesbian and mother, illustrate the extent to which 'mother' and 'lesbian' remain mutually exclusive categories within the popular imagination, despite the existence of the 'lesbian baby boom' and growing representation of lesbian parents within popular culture narratives. This new femininity is still struggling for wider acceptance and recognition, as well as equality in relation to sexual citizenship. As lesbian parents, the participants in this research struggled to create spaces that recognized their family form. The continuous efforts to have their families validated created an extra burden for them, as they struggled to communicate their family identities and needs. These efforts often occurred at very vulnerable moments, from prenatal to postnatal care. Lesbians who embark on parenthood are creating family forms that reflect new narratives of kinship and it is notable that considerable work remains to be done in order to create sufficient awareness and tolerance among health care providers.

The tendency in theory and research on lesbian parenthood to explore the ways in which these families are either similar to, or different from, a heteronormative family standard, obscures the complexities that lesbian parents negotiate in their every day lives. Lesbian parenthood is fundamentally subversive in the face of societies that deny or prohibit their very existence. Nonetheless, lesbian parents may utilize heteronormative discourses or practices in their efforts to secure their families' safety within a wider homophobic context. Irrespective of whether or not these families do in fact 'transgress' or reinforce heternormativity, this pioneering generation of families offer a unique insight into broader understandings of intersections of new femininities, kinship, culture and sexual citizenship.

Notes

1. The law on registered partnership was passed in 1994 (Lagen, 1994, p. 1117) om registrerat partnerskap and came into effect in 1995.
2. Äktenskapsbalk (1987, p. 230).
3. http://www.regeringen.se/content/1/c6/01/63/49/c6eb469c.pdf
4. Lag (2006, p. 351) om genetisk integritet m.m. (Chapter 6, Insemination).
5. For example, NRTs are often presented as a means to enable a heterosexual couple to have a longed-for child, while opponents of NRTs may deride them as unnatural and actively utilize the example of lesbian parents as representative of the dangers of technology (Liljestrand, 1995).
6. This interview has not been included in the wider study, apart from the reference to it here.
7. The same is also true of heterosexual women who experience infertility but choose not to adopt or undergo medical interventions such as IVF.
8. See, for example, the third feature in the (2000) HBO film *If These Walls Could Talk 2*.
9. Riksförbundet för sexuellt likaberättigande.

Bibliography

Agigian, A. (2006) *Baby Steps: How Lesbian Alternative Insemination Is Changing the World* (Middletown, CT: Wesleyan University Press).

Bell, D. and Binnie, J. (2000) *The Sexual Citizen* (London: Routledge).

Dunne, G. (1998a) *Opting into Motherhood: Blurring the Boundaries and Redefining the Meaning of Parenthood*, LSE Gender Institute discussion paper series (London: London School of Economics and Political Science, Gender Institute).

Dunne, G. (1998b) 'Pioneers Behind Our Own Front Doors': New Models for the Organization of Work in Partnerships, *The Journal of Work Employment and Society* 12: 273–97.

Halberstam, J. (2003) 'The Brandon Teena Archive' in R. Corber and S.Valocchi (eds), *Queer Studies: An Interdisciplinary Reader* (Oxford: Blackwell).

Knopp, L. (1998) 'Sexuality and Urban Space: Gay Male Identity Politics in the United States, the United Kingdom and Australia' in R. Fincher and J. Jacobs (eds), *Cities of Difference* (London: Guilford Press).

Liljestrand, P. (1995) 'Legitimate State and Illegitimate Parents: Donor Insemination Politics in Sweden', *Social Politics: International Studies in Gender, State and Society* 2: 270–304.

McDonnell, O. (1999) 'Shifting Debates on New Reproductive Technology: Implications for Public Discourse in Ireland' in P. O'Mahony (ed.), *Nature, Risk and Responsibility: Discourses of Biotechnology* (Basingstoke: Macmillan).

Mohler, M. and Frazer, L. (2002) *A Donor Insemination Guide Written by and for Lesbian Women* (New York: Haworth Press).

O'Sullivan, M. (2004) *The Family of Woman: Lesbian Mothers, Their Children, and the Undoing of Gender* (Berkeley: University of California Press).

Pepper, R. (1999) *The Ultimate Guide to Pregnancy for Lesbians* (London: Cleis Press).

Pies, C. (1988) *Considering Parenthood* (London: Spinsters Book Company).

Plummer, K. (2003) *Intimate Citizenship: Private Decisions and Public Dialogues* (London: University of Washington Press).

Podmore, J. (2001) 'Lesbians in the Crowd: Gender, Sexuality and Visibility along Montréal's Boul. St-Laurent', *Gender, Place and Culture* 8: 333–55.

Ryan-Flood, R. (2005) 'Contested Heteronormativities: Discourses of Fatherhood among Lesbian Parents in Sweden and Ireland', *Sexualities: Studies in Culture and Society* 8(2): 189–204.

Ryan-Flood, R. (2009a) 'Keeping Mum: Secrecy and Silence in Research on Lesbian Parenthood' in R. Ryan-Flood and R. Gill (eds), *Secrecy and Silence in the Research Process: Feminist Reflections* (London: Routledge).

Ryan-Flood, R. (2009b) *Lesbian Motherhood: Gender, Families and Sexual Citizenship* (London: Palgrave Macmillan)

Saffron, L. (1999) 'Meeting the Needs of Lesbian Clients', *The Practising Midwife* 2: 18–19.

SOU (2001) *Barn i homosexuella familjer: betänkande av Kommittén om barn i homosexuella familjer* [Children in Homosexual Families: Report from the Commission on Children in Homosexual Families].

Stacey, J. and Biblarz, T. J. (2001) '(How) Does the Sexual Orientation of Parents Matter?', *American Sociological Review* 66: 159–83.

Part V
New Feminisms, New Challenges

17
The New German Feminisms: Of Wetlands and Alpha-Girls

Christina Scharff

It has been widely documented that women, and particularly young women, do not identify with feminism as a label or political movement (Aapola et al., 2005; McRobbie, 2004, 2009; Scharff, 2012). Indeed, McRobbie (2003, p. 133) argues that feminism has been expelled to an 'abject state'. It seems that new femininities can do without feminism in the postfeminist era where feminism is taken into account, and simultaneously repudiated (Gill, 2007; McRobbie, 2004, 2009). Against this context, it is notable that since 2006 the emergence of 'new' feminisms has been proclaimed in Germany, triggered by a public debate on demographic changes. While there was an active women's movement in West Germany in the 1970s and 1980s (Lenz, 2001) and in East Germany in the 1980s (Miethe, 2002),[1] subsequent years were constituted by a quieter period for feminist activism (Gerhard, 1999). However, this has changed. 'Without any doubt', argue Hark and Kerner (2007),[2] 'the embarrassment is over and also in this country feminism has come back onto the discursive stage.'

By analysing various texts that call for a revised feminist politics, and situating them into wider media and academic debates, this chapter highlights some characteristic features of the new feminisms. I will explore the emancipatory potential of this political 'movement' and demonstrate that it negotiates cultural divisions and phenomena that reach beyond the new feminisms and Germany. My focus will be on difference (particularly in relation to race, class and sexuality), processes of individualization (Bauman, 2000) and the portrayal of 1970s feminism. While the new feminisms challenge contemporary socio-cultural trends that facilitate the widespread rejection of feminism, I will argue that their main themes exhibit problematic tendencies. The new feminists, for example, distance themselves from 1970s feminism, mainly because they associate it with man-hating and lesbianism. The homophobic rejection of the 1970s raises questions about the new feminisms' critical and emancipatory potential. It seems that the new feminisms do not sufficiently interrogate the social constellations that initially gave rise to the felt need for a new feminist politics.

Mapping the field

German journalists (Ritter, 2008) as well as academics observe that public negotiations of feminism are changing. While feminism figured as a swearword in the past, it has recently become more popular. One important trigger for the revival of public debates on feminism was the so-called *Demographiedebatte*, a public debate on demographic change in Germany which began in 2006 (Klaus, 2008). The forecasted shrinking and ageing of the 'German population' gave rise to a conservative backlash against feminism: several journalists and public commentators blamed the integration of women into the (paid) labour force for the predicted demographic changes, arguing that it had led to a decrease in stay-at-home mothers and a low birth rate. The debate on demographic changes is disconcerting because of its anti-feminism and its troubling concern with the decline of the 'German people'. The *Demographiedebatte* also figured as a catalyst for another curious discussion on gender mainstreaming, whose main critical object was gender studies (Thorn, 2007). Critics of gender mainstreaming (e.g. Zastrow, 2006) argued against the conceptualization of gender as a social construct and against queer theory approaches. They also stated a direct correlation between feminism and lesbianism (Thorn, 2007), where the latter was cast in a negative light. Such overt anti-feminism, homophobia and conservatism have given rise to a range of critical responses and the emergence of a complex discursive field with various feminist strands. The voices of journalists, politicians and public commentators are loudest, and perspectives emanating from gender studies are rarely provided (Klaus, 2008).

The field is mapped differently by various researchers (cf. Dölling, 2007; Hark, 2008a; Klaus, 2008), but all concur that the new feminisms represent the views of a homogeneous and privileged group of women (most authors are white, well-educated and heterosexual), are neoliberal in outlook and characterized by a fierce repudiation of second-wave feminism, which is dubbed the 'old' women's movement. This is why the feminisms are most commonly referred to as 'new'. In Germany, the wave metaphor is less frequently used: what is called 'second-wave' in an Anglo-American context tends to be labelled the 'old' women's movement or '1970s feminism'. While these new feminisms are evoked in a range of areas, such as popular culture and politics, I will focus on several books and media articles that have been published since 2006. The analysis presented here does *not* seek to provide a complete overview of the new feminisms in Germany, but instead attempts to analyse some characteristic features and their interplay with broader cultural trends.

In her book *Die neue F-Klasse: Wie die Zukunft von Frauen gemacht wird* (The New F-class: How the Future Is Made by Women), the novelist Dorn (2006) interviews eleven successful women. Distancing herself from the old feminism in the introduction, Dorn advocates a new F-class, which is elitist and strongly neoliberal in its focus on women as self-responsible managers of their own lives. Dorn's outlook is similar to the book *Schwestern: Streitschrift für einen neuen Feminismus* (Sisters: Pamphlet for a New Feminism) written by one of Dorn's interviewees, the politician Koch-Mehrin (2007). Focusing primarily on the difficulties in combining a family and career, Koch-Mehrin advocates for better child-care provisions and argues against the *Muttermythos*, which she regards as a specific 'German' idealization of the 'biological' mother as primary caregiver.

The year 2008 saw the publication of three books that received considerable media attention. In their text *Wir Alphamädchen: Warum Feminismus das Leben schöner macht* (We Alpha-Girls: Why Feminism Makes Life More Beautiful), the journalists Haaf, Klingner and Streidl endorse a new feminism that resonates with the experiences of young German women. Distancing themselves from 1970s feminism, and most notably the widely known German feminist Alice Schwarzer,[3] the alpha-girls address issues of identity, sex, media and power. While the authors claim that every woman who thinks critically and has goals in her life can be an alpha-girl, the book addresses differences between women only in the foreword and conclusion. Pursuing a similar agenda, the novelist Hensel and journalist Raether published *Neue Deutsche Mädchen* (New German Girls) at around the same time.[4] Also distancing themselves from 1970s feminism – which they view as being personified by Alice Schwarzer – Hensel and Raether's book describes what it is like to be a woman today. Like the alpha-girls, Hensel and Raether focus on themselves, thereby failing to acknowledge differences amongst women. Both books carry strangely elitist and exclusionary titles, revealing that the experiences addressed are those of a privileged, comparatively small group of women.

The third book that addressed feminist issues in Germany in 2008 is Roche's hotly debated *Feuchtgebiete* (Wetlands). By 2009, *Feuchtgebiete* had sold almost 700,000 copies (Kean, 2009) and been translated into English (2009). The novel tells the story of Helen Memel, who lies in a hospital, exploring every part of her body and rebelling against bodily hygiene. Numerous passages in the book provoke disgust: the press reports that audience members have fainted at public readings and the journalist Aitkenhead (2009) claims that the book 'makes the *Vagina Monologues* sound like *Listen With Mother*'. The novel is hugely popular amongst young women and men over the age of 55. Roche openly admits that her novel can serve as a masturbation pamphlet and adds that she wishes women would use it in such a way too (Mueller and Ritter, 2008). While the term 'feminism' does not appear in the book, Roche (quoted by Caesar, 2009) describes her book as a 'feminism of the body':

> The feminist angle to the book is this: I think women, now, have to have this clean, sexy, presentation side to their body. At any time, you must

be available for sex, and you can just strip naked and look super. That's a high pressure, and the joke in this book is saying, 'Women shit, too, you know'. I know there are men who will find that hard to accept, because they are thinking, 'I want to f*** a clean woman.

In the German-speaking context, there have been (at least) two more recent publications by young women which promote feminism. These texts differ from the books that I have discussed so far in that they also incorporate academic, feminist work and do not forcefully reject 1970s feminism. Stöcker's (2007) *Das F-Wort: Feminismus ist sexy* (The F-Word: Feminism Is Sexy) as well as Eismann's (2007) *Hot Topic: Popfeminismus heute* (Hot Topic: Pop Feminism Today) are both edited collections that explore a range of feminist issues. Stöcker's collection seeks to challenge negative stereotypes of the women's movement. Eismann, a journalist who works on feminism and popular culture, provides a platform for a German-speaking, critical and radical feminism that is informed by popular culture. Referring to ladyfests, feminist workshops and drag-king shows, she wants to move the (media's) focus away from Alice Schwarzer's and Roche's feminisms to explore German-speaking pop feminism in its various forms and manifestations. Her edited collection draws on a range of feminist, academic literature and also seeks to represent the views of a diverse group of women. Stöcker's and Eismann's collections have received considerably less media attention, but are included here because their more critical and radical perspectives (particularly Eismann's collection) represent important exceptions to the exclusionary, neoliberal and anti-1970s outlook of the mainstream new feminisms.

Ambivalently, and in various forms, the new feminisms proclaim a feminist politics. In this regard, the recent support for a new feminism differs from (young) women's reported reluctance to claim feminism in the postfeminist era. The call for a new feminism breaks with the postfeminist logic in that the need for a continued feminist politics – in whatever form – is asserted. On a different level, however, the majority of new feminisms contain fierce repudiations of 1970s feminism not dissimilar to the ambivalent negotiations of feminism that characterize young women's talk (Scharff, 2012), the media (Gill, 2007) and the cultural realm (McRobbie, 2009). Arguably, the fierce repudiation of feminism that McRobbie claims is part of the postfeminist double entanglement is projected onto an older feminism from which the new feminists desperately seek to distance themselves. In this respect, the new feminists still follow a postfeminist logic: they acknowledge feminism – indeed they call for a renewed feminism. Through their call for a renewal of feminism, the new feminists nevertheless allocate a certain type of feminism (read 'old') to the past, and even engage in a forceful repudiation of it. They renew and refresh the feminist common sense; however, the rebranding of feminism as new and different constructs and constitutes the old feminism as 'almost hated' (McRobbie, 2003, p. 130). Therefore, the postfeminist negotiation of feminism as both valuable and hated also features in the mainstream German feminisms through the call for a renewed feminism which relies on discarding its older variants.

(Dis-)regarding differences amongst women

Feminist debates have shown that female identity is not determined by sex alone but is constituted through the complex interplay of a variety of factors such as race, socio-economic status, cultural background, ability and sexuality. For example, the German feminist movement has been critiqued for its white bias (Gutiérrez Rodríguez, 1999), calling for an awareness of differences amongst women. As several researchers (Dölling, 2007; Hark, 2008b; Hark and Kerner, 2007; Klaus, 2008) have pointed out, the new feminisms are elitist and only reflect the views of a privileged group of women. As my analysis of exclusionary tendencies in the new feminisms will demonstrate, I agree with these claims. However, I think it is important to highlight the existence of different strands in the new feminisms: Eismann's edited collection, for example, addresses issues of class and racial inequalities, as well as queer politics. Numerous contributors provide an intersectional analysis which also comes to the fore in Stöcker's edited collection (notably Haas's analysis of the TV show *Germany's Next Topmodel*). While Hark, Kerner, Dölling and Klaus are right in challenging the alpha-girls and F-class proponents for providing an elitist perspective, I want to stress the complexities of the field before developing my argument that the new feminisms predominantly exhibit exclusionary tendencies.

The focus on privileged, white, heterosexual and German women is striking in mainstream endorsements of a new feminism. Dorn's and Koch-Mehrin's acknowledgement of difference is limited to a few references to the oppression of Muslim women (Dorn, 2006, p. 24; Koch-Mehrin, 2007, p. 67). These passing remarks are highly problematic because they resonate with colonial discourses about the 'other' where a knowing gaze asserts Western superiority, legitimizes civilizing missions and overlooks differences amongst women (Khan, 2005; Pedwell, this volume). The evocation of difference – in relation to the 'oppression of Muslim women' – is also apparent in *We Alpha-Girls*. Haaf, Klingner and Streidl (2008, p. 202) draw attention to 'backward' and 'cruel' traditions in 'several Islamic cultures' and refer to genital cutting in particular. More generally, the alpha-girls make a weak attempt at discussing diversity in their book. Differences amongst women are referred to at the book's beginning and end. This indicates to me that the theme has been added on to an already-existing analysis whose prime focus is on younger, able-bodied, white, straight and well-educated women. Having discussed the lives of German women for almost 230 pages, the alpha-girls (2008, p. 237) take a look around the world. In the space of four pages, they talk about global issues and refer to Mexico, Guatemala, Pakistan, Iran, India, the Sahel zone and the Congo. Their knowing gaze on other parts of the world does not include the perspectives of women other than the authors. While the book *We Alpha-Girls* demonstrates that feminism can improve the lives of a privileged few, its claims for inclusiveness paradoxically reproduce exclusions. The possibility of competing perspectives or experiences is evoked, but the authors fail to analyse how this might affect their analysis. As Hark (2008b) points out, the focus on a certain group of women that is similar to oneself constitutes a solipsist feminism that can only inadequately deal with a range of challenges. The new feminisms' focus on the privileged few reactivates and potentially reinforces existing hierarchies and inequalities, rendering it more difficult to regard critical engagements with various forms of (global) inequalities as feminist concerns (Hark and Kerner, 2007).

An equally uncritical engagement with difference, namely racial difference, occurs in Roche's (2009) *Wetlands*. The narrator Helen visits brothels to look at other women's genitals – in her words: '[s]tudying pussy' (2009, p. 116). She only goes to 'black hookers', after 'having learned that black women have the reddest pussies' (2009, p. 125). I am citing the following passage at length to convey Helen's exoticizing description:

> That's something. Because they have dark skin, the interior colours of the pussy really pop when it's spread open. Much more than with white women, where the contrast isn't as extreme. Something to do with complementary colours, I think. Pussy-pink next to light-pink skin tone looks a lot more boring than pussy-pink next to dark-brown skin tone. (2009, pp. 124–5)

To my surprise, none of the media articles that I read on *Wetlands* picked up on Roche's exoticizing portrayal of black women's vaginas. The detailed description of black women's sexual organs, and how they differ from those of white women, resonates with colonial fascinations with black female sexuality (Gilman, 2005 [1992], p. 180). Helen's engagement with black women's genitalia is exoticizing, treating them as special, and worthy of investigation. Roche's feminism of the body others blackness. This is enhanced by Helen's (2009, p. 126) claim that 'there are no black women in my world' which overlooks diversity in Germany and resonates with exclusionary discourses of ethnic and national homogeneity (Solanke, 2000).

Roche's, or for that matter Helen's, account of seeing prostitutes is not only disturbing because of its exoticizing fascination with black female sexuality, but is also of interest because of the way in which homosexuality is to some extent evoked in the book, but always repeatedly foreclosed. Helen has sex with the female sex workers she visits. In talking about her only experience with a white woman, Helen provides one of numerous pornographic descriptions: 'I lick her and grind my pussy on her bent knee. I come fast.

I'm the queen of coming.' However, Helen repudiates the possibility of lesbianism by arguing she goes to brothels only to 'study pussy'. This repudiation does not seem to be a (potentially critical) rejection of a label or an identity. Nowhere in the book does she express a sexual *desire* for women, other than her 'scientific' interest in their genitals and bodies. Throughout the book, Helen mainly talks about her sexual adventures with men. Indeed, the novel has a conventionally romantic twist as it also tells the story of Helen falling in love with one of the male nurses in the hospital.

Helen's experience of orgasms with women does not mean she identifies as lesbian or bisexual. What I find noteworthy is that Helen's story is so safely embedded in a heteronormative account, resonating with the heteronormativity of the new German feminisms more generally. While Eismann's and Stöcker's edited collections contain queer perspectives, the majority of the new feminist texts are written for and by heterosexual women. As I will explore below, the new feminisms are characterized by a repudiation of lesbianism through the rejection of 1970s feminism, which they associate with man-hating and homosexuality. The alpha-girls (2008, p. 23) state that 'the new feminism has a more relaxed attitude towards sex [in comparison to the old feminism]. Feminists are for a lot of sex and good sex.' However, the alpha-girls talk about penile-vaginal sex, focusing on heterosexual encounters only. Their attitude towards sex is 'relaxed' on the condition that lesbianism and bisexuality are excluded: they are for 'a lot of sex' and 'good sex' between men and women. Non-heterosexual encounters are foreclosed and heterosexual sex is understood in narrow terms as primarily referring to penile-vaginal intercourse.

On the whole, most strands of the new feminisms do not reflect, address or attempt to represent the experiences of a range of women. With the exception of the two edited collections, the new feminisms normalize the views of a small group of privileged women by proclaiming feminism for the many, which turns out to be feminism for the few. Finally, it is curious that none of the authors explicitly asks whether the history of a divided Germany continues to differently affect women's lives. As Miethe (2002, p. 52) emphasizes, 'the German unification threw together two systems that could hardly have been more different from another'. In relation to feminist and/or women's issues in particular, there were numerous differences between the capitalist Federal Republic of Germany and the socialist German Democratic Republic, ranging from abortion rights and employment to the public/private distinction (for a detailed exploration see Miethe, 2008).The new German girls indicate that they were raised in Eastern and Western Germany, but the potential implications of this fact remain undeveloped. This is not to argue that the East/West divide necessarily mediates women's stances on feminist issues. However, this omission points to the neglect of differences amongst women that characterizes the mainstream variants of the new German feminisms.

Challenging individualization through individualism

The new German feminisms are also marked by a pronounced individualism. Dorn's *The F-class* and Koch-Mehrin's *Sisters* represent the most individualist strands of the new feminisms. Dorn (2006, p. 37) openly lays out her individualist perspective by arguing: 'Why not admit that this book is not about solidarity amongst women at any cost, but about a certain class of women, who are not defined by their privileged background, but solely by their individual achievements and experiences?' Dorn seeks to pre-empt the criticism of elitism by refuting that the F-class comes from a privileged background. Nevertheless, her account elides structural constraints and reflects individualizing tendencies that Bauman (2000) and McRobbie (2009) regard as crucial markers of the contemporary era. Arguing that modernity and individualization are the same social condition, Bauman (2000, p. 652) states that 'everything is now down to the individual'; the conditions in which individuals live, their experiences and narratives undergo a relentless process of individualization so that individuals' achievements are disembedded from the wider context in which they occur.

The new feminisms contain different strands, however, and Eismann's edited collection investigates personal experiences in order to relate them to broader structural constraints, and to offer a critical perspective. Moving away from Eismann's book to the more mainstream versions of the new feminisms, the alpha-girls and new German girls also engage with structural constraints, albeit in unsatisfactory ways. They are aware of persisting inequalities and acknowledge them explicitly in their texts. Indeed, they critically engage with individualist perspectives. Hensel and Raether (2008a, p. 72) argue that we now sense that success is determined by more than hard work and that those who have failed might not be solely responsible for that. 'Perhaps this is why we can again speak about the social constraints that women encounter: because we can again speak about social constraints existing at all, not being less powerful only because some are capable of superseding them' (2008a, pp. 72–3). Equally, the alpha-girls critically refer to the current 'individualist-neoliberal climate' (2008a, p. 19) and the fact that the young generation regards inequalities as individual problems (2008a, p. 196).

It could be argued then that alpha-feminism addresses structural constraints, but I want to suggest that the manifested awareness of broader inequalities is frequently undone and rendered irrelevant, most often through a renewed uptake of individualist rhetoric. The alpha-girls, for example, critically discuss ever increasing beauty standards. Nevertheless, they undo their critical analysis by making the individualist claim that every woman should be allowed to look the way she pleases (2008a, p. 22). Arguably, their negotiation of individualization follows a postfeminist logic, in that they take into account critiques of individualizing processes, but similarly undo such challenges through the renewed uptake of individualist rhetoric. On a more general level, the two books do not offer much in terms of a new feminist politics. While they distance themselves from 'the old feminism' by arguing that it is time to modulate feminism to meet the requirements of contemporary young women, they do not provide a political agenda. On the contrary, it seems that they are reluctant to do so. In an interview, Hensel (2008b) states that she and her co-author do not want to instigate a political movement. Hensel (2008c) does not even like the term 'feminism'. 'It sounds like movement, struggle, bad conscience and a patronizing know-it-all attitude. I avoid it whenever I can.' The alpha- and new German girls critically engage with processes of individualization to a certain extent, but an investment in individualist perspectives transpires throughout the texts. While the new German feminists do not reject feminism, their engagement with it remains ambivalent and fraught. This becomes particularly apparent in their negotiation of 1970s feminism.

Repudiating 1970s feminism

Numerous new feminist texts distance themselves from the old German women's movement. In particular, they seek to counter common stereotypes of feminists as unfeminine, man-hating and lesbian (Scharff, 2012). The mainstream variants of the new feminisms exhibit a strong investment in distancing themselves from commonly made assumptions about feminists by repeatedly emphasizing that they are not anti-man. The alpha-girls (2008, p. 25) stress that men should not be turned into enemies. When being interviewed and asked what exactly is new about their feminism – given that their book addresses issues traditionally perceived as feminist – they first and foremost emphasize that their feminism includes men (2008b, p. 50). This emphasis on not being anti-man should be placed in the context of heterosexual conventions where heterosexual desire is privileged (Berlant and Warner, 2000, p. 328). Drawing on the insights of Butler's (1993) work, and queer theory more broadly (Sedgwick, 1990), I regard the alpha-girls' assertion that they are pro-men as arising from the heteronormative requirement that women like (and desire) men. By stressing their positive attitude towards men, the new feminists seek to pre-empt common accusations that feminists are anti-men.

Like the feminism of the alpha-girls, the alleged novelty of Koch-Mehrin's (2007, p. 16) approach consists in being pro-man: 'No feminism of women against men – that was yesterday – but a feminism with men, which immensely enriches the lives of all of us, women, men and children.' Koch-Mehrin's portrayal of the old feminism fails to account for the involvement of men in feminist activism. Indeed, if the novelty of the new feminism is based around the inclusion of men, the old feminism has to be portrayed as excluding men for the new feminism to be new. Equally, Dorn (2006, p. 36) argues that one difference between her F-class and 1970s feminism consists in not seeing the root of all evil in compulsory heterosexuality. The new feminists dis-identify with the allegedly man-hating and homosexual old feminism. They frequently evoke stereotypical views of feminists in order to distance themselves from them. In doing so, they collude with, if not reproduce, ideological accounts of feminism (Gill, 1997). Instead of challenging hostility towards feminism and highlighting the homophobic and sexist undertones of such portrayals, the disavowal of the old women's movement reifies feminism and overlooks its diversity.

The reification and homogenization of feminism is an attribute of all mainstream strands of the new feminisms. With few exceptions, the new feminists offer simplistic, generalizing, and historically inaccurate portrayals of 1970s feminism that is, of course, always referred to in the singular. What struck me in particular is the absence of a thorough engagement not only with the history of the women's movement in Germany, but also with academic feminism (also see Klaus, 2008). The F-class feminists write books about feminism that, in some cases, draw on a range of 'scientific' studies. But none of these texts makes a serious attempt at engaging with academic feminist approaches. This lack of engagement speaks volumes about the 'epistemic status' (Pereira, 2008) of gender and women's studies (in Germany). Decades of feminist academic research are overlooked and simultaneously caricatured. Arguably, feminist research has to be ignored for the negative portrayal of the old feminism to remain intact.

The rejection of the old, second-wave, 1970s feminism is not unique to the new German feminisms, but also features in the Anglo-American third wave (Budgeon, this volume; Gillis et al., 2007; McRobbie, 2009, pp. 156–9). Since the mid-1990s, there have been numerous academic texts claiming the existence of a 'third wave'. Similar to their German counterparts, '[t]hird wave feminists have been extremely eager to define their feminism as something "different" from previous feminisms' (Gillis et al., p. xxii). Waters (2007, p. 258) claims that the third wave's foregrounding of pleasure involves the 'attempt to make feminism more agreeable to a generation of young women who have been fed the myth that feminists are the fat, man-hating, no-fun lesbians'. I argue that such a strategy is politically ineffective because it does not address the homophobia, sexism and exclusionary norms underlying the stereotypical portrayal of feminism. Indeed, the repudiation of feminists' alleged man-hatred, lesbianism and unfemininity parallels, rather than challenges, broader dynamics at play in repudiations of feminism. The mainstream of the new feminisms, with their disregard for feminist and queer theory approaches, is ill-equipped to transform the heteronormative attitudes which, amongst other dynamics, facilitate the rejection of feminism. Their emancipatory potential is limited through the absence of intersectional analyses and lack of understanding of the social forces that give rise to continuous calls for feminist/queer politics in the first place.

Conclusions

The emergence of the new German feminisms complicates the common finding that postfeminist femininities repudiate feminism. At first glance, the endorsements of a revised feminist politics break with a postfeminist logic that entails the fierce repudiation of feminism in that they actively call for a new feminism. My analysis, however, revealed that the mainstream strands of the new feminisms do not critically engage with exclusionary and oppressive socio-cultural convergences. The new feminisms are mainly written by and for a homogeneous and privileged group of women, seek to challenge individualization through individualism and reiterate heteronormative conventions through their representation of 1970s feminism as man-hating. The mainstream versions of the new feminisms fail to critically interrogate the political implications of the claims they are making, thereby limiting their emancipatory potential. The coexistence of recent feminist texts that adopt an intersectional and critical perspective demonstrates that it is possible to engage in forms of critique that interrogate, rather than reproduce, exclusionary constellations and processes.

Notes

1. Independent women's groups organized under the roof of the Protestant church to obtain publicity, focusing on similar issues that the West German movement discussed. However, the themes of non-ideologized childrearing, as well as combining a family with a career, were more important in the East German women's movement (Miethe, 2002, p. 45). It is difficult to estimate the scale of this movement, but researchers believe there were up to 100 women's groups (ibid.).
2. All translations are mine. The texts under discussion are written in German, except for Roche's *Feuchtgebiete* which has been translated into English. The absence of page numbers in in-text citations indicates that the quote was published in the print media, and/or accessed online.
3. Alice Schwarzer is a well-known German feminist activist and controversial public figure. She is founder of *Emma*, a German feminist magazine which began publication in 1977. Her political views are problematic for various reasons. For example, she draws parallels between Islamicists and Nazis.
4. I will use the expressions 'alpha-girls' and 'new German girls' when referring to the authors of the so-called books. I therefore only use 'girl' when writing about young women who call themselves girls. When discussing the 'alpha-girls' and 'new German girls', I do not seek to convey a lack of status that is potentially signified by the term 'girl' (Aapola et al., 2005, p. 6). For stylistic reasons, I sometimes write about the 'F-class' when talking about the new feminists, paralleling how Hark refers to the authors.

Bibliography

Aapola, S., M. Gonick and A. Harris (2005) *Young Femininity: Girlhood, Power and Social Change* (Basingstoke and New York: Palgrave Macmillan).

Aitkenhead, D. (2009) 'It Should Make You Blush', *The Guardian*. Available at http://www.guardian.co.uk/books/2009/jan/17/interview-charlotte-roche-debut-novel-wetlands [accessed 8 October 2009].

Bauman, Z. (2000) *Liquid Modernity* (Cambridge: Polity Press).

Berlant, L. and M. Warner (2000) 'Sex in Public' in L. Berlant (ed.), *Intimacy* (Chicago: University of Chicago Press).

Butler, J. (1993) *Bodies that matter: On The Discursive Limits of "Sex"* (London and New York: Routledge).

Caesar, E. (2009) 'Charlotte Roche Is an Unlikely Shock Artist', *Timesonline*. Available at http://entertainment.timesonline.co.uk/tol/arts_and_entertainment/books/article5612411.ece?print=yes [accessed 8 October 2009].

Casale, R., U. Gerhard and U. Wischermann (2008) 'Einleitung', *Feministische Studien*. Available at http://www.feministische-studien.de/index.php?id=25&no_cache=1&paper=39&intro=1 [accessed 8 October 2009].

Dölling, I. (2007) ' "Eva-Prinzip"? "Neuer Feminismus"? Aktuelle Verschiebungen in Geschlechterbildern im Kontext gesellschaftlicher Umbruchsprozesse'. Beitrag zum Thema 'Geschlecht Macht Arbeit des Graduiertenkollegs, Geschlechterverhältnisse im Spannungsfeld von Arbeit, Politik und Kultur', Universität Marburg, 10–12 October, Unpublished conference paper.

Dorn, T. (2006) *Die neue F-Klasse: Wie die Zukunft von Frauen gemacht wird* (Munich, Zurich: Piper).

Eismann, S. (ed.) (2007) *Hot Topic: Popfeminismus heute* (Mainz: Ventil Verlag).

Gerhard, U. (1999) *Atempause: Feminismus als demokratisches Projekt* (Frankfurt am Main: Fischer).

Gill, R. (1997) 'Colluding in the Backlash? Feminism and the Construction of Orthodoxy', *Soundings* 5: 21–8.

Gill, R. (2007) *Gender and the Media* (Cambridge: Polity Press).

Gillis, S., G. Howie and R. Munford (2007) *Third Wave Feminism: A Critical Exploration* (Basingstoke: Palgrave Macmillan).

Gilman, S. L. (2005 [1992]) 'Black Bodies, White Bodies: Toward an Iconography of Female Sexuality in Late Nineteenth-Century Art, Medicine and Literature' in J. Donald and A. Rattansi (eds), *'Race', Culture and Difference* (London: Sage).

Gutiérrez Rodríguez, E. (1999) *Intellektuelle Migrantinnen – Subjektivitäten im Zeitalter von Globalisierung* (Opladen: Leske & Budrich).

Haaf, M. and S. Klingner (2008b) 'Politik oder Werbung', *EMMA* 3(284): 50–1.

Haaf, M., S. Klingner and B. Streidl (2008) *Wir Alphamädchen: Warum Feminismus das Leben schöner macht* (Hamburg: Hoffmann & Campe).

Hark, S. (2008a) 'Die Zeit und Zukunft von Feminismus. Zwischen Verona-Maxime und Gender-Kompetenz', *Kofra 127. Zeitschrift für Feminismus und Arbeit* 26 (July and August): 3–10.

Hark, S. (2008b) 'Solipsismusfeminismus', *Freitag 20*. Available at http://www.freitag.de/pdf-archiv/Freitag-2008–20.pdf [accessed 8 October 2009].

Hark, S. and I. Kerner (2007) 'Eine andere "Frau" ist möglich', *Freitag 30*. Available at http://www.freitag.de/2007/30/07301701.php [accessed 8 October 2009].

Hensel, J. (2009) ' "Wer sind unsere Feinde?" Bundeskanzlerin Angela Merkel und Jana Hensel diskutieren über "Wellness-Feminismus", verunsicherte Männer und den Vorzug, eine Frau zu sein', *Die Zeit* 5: 8–9.

Hensel, J. and E. Raether (2008a) *Neue Deutsche Mädchen* (Reinbek bei Hamburg: Rowohlt).

Hensel, J. and E. Raether (2008b) 'Neue Mädchen. Feminismus 2008: Jana Hensel und Elisabeth Raether zum überfälligen Generationswechsel', *Frankfurter Rundschau*. Available at http://www.fr-online.de/in_und_ausland/panorama/?em_cnt=1344170& [accessed 8 October 2009].

Hensel, J. and E. Raether (2008c) 'Interview for satt.org'. Available at http://www.satt.org/gesellschaft/08_03_ndm.html [accessed 8 October 2009].

Kean, D. (2009) 'Art or Porn? Publishers Love it When Women Talk Dirty, as the Success of Charlotte Roche's Sexually Explicit Novel "Wetlands" Once More Shows. Danuta Kean Lifts the Covers on a Dubious Genre', *The Independent*. Available at http://www.independent.co.uk/arts-entertainment/books/features/are-these-taboobreaking-novels-art-or-porn-1501292.html [accessed 8 October 2009].

Khan, S. (2005) 'Reconfiguring the Native Informant: Positionality in the Global Age', *Signs: Journal of Women in Culture and Society* 30(4): 2017–35.

Klaus, E. (2008) 'Antifeminismus und Elitefeminismus – Eine Intervention', *Feministische Studien* 26(2): 176–86.

Koch-Mehrin, S. (2007) *Schwestern: Streitschrift für einen neuen Feminismus* (Berlin: Econ).

Koffman, O. and R. Gill (2013) ' "i matter. And so does she": Girl Power, (Post)feminism and the Girl Effect' in D. Buckingham, S. Braggs and M.-J. Kehily (eds) *Youth Cultures in the Age of Global Media* (London: Palgrave).

Lenz, I. (2001) 'Bewegungen und Veränderungen. Frauenforschung und Neue Frauenbewegung in Deutschland' in U. Hornung, S. Gümen and S. Weilandt (eds), *Zwischen Emanzipationsvision und Gesellschaftskritik: Rekonstruktion der Geschlechterordnung* (Münster, Westfählisches Dampfboot).

McRobbie, A. (2003) 'Mothers and Fathers, Who Needs Them? A Review Essay of Butler's Antigone', *Feminist Review* 75: 129–36.

McRobbie, A. (2004) 'Post-feminism and Popular Culture', *Feminist Media Studies* 4(3): 255–64.

McRobbie, A. (2009) *The Aftermath of Feminism: Gender, Culture and Social Change* (London: Sage).

Miethe, I. (2002) 'Women's Movements in Unified Germany: Experiences and Expectations of East German Women' in S. Roth and S. Lennox (eds), *Feminist Movements in a Globalising World: German and American Perspectives* (Washington, DC: American Institute for Contemporary German Studies, 1–3. Harry & Helen Gray Humanities Program Series 11).

Miethe, I. (2008) 'From "Strange Sisters" to "Europe's daughters"? European Enlargement as a Chance for Women's Movements in East and West Germany' in S. Roth (ed.), *Gender Politics in the Expanding European Union: Mobilisation, Inclusion, Exclusion* (Oxford and New York: Berghahn Books).

Mueller, S. and A. Ritter (2008) 'Interview Roche/von Schirach: Wir muessen den Sex zurueckerobern!' *Stern*. Available at http://www.stern.de/lifestyle/leute/:Interview-Roche-von-Schirach-Wir-Sex-/614438.html [accessed 8 October 2009].

Pereira, M. d. M. (2008) 'The Epistemic Status of Women's, Gender, Feminist Studies: Notes for Analysis' in B. Waaldijk, M. Peters and E. van der Tuin (eds), *The Making of European Women's Studies* (Utrecht: Drukkeriy Zuidam and Uithof).

Ritter, A. (2008) 'Die Zotenkönigin von Muschiland', *Stern* 19: 163–75.

Roche, C. (2009) *Wetlands* (London: Fourth Estate).

Scharff, C.M. (2012) *Repudiating Feminism: Young Women in a Neoliberal World* (Farnham: Ashgate).

Schwarzer, A. (2007) *Die Antwort* (Cologne: Kiepenheuer & Witsch).

Sedgwick, E. K. (1990) *Epistemology of the Closet* (London: Harvester Wheatsheaf).

Solanke, I. (2000) 'Where Are the Black Lawyers in Germany?' in M. M. Eggers, G. Kilomba, P. Piesche and S. Arndt (eds), *Kritische Weissseinsforschung in Deutschland: Mythen, Masken und Subjekte* (Münster: Unrast Verlag).

Stöcker, M. (ed.) (2007) *Das F-Wort: Feminismus ist sexy* (Königstein: Ulrike Helmer Verlag).

Thorn, C. (2007) ' "Gender Mainstreaming" im Gegenwind: Die Kontroverse in den Medien und Möglichkeiten feministischer Gegenrede(n)'. Available at http://www.gender.hu-berlin.de/w/files/sozak/thorngenderdiskursemai07.pdf [accessed 8 October 2009].

Waters, M. (2007) 'Sexing it Up? Women, Pornography and Third Wave Feminism' in S. Gillis, G. Howie and R. Munford (eds), *Third Wave Feminism: A Critical Exploration* (Basingstoke: Palgrave Macmillan).

Zastrow, V. (2006) ' "Gender Mainstreaming": Politische Geschlechtsumwandlung', *Frankfurter Allgemeine Zeitung*. Available at http://www.faz.net/s/RubFC06D389E E76479E9E76425072B196C3/Doc~E19A6FC7720554E81829007B25E33D7E4~ATpl ~Ecommon~Scontent.html [accessed 26 April 2009].

18
The Contradictions of Successful Femininity: Third-Wave Feminism, Postfeminism and 'New' Femininities

Shelley Budgeon

In contrast to claims that feminism no longer retains currency in late modernity third-wave feminism asserts that feminism continues to be both possible and necessary.[1] This position proceeds on the basis that the applicability of second-wave feminism to contemporary gender relations and social conditions is limited because the lived experience of femininity has become increasingly complex. Accordingly, third-wave feminism claims to offer a corrective to this situation by allowing women to develop their relationship to feminism in ways that are more relevant to the contradictions which characterize their lives. In reconstituting the subject of feminism for a 'new generation', in often ambiguous ways, an interesting challenge to established definitions of feminist values and practices is waged. However, this challenge is not without problems or conceptual inconsistencies. This chapter will consider what third-wave feminism offers to our understanding of new femininities emerging in late modernity and the relationship these emerging subjectivities have to both feminism and postfeminism.

Context

Third-wave feminism is a contested term and as such does not easily lend itself to a straightforward definition. However, in order to explore its relevance to new femininities it is useful to examine some key characteristics of the socio-cultural context which provide the backdrop for its emergence. Third-wave feminism has sought to respond to a wide range of economic, political and cultural features of contemporary Western society which have affected the ways in which gendered subjectivities are articulated and enacted. Broadly speaking key factors include the rise of global capitalism, the expansion of information technologies, crises of environmental degradation, 'multiple modes of sexuality, changing demographics, and declining economic vitality' (Dicker and Piepmeier, 2003, p. 14).

Heywood and Drake[2] (2004) explain how a number of demographic and economic determinants shape third-wave feminism. New levels of gender parity in educational attainment and occupational success mean that women are as likely, or perhaps even more likely, to identify with their *generation* than their *gender*. Under these circumstances a feminism which relies upon intergenerational identification is less effective than one which speaks to newly forming feminine subjectivities. Secondly, third-wave feminism is heavily influenced by the proliferation of visual culture and the circulation of media representations of femininity. For third-wave feminism it is possible to approach popular culture simultaneously as a site of pleasure and an object of critique. By refusing to deploy straightforward codes to designate contemporary gender ideals in terms of simple binaries such as 'good' or 'bad', third-wave feminism insists on the necessity of straddling binaries and working with the contradictions that result. Negatively coded terms such as 'bitch', 'slut' or 'girl' are often reappropriated in an ironic stance in order to express new amalgamations of contradictory feminine subjectivities. These are subjectivities expressed through acts of cultural production and consumption that seek to run counter to and subvert dominant representations of femininity yet often draw upon the products of popular culture as resources (Garrison, 2000; Klein, 1997; Reed, 1997).

Thirdly, the tenets of third-wave feminism are consistent with the view that late modern lifestyles are characterized by increased levels of insecurity and that this state of uncertainty prevents individuals from investing their identities in any one specific site, particularly a job or a profession (Heywood and Drake, 2004, p. 16). The destandardization of life courses in late modernity underscores the multifaceted nature of late modern identities which by necessity have become more flexible, mobile and complex (Beck and Beck-Gernsheim, 2001).

Fourthly, third-wave feminism attempts to articulate a response to qualitative shifts taking place in the restructuring of contemporary power relations. Globalization and the resulting world economic order it fosters has in many complex ways altered the concentration of wealth and power. For third-wave feminists the site for political struggle has been affected in this shift as the 'enemy' has been increasingly decentralized and patriarchy itself dismantled as a primary object of critique (Heywood and Drake, 2004, p. 16). As such third-wave feminism does not privilege gender or sexual difference as its key site of struggle nor does it limit itself to any single issue.

This range of socio-cultural transformations, alongside advances made by women, has produced a context within which the meanings that attach to femininity are increasingly being questioned. Since feminism itself is characterized by diversity, fragmentation and a series of contestations its meaning is also often questioned. One response to the uncertainty resulting from these developments is to declare that feminism and the study of gender is characterized by a crisis in which there is little agreement about *why* the study of gender is still relevant and *how* to best proceed with the project of feminism. Indeed, popular perceptions of gender relations often suggest that feminism can now safely be relegated to the past. This discourse, widely circulating in popular cultural forms, is characterized by a dismissal of feminism as something from the past (Tasker and Negra, 2007). Far from being a simple backlash against feminism this discourse depends upon the selective incorporation of feminism for its efficacy. Only by recognizing the legitimacy of feminist successes can feminism then be declared redundant; the suggestion is that gender equality is important and thankfully has now been achieved (McRobbie, 2004a). Postfeminism, as such, relies upon a fundamental contradiction – feminism is both incorporated but simultaneously reviled.[3] By asserting that equality has been achieved postfeminist discourse focuses on female achievement, encouraging women to embark on projects of individualized self-definition and privatized self-expression exemplified in the celebration of lifestyle and consumption choices.

In opposition to this postfeminist position third-wave feminists assert that feminism continues to be an active and important force in contemporary society but often materializes in identities and practices that are not immediately associated with previously established forms of feminism. Third-wave feminists accept that feminism has been fundamentally challenged by both the loss of a unified subject 'woman' and a perceived lack of relevance to women's lives but attempt to develop ways of rethinking gender from a perspective that may still be named as feminist. Indeed third-wave writers view the uncertainty that contemporary social change has brought to an analysis of gender relations as an opportunity for a revitalized feminist project. This aim requires third-wave feminism to work productively with significant levels of ambiguity existing as it does within a 'precarious space' located in between the tension of second-wave feminism and postfeminist discourse (Kinser, 2004).

Third-wave feminism: central aims

Third-wave feminism begins from the position that any understanding of the relationship between feminism and women's lives must work consciously with women's wide-ranging differences (Heywood and Drake, 1997, p. 9). It has been argued that because third-wave feminists have come of age in a society that is transgender, bisexual and interracial they 'have trouble formulating and perpetuating theories that compartmentalize and divide according to race and gender and all other signifiers'. This is a world constituted through hybridity in which 'lines between Us and Them are often blurred' making identities 'that accommodate ambiguity and our multiple positionalities' a necessity (Walker, 1995, p. xxxiii). As Reed (1997, p. 124) argues, 'one of the strengths of third wave feminism is its refusal of the singular liberal-humanist subjectivity'. Heywood and Drake (1997, p. 3) echo this refusal when they explain that the impossibility of escaping contradictions 'marks the desires and strategies of third wave feminism'.

Given the emphasis on multiple and unpredictable positioning of gendered subjects third-wave feminism embraces the principle of inclusivity in its attempts to develop an understanding of how a feminist practice or identity might be defined. Third-wave feminism seeks to work with a proliferation of feminine subjectivities and multiplying forms of feminist affiliation including 'power feminism', 'victim feminism', black feminism, women-of-colour feminism, working-class feminism and pro-sex feminism (Heywood and Drake, 1997, p. 3).

> Since no monolithic version of 'woman' exists, we can no longer speak with confidence of 'women's issues'; instead we need to consider that such issues are as diverse as the many women who inhabit our planet. (Dicker and Piepmeier, 2003, p. 10)

Multiplicity is endorsed often at the expense of definitional consistency or reliability. However, the positive effect of opening out definitional boundaries is seen to be an increased awareness and recognition of the diffuse spaces within which feminist identities are now being practised. It is argued that there are numerous ways in which one may be a feminist and that there is no one 'right' way of being one. As Walker states (1995, p. xxvi) 'there are an infinite number of moments and experiences that make up female empowerment'.

The theme of 'empowerment' runs through third-wave discourse drawing both upon critiques of gender inequality *and* postfeminist discourses which emphasize the establishment of female success. Third-wave feminists have come of age with a 'sense of entitlement' – a context that often problematizes the assertion that gender inequality requires sustained political critique (Findlen, 1995, p. xii). Although the continued salience of gender inequality is acknowledged third-wave feminism tends to look with scepticism upon claims that women's oppression is systematic and that the occupation of a similar structural position creates an identity that women share. As such, a 'foundational project of naming shared themes' has become too complicated for third-wavers to pursue with any confidence (Siegel, 1997, p. 57).

By advocating an analytical move away from understanding gender in collective terms third-wave feminism often promotes a 'politics of difference' starting from the specificity of individual experience. Since there is no 'pure' definition of either the category woman or feminist[4] there is no 'real' feminist identity that transcends the culture within which it is produced. From this perspective identity projects have only the cultural resources within which they are embedded as tools for resistance. These projects of selfhood and the practices which constitute them are cast as a form of feminist activism.[5] Particular attention is given to those sites in which lived contradictions associated with new femininities reveal the instability of gender categories and create the possibility for reclaiming femininity through the reappropriation and resignification of dominant codings of femininity.[6]

> Our politics reflects a postmodern focus on contradiction and duality, on the reclamation of terms. S-M, pornography, the words cunt and queer and pussy and girl – are all things to be re-examined or reclaimed. In terms of gender, our rebellion is to make it camp. The underground music community has served as a particularly fertile breeding ground for redefining a feminism to fit our lives. (Klein, 1997, p. 208)

Licona (2005) borrows the concept of a 'third space' from US Third World feminism to describe third-wave political practices. Within these 'spaces subjects put perspectives, lived experiences, and rhetorical performances into play ... (b)orderlands' rhetorics move beyond binary borders to a named third space of ambiguity and even contradiction' (Licona, 2005, p. 105). The practices which constitute these spaces are both subversive and generative. They are *subversive* because by deploying disruptive discursive strategies third-wave subjects create self-representations which evade the effects of phallogocentric representational practices. These spaces are also *generative* because they allow for the production of new subjectivities and the legitimation of new forms of knowing (Licona, 2005, p. 106).

The aim is not to develop a feminism which makes representational claims on behalf of women but to advance a politics based upon *self-definition* and the need for women to define their personal relationship to feminism in ways that make sense to them as individuals. This is evident for instance in the D.I.Y. ethic of Riot Grrrl[7] which promotes self-empowerment and independence as the motivating force behind its pursuit of a politics that will allow women to develop an understanding of the personal realm focusing 'more on the individual and the emotional than on marches, legislation, and public policy' (Rosenberg and Garofalo, 1998, p. 810).

The 'postmodern individualism' characteristic of third-wave discourse is partly a legacy of second-wave feminism's contribution to making female ambition a realizable prospect (Heywood and Drake, 1997, p. 5). Female success is perhaps the area where the most challenging tensions emerge for third-wave feminism in developing its position in relation to second-wave feminism, postfeminism and the current gender order. This is a context where a discourse which focuses on the selective successes certain women enjoy is often universalized and used to justify the postfeminist argument that feminism, with its focus on inequality, discourages women from embracing female empowerment and as such encourages detrimental identifications. For example, Roiphe (1993, p. 6) argues that 'the image that emerges from feminist preoccupations with rape and sexual harassment is that of women as victims' and Wolf (1994, p. 147) similarly claims that the culturally dominant form of feminism has become 'victim feminism' which incites women to seek power through an 'identity of powerlessness'.

Successful femininity

Third-wave feminism represents one strategy for negotiating the contradictions that constitute a late modern female empowerment discourse. This discourse is underwritten by the assertion that women's access to an autonomous subject position increased significantly in the latter half of the twentieth century resulting in women's ability to define their own identities independent of their relations to others. This transformation is described by theorists of reflexive modernization as a shift from 'living for others' to 'living a life of one's own' (Beck and Beck-Gernsheim, 2001, p. 55). With this shift in orientation women have been able to enter as full participants into a late modern culture of the self that endorses self-invention, autonomy and personal responsibility alongside key competences of reflexivity, self-observation and personal biographical narration, all of which are traditionally associated with femininity (Nielsen, 2004, p. 11) and have increasingly come into demand in a context governed by a neoliberal ethos and market demands (Ringrose, 2007, p. 483).

As argued by Harris (2004a, p. 16) the idealized subject of late modernity is one who is 'flexible, individualised, resilient, self driven and self made and who easily follows nonlinear trajectories to fulfilment and success'. Increasingly these are the characteristics that are demanded of young women because they are perceived to be the 'most confident, resilient, and empowered of all the demographic groups affected by risk' (Harris, 2004a, p. 16). Young women are often held to be key beneficiaries of a range of socio-economic changes that now characterize Western societies and the neoliberal tropes of freedom and choice are increasingly associated with the category 'young women' (McRobbie, 2004b, p. 255). Far from being neatly compatible with feminist goals the discourse of female success requires interrogation. On one level this discourse is overtly, and often *overly*, celebratory of women's increased independence and levels of educational and workplace success. Yet on the other hand, this discourse is also shaped by a deep sense of unease and ambivalence regarding the role that gender now plays within a transforming social order characterized by rapid change and uncertainty. Anxieties surround what is often perceived as the feminization of the spheres of work, consumption and education where young women are seen to flourish while young men are left at a disadvantage (Gonick, 2006; Ringrose, 2007).

The production of these successful femininities depends very much upon placing an emphasis on gender equality, and hence its irrelevance, at the expense of understanding how gender continues to operate in complex ways in the structuring of new femininities (Baker, 2008; Gonick, 2004; Rich, 2005). Volman and Ten Dam (1998, p. 539) summarize the dilemma that gender equivalence presents for young men and women who are negotiating their gender identities within a context where gender difference continues to be relevant:

> The message seems to be: you must be a girl or a boy, but traditional gender identities are no longer desirable ... multiple forms of masculinity and femininity exist, but the legitimacy of difference between gender groups that implies inequality is under pressure, whereas equality in the sense of sameness is unthinkable.

Within this climate new femininities provide far from straightforward subject positions as they produce both possibilities and troubles for young women attempting to manage the difficulties of enacting ideals associated with both traditional femininity and masculinity (Ringrose, 2007). Because 'girls as a category are positioned as a new social and economic force in ways that have previously been the reserve of boys' (Gonick, 2006, p. 17) successful femininity now involves living a tension between exercising the traditional feminine mode of relationality and the exhibition of individualized agency previously associated with masculinity (Gonick, 2004, p. 191). This tension places demands on young women which are difficult to resolve within current social arrangements.

Negotiating contradictions

The contradictions that result from attempting to occupy the subject position of successful femininity are not lived unproblematically but are experienced in ambivalent ways for which resolution is often sought through highly individualized strategies that do not necessarily work to women's advantage nor do they result in the expansion of their capacity to exercise autonomy. For example, maintaining a coherent empowerment narrative consisting of autonomy, individuality and personal choice requires a denial of the effects that external influences have on the realization of individual success and as such the classed and raced constitution of the 'successful' feminine subject is obscured. This leads to a fundamental misrecognition of the causes of social disadvantage as explanations for inequality are seen to reside in the ability or motivation of individuals to make 'good' choices (Rich, 2005; Walkerdine et al., 2001). Although constructing an unfettered relationship to choice may enhance a sense of personal empowerment it also places incredible pressure on individuals to make the 'right' choices

(Baker, 2008). The struggle to incorporate the new cultural ideal of feminine success is particularly complex for young working-class women for whom the limits to doing so are attributed to individualized failure and borne at an inordinate psychic cost (Walkerdine et al., 2001).

An uncontextualized understanding of the ideal of 'choice' reinforces a regime of personal responsibility (McRobbie, 2004a) and a separation of self from gendered contexts (Rich, 2005). The effects of this separation are seen in the disavowal of feminism on the part of young women who associate feminism with narratives of female disadvantage. Within this context making a positive identification with feminism threatens to rupture a carefully constructed narrative of self-determination (Rich, 2005). It would seem as though there is a difficulty in recognizing that gender inequality does not cancel out but exists in tension with female success. Rather than being 'held' in such a tension young women often adopt a stance of gender neutrality which functions to dissolve this tension while preserving the consistency of a narrative of self-empowerment (Baker, 2008; Volman and Ten Dam, 1998).

Baker (2008, p. 56), for example, found that women in her study imagined gender relations were defined by a progressive linear trajectory towards equality and that men no longer enjoyed greater advantages compared to women. Being a man or a woman, therefore, was seen to be less meaningful than what one could claim to be as an *individual*. Similarly, Volman and Ten Dam (1998) found gender was often denied as a factor that could feasibly account for the different behaviours of girls and boys in educational contexts. The girls and boys in this study refused to apply gender as an explanatory frame because to talk about difference in gendered terms was conflated with endorsing gender inequality – a position that they were aware held no social legitimacy. The recognition that gender differences were evident required a strategy that could render these meaningful without suggesting that girls were inferior to boys and this was found by explaining difference as just being a matter of *individual* preference.

In these examples gender equivalence is invoked in ways that downplay the significance of gender difference and bolster a sense of individual self-efficacy. However, a set of ambivalences remain because many aspects of gender difference continue to be valued and as such are required of women who wish to be recognized as 'successful'. Traditional dictates of femininity including physical attractiveness, bodily ideals and heterosexuality are not easily rejected as matters of individual 'choice'. Young women must be ' "bright and beautiful", "heterofeminine/desirable and successful learner", "aggressor and nurturer" ' (Ringrose, 2007, p. 485) and autonomous but still connected in significant ways to their families and communities (Gonick, 2004). Many norms associated with traditional femininity operate to cordon off particular choices which threaten the coherence of its boundaries including choosing to be a lesbian, childless, single or a feminist (Baker, 2008; Rich, 2005). Indeed a fanaticized feminism operates at the edges of acceptability indicating where female empowerment has 'gone too far'.

Third-wave resolutions

The findings from these various studies indicate that young women's lives are indeed characterized by a series of ambivalences and that many lack resources which might allow them to find adequate resolution to dilemmas they face. Complex contradictions which constitute the discourse of female success are socially systemic in nature and as such cannot be resolved through biographical solutions (Gonick, 2004). There is an apparent need to develop ways of negotiating the discourse of female success and its incitement to construct oneself through the ideal of unencumbered 'choice'. These strategies would allow more creative responses rather than the foreclosures described above. The possibility of doing so is the very claim third-wave feminism places at the centre of its politics of ambiguity and its analysis of hybrid subjectivities. According to this analysis by straddling the intersections of what are often impossible sets of demands new femininities potentially destabilize prevailing gender norms. However, as the studies discussed above show, rather than produce such a destabilization contradictions are not left open as sites of production. Instead their resolution is sought in often highly unsatisfactory ways that limit positive identifications with feminism. The generative potential for third-wave spaces to produce new articulations of a *feminist* femininity, therefore, demands closer examination.

Two main challenges demand consideration. Firstly these spaces must provide opportunities to evade the co-optation and commodification of pro-girl discourses (Kinser, 2004; Riordan, 2001). Female empowerment has been transformed into an extremely attractive commodity that 'contributes to rearticulating dominant patriarchal and capitalist values, while not substantially disrupting power relations' (Riordan, 2001, p. 282). The consumption of female empowerment in its various forms merely offers 'a celebration of what girls already do rather than encourage girls to seek power through direct economic and political means' (Riordin, 2001, p. 291). Buying into feminine empowerment may enhance a sense of agency associated with individualized identities but leaves little room to develop an awareness of the full complexity of self-empowerment or to develop a sustained critical understanding of the social context where female empowerment and feminist values are appropriated in the name of reproducing the status quo at the expense of understanding the classed and 'raced' divisions which render empowerment discourses so problematic.

McRobbie (2004b, p. 260) effectively argues that to count as a 'modern sophisticated girl' who is free to choose, young women must withhold critique and maintain

> an uncritical relation to dominant commercially produced sexual representations which actively invoke hostility to assumed feminist positions from the past in order to endorse a new regime of sexual meanings based on female consent, equality, participation and pleasure, free of politics.

This suggests that third-wave feminism must go beyond advocating for women's right to choice and self-expression and interrogate the substance of those choices in a critical way but third-wave feminism is often uncertain about the role of prescription in feminist politics. This is manifest in the rhetorical strategies third-wave feminism deploys to differentiate itself from second-wave feminism with its now almost customary characterization as overly dogmatic and hence incompatible with new feminist subjectivities. As one of the early proponents of third-wave feminism explains, 'Young women coming of age today wrestle with the term [feminist] because we have a very different vantage point on the world than that of our foremothers...For many it seems that to be a feminist in the way that we have seen or understood feminism is to conform to an identity and way of living that doesn't allow for individuality, complexity, or less than perfect personal histories' (Walker, 1995, pp. xxxii–xxxiii). This position accounts for why the specificity of individual experience is placed at the centre of third-wave politics. Ideally spaces of self exploration provide women with the opportunity to lay claim to personalized feminist identities without facing judgement or condemnation but is laying claim to the legitimacy of one's experience always a feminist act? Third-wave spaces are located within a context where the undertaking of a project of self-definition is valued in and of itself and as such constitutes a contemporary normative expectation of 'modern', liberated femininity celebrated for its amenability with neoliberal governance.

Herein lies the second challenge. Contemporary femininities are celebrated by definition for the skills that constitute them: self-definition, self-responsibility and *independence* from a collective identification with gender or feminism. Postfeminist popular discourses continue to suggest that feminism places limits on women's ability to construct their own identities in ways they feel best suit their circumstances. Being able to do so, however, does not necessarily stand as a form of feminist politics. The ascendancy of postfeminism to one of the dominant logics of late modernity requires a more strategic position to be developed on the part of third-wave feminism so that the projects of self-definition which they valorize do not simply become conflated with taking up a position that celebrates individualized experiences of empowerment. In order to produce feminist articulations of femininity third-wave feminist political strategies must provide opportunities to transcend the ideological incitement to engage *uncritically* in a project of self-definition founded upon individualized female success and the values of choice, freedom and self-sufficiency. It is a difficult task to simultaneously give recognition to the multiple positionings, experiences and priorities which constitute women's lives *and* place limits on the ethic of inclusivity in order to demarcate where a feminist articulation of identity lies. The risk for third-wave feminism in not exploring how this might be negotiated is that a call to the practice of inclusivity easily mutates into an indiscriminate invitation to construct any claim to feminist membership as equally valid or radical.

> Resistance per se does not equal feminism; consumerism for women does not equal feminism. Some choices *are* more compromising to women's lives than others, and third-wave feminists have no business shutting down the discussion about which choices accomplish what all in the name of pluralistic thinking. Pluralism, multiplicity, polyphony, all of these suggests a willingness to hear; they do not imply *ipso facto* acceptance of what is heard. (Kinser, 2005, p. 145)

Current social conditions require a more sustained analysis of how definitional boundaries might be drawn around a *feminist* project of resistant self-transformation. The problem to consider further is whether or not 'anything that looks like one is casting off any cultural restriction whatsoever, and in particular if the one doing so is female, counts as feminism' (Kinser, 2005, p. 144). This conflation requires a critical engagement with the experience of resistance and the tendency to overestimate its efficacy. Postfeminism reduces politics to the right to self-expression, regardless of its form or substance but just because a particular act is experienced as resistant does not make it a feminist act per se. As argued by Riordin (2001, p. 283) there is a propensity within a politics of resistance to put an accent on *individualized* agency which is why resistance has also become the preferred idiom of postfeminism whose discourse of empowerment relies upon casting off prescriptive codes, particularly those associated with so-called victim feminism (Denfeld, 1995; Roiphe, 1993; Wolf, 1994). ' "We feminists" has come to mean, unilaterally and unequivocally, "we victims" ' (Siegel, 1997).

The discourse of female success introduces a new set of contradictions for femininity that profoundly complicates young women's struggle for self definition. Third-wave feminism has identified that femininity in late modernity is far from unproblematic and presents both opportunities and challenges. While focusing on the opportunities that contradictions might bring to the analysis of new femininities the third-wave project must also engage with the limits set by these contradictions and offer a more critical analysis of how and why they are sustained. Individual empowerment is an important element in transforming current social arrangements but while necessary it is not sufficient. As argued by Orr (1997, p. 33) a sense of entitlement is not enough to transform a culture where that entitlement is not yet fully recognized.

Notes

1. A number of key texts are now associated with the emergence of third-wave feminism. These include Baumgardner and Richards (2000); Dicker and Piepmeier (2003); Findlen (1995); Heywood and Drake (1997); Walker (1995); and a special issue of *Hypatia* (Zita, 1997). Critical approaches to third-wave feminism are addressed in Gillis et al. (2004). While third-wave seeks to develop a more global feminism its origins are firmly rooted in an Anglo-American feminist tradition.
2. According to Heywood and Drake (2004, p. 13) third-wave feminists are part of the generation born between 1963 and 1974. Other theorists avoid clear demarcations, preferring to engage with the problem that definitional debates present. Siegel (1997, p. 77) leaves the term relatively open using it to connote 'the diversity of feminisms articulated and practiced by contemporary young women'. See also the discussion in Gillis et al. (2004).
3. For further discussion of the relationship between feminism, postfeminism and third-wave feminism see the analysis by Braithwaite (2002).
4. See Reed (1997, p. 14) on the politics of purity.
5. Third-wave feminism is heavily influenced by poststructuralist theory but is firmly committed to promoting activism outside the academy.
6. See Gillis and Munford (2004) for an examination of 'girl culture' which includes Riot Grrls, Girlies and Girl Power. These cultures have in common 'a vigorous reclamation and recuperation of the word "girl" as no longer a simply derogatory and disrespectful term but one that captures the contradictions shaping female identity for young women whose world has been informed by the struggles and gains of second wave feminism' (Gillis and Munford, 2004, p. 169).
7. Riot Grrrl is an often cited exemplar of early third-wave activism. See Garrison (2000).

Bibliography

Baker, J. (2008) 'The Ideology of Choice: Overstating Progress and Hiding Injustice in the Lives of Young Women. Findings from a Study in North Queensland, Australia', *Women's Studies International Forum* 31: 53–64.

Baumgardner and Richards (2000) *Manifesta: Young Women, Feminism, and the Future* (New York: Farrar, Straus and Giroux).

Beck, U. and E. Beck-Gernsheim (2001) *Individualization: Institutionalised Individualism and Its Social and Political Consequences* (London: Sage).

Braithwaite, A. (2002) 'The Personal, the Political, Third Wave and Postfeminisms', *Feminist Theory* 3(3): 335–44.

Denfeld, R. (1995) *The New Victorians: A Young Woman's Challenge to the Old Feminist Order* (New York: Warner Books).

Dicker, R. and A. Piepmeier (2003) 'Introduction' in R. Dicker and A. Piepmeier (eds), *Catching a Wave: Reclaiming Feminism for the 21st Century* (Boston: Northeastern University Press).

Findlen, B. (1995) 'Introduction' in B. Findlen (ed.), *Listen Up: Voices from the Next Feminist Generation* (Seattle: Seal Press).

Garrison, E. K. (2000) 'US Feminism-Grrrl Style! Youth (Sub)Cultures and the Technologies of the Third Wave', *Feminist Studies* 26(1): 141–70.

Gillis and Munford (2004) 'Genealogies and Generations: The Politics and Praxis of Third Wave Feminism', *Women's History Review* 13(3): 165–82.

Gillis, Stacy, Gillian Howie and Rebecca Manford. (2004) *Third Wave Feminism: A Critical Exploration* (Basingstoke: Palgrave MacMillan).

Gonick, M. (2004) 'Old Plots and New Identities: Ambivalent Femininities in Late Modernity', *Discourse* 25(2): 189–209.

Gonick, M. (2006) 'Between "Girl Power" and "Reviving Ophelia": Constituting the Neoliberal Girl Subject', *NWSA Journal* 18(2): 1–22.

Harris, A. (2004a) *Future Girl: Young Women in the Twenty-First Century* (London: Routledge).

Harris, A. (2004b) 'Introduction' in A. Harris (ed.), *All About the Girl: Culture, Power, and Identity* (London: Routledge).

Heywood, L. and J. Drake (eds) (1997) *Third Wave Agenda: Being Feminist, Doing Feminism* (Minneapolis: University of Minnesota Press).

Heywood, L. and J. Drake (2004) 'It's All About the Benjamins: Economic Determinants of Third Wave Feminism in the US' in S. Gillis et al. (eds), *Third Wave Feminism* (Basingstoke: Palgrave Macmillan).

Kinser, A. E. (2004) 'Negotiating Spaces for/through Third-Wave Feminism', *NWSA Journal* 16(3): 124–53.

Kinser, A. E. (2005) 'Negotiating Spaces For/Through Third-Wave Feminism', *NWSA Journal* 16(3): 124–53.

Klein, M. (1997) 'Duality and Redefinition: Young Feminism and the Alternative Music Community' in L. Heywood and J. Drake (eds), *Third Wave Agenda: Being Feminist, Doing Feminism* (Minneapolis: University of Minnesota Press).

Licona, A. C. (2005) '(B)Orderlands' Rhetorics and Representations: The Transformative Potential of Feminist Third- Space Scholarship and Zines', *NWSA Journal* 17(2): 104–29.

McRobbie, A. (2004a) 'Notes on Postfeminism and Popular Culture: Bridget Jones and the New Gender Regime' in A. Harris (ed.), *All About the Girl: Culture, Power and Identity* (London: Routledge).

McRobbie, A. (2004b) 'Post-Feminism and Popular Culture', *Feminist Media Studies* 4(3): 255–64.

Nielsen, H. B. (2004) 'Noisy Girls: New Subjectivities and Old Gender Discourses', *Young* 12(9): 9–30.

Orr, C. M. (1997) 'Charting the Currents of the Third Wave', *Hypatia* 12(3): 29–45.

Reed, J. (1997) 'Roseanne: A "Killer Bitch" for Generation X' in L. Heywood and J. Drake (eds), *Third Wave Agenda: Being Feminist, Doing Feminism* (Minneapolis: University of Minnesota Press).

Rich, E. (2005) 'Young Women, Feminist Identities and Neoliberalism', *Women's Studies International Forum* 28: 495–508.

Ringrose, J. (2007) 'Successful Girls? Complicating Post-feminist, Neoliberal Discourses of Educational Achievement and Gender Equality', *Gender and Education* 19(4): 471–89.

Riordan, E. (2001) 'Commodified Agents and Empowered Girls: Consuming and Producing Feminism', *Journal of Communication Inquiry* 25(3): 279–97.

Roiphe, K. (1993) *The Morning After: Sex, Fear and Feminism* (London: Hamish Hamilton).

Rosenberg, J. and G. Garofalo (1998) 'Riot Grrrl: Revolutions from Within', *Signs: Journal of Women in Culture and Society* 23(3): 809–41.

Siegel, D. L. (1997) 'Reading between the Waves: Feminist Historiography in a "Postfeminist" Moment' in L. Heywood and J. Drake (eds), *Third Wave Agenda: Being Feminist, Doing Feminism* (Minneapolis: University of Minnesota Press).

Tasker, Y. and D. Negra (eds) (2007) *Interrogating Postfeminism* (London: Duke University Press).

Volman, M. and G. Ten Dam (1998) 'Equal but Different: Contradictions in the Development of Gender Identity in the 1990s', *British Journal of Sociology of Education* 19(4): 529–45.

Walker, R. (1995) 'Being Real: An Introduction' in R. Walker (ed.), *To Be Real: Telling the Truth and Changing the Face of Feminism* (New York: Anchor Books).

Walkerdine, V., H. Lucey and J. Melody (2001) *Growing up Girl: Psychosocial Explorations of Gender and Class* (Basingstoke: Palgrave Macmillan).

Wolf, N. (1994) *Fire with Fire* (London: Vintage).

Zita, Jaqueline (ed.) (1997) 'Third Wave Feminisms', special issue of *Hypatia* 12(3): 1–6.

19
Skater Girlhood: Resignifying Femininity, Resignifying Feminism

Dawn H. Currie, Deirdre M. Kelly and Shauna Pomerantz

While there is general consensus that 'gender' is a socially and theoretically significant identity category, there is less agreement on exactly how. Disagreement reflects the emergence of previously unthinkable possibilities and an accompanying sentiment – expressed in both popular and academic thought – that identities are now self-constructed. As traditional markers of 'femininity' and 'masculinity' are being challenged, what it means to be a 'gendered subject' is a matter of everyday as well as scholarly speculation. Informing the latter is the notion that the current neoliberal context favours what has been associated historically with femininity – the flexible, self-fashioning subject (Walkerdine, 2003).[1] Within this context, girlhood is being redefined; as girls are reported to outperform boys academically, and young women defer marriage and motherhood in order to pursue careers, characterizations by second-wave feminists of girlhood as preparation for subservient roles associated with conventional femininity have been replaced by what Harris (2004, p. 17) calls 'future girls':

> a unique category of girls who are self-assured, living lives lightly inflected but by no means driven by feminism, influenced by the philosophy of DIY (do it yourself), and assuming they can have (or at least buy) it all.

Harris and others link the emergence of this new category to a 'girl power' culture of the 1990s. Often missing from this characterization of girlhood are voices of girls themselves.

In this chapter we explore what it means to be a 'girl' today, drawing on research with girls between the ages of 12 and 16 living in and around Vancouver, Canada. Semi-structured interviews focused on how study participants negotiated social identities as 'girls' and, in the context of their identity practices, what 'girl power' – with its feminist connotations – meant to these young women. Practices that distanced girls from conventional femininity intrigued us. By 'conventional' we refer to an appearance-based femininity rooted in girls' preoccupation with gaining boys' approval and sexual interest.[2] Skateboarding engaged girls in practices that challenged this femininity, and we purposely set out to recruit girls whom we dubbed 'Skaters'. While our larger study includes 71 participants, here we draw on interviews with 20 girls who ranged from 13 to 16 years of age.[3] Eleven of these girls were white Euro-Canadian, four Chinese-Canadian, three multiracial and two Aboriginal. Based on their parents' occupations, educational backgrounds and their current living arrangements, we classified one participant as coming from an upper-middle-class family, fourteen from middle-class, and five from working-class family backgrounds.

To be clear, our goal was not to 'discover' new femininities. Rather, we are interested in sociocultural conditions facilitating 'alternative girlhoods': ways of being gendered that consciously reject the conventional mandate for girls to be 'skinny', 'pretty' and 'sexually pleasing to boys'. Born during the decade wherein 'girl power' rhetoric reached a frenzy in popular, commercial and academic culture, our study participants grew up amidst slogans that 'girls rule' and a growing sentiment that feminism, whether a political or an academic movement, is no longer relevant to young women.[4] Interviews with Skater girls, who for us embodied an alternative girlhood, enable us to explore questions addressed by this collection: To what extent are girls free to fashion new femininities, in ways claimed by much popular culture? Which girls can participate in rewriting girlhood? And what does their rewriting tell us about the future of feminism as a movement for social justice?

In our study Skater girls consciously positioned themselves against both conventional girlhood and the mainstream in youth culture. Our interest lies in girls' agency; Skater girls rejected conventional femininity as enacting a passive bid for boys' attention. At the same time, girls' involvement in skater culture put them into conflict with more than gendered norms. Skateboarding is organized around a distinct culture (see Beal, 1996; Borden, 2001). Most of the Skater girls in our study identified with alternative rock, punk or metal music that emphasizes the importance of being oneself amidst pressures to conform. Thirteen-year-old Jessica[5] (white, upper-middle-class) maintained that these themes are 'meaningful' and 'worth hearing'. They are 'about growing up or having trouble with friends, not liking school or dropping out'. We find it interesting that, at the time of our fieldwork, little academic interest had been shown in girls as skateboarders. This lack of academic interest stands in direct contrast to growing commercial interest, evident in magazines, web pages and fashion targeting girl skaters. We hope to inspire further research into girls' involvement in skateboarding, as well as other alternative cultures for girls.

Drawing on our participants' experiences of being skaters, we begin this chapter by describing 'skater girlhood'. At the same time, however, we trouble our own category by exploring the unstable and contingent nature of girls' identities that are always mediated by relations of racialization[6] and class as well as age and gender. While some Skater girls could move freely between and among competing ways of doing girlhood, other girls were much more 'bound' by their social positioning: in our (limited) study, the ability to move between social groups – hence identity categories – was more evident among girls who enjoyed material and cultural privileges. What can their practices tell us about the malleability of gender? About the ability for girls today to be 'whatever they want to be'? We conclude by considering how skateboarding – as an example of new, emergent femininities – is not only a resignification of femininity, but potentially also of feminism.

Emergent femininities: resignifying girlhood

We discerned three distinct ways that girls participated in what we call Skater girlhood. 'Hardcore' or 'serious skaters' frequented skate parks, had mastered a number of tricks, and knew how to assemble their own boards. Those we designated, more simply, as 'Skaters' enjoyed the lifestyle but skated less frequently than hardcore Skater girls. They had mastered only the basics, although some knew a few tricks. Finally, Skater girlhood includes 'skater affiliates'. These girls were identified or known as 'skaters' among their peers based on their friendship with other skaters, an affinity for skater culture, or both. These diverse positionings within skater culture reflect the way that identities are ongoing projects of becoming; girlhood is always in the process of formation, never fully formed. What the Skater girls in this chapter shared, and what initially brought them to our attention as performing an 'alternative' girlhood, was the way that they consciously distanced themselves from conventional femininity.

No matter what degree of involvement girls maintained in skateboarding, Skater girls in our study refused to waste their energy by worrying about clothes, looks and boyfriends. The tight low-cut tank tops and low-riding jeans from expensive, brand name stores that made many of their female classmates popular among boys were a particular point of derision. While some skater boys were attracted to girls' overt displays of heterosexuality, Skater girls generally tried to resist enacting this kind of feminine power, calling it 'fake'. Fifteen-year-old Gracie (white, middle-class) complained that popular girls often played at being seen as 'dumb', while 15-year-old Sandy (Chinese-Canadian, middle-class) described their performance as 'a façade'. As Zoe (15 years old, part First Nations, middle-class) explained:

> 'You know, the whole thing, like, where a lot of girls want to be sexy? That is totally the opposite of us. We don't. We don't and we kind of don't really like those kind of girls that do, because it's for popularity and stuff like that.'

By adopting skater style, these girls wanted to 'be their own person', 'to stand out' or be 'funky'. They shopped and dressed to make a statement about their individuality and difference from mainstream kids. As described by 14-year-old Sara (Jewish, middle-class), mainstream kids were into 'Roxy shoes, Mavi jeans. Like blond hair, baby blue visors, poofy white vests – stuff like that'. In a seeming protest against the corporate consumerism embodied by this style, a number of Skater girls made a point of saying that they shopped at second-hand clothing stores, while Tori (14-years old, white, working-class) designed her own clothes. Grenn and Lexi (both white from working-class families) insisted that they were following 'no fashion trend at all' and that, as a result, their preppy classmates designated them as 'weird'. Whatever image they intended to convey, skateboarding required these girls to wear comfortable clothing in order to move with ease on their boards. As Zoe complained, 'that really tight stuff can get annoying after a while. You can't do anything on a board in it.'

Given their conscious rejection of commodified expressions of selfhood, the increasing adoption of skater style among non-skating peers complicated the otherwise mundane act of adopting casual or alternative clothing. Sixteen-year-old Madeline (white, middle-class) pointed out that some girls at her school bought expensive skater paraphernalia that they did not use, or even need, for skateboarding. These kids were called 'posers'. A poser wears the right clothing, such as wide sneakers with fat laces, brand name pants and hoodies and, of course, carries a skateboard. But posers do not really skate. Although boys can be posers too, girls are more usually singled out for this derogatory title. It is assumed that poser girls hang around the skate park to meet skater boys. Posers were targets of derision among 'real' Skater girls who themselves were often accused, especially by boys, of being posers.

The tendency for 'rich' kids to encroach on skater culture because of their ability to sport skateboard props annoyed working-class Tori:

'It bugs me 'cause you see all these preppy little kids and they are going and buying skate shoes and skate clothing, which makes the price go up for people like us who depend on that.'

Tori went on to explain that she used to be able to replace her shoes for $30, but now the 'cheapest shoe' cost $120. As a consequence of this kind of problem, the commodification of skater culture could sharpen awareness of class relations. At first it seemed a bit odd to us that, despite her skating ability, when asked if she was 'into other sports', Grenn insisted, 'No, I *hate* sports! Skateboarding is not a sport!' Although there is no doubt that skateboarding requires physical strength, balance and agility, to call it a 'sport' seemed to associate it with the much-hated preppies, who traditionally have used sports as a route to social status within school-based culture (see Eder, 1995).

Like Tori, Grenn and Lexi's roots were solidly working class. Grenn lived in a town divided by social class: 'There's this side [where we are], and then there's this side over there. *Those* are the rich people.' Her school was ruled by 'snobby preps', who had 'blonde hair', wore 'lots of makeup', and were 'very slim', almost 'anorexic'. Preps were described as 'rich', they followed 'the trends' and wore 'good clothes'. Skaters were far from popular, and, in fact, some were labelled 'losers' by their peers, reflecting the fact that a small group of skaters were either 'into drugs', had left school, or both. Relations between the preps and non-preps, including the skaters, were antagonistic:

'They [the preps] don't agree with the way I look. They don't agree with the way I act. They just don't agree with my music. They don't agree with like anything about me, right?' (Grenn)

When asked why the preps gave her such a hard time, Lexi explained, 'Because I don't dress like *they* do [in tight clothes].' In a passionate statement in support of the 'underground culture' of skating and against 'preppy culture', Tori evinced at least a partial class-consciousness:

'I don't want to be a part of that [preppy culture], because you see the way people treat each other. You see the way things are stacked up. Like, it's all about what you have and what you don't have [by way of material goods] that makes you who you are.'

By contrast, she argued that 'skaters don't expect anything from you – except *you*'.What do these kinds of dynamics tell us about the 'malleability' of gender?

Rewriting girlhood as 'self-invention'

As already noted, it was Skater girls' self-conscious rejection of conventional femininity that initially attracted our interest and led us to view them as embodiment of an emergent, 'alternative' femininity. And yet, by characterizing their identity practices as a new expression of girlhood, there is the danger of implying that we see embodied identities as unified and stable, seamlessly organized around the academic categories used to 'classify' youth. In actuality, girls' practices often demonstrated complicated, shifting relationships to the identity-based groups characteristic of youth culture. For example, Zoe claimed that she and her skater girlfriends moved between 'the studying group' and the skaters. This dual affiliation allowed them to resolve the dilemma of avoiding the 'mean' set of skaters, while remaining distinct from the 'goody-goody' students who focused on academic work and were labelled 'geeks' by the popular clique. As Skater girls, Zoe and her friends were respected as fun loving and open-minded. Yet, because they were girls and good students, they avoided the stereotypes associated with boy skaters – as 'into drugs', acting 'punky' and 'tough'. Moving between groups, these Skater girls felt relatively free to select what they liked from mainstream culture, and turned their eclectic taste (in music, clothing style) into a mark of their individuality.

Madeline likewise moved between skater and academic groups to powerful effect. At her large, inner city but gentrifying high school, she described knowing 'so many people from different groups [academic students, French Immersion students, the Asian 'fashionable group' and the skaters] that I can basically go in to any group and … hang around'. Being a hardcore skater helped to offset the 'smart student' stigma of having received the top academic achievement award at her school for two years running. Among these girls – whom we dub 'in-betweeners' – Sara was proud of the fact that other kids positioned her as 'weird'. She boasted:

> 'I can sometimes be very mainstream, sometimes I can be like more dark, and sometimes I can be punk. Uhm, right now I'm wearing plaid (laughs)! Plaid pants and a black studded shirt. I'm also into like studded belts and studded collars and I have a bike chain bracelet. … Uhm, I'm not really sure. I guess purple is my favorite color. I wear black a lot. Uhm, I have spiked whore boots (laughs). Like up to the knee, with big platforms.'

Sara claimed, 'I can just hang out with the poppy people and be really ditzy and like "ah hah hah", and then I can hang out with the intellectual people and be very like deep and "blah blah blah", and hang out with the skaters and be a moron.'

Thirteen-year-old (white) Vanessa, the only working-class in-betweener in our study, described the social scene at her small, urban, largely working-class and immigrant school as consisting of the 'popular people' ('girls that are airheads and anorexic, and guys that play basketball and try to score with the anorexic girls'); the 'geeks' ('who study at home constantly'); the 'punk kids' (who 'make a lot of trouble and a lot of noise in the halls and they're sort of off the beat, and they have friends that wear all black clothes and wear goth makeup, and they sort of get picked on, but people sort of accept them at the same time because they're pretty cool'); and the 'immature, nerdy people'. Vanessa described liking school, loving and excelling at sports, joining the dance club and having 'a lot of friends'. These friends included members of the popular group as well as the punk crowds, while Vanessa did not display full membership in either group. Her punk friends (all girls) 'listen to music like the Ramones and Bikini Kill [all-female punk band] … one of them, she shops at like Value Village for all the like vintage clothes and stuff like that. And they dye their hair funky colors, like blue or purple.'

When probed, Vanessa stated that while her personality is more like her punk friends, the way she looks 'is probably not'. She also revealed that she had a high Grade Point Average and was known as 'smart' but not 'nerdy'. She attributed this reputation to the time she spent shooting pool at a downtown establishment and playing online games in internet cafés. She also claimed: 'What helps... I have like a really good memory, so I don't have to study or anything – I just do well.' In these kinds of narratives, we detect the capacity of these girls to flexibly fashion identities that enabled them to move among social groups, forging positive, multiple and shifting identities for themselves. Does this mean that today girlhood is a matter of self-invention? That girls can be 'whatever they want'?

In our (limited) study, developing the discursive and social repertoire to recognize and enact several distinct ways of being, based on interaction with others in particular contexts, depended on certain privileges (that is, economic and cultural resources from home). With the exception of Vanessa, it was middle-class girls who strategically negotiated girlhood in this way. Working-class participants who attended working-class or class-divided schools more strongly identified with the underground culture of skateboarding, which they saw as diametrically opposed to 'preppy culture' so that being a 'skater' was more likely to be an all-encompassing, nonconformist identity. Reflecting this position, Grenn evinced a clear class antagonism when she implied that to call skateboarding a 'sport' mistakenly associates it with middle-class (school) conformity. Moreover, hardcore skaters pointed out that there are no rules in skateboarding so that, unlike a sport, there are no winners and losers.

In sum, 'in-betweeners' capture the fluidity, segmentation and hybridity of social identities. Their ability to consciously carve out flexible femininities, however, does not signal that gender is infinitely malleable and that girls can be 'whatever they put their minds to'. Such a claim sells many girls short because the flexibility of femininity remains bounded by class privilege as well as the patriarchal mandate for girls to be 'demure, attractive, soft-spoken, fifteen pounds underweight, and deferential to men' (Adams, 2005, p. 110).

Given these types of constraints on girls' ability to reconfigure their identities, Skater girls talked about the importance of support from friends and others. As Gracie explained, among friends 'We don't really care what others think, and we don't laugh at each other when we try things... When we're all together, I think it's easier for us to be more outgoing and more ourselves. I don't really feel like I'm all myself at school unless I'm with my skater friends.' In these words and practices, we discerned the importance of girls supporting one another when doing girlhood in ways that, in defiance of conventional femininity, gave them a sense of control over their lives. Do we also discern the emergence of a youthful feminism in this collective agency, one that can enlarge girls' opportunities to explore and expand the boundaries of what it means to be 'a girl'?

Re/inventing girlhood, re/inventing feminism

Because many of the identity practices of 'alternative' girls in our study seemed to signal a feminist subjectivity, near the end of interviews they were asked what they knew about 'girl power' and feminism. For the large part, girls' knowledge of, and relationship to, feminism was 'mixed'. On the one hand, Gracie reasoned, 'If there weren't feminists, then we would go backwards. And men would get back the power. Feminism is just like making sure that there is always that equal power.' At the same time, 15-year-old Emily (white, middle-class) claimed 'it's pretty much even with guys now'. As a consequence, Emily argued that feminists 'just want to be better than men'. It interested us that, no matter how they viewed feminism, Skater girls actively fought against the sexism characteristic of skateboarding culture. This struggle is exemplified in the actions of a group of eight girls we dubbed the 'Park Gang'.

Members of the Park Gang were 14 and 15 years old at the time of their interviews. They all lived in an area known for its family orientation, professional demographics and urban chic. Four were Canadian-born Chinese, two were white, one was a Canadian-born Latina and one was half First Nations, half white. With the exception of one girl, who attended a Catholic school, the girls all attended a large urban high school known for its Asian population and academic achievement. Skateboarding was a passion for four of the girls; two girls called themselves 'coaches' in that they skated but preferred to 'just help'; and two were skater affiliates – they were involved in skate culture, music and style as were all of the Park Gang, but without the desire to actually skate. Together, the Park Gang hung out at a skate park that, located in an affluent neighbourhood, was relatively clean and safe. Perhaps as a consequence, it was a hangout for youth, many of whom did not skate but instead socialized on the benches, picnic tables and steps surrounding the area designated for skating.

Members of the Park Gang were relatively new skaters when recruited into our study. To their disappointment, the park proved to be 'owned' by skater boys who put the girls under surveillance when they first showed up with their boards. Being the only girl skaters at the park singled the Park Gang out for harassment. The boys made very little room for girls unless they took up the traditionally feminine positions of watcher, fan or girlfriend. Fifteen-year-old Grover (Latino-Canadian, middle-class) claimed that the Park Gang threatened skater boys 'because, you know, girls are doing *their* sport. Sometimes, they'll be kind of rude, like, I don't know if it's on purpose, but they just, you know, have this kind of attitude.'

The girls understood that the boys were threatened by their presence, but wished these boys could appreciate how hard it was for girls to get started. They wanted the boys to see them as equals who deserved the camaraderie that the boys gave each other. Instead, the boys saw the Park Gang as interlopers with little legitimate claim to their space:

'...a couple of the guys thought we were just – they said it [that we were posers] out loud, that we're just there for the guys and we're like, "No!" And they're like, "But you're here all the time, like almost every day, skateboarding, and so are we."' (Zoe)

To avoid boys' harassment, the Park Gang boycotted the park, instead practising at an elementary school for two weeks. Upon returning to the park the girls suddenly received more respect from the skater boys. Instead of placing the girls under surveillance, skater boys took an interest in the girls' progress. Zoe noted 'to some level, they treated us like an equal to them, kind of'.

In essence, the girls involved in the boycott retreated to a safe space where they were not being monitored. By monitoring the identity of 'skater', the boys not only guarded the 'purity' of the masculinity that characterized their skateboarding group, they retained some control over the girls' sense of who they were. When they re-emerged, the Park Gang was ready to fully occupy the subject position of 'skater'. In so doing, the girls challenged the skater boys' power to name who had a legitimate claim to the park. Working together, the girls altered how the boys thought of them and, more significantly, how they thought of themselves.

By challenging not only the male domination of skater culture, but also the tenets of 'proper' feminine decorum, the Park Gang expanded the possibilities for other girls:

'Lots of girls have actually started [skating] because my group started and then they kind of feel in power. I think they kind of feel empowered that they can start now, that it's okay for girls to skate.' (15-year-old Pete, Chinese-Canadian from a middle-class family)

Their resignification of girlhood enacted a politics that worked to reshape gender categories in a male-dominated locale. Does this politics entitle us to claim their actions as 'feminist', regardless of these girls' self-definitions?

As noted above, despite their struggle against the sexism of skater boys, Skater girls did not necessarily identify with feminism. More prominent in their talk was a discourse of 'authentic individualism'. As seen above, this discourse emphasizes the importance of 'being yourself'. For example, 15-year-old Onyx (Chinese-Canadian, middle-class) reasoned, 'everyone's unique and if you change that you wouldn't be unique any more. You'd just be like wanting to be something else. And that's not *you.*' 'Being yourself' enabled Skater girls to go against convention by labelling girls who pursued what we call conventional femininity as 'fake', because they were 'not really their *own* person'. According to Onyx, 'if you keep adjusting yourself to fit in' you could lose yourself:

> 'Not finding yourself again. Not knowing what you're worth. Thinking that you are only good if someone else finds you to be who they think you should be.'

This reasoning was shared by Grover who exclaimed 'I know who I am and I am confident with who I am':

> 'I think you should just let someone, you know, express themselves the way they want to be expressed. And I am against people, you know, saying "You shouldn't look a certain way" like that because, you know, "it's not pleasing", "it's degrading" or something like that.'

As other writers have noted, the tendency to emphasize personal oppression, celebrate localized acts of transgression, and frame liberation in terms of expanding girls'/women's lifestyle 'choices' has been accused of operating against the legacy of a unified, collective women's movement (see Lorber, 2005). Against these claims, and despite our theoretical rejection of individualism, in our fieldwork a discourse of 'authentic individualism' empowered girls to position themselves against a femininity that would subordinate their interests to those of boys.

Also finding this kind of talk in her interviews with young women, Budgeon (2001, p. 18) maintains that what she heard is not an outright rejection of feminism as much as feminism 'in process', a feminism wedded to individualism. She argues that if feminism is to be relevant to young women today, it must resonate with the sociocultural context; today these conditions include a mandate for girls to 'choose' their selfhood. In the short span of about three decades, we have witnessed a transformation of struggles by women to gain control over 'Who they are' into a mandate for women to take responsibility for the new choices they face. The problem is that this responsibility takes place in a postfeminist context devoid of cultural evidence that 'race, class and gender' matter because social differences have been recoded as 'lifestyle choices' (such as that of skateboarding). Thus we agree with Budgeon that girls' struggles for self-discovery are not so much a celebration of a depoliticized individualism as a signal of a more general transition within late modernity that directs youth towards self-actualizing selfhoods (Budgeon, 2001, p. 22). To be critical of the latter does not require us to be critical of the ways girls incorporate this modern individualism into their identity practices. After all, this discourse gave Skater girls a sense of entitlement to the public space historically controlled by boys.

With Misciagno (1997) – and consistent with our view of culture as practice – we see feminism in Skater girlhood. Misciagno argues that today feminism is better understood through the individual and small group practices of girls and women, rather than looking for the large-scale social action and explicit political agendas that characterized second-wave feminism. What she calls *de facto* feminism arises from the everyday efforts of individual girls and women to grapple with the inequities and contradictions in their lives. Thus, *de facto* feminism embraces the practices of girls and women who do not necessarily explicitly identify as feminists but whose everyday actions create greater freedom for girls and women generally. At the same time, however, we do not claim that every transgression of conventional femininity constitutes *de facto* feminism. Pushing against the boundaries of what constitutes acceptable femininity does not necessarily mean that gendered power inequalities are being challenged,[7] let alone transformed. Political agency arises when people, interacting in groups, identify an issue or structure of inequality that becomes the conscious object of their resistance through collective action to redress institutionalized privilege. We leave open the possibility that (some) Skater girls will claim future identities as 'feminists'. Because experience is a potent venue of politicization, the future of feminism is thus a 'historical' and not (simply) theoretical question.

Conclusion

In conclusion, Skater girls can be credited with resignifying girlhood. They did so by rejecting an appearance-based femininity that requires girls to be preoccupied with gaining boys' approval and sexual interest. By rejecting this girlhood, Skater girls refused to subordinate their interests to those of boys. As illustrated by the Park Gang, this refusal can engage girls in a struggle against sexism. The story of the Park Gang also illustrates how gendered identities are never fixed, but open to negotiation. While feminism as a discourse aims to facilitate this kind of renegotiation, these girls did not always adopt an identity 'as feminist'. More influential was a discourse of 'authentic individualism'. In the final analysis, we claim that while the actions of the Park Gang were not necessarily feminist in *intent*, by opening new possibilities for girlhood they are feminist in *effect*. We are therefore open to the idea that feminism is being resignified through the actions of girls who struggle to redefine the parameters of girlhood because feminism, as well as femininity, is in a constant state of becoming.

Notes

1. But see Francis and Skelton (2005, p. 126) who argue that neoliberalism calls for both masculine (independence, competition, risk-taking) and feminine traits (flexibility, conscientiousness, reflexivity). A similar mix of feminine and masculine traits is called for in the current construction of the ideal achieving student.
2. We do not want to imply a monolithic, stable category, but rather signal a relational category that gives meaning to the notion of 'alternative' femininity (see Connell, 1987, pp. 183–4).
3. For a fuller discussion see Currie et al. (2009).
4. A claim often contested by young women themselves (see Bryn Rundle et al., 2001; Schilt, 2003).
5. The girls chose pseudonyms; as each girl is introduced into our narrative, we note her age, class and racialized identity.
6. Due to lack of space we do not elaborate on the ways that racialization shaped the gendered practices of our participants. Suffice it to say that what we call 'conventional' femininity was a socially valued way of 'doing girlhood' across differently racialized groups. See Currie et al. (2009).
7. As shown by the commodification of Skater style.

Bibliography

Adams, N. G. (2005) 'Fighters and Cheerleaders: Disrupting the Discourse of "Girl Power" in the New Millennium' pp. 101–14 in P. J. Bettis and N. G. Adams (eds) *Geographies of Girlhood: Identities in-between* (Mahwah, NJ: Lawrence Erlbaum Associates, Publishers).

Beal, B. (1996) 'Alternative Masculinity and Its Effects on Gender Relations in the Subculture of Skateboarding', *Journal of Sport Behavior* 19(3): 204–20.

Borden, I. (2001) *Skateboarding, Space and the City: Architecture and the Body* (Oxford: Berg).

Bryn Rundle, L., L. Karaian and A. Mitchell (2001) *Turbo Chicks: Talking Young Feminisms* (Toronto: Sumach Press).

Budgeon, S. (2001) 'Emergent Feminist (?) Identities: Young Women and the Practice of Micropolitics', *The European Journal of Women's Studies* 8(1): 7–28.

Connell, R. W. (1987) *Gender and Power* (Stanford: Stanford University Press).

Currie, D. H., D. M. Kelly and S. Pomerantz (2009) *'Girl Power': Girls Reinventing Girlhood* (New York: Peter Lang).

Eder, D. (1995) *School Talk: Gender and Adolescent Culture* (New Brunswick, NJ: Rutgers University Press).

Francis, B. and C. Skelton (2005) *Reassessing Gender and Achievement: Questioning Contemporary Key Debates* (London: Routledge).

Harris, A. (2004) *Future Girl: Young Women in the Twenty-First Century* (New York: Routledge).

Lorber, J. (2005) *Gender Inequality: Feminist Theory and Politics* (Los Angeles: Roxbury Publishing Company).

Misciagno, P. S. (1997) *Rethinking Feminist Identification: The Case for* De Facto *Feminism* (Westport, CT: Praeger).

Schilt, K. (2003). ' "I'll Resist with Every Inch and Every Breath": Girls and Zine Making as a Form of Resistance', *Youth and Society* 35(1): 71–97.

Walkerdine, V. (2003) 'Reclassifying Upward Mobility: Femininity and the Neo-liberal Subject', *Gender and Education* 15(3): 237–48.

20
Will These Emergencies Never End? Some First Thoughts about the Impact of Economic and Security Crises on Everyday Life

Gargi Bhattacharyya

In a time of crisis there is a question about the extent to which previous approaches to understanding can fit to the fast moving terrain that lies before us. In many ways we are clearly living through a period of accelerated and immense change, for many groups of people in many parts of the world. Whatever the shortcomings of the so-called global economy, the apparently endless restructuring of local economy in response to the pressures and pulls of that nebulous creature the global market continues to result in large-scale population movement (Cohen, 2006), the growth of mega-slums (Davis, 2006), the dispossession of rural communities (Manyathi, 2008), and greater and greater immiseration of labour, perhaps most of all in those spaces that seek to manufacture the frippery of throwaway consumer society (Huang, 2009).

At the same time, the world is being reshaped by the still unfinished process of accelerated militarization. For all the extensive talk about a new world order, and then later the new new world order, the disciplinary logics of twenty-first-century geopolitics have surprised us all. While we may try to grasp a little hope from the Obama administration's initiation of some forms of disarmament, the reinvention of occupation as an ongoing and endless task by which military powers seek to discipline more unruly segments of the globe, ostensibly for the good of all, somewhat limits the celebratory potential.

If we are living in a new time, or even if we seek to unpack the uncanny familiarity of apparently recent and new events, then these two themes must occupy our attention. What happens to labour, most of all the labour that is mobile, hidden, always on the edge of official labour markets, when capitalism itself declares its own crisis? And how does the remilitarization of the world intersect with such economic processes, and with what constrained possibilities for the least privileged?

It has not been the habit of my own feminist education to begin enquiry with such large-scale questions, although much of what I have learned about both militarism and the exploitation of vulnerable workers comes from the work of feminist scholars (for example Enloe, 1988; Mies and Shiva, 1993). However, it seems that in recent years (and I admit I may be revealing the limits of my own reading), discussion amongst feminist scholars more often begins from the impact on women, from the detail and deprivation of everyday life, from the manner in which new/old incarnations of gender subjugation enter public consciousness. I, too, have been accustomed to these habits. And am barely equipped to ask questions that I think must be asked, let alone with the expertise to answer them.

For these reasons, I am trying to outline here a programme of study in a spirit of invitation. Some of us have some expertise in some aspect of these questions. Others bring skills from very different areas and approaches to learning. But I don't believe that any one of us knows all of the answers already. After the demands that proper respect is shown to disciplinary expertise, professional status, publication record, overall place in the hierarchy of the conflicted space of the Academy, after all of that, who among us is so cynically knowing that they cannot look at the horror before us and ask 'must it be so?'

So the programme of enquiry that I advocate is amateurish, I hope in its best sense of being free of the arbitrary limitations of professionalism – but it is also ambitious. And although I also treasure the small, the detailed, the fleeting pleasure and resistance of the everyday, we must retrain our feminism to also engage with the most sweeping and abstract occurrences of our time.

Losing our jobs

We have learned over a period of years to appreciate the additional impact of gender in the exploitation and marginalization of the most disenfranchised in the labour market. The various hidden and semi-visible activities that enable the more celebrated aspects of the global economy rely disproportionately on migrant labour, including the labour of women, many of whom continue to carry out the 'gendered' tasks of cleaning and caring for others in order to support their own loved ones and dependants (Ehrenreich and Hochschild, 2003). However, as others have pointed out, despite this dependency there continues to be an active persecution of migrant workers and an ongoing controversy about how affluent national spaces can reconcile their need for cheap labour with their addiction to cheap racism (Fekete, 2009).

In a time of economic crisis and contraction across many developed economies, there is a question about the impact on the lives of these already marginalized workers. For those working in the underground economy, and most of all for those whose immigration papers are not in order, employers can wield an almost feudal power over the conditions of life. One focus of our attention must be the reshaping of the shadow economy in times of economic crisis and the impact on everyday life for women and for men.

Alongside the ongoing reconstitution of the nation as a space with simultaneously permeable and well-protected borders, we are living through a time in which securitization has become an inescapable element of the repertoire of day-to-day government. By securitization I mean both the overt display of state power and security measures and the more hidden integration of security-related measures into a range of state practices. Influential feminist scholarship has taught us of the impact of war on whole societies, including on the playing out of gender relations. For example, Cynthia Enloe has encouraged us to rediscover our feminist curiosity and to transfer lessons learned from an analysis of previous war states to a more systematic understanding of our own violent present (Enloe, 2004). Despite its uncertain location, boundaries, enemy, participant forces and overall objective, the war on terror has transformed many of our 'homes' (or should that be 'homelands'?) into states of war. In an echo of textbook accounts of the war state, the expectation of ongoing armed conflict shapes internal government, resource allocation and overall representation of the nation. Most obviously, the seeming acceptance of a state of war without end reshapes social relations within the nation and, increasingly, is linked to institutional techniques designed to survey, police and demonize particular groups.

In both themes, that of contradictory accounts of migrant labour and that of the urgency of embracing securitization, we can discern the revamping of old and familiar techniques to identify, contain and exclude the alien body. Yet there is also something in our time which seems to make all of us into alien bodies. Somewhere in the overlap between us all being suspects and this translating into violent dispossession only for some, I think there might be some answers about questions of power, status and human worth in our time.

Thinking like a feminist

Although this refashioning of borders and divisions between people has an impact on the vulnerability of actual real-life women to exploitation and violence, I am not sure that a focus on women's lives helps me to understand these processes. Perhaps because my recent work has been in this area, I am more comfortable (perhaps wrongly) with the framework of racialization and the changing terrain of class divisions. Despite the well-practised discussions about denaturalizing gender, it is hard to use the reference point of gender to analyse significant changes in social power without, sooner or later, returning to assumptions about the knowability and pretty much the unchanging nature of gender divisions. In an uncertain space of change,

I am reduced once again to looking for the women – as if I know who the women are and what that category means. However, gendering also works in peculiar and changeable ways – remaking boundaries and occupying familiar divisions at the same time. Perhaps we can remember approaches to feminist thinking that see gendering as an ongoing mystery and the apparent solidity of the categories of women and men as a distracting cover for the endless negotiation of power, privilege and embodiment that is gendering.

Racialization has become an overused and undoubtedly too elastic term. I understand David Goldberg's criticism of racialization-speak and the manner in which so broad and directionless a concept lacks analytic precision (Goldberg, 2009, p. 67). How does such a woolly process happen? Who are the perpetrators? Where is agency of any kind if we conceive of the world as shaped by forces that appear so indeterminate and yet so inescapable? At worst, it is true that the concept of racialization can appear to legitimize racial hierarchy, because this is a way of understanding social formation as if it is as inescapable as biological essence.

And yet there is still something in the openness of the category that seems useful. Racialization allows us to comprehend the manner in which human beings may be allocated differential value and status and that this may be made to seem as natural and as inevitable as the changing of seasons – and yet the changeability of racial categorization reveals how arbitrary these attributions are. Race remains an empty category, still a handily floating signifier, and in the right circumstances any of us could be blighted by the accusation of a lesser association or lifted up through some equally spurious attribution of social worth. In a time when hierarchies of human worth once again appear both changeable and yet almost impossible to escape, even the reminder that the meanings of bodies, or of cultures, or of religions can change and change all the time seems important to hang on to.

When looking at where the women are, on the other hand, however unexpected the twists of a constantly recalibrating gender politics, it is hard not to regard men and women as timeless players in a battle that has continued since battles were recorded. Of course, none of us really thinks this and gender has been decentralized and de-essentialized along with all other identities. However, the quest to uncover the contours of new femininities can move too quickly to an exploration of the lives, experiences and representations of those named 'women'. The disciplinary division of labour within scholarship can lead to a parallel division between those who analyse the worlds of representation and fantasy and assume that gender is always radically contingent and those who document and inform the worlds of more traditional politics and policy and who, from a sense of urgency, can speak as if gender is solid and decided and demanding immediate documentation. I hope that feminist responses to both the new and familiar injustices of our time can reconcile these two approaches again, so that we both remember why we wished to dismantle and question the category of 'woman', not only for the purposes of understanding representations but also because of what is added to our understanding of how gender works, but also return the focus of (some) feminist theory to questions of global injustice. This is not a project for any one person to undertake – but it is an important conversation for those of us who think that feminism matters. The only point I can make for now is to say again that feminist thinking can help me to look at seemingly solid identities with a questioning eye, but without convincing me that 'gender' is necessarily a central dynamic in the changes around us. So, let us say that I assume that shifts in state practices and modes of cooperation between states intertwine with economic uncertainty in a manner that reshapes the lives of ordinary women and men and is likely to inhabit structures of existing gender inequalities when it suits – but also that the realignments of securitization plus economic restructuring in some circumstances may rework or confound gender expectations for some other purpose. If there is an overarching gendering logic playing through these parallel processes, I have not yet learned how to discern and map it.

Gendering migrant workers

In previous recessions, women have been regarded as particularly vulnerable to the impact of economic downturn. In economies where women's work has been recognized and socially validated only quite recently, economic downturn has been seen as a time when underlying social prejudices against women working can shape patterns of job loss and redundancy. Trade unions have become accustomed to warning that economic downturn threatens to exacerbate existing social divisions and inequalities (TUC, 2009).

However, in the aftermath of this early twenty-first century financial crisis, it has been asserted that women are no more vulnerable to job loss than their male colleagues (Ludden, 2009; Tyler, 2008). In fact, the misery tales of this recession have focused on the disproportionate impact on previously privileged groups of workers, with a particular emphasis on the suited armies that emerged with the expansion of financial service industries.

The other army of low-paid service workers who serviced this affluent group – peopling the cleaning, security, hospitality services that have surrounded the well-paid jobs of the south-east boom – suffer a less discussed and documented fall-out from recession.

We have become accustomed to depicting the different tiers of work in the global economy and their interrelation – influential studies have taught us to understand that the global city operates through the undervalued labour of migrant workers (Sassen, 1999), that elite workers pass on their caring responsibilities to less privileged women, who themselves use their wages to pay for the care of their own dependants, often many miles away (Parreñas,

2005). Although less explicit in the literature, we can surmise that the emergence of relatively well-paid work and a diversion into far greater consumer expectations for some in more developed economies cannot occur without greater access to a range of personal services, an expansion of the activities and expectations in the public spaces of privileged work that requires feeding, cleaning, guarding and, of course, and this is widely documented, the rapid rise of mass production of all sorts of low-cost consumer items in other regions (Klein, 2002).

Already there has been some discussion of the impact of financial crisis on the manufacturing centres of China – and the traumatic experiences of migrant workers suddenly unable to send payments to dependants and unable to maintain themselves without their factory wage. But what happens to the undocumented and semi-documented workers of affluent regions when affluence is under attack? My suspicion is that long-running anti-migrant campaigns from government and media combine with the highly developed processes for detaining, degrading and excluding migrants when this is deemed necessary to demonstrate how truly vulnerable 'surplus' labour can be.

Demonizing migrants

The demonization of migrants is not a new phenomenon. Britain has experienced at least a century of anti-migrant politics, a politics that can be discerned in racist legislation, political debate and popular representation (Panayi, 1994). However, it does seem that in recent years we have reached a stage of greater tension between the amplified level of concern about the 'problem' of migrants and our societal dependency on the hidden labours of these same people. I have suggested that in times of relative affluence and prosperity, migrant workers provide the luxurious extras of personal services, or, less titillatingly, the necessary army of low-paid labour that maintains many new service industries. At the same time, in periods when more enfranchised citizens can aspire to less dirty and dangerous forms of work, migrants have carried out the various picking, gutting, cleaning and packing tasks that keep agriculture and food processing just about profitable (Byrne, 2008).

Much of the work of migrant workers continues to be semi-documented or undocumented. Even where migrants have the right to work, they remain vulnerable to exploitation by those willing to prey on their lack of knowledge, limited knowledge of English, and inability to seek support and advice (Commission on Vulnerable Employment, 2005). When people like this lose their jobs, or have their hours cut or don't get paid at all, we are unlikely to know about it. Official accounts of unemployment will not register those whose employment was informal or semi-formal in the first place. When workers like these are abused by employers, or denied their basic employment rights, or ripped off and have their wages stolen, they have few avenues of complaint.

Instead, in these times of so-called economic downturn, the semi-formal economy (that is, all those forms of employment that profit from some element of unofficialness whether that is through avoidance of National Insurance payments, cash payments with no records, lack of employment records, failure to pay the minimum wage or to offer other statutory employment benefits) can contract and/or restructure with little or no official acknowledgement. Just as these workers provided an extra cushion for the newly affluent in times of boom, often at great expense to themselves and their families, now the undocumented precariousness of their employment serves to hide the full extent of the human losses sustained through recession.

We know already that this group includes both women and men, and that these forms of shadow employment cut across sectors (Commission on Vulnerable Employment, 2005; Evans et al., 2005; Markova and McKay, 2008). It is likely that most of our lives are touched in some way by these poorly rewarded labours. However, this is not an injustice borne more by women or by men. The detail of exploitation or the manner of workplace abuse, perhaps the sector or the coercive methods used might play upon gender expectations. But this is not easily understood as a set of happenings motored by the logic of gender inequality.

Instead and predictably, the misfortunes of these lives take shape through what Liz Fekete has called 'xenoracism' (Fekete, 2001), the heavily policed border between citizen and non-citizen, between native and foreign, with all of this heavily overladen with long-running practices of racism. This is the point where the demonization of foreign workers becomes folded into wider depictions of border dangers and national security.

Here there is a blurring between accounts of national security that point to the threat of terrorism, including the internal threat of radicalization and so-called home-grown terrorists, and accounts of national security that point to migrants as a drain on the national economy. In both narratives, beleaguered citizens (and here citizenship regains its racial connotations in distinction to those formal citizens of questionable allegiance) must navigate a world where shadowy and yet seemingly familiar figures constantly threaten national well-being with the possibility of explosions, demands for public services or an undercutting of wages or working conditions.

One outcome of these overlapping fears has been an augmentation of security measures across both public services and public spaces. While it remains relatively easy to exploit the uncertain status of migrants in the workplace and there are few bodies with either the resources or the responsibility to monitor such things, other arenas of life have experienced far greater levels of surveillance in recent times (Duvell and Jordan, 2003). Increasingly public services are tasked with monitoring the immigration status of prospective clients and employers that seek or require cooperation with the state must demonstrate their systems for checking the immigration status of prospective staff in similar ways (Home Office, 2006). The undocumented and the semi-documented can remain invisible while suffering the exploitation of the semi-formal economy and in the process ensure cheaper goods and services for the newly affluent, or at least slightly more affluent, but if in times of trouble they seek emergency support or assistance their uncertain status threatens to be revealed. The anti-migrant state is far more diligent in denying services to migrants than it is in exploring the working conditions of that same group.

Securitization is all

The constant reiteration of the need to survey, monitor, track and contain security threats combines appeals to anti-migrant and anti-terrorist agendas. It is not that anti-migrant politics is ushered in surreptitiously under the cover of national security. Both political pronouncements and popular media assert continually that the migrant threat is a close cousin of the terrorist threat – with precisely this allusion to dangerous kinship (for a vivid example of this logic, see Howells, 2009). However, although anti-migrant politics has provided some of the most developed institutional practices for the everyday securitization of the war on terror, including approaches to indefinite detention and a ready-made template to justify and operationalize the exclusion of particular demonized groups from the exercise of law as experienced by citizens, it has been the announcement of the emergency without end of the war on terror that has enabled an expansion and consolidation of these tendencies in other spheres of life.

If states have learned to assert their sovereignty and control of their borders through stripping illicit and/or unwanted migrants of human dignity and rights to legal redress, then this has occurred, until recently, with relatively little fanfare. States such as Britain may wish to declare their toughness in relation to irregular migration, but they do not tend to trumpet their abandonment of human rights or to publicize the detail of violence and degradation that clamping down on immigration entails (for a heartbreaking account, see Madill, 2009).

The threat of terrorism, on the other hand, has heralded a different rhetoric of security and a different tone of public debate. It is this new/old threat that has enabled states of different political hues to not only justify but to actively celebrate the abuse and degradation of enemies of different kinds. In the face of terrorism, government abuses can be represented as tough but legitimate responses to a threat to our way of life – as seen in locations as diverse as Chechnya (Eke, 2005), Sri Lanka (Human Rights Watch, 2009b), India (Nelson, 2005), Egypt (Amnesty, 2009) and, of course, Britain (Human Rights Watch, 2009a) and the United States.

In recent years, participation in the war on terror has revealed the willingness of states to abandon previous codes of acceptable conduct and to publicize these methods as part of their own propaganda and as evidence of their strength of purpose. Here the display of excessive violence, of abuse and degradation and a disregard of previously understood rules of war all become part of the battle of wills between us and them. It seems that this process is continuing even now, after the rhetoric of us and them has been discredited and the concept of a war on terror has been abandoned (Branigan, 2007). This seems to be quite distinct from earlier semi-covert campaigns of violence and intimidation against migrants, where, although rumoured knowledges of what happens in detention and deportation formed part of the intimidation of migrant communities, the public at large remained comfortably unaware of the horrors carried out in their name.

To a large extent, this ground has been well-trodden already. The war on terror has brought a renewed discussion of the concept of bare life. A number of commentators have returned to Agamben's writings in order to examine that double consciousness of our time, where some are regarded as holders of rights, and deserving of untold resource-heavy protection, while others are deemed to be superfluous people, those with no value or rights (Agamben, 1998).

These discussions have tended to describe the changing map of contemporary geopolitics, describing relations between spaces and places and the parallel orders of national belonging and citizenship and zones and routes that carry the dispensable bodies of the enemy combatant. Mark Duffield has suggested that others too hold the status of homo sacer – and he argues that the non-insured populations of the poor world, those subject to the complex disciplines of development, may also be understood to be holding the status of dispensable bodies (Duffield, 2007).

My interest is in what happens to this logic and to these practices when they become folded into the same space. The everyday and mundane practices of securitization that increasingly shape the home spaces of occupying and/or aggressor nations tend to lack the theatrical fanfare of some other security measures. As others have noted, even the embarrassment of Guantanamo can also be understood as a display of force and will, and, however bizarrely, an aspect of propaganda in favour of military aggression (Willis, 2006).

The integration of security practices into the delivery of public services and administration of other activity is less showy. Although securitization within the nation includes more recognizable alerts such as government warnings and media releases, sporadic raids for unspecified offences and ongoing discussion about the close connections and networks of radicalization that link, allegedly, some UK communities and some zones of war, there is also a swathe of activity that is barely public. So we see colleges and universities tasked with monitoring students for any trace of dangerous radicalism (BBC, 2006, 2008); banks and building societies revealing client details in the interests of security (Hayes, 2009); community and youth groups charged with preventing extremism, but under cover of their usual activity (Kundnani, 2009); and public services of all kinds coerced into checking the immigration status of prospective clients, quietly, as part of the normal routine of everyday life.

In one sense the primacy of the security agenda has contributed to the displacement of the so-called social wage. The ongoing emergency of security threats has added to a public discussion where resources are siphoned away from welfare services and a safety net for the poor and increasingly towards different forms of the militarization of everyday space. Some of this work focuses on the US city, and therefore can point to quite explicit military reference points and practices in city governance (Gray and Wyly, 2007). Although there has been some increase of the use of armed police and military tactics of policing, British and perhaps other European cities have tended not to be characterized by the overt use of a militarized security presence. In the British context what I am discussing is far more hidden, yet there is still an appeal to the rhetoric of emergency in its imposition.

In practice, different factors and organizations do their best to adapt to the circumstances of securitization. Certainly for community organizations and the black voluntary sector, the parallel agendas of worklessness and preventing violent extremism (PVE) have replaced the only recently learned languages of community safety, regeneration and social inclusion in the framing of both funding and the explanation of services. In relation to PVE, the admirable flexibility shown by sections of the voluntary sector has been criticized by proponents of the programme. Whereas the intention was to uncover the dangerously radicalized and proto-terrorist heart of particular, read Muslim, communities including through the engagement of women, young people and children in a surveillance exercise without end, the diversion of PVE funding into a very familiar range of community-led services has raised questions about the focus and the efficacy of this approach (Kundnani, 2009). Although this pot of funding has been controversial, an already stretched voluntary and community sector has, in large part, played along with its strange demands for native performance and informants. Despite my own scepticism, it seems unlikely that the various women's groups, outdoor pursuits activities, supplementing of training or other business as usual activity funded through this programme will offer either great benefit to the security services or too intrusive a surveillance into communities on the ground.

However, despite the apparently easy adaptation to these new demands, each reshaping of funding policy in relation to local services delivered over the sector has an impact on practice on the ground. Although organizations may learn to represent themselves for different purposes to different audiences – those most valuable attributes of any third sector organization – new funding regimes clearly determine what can no longer be done. Therefore, the PVE agenda brings unlikely critics from other BME communities and organizations who are not able to occupy the role of 'minority most dangerous to national security' (Kundnani, 2009). In order to qualify for increasingly rationed state assistance, disadvantaged communities must learn to present themselves as potential security threats (although not so dangerous that they cannot be diverted by suitable intervention) and/or open to training to become market-ready. Everyone else learns to get along with increased levels of intrusive surveillance and the various annoying curtailments that accompany a state of emergency. Those too dangerous to save, whether due to immigration status, national or religious allegiance or overall outlook, can be excised from the national space. After a while, it becomes hard to distinguish between civilizational tests of allegiance and demonstrations of being ready for the workplace, at whatever price and in whatever conditions.

In the end, I am still stuck at thinking about 'why'. It does seem that everyday securitization extends the practices of monitoring, harassing and demonizing migrants to the rest of the population – while also adding some new elements of information gathering and sharing across borders. I also suspect that there is a complementarity between economic exploitation and securitization – not that they are the same agenda or even that there is some master plan or foundational logic – but a hunch that the exercise of power includes a habit of replicating its own conditions of existence and that overlapping groups of resource-rich interested parties are likely to reach an understanding about how to pursue their respective interests. There is no space here for further discussion of this new transnational incarnation of the military-industrial complex, but, again, others have sought to document some of its activity (Klein, 2008).

Is any of this about feminism? Where are the women? And if my questions do not include a focus on the particularity of women's experience and position in these processes, are they the business of a volume about feminism at all? Can I be a feminist scholar if my work no longer (for now) talks much about gender? Of course, I think it is (about feminism) and I can (be a feminist scholar, at least of a sort) – but I also think that feminists need to engage in some active remembering again about the extent of feminism's ambitions. Whatever the pressures of institutionalization and professionalism, a feminism for difficult times needs to remember our dreams of earth-shattering change, our most inclusive traditions of radicalism, critique and irreverent and bloody-minded activism and our impatience with a world that is just not good enough, for any of us, not yet.

Increasingly I think that learning about the ordinary lives of women and of men might demand a detour through other forms of learning. I realize that in part this may be nothing more than a recognition of my own partial education – perhaps I should have learned all this stuff much earlier and perhaps most if not all others are already ahead of me and know what all of these things mean. But it feels to me that we are living through a time when the battle lines between the powerful and the vulnerable, between those who can have and choose and those who cannot, are becoming harder and fiercer. If feminism is a politics against injustice, occasionally we may need first to examine the character of injustice in our time, and only later consider the place and misuse of gender, because how will women's lives get better if we do not learn to combat this?

Bibliography

Agamben, G. (1998) *Homo Sacer: Sovereign Power and Bare Life* (Palo Alto, CA: Stanford University Press).

Amnesty (2009) *Amnesty Country Report – Egypt*. Available at http://thereport.amnesty.org/en/regions/middle-east-north-africa/egypt [accessed 2 December 2009].

Anderson, B. and H. Jayaweera (2009) *Migrant Workers and Vulnerable Employment: A Review of Existing Data* (Oxford: Centre on Migration, Policy and Society (COMPAS), University of Oxford).

BBC (2006) 'Campus Radicals "Serious Threat"', *BBC News*, 17 November.

BBC (2008) 'Tackle Extremism, Academics Urged', *BBC News* 22 January.

Branigan, T. (2007) 'Bush's "War on Terror" Phrase Helps Terrorists, Minister Warns', *The Guardian*, 17 April.

Byrne, J. (2008) 'Labour Shortage Puts UK Food Sector at Risk – Claim', foodproductiondaily.com, 22 August. Available at http://www.foodproductiondaily.com/Supply-Chain/Labour-shortage-puts-UK-food-sector-at-risk-claim [accessed 2 December 2009].

Cohen, R. (2006) *Migration and its Enemies* (Farnham, Surrey: Ashgate).

Commission on Vulnerable Employment (2005) *Hard Work, Hidden Lives: The Full Report of the Commission on Vulnerable Employment* (London: TUC).

Davis, M. (2006) *Planet of Slums* (London: Verso GB).

Duffield, M. (2007) *Development, Security and Unending War: Governing the World of Peoples* (Cambridge: Polity Press).

Duvell, F. and B. Jordan (2003) 'Immigration Control and the Management of Economic Migration in the United Kingdom', *Journal of Ethnic and Migration Studies* 29(2): 299–336.

Ehrenreich, B. and A. R. Hochschild (2003) *Global Woman: Nannies, Maids and Sex Workers in the New Economy* (London: Granta).

Eke, S. (2005) 'Russia "Committed Chechnya Abuse"', *BBC News*, 24 February. Available at http://news.bbc.co.uk/1/hi/world/europe/4295249.stm [accessed 2 December 2009].

Enloe, C. (1988) *Does Khaki Become You? The Militarization of Women's Lives* (London: Pandora Press).

Enloe, C. (2004) *The Curious Feminist: Searching for Women in a New Age of Empire* (Berkeley: University of California Press).

Evans, Y., J. Herbert, K. Datta, J. May, C. McIlwaine and J. Wills (2005) 'Making the City Work: Low Paid Employment in London', November, Department of Geography, Queen Mary, University of London.

Fekete, L. (2001) 'The Emergence of Xeno-Racism', *Race and Class* 43: 23–40.

Fekete, L. (2009) *A Suitable Enemy: Racism, Migration and Islamophobia in Europe* (London: Pluto).

Goldberg, D. T. (2009) *The Threat of Race: Reflections on Racial Neoliberalism* (Oxford: Wiley-Blackwell).

Gray, M. and E. Wyly (2007) 'The Terror City Hypothesis' in D. Gregory and A. Pred (eds), *Violent Geographies* (London: Routledge).

Hayes, B. and TNI (2009) *Neoconopticon: The EU Security-Industrial Complex* (London: Statewatch).

Home Office (2006) *A Points-Based System: Making Migration Work for Britain* (London: HMSO).

Howells, K. (2009) 'It's Time to Pull Out of Afghanistan and Take the Fight to Bin Laden in Britain', guardian.co.uk, Comment is free, 3 November. Available at http://www.guardian.co.uk/commentisfree/2009/nov/03/afghanistan-terror-taliban-al-qaida [accessed 2 December 2009].

Huang, C. (2009) 'Migrant Workers Struggle as China's Factories Slow', *Christian Science Monitor*, 28 January.

Human Rights Watch (2009a) *Cruel Britannia, British Complicity in the Torture and Ill-treatment of Terror Suspects in Pakistan* (New York, Human Rights Watch).

Human Rights Watch (2009b) Sri Lanka: Domestic Inquiry into Abuses a Smokescreen, 27 October. Available at http://www.hrw.org/en/news/2009/10/27/sri-lanka-domestic-inquiry-abuses-smokescreen [accessed 2 December 2009].

Klein, N. (2002) *No Logo* (London: Picador).

Klein, N. (2008) *The Shock Doctrine* (London: Penguin).

Kundnani, A. (2009) *Spooked! How Not to Prevent Violent Extremism* (London: Institute of Race Relations).

Lawton, K. (2009) *Nice Work If You Can Get It, Achieving a Sustainable Solution to Low Pay and In-work Poverty* (London: IPPR).

Ludden, J. (2009) 'Recession Drives Women into Role of Breadwinner', NPR, 6 November. Available at http://www.npr.org/templates/story/story.php?storyId=120146408 [accessed 2 December 2009].

Madill, E. (2009) 'End the Inhumanity of Child Detention', *The Independent*, 20 October.

Manyathi, T. (2008) 'New Forms of Land Dispossession'. Available at http://www.afra.co.za/default.asp?id=1091 [accessed 1 December 2009].

Markova, E. and S. McKay (2008) 'Agency and Migrant Workers: Literature Review', Working Lives Research Institute (London Metropolitan University).

McVeigh, K. (2009) 'Children Made "Sick With Fear" in UK Immigration Detention Centres. Paediatricians' Report Condemns the Effect of Incarceration At Yarl's Wood', *The Independent*, 13 October.

Mies, M. and V. Shiva (1993) *EcoFeminism* (London: Zed).

Milne, S. (2009) 'Spying On Us Doesn't Protect Democracy, It Undermines It', guardian.co.uk, Wednesday, 28 October.

Nelson, D. (2005) 'India Fences off Bangladesh to Keep Out Muslim Terror', *The Sunday Times*, 13 November.

Panayi, P. (1994) *Immigration, Ethnicity and Racism in Britain, 1815–1945* (Manchester: Manchester University Press).

Parreñas, R. S. (2005) *Children of Global Migration: Transnational Families and Gendered Woes* (Palo Alto, CA: Stanford University Press).

Reuters (2009) 'U.N. Calls for Nuclear Disarmament, Obama Presides', 24 September. Available at http://www.reuters.com/article/topNews/idUSTRE58M0VN20090925 [accessed 1 December 2009].

Sassen, S. (1999) *Globalization and its Discontents* (New York: New Press).

Triggle, N. (2006) 'NHS "in Illegal Immigrants Mess"', *BBC News*, 22 August 2006. Available at http://news.bbc.co.uk/1/hi/health/5275586.stm [accessed 2 December 2009].

TUC (2009) Women and Recession (London: TUC).

Tyler, R. (2008) 'Women Better Placed to Survive Recession than Men', *The Telegraph*, 17 November.

Verkaik, R. (2009) 'Immigration Centre's Toll on Children's Mental Health', *The Independent*, 13 October.

Willis, S. (2006) 'Guantanamo's Symbolic Economy', *New Left Review* 39, May–June.

Index

Printed and bound in Great Britain by
CPI Antony Rowe, Chippenham and Eastbourne